Veronica Cook

Veronica is a survivor, her childhood experiences were challenging, but she has come through trauma and heartache with a message for others in drug-taking families. She always wanted a normal life, which she now has with her own loving family. She is reaching out to help others like her.

DEDICATION

I would like to dedicate this book in memory of my mum Paula who tragically died prematurely due to drug addiction. The shock and heartache of losing her is what spurred me on to write this book.

Veronica Cook

VERONICA, HIDDEN HARM

AUSTIN MACAULEY
PUBLISHERS LTD.

A CIP catalogue record for this title is available from the British Library.

ISBN 9781786930422 (Paperback)
ISBN 9781786930439 (Hardback)
ISBN 9781786930446 (E-Book)

www.austinmacauley.com

First Published (2017)
Austin Macauley Publishers Ltd.
25 Canada Square
Canary Wharf
London
E14 5LQ

ACKNOWLEDGMENTS

I would like to thank my husband Rae, who has been my hero over the last seventeen years. My children for inspiring me to be a better person and bringing me so much joy and hope. I would also like to thank Steve Orwin my counsellor and friend for working tirelessly over the last few years, encouraging me to write about my life and providing me with his endless knowledge and kindness.

PREFACE

This is a story of survival; how a baby born prematurely to drug taking parents, who spent the first three months of her life in an incubator then her early years living in London squats, coped with an unusual childhood. With many struggles along the way to discard the influences of her past, Veronica emerged with a passionate desire to tell people what it was like, as a voice of the least addressed and understood part of a drug user's life, the user's children. The events are true, they are not glamorised for effect, but are reported to inform the reader's understanding of the interaction between drug culture and society, from a child's perspective.

Veronica's life experiences ranged from exciting to horrifying, against the constant backdrop of her parents' drug taking and dealing. She suffered emotional abuse, neglect and bullying, which made her street-wise but deeply troubled. Something in Veronica saw her through though, an inner strength, a sense of hope and decency; and a desire for change. She endured worry and boredom, yet there were good times when Veronica wished things could be that way for ever. All she wanted was for her parents to get clean and live a normal life.

There was a time when it almost happened and she was full of hope. Her dad bought a yacht which they sailed back from Turkey with the intention of going round the world, but things changed and they went back to their old ways.

This finally prompted Veronica to leave home and set off on her own adventures in Mexico, where her confidence and self-respect grew. When she returned, she was treated as an outsider, except for when her family could use her to their advantage. But she still loved them passionately, and did everything she could to help them. Finally, to her great distress, her mum died at an early age from liver cancer, caused by Hepatitis C from a dirty needle.

This book is Veronica's emotional biography as well as a recounting of events, and is deeply touching.

In her own words, "I have cried so many tears over the fact that my mum's passing was a direct outcome of all of her choices in life with regard to getting heavily addicted to heroin which my dad introduced her to. I paid the price all my life for their choices, having to live with their addiction and the life style that went with it, the dealing of drugs and having many addicts around me throughout my childhood and early adulthood. Their lifestyle plagued me with bouts of depression, not being able to see an end to the situation. As a child I feared their premature death through using drugs, or them going to prison for years for dealing and me being taken away by social services. I also felt responsible for my younger sisters, which was what kept me bound to them."

Though she loved her parents Veronica eventually despaired of them, seeing how they wasted their talents and damaged their health and personalities through drugs.

There are people in this book whose lives reveal the sad unfulfillment of their potential, people who you would probably have liked if you'd known them, but not realised what they were hiding. There are some whose lives were blighted by living with and supporting addicts; and others who can't be mentioned because they were 'celebrities', artists in the public eye, who 'scored' from Veronica's parents. Veronica sometimes thought of the contrast of their lives, how she nearly rubbed shoulders with them, but how far apart they really were.

There are a lot of 'if only' situations in this story, which underline the relentless tragedy of being part of the drug culture. Sadly it is a tragedy without a fully happy ending, as though Veronica has left that life style behind, she deeply regrets the things that could have been but weren't, and the loss of relationships with friends and family who haven't changed or moved on; and of course those who have passed away. It is hard for any of us to relinquish our attachment to our early lives, to re-evaluate the things we grew up with and the people who influenced us. It is painful to swap loyalties, to make positive choices and try to fit into a culture with different values to the one in which we were raised. Though Veronica has made the shift, the conflicts remain, which is partly why she wanted to write this book.

For anyone who thinks it is easy to give up drugs and the associated lifestyle, let this book tell you it isn't. For anyone who is or has been in a similar situation, let this book give you hope and comfort. For anyone who is wanting to change their lives, let this book tell you it is worth the struggle for yourself and your family. For anybody who is worried about children living in a similar situation, it may be a hard choice to take action, but children's needs must come first. If you think that drug taking is okay, consider the damage drugs have done to these people's lives and think again.

Veronica is an articulate, talented and motivated person who has worked hard to change her life and expectations. How many more people are out there who are having the same experience, but without the capacity or opportunity to make the change?

Veronica hopes that this book will help them.

CHAPTER 1

The Raid

Veronica's cosy evening was about to come to an abrupt end. One moment she was comfortably lounging on the sofa with her Nan watching TV, when suddenly there was an almighty bang. The sound of shattering glass and heavy footsteps pounding down the stairs terrified her; she knew in an instant that they were back again. She jumped to her feet full of fear, but within a moment she and her Nan were surrounded by armed men dressed in black, only their eyes and lips showing through their balaclavas.

Barely thinking, Veronica ran behind the sofa in a vain attempt to hide, but one of the men pointed his gun at her and told her to get out of the room. She froze, her heart pounding so fast she could hardly breathe, then she felt a warm trickle down her legs, and realised with horror, that she'd wet herself. Her Nan, Rose, was trying to stay calm, she called Veronica to come and sit with her. Rose was just as terrified, never having experienced anything like this before. She was a convent educated lady, whose destiny was to become a nun until she met the man who became Veronica's Grandfather. Veronica ran into her Nan's arms, they huddled together shaking.

"We have a warrant for the arrest of Philip Baker for supplying class A drugs," said one of the men who was now evidently a police officer.

As his words echoed in her mind, Veronica remembered when her dad went away a few years ago. She was around six years old and missed him desperately. Every day after school she would rush home and ask her mum to put her favourite song on the record player. It was 'Go Your Own Way' by Fleetwood Mac. She would sing it over and over and dance around the room reminiscing about her dad. Philip was a talented guitarist and Veronica was his biggest fan, she idolised his musical ability.

One of the officers had removed the Christmas presents from under the tree, and was busy opening them when her mum came into the room and pleaded with him not to.

"Do you think we would stoop so low as to hide drugs in our kids' presents?" Paula exclaimed. Her pleas were ignored and the police officer continued unwrapping the presents.

Veronica was beside herself, Christmas had been devastated right there in an instant; and she had no doubt in her mind that her daddy wouldn't be at home this Christmas either. There was a sound of scuffling upstairs from her parents' bedroom; and her dad yelping in pain. The officers were shouting and beating him. Veronica wanted to run upstairs to her dad's aid, but she knew there was nothing she could do to help.

The officer destroying the presents then ushered Veronica into the kitchen, as they had decided to strip search her Nan. Rose was absolutely horrified that she was being treated like a criminal, "how dare you?" she demanded as they forced her by the arm. She was a law-abiding citizen who had always worked hard to pay her way in society; and here she was, a pensioner being forced to strip naked in front of a stranger. Veronica walked into the kitchen; there were officers searching through drawers and cupboards there too, and one of her dad's friends who had been visiting was also under arrest. Graham was seated at the kitchen table, he could see that Veronica was extremely upset and called her to sit on his lap to comfort her.

As she sat there one of the officers sneered, "Do you know what your dad is Veronica? He is dirt!"

Veronica became hot with anger and spat in the officer's face, retorting, "No, you are dirt for picking on my dad who hasn't hurt anyone, why don't you do a proper job and go arrest the murderers out there?"

The officer was gob-smacked. He turned to Paula who had also been led into the kitchen and said, "Your daughter has a chip on her shoulder!"

"Well what do you expect?" she replied.

Just then, one of the officers came into the kitchen with a bag of heroin. He was very pleased with himself as he'd found a substantial amount. Another officer had found some marijuana and electronic scales. They continued searching the house, leaving a trail of destruction along the way. Philip was led downstairs in handcuffs; he was read his rights and arrested. He looked weary; his hand was swollen black and blue. There was a huge abscess on his hand that had become infected from using dirty needles and he'd been in hospital because of blood poisoning from it. Now the police had crushed his hand by stamping on it. Veronica cried inconsolably, she couldn't bear her dad being treated like that.

"No," she cried, "don't take my dad." She was nearly hysterical with worry, "What are we going to do now?" she thought to herself.

Paula was cradling baby Ella, Veronica's little sister; and Veronica wondered how they would cope without her dad. Rose came out of the bathroom looking disgusted and dishevelled; they had found nothing on her of course. The police left the house one by one and put Philip into a van waiting outside, then drove him away. Paula was crying, she called the council to send a maintenance man to make good the upstairs balcony door that had been smashed to smithereens, and Veronica was sent to bed so that her mum could start cleaning up the mess.

CHAPTER 2

Tangiers

Veronica was not surprised that the police had found the drugs, and she knew it would not really have been beyond her parents' guile to hide them under the Christmas tree. The scene took her back to when she was seven years old and went to North Africa in a Volkswagen Camper with Mum, Dad and an 8 year old cousin. Her dad had saved up enough money to travel there, firstly to come off heroin, secondly for the experience of it, or so Veronica was told. Drugs were never far from his mind though, as Veronica discovered on their way back from Morocco. While they were queuing in traffic to go through customs in Tangiers on their way to get the ferry to Spain, some customs officers who were randomly stopping cars and vans to search for drugs or other smuggled goods pulled them over. Alsatian sniffer dogs were set to work in their camper van. The dogs sniffed and snarled all over the van whilst the officers with them rummaged through cupboards, pulling out bedding and clothes. Veronica knew what they were looking for and wondered if the hash oil that had been kept in a glass in the fridge, had been moved and hidden well. She sighed with relief when she realised that fortunately it hadn't been found.

The officers decided to take Philip and Paula off to the cells to be searched. A woman officer took Veronica and her cousin Selina to a waiting room. Veronica was worried but she busied herself by playing with her cousin. She had learnt to use her imagination to escape the reality of her parents' drug addiction, and had imaginary friends who helped comfort her at times like these when she was anxious, but at least she had her cousin for company this time.

A while later the girls were reunited with Philip and Paula, and they all returned to the camper van. Philip was relieved that Paula had surreptitiously got rid of a handful of condoms full of hash oil, which she had carried hidden in her clothing. She managed to throw them out of her pockets as they were walking down a corridor in the customs building, without being seen. One of the condoms had landed next to a lady's bag which was being searched by other officers. It was picked up; and they assumed it had come from that woman's bag which was unfortunate for her, as clearly Paula could say nothing in the circumstances.

As they had missed the ferry due to the customs search, they had to wait for the next sailing.

This gave Paula time to notice that some of the condoms were still lying where she'd discarded them. She wanted to get them back; and told Veronica to pretend to drop a toy next to them, then as she picked it up, to hide the condoms down the front of her dungarees. She told her to make really sure that no one saw her do it. To Veronica, this was like a game; she was excited by the idea of retrieving the items without being noticed. She would be seen as a hero in her parents' eyes and that spurred her on. Veronica did her job well, and they soon continued their travels to Spain. The camper van broke down there though; and Veronica, her mum and cousin returned to England on ferries via France, whilst Philip stayed away for a further three months. Paula had sewn the condoms into fluffy rabbit pyjama cases, which Veronica and Selina carried all the way home. It was a difficult journey; they had very little money for food or comfort, which seemed ironic given the value of the drugs they were carrying.

CHAPTER 3

Tied Up and Burgled

Phil and Paula had been dealing heroin for over a year, they felt they had no choice but to supply drugs to fund their own habit. Their house became so busy that little Veronica would be up and down the stairs all day answering the door and making cups of tea. Sometimes she would answer the door, run upstairs and before she reached the top, the bell would ring again.

Veronica knew never to just open the door. She or her parents would look out of the first-floor window of their second-floor maisonette; then only open the door if they knew who the person was.

One early Sunday morning in October 1982, the bell rang and Veronica went to the window as usual. There were two foreign men outside speaking to each other in another language. Veronica called down to them and asked them what they wanted. One replied, "Philip."

Veronica went upstairs to the top floor loft room, where her parents were in bed. She woke her dad and told him about the strange men outside.

Paula was asleep and heavily pregnant; in fact it was her due date to give birth.

Philip got up, put on his jeans and went downstairs to the lounge to open the window.

The men couldn't really speak English; they were French but knew his name.

Philip sent Veronica to open the door and when the men came upstairs, Philip invited them to sit at the kitchen table.

Philip and Paula had known a French lady called Evelyn for some years before she moved back to France. Evelyn had sent two male friends over to Phil and Paula a few months earlier, as one of the guys was interested in purchasing a motor bike and she knew that Phil knew a lot about motorbikes. These guys were also interested in buying drugs. Phil and Paula had put them up for a few days, helped them get a bike; and sold them various drugs.

Phil and one of the guys had a difference of opinion before they left for France, but Phil didn't put any thought into it and assumed these other two men were also friends sent by Evelyn.

Philip gave Veronica some money and told her to go across the road to get some milk and biscuits from the shop.

When Veronica returned, she rang the bell and was surprised that one of the French men let her in. As she reached the top of the stairs, the man put his hand on the back of her neck and pushed her into the kitchen where Philip was sitting at the table. Veronica knew something was wrong because the other man was shouting in French and waving a knife at him.

Philip tried to keep the situation calm by telling the men where there was money and to just take it. Veronica began to cry which made the knife man even more agitated. He stank of vodka; they had brought a bottle of vodka with them which showed they had just come off the ferry, as the label clearly stated 'duty free'.

Veronica was made to sit on her dad's lap and as she did so, Philip whispered in her ear to keep calm and not to worry. The man who had answered the door to Veronica then dragged Lennon, Veronica's pet dog, into the bathroom and shut the door, before going up the stairs to the loft room where Paula was still sleeping.

As he was searching the room for valuables and drugs, Paula woke up startled and told him to fuck off. He started yelling in French and pointing a knife at her; he made her get up and go down stairs. Paula was shouting down to Philip, who told her to keep calm and do as the man said. When she came into the kitchen she was made to sit beside Phil and Veronica.

The man who'd been drinking was becoming hysterical, it was obvious he wanted the drugs stash, but Philip was not going to give that away. He kept telling him, "I gave you everything, you have it all." He grabbed a gold necklace around Paula's neck and snapped it off. Paula shouted at him as he had hurt her.

Phil told Paula to pretend she was going into labour and make loud panting noises, he hoped the blokes might panic and leave. At first it didn't work, the drunken man just became more impatient with Philip and started waving his knife around. Then they decided to take Phil, Paula and Veronica upstairs to the loft room. The men had already cut the wires from the telephone, so they used these and Philip's electric guitar leads, to tie Phil and Paula up.

They tied Phil to the headboard post of their bed, whilst Paula was tied with her hands behind her back and feet together. They didn't seem to care that she was heavily pregnant and continued by stuffing a baby's nightie, which was in a pile of newborn clothes ready in a basket beside the bed, into her mouth.

The quieter of the two men seemed to argue with the louder, drunk man. He obviously didn't want to tie Veronica up, but he did so in the end. Her hands were tied behind her back with a scarf, and then the men went downstairs to continue their search for valuables.

Philip told Veronica to be brave and keep calm and wait for the men to leave.

Eventually the door slammed and the house became quiet. Philip struggled to get free but was tied very tightly with the guitar leads. He told Veronica to wriggle her wrists to see if she could get one of her hands free. Veronica did as she was told and eventually she managed to free herself. Then she took the nightie from her mum's mouth and ran to the kitchen to fetch a sharp knife as her dad had instructed. She cut the wire from her mum's ankles and wrists, then once Paula was free, she was able to cut Philip free too.

They went downstairs to find the house had been turned upside down, vases had been broken and ornaments strewn all over the floor. There was a trail of destruction in every room as the men had taken many valuables, but they didn't get what they had come for, the drugs.

CHAPTER 4

Philip's Early Years

Philip was the youngest of four children and grew up in Marylebone with his mum and dad, sister and two older brothers.

His dad had been a medic in the Second World War, who was posted to Malta to help with the dead and wounded. This had affected him enormously for years afterwards. He started a family with Philip's mum, Emily, after the war, but he was a heavy smoker, which led to his death from lung cancer when Philip was only six years old. Emily had to play the role of mum and dad from then on, and work all the hours she could to keep the roof over their head. Philip's last memory of his dad was of him being quite sick and asking Philip to go the shop for him. Philip's response was, "Only if you fix my bow and arrow by the time I get back," which his father did.

Later in life, Philip said how selfish he felt for years after, for demanding that of his dad whilst he was so poorly. He said no one explained how serious it was; and when he died, he wasn't allowed to go to the funeral. It was years later when he was about ten or eleven years old, that his mum let him go to Finchley Road cemetery to lay flowers. She got lost in there and couldn't remember where his dad's plot was, but Philip seemed to know instinctively; and took her to the grave.

Philip's eldest brother and his sister were much older than him and left home whilst he was still young. His sister joined the army, where she met the man she would marry.

Philip's brother Michael, who was only eighteen months older, was still at home, but Philip found it difficult to get along with him. He was always lying and cheating people out of money, especially his own family and friends. Philip didn't like this about his brother one bit, but loved him wholeheartedly nevertheless.

Philip found life without his dad difficult. His mum would leave for work at the crack of dawn and some days would not return until late into the evening. Philip and Michael would have to come home from school and fend for themselves until their mother came in from work.

Left to his own devices, Philip got involved with older lads in the area. He was very interested in motorbikes, and had built his own by the time he was twelve. This got him involved with a gang of Hells Angels, who were mostly about eighteen. Philip looked up to them and wanted to be accepted as one of them. He decorated his leather jacket with the words 'All Coppers are Bastards', plastered across the back, and was pleased when the gang involved him as an accomplice in a bank robbery when he was just twelve years old. He got away with hundreds of pounds, which he hid at home. When his mum found out, she was very disapproving, but Philip offered her some money, which she needed to pay for her daughter's wedding. Emily knew that the money had come from some illegal means but didn't know exactly how. She didn't want to know either, so she turned a blind eye and accepted the gift.

Michael found what Philip had left under his bed and stole a substantial amount of it. Then he produced the remainder to their mum to grass his brother up to her.

Emily slapped Michael and told him to mind his own business and put the money back! He never owned up to stealing some of it though, but Philip knew. This was just one of the many occasions when Michael would steal from, or cheat his brother or his own mother, out of money.

Philip had spent some years through his adolescence in approved schools because he'd been in a lot of trouble with the law for robberies and other crimes, but this didn't change him. As soon as he got a chance, he would escape and go on the run.

He grew up fast and was having intercourse with fourteen year old girls by the time he was twelve. He even fathered children at the ages of twelve and fourteen. Nothing seemed to have stopped Philip from getting into trouble; which probably had a lot to do with the fact that his Hells Angels friends had given him a hit of heroin when he was just twelve; which created a massive problem for the rest of Philip's life.

By the time he bumped into Paula at seventeen, he had acquired a taste for marijuana and had experimented with acid and poppers, but he was well and truly addicted to heroin. He was very much into the latest scene of music culture and taught himself to play the guitar. His idols were Jimmy Hendrix, The Who, Fleetwood Mac, David Bowie and Pink Floyd to name a few.

Phil became an extremely talented lead guitarist in a band that played local gigs, and which even supported 10CC briefly. They had an opportunity to go on tour with 10CC, but relationships and drug abuse prevented that. Other band members dropped out for various reasons, but Philip had already fallen in love with Paula; and so the next year would see them shack up together in various squats around London, with their newborn baby girl; Veronica.

CHAPTER 5

Paula's Early Years

Paula grew up in Capland Street, Marylebone, with her mum, Rose and her dad, Bill. Her father was an alcoholic who spent most of his time in the local pubs drinking Guinness, whilst his wife worked hard, often holding down three jobs in a day, cleaning for various clients.

Paula was a shy and quiet child, the youngest of four daughters. She was sweet and innocent, with a very mild mannered temperament.

Paula went to Gateway Primary School, where she first met Veronica's dad Philip. They became 'boyfriend and girlfriend' when Paula was only six. She was too shy to kiss Philip then, so he packed her in, choosing her cousin Christine instead, who was happy to oblige.

As Paula went through puberty she began to become interested in boys; and like most teenagers, was also into the latest popular music scene. She too liked Jimmy Hendrix and David Bowie, but had a particular crush on Marc Bolan; and even as an adult she often cooed over him when he was on TV, even in front of Veronica.

Experimenting with drugs was part and parcel of the underground hippy era which Paula began to become a part of. When she was around twelve to thirteen years old she tried poppers and acid pills, along with her first sexual experiences with a few of the local lads.

Her cousin Christine lived in the same block of flats and was the same age as Paula. They were the best of friends and often hung out together. They went to parties, took ecstasy, acid and other similar drugs; and met lads. Christine often climbed out of the window of the high storey flat where she lived with her parents, as they would not allow her out at night, let alone go to parties. So Christine would climb onto a narrow drain pipe, which she would shimmy down, to get to the bottom.

One day Christine fell and ended up in a coma for two months before she passed away, at the age of fifteen. This had a massive impact on Paula as they had gone to school together and had been the best of friends for most of their childhood. Paula was beside herself.

Around this time Paula was dating a lad called Derek. She had been going out with Derek for a couple of years. He was a few years older than Paula and his experimenting with drugs had led him into a heroin habit. He treated Paula quite badly, always taking her wages to buy heroin. She was quite used to this kind of treatment though, as her own father was always taking money from her to pay for his alcohol. She was also used to seeing her mum being treated quite badly.

Unfortunately for Paula, she soon realised that she had become pregnant by Derek at the age of fifteen, but when she broke the news to him, he insisted it wasn't his and accused her of sleeping around. Paula knew in her heart that she couldn't have a baby at the age she was, by a heroin addict who clearly had no real feelings for her. She confided in her mum, who arranged for Paula to have an abortion.

This was still very taboo back in the early 1970s, and women wanting abortions were treated terribly by medical staff. Under-age girls who were pregnant and wanting an abortion were made to feel dirty; and treated like a disgrace to their families and society.

Paula was ushered into a room where she waited for a doctor to examine her. It was a horrifying experience. She felt as though she was invisible, the doctors only spoke to ask her name, age and address. After the procedure she was ushered out of the clinic with her mum.

Having been educated in a convent, Rose wasn't equipped to deal with her daughter's situation. She didn't know how to talk openly about sex with Paula. In fact when Paula started her period around the age of twelve, Rose told Paula, 'Just stay away from boys.' Paula thought she had a disease and was dirty. It would take some time for Paula to work it all out for herself, as talking openly about sex, boys, drugs and life wasn't an option. Even though she had three sisters, they were much older and had already left home to begin their own lives.

Paula and Derek split up; then within a year, Derek died of sclerosis of the liver through alcohol abuse. Paula bumped into Philip again, and they began dating. She was smoking marijuana and on occasion taking various other drugs. Philip was using heroin; and although Paula wasn't happy about this, she continued to see him.

Their union was to become a life of addiction, drug abuse and much more. They were infatuated with each other, and Paula was head over

24

heels in love. Philip quite openly said over the following years, that they didn't leave his bedroom for days while making love.

Paula conceived within a year; she was over the moon with happiness. She had not had the best of childhoods watching her mum struggling to make ends meet whilst her dad drank it all away down the pub. Rose was a beautiful petite lady who wouldn't say "boo" to a goose, but Bill was always foul-mouthed and drunk. He abused poor Rose and never had a nice word to say to her. Paula wanted a better life, with someone who loved her; and she had found that in Philip, all she had to do was get him to stop taking the drugs.

CHAPTER 6

Veronica's Early Years

During Veronica's early life, Phil and Paula moved from one squat to another, getting more heavily involved in drugs. Veronica wasn't well during this period and spent a lot of time going in and out of hospital with chest infections and pneumonia, seven times in one year.

From birth until she was around seven years old, Veronica spent months in hospital. Sometimes it would just be for a matter of days, then she'd be sent home only to return a few days later, worse than she was before.

The doctors carried out various tests including sweat tests, which ruled out cystic fibrosis, but they never came to any real diagnosis, just concluding that it was because she was premature at birth. Veronica hated the sweat tests; she had plasters applied all over her back, attached to little wires or tubes. She felt like a freak and cried the hospital down every time they did this. She also had to have an operation to straighten her lazy eye when she was five years old; and when she was six, she came down with measles and pneumonia, both at the same time.

Veronica was extremely poorly then and had to stay in isolation for 3 weeks. She remembers looking out of the hospital window and peering down at the streets, she could see the sun was shining and children were playing in a nearby park. She noted how the kids were wearing nice clothes and pretty dresses. She desperately wanted to be wearing her own clothes and be able to play in the park with her mum. Veronica got on a mission to perk herself up and told the nurses that she was feeling much better and needed to go home. They assured her that she would be going home just as soon as she was all clear.

Veronica was frustrated; she found some clothes in her room, got dressed and waited.

When her mum arrived she told her that she was much better and could go home now.

Veronica was so persuasive that she managed to get Paula to take her out of the room and towards the ward exit, but Paula spoke to a nurse who informed her that Veronica was in no fit state to leave yet. Veronica found being so poorly in her early years to be quite traumatic; and having to stay in hospital meant being apart from her mum so much. Once, when Veronica was just two years old, she was in hospital with pneumonia; and when Paula came to visit her, she punched her mum. Veronica was too young to understand why she had been left in there and it had obviously affected her a great deal.

As time went by and Veronica got older, she understood more about what was happening, and fortunately her pneumonia stopped when she was seven years old. By this time, she and her parents were living in a two-bedroom maisonette provided by Camden council; and paid for by social security benefits. This should have been a fresh start for the family, but the heroin had by now taken a strong hold on Phil and Paula; and life was to become a peculiar existence for Veronica. She would have to learn to use her imagination to keep herself company, as she would spend many hours alone in a room whilst her parents were out of their heads.

CHAPTER 7

Sedating Veronica with Marijuana

Phil and Paula were typical hippies during the seventies and strict vegetarians.

Paula baked a lot of homemade bread and also made Hash Cakes. When Phil and Paula held social gatherings with their friends, they sometimes invited their neighbours around and offered them some of the cakes. Their neighbours were straight laced normal types, who had never touched anything drug related in their lives. They had no idea what was in the cakes, yet here they were, high on marijuana without even realising it. Phil, Paula and their friends found this very amusing, it was like a scene out of the Cheech and Chong movie: 'Up in Smoke'.

Veronica would scoff her share of the cake too, she was only around 2 or 3 years old when she first remembered eating marijuana, she acquired a taste for it and would plead for more. Veronica can remember playing with different coloured bouncy balls and being mesmerised by their colours and shapes. Everything felt slower, and she would soon feel tired and go to sleep.

When Veronica was 5 years old she remembers her mum and dad getting ready to go out looking for empty houses. They had given Veronica some marijuana to sedate her but she felt hungry, it was late and she wanted her mum to cook her some food. Paula prepared some scrambled eggs and beans on toast for Veronica, but as she began to eat, she started to feel funny. A dizzy feeling washed over her and as she looked down at her red paisley dress, she noticed the pattern had started to move. The shapes began to change into long slithering snakes and they were winding upwards out of her dress towards her face. This scared Veronica terribly and she began to panic and cry. Her mum came into the lounge to see what the matter was and told Veronica that it was in her imagination and not to worry, as it wasn't real.

Paula got Veronica ready for bed, tucked her in and gave her a kiss goodnight. This was the last time Veronica remembered eating marijuana, maybe her mum realised that it was having a negative effect.

As Veronica got older, she questioned her parents about this. She told them she remembered asking for more cakes and remembered the taste of marijuana and the frightening episode when she was five years of age. Her dad denied this, he was either ashamed of these actions as time went on, or worried that Veronica may spill the beans to the wrong ears, but Paula never denied it. She admitted that they had given Veronica minute amounts of marijuana to quieten her down.

She said Veronica had such a lot of energy and they only wanted to calm her on occasions.

Paula said they were young themselves and didn't see the harm, but realised as they were growing up that it wasn't a clever idea. She told Veronica to not ever tell anyone, as her mum and dad would be in a lot of trouble; and Veronica would be taken away by Social Services. Veronica loved her parents and never wanted this to happen. She loved her mum and dad so much, she couldn't live without them. Veronica agreed it would always remain a secret.

CHAPTER 8

Nocturnal Events

Phil had many practical skills which he had learned whilst working for St Mary's hospital in Paddington, before Veronica was born. He was a good plumber and also good with electrics. He could rewire electrical circuits and was confident in handling gas boilers.

During the first five years of Veronica's life, Phil used his expertise to operate the gas and heating systems in the squats where they lived. He often wired into the legitimate tenants' systems, so that they were unknowingly footing the bill for the squatters using their utilities. Phil and his hippy friends thought it was harmless and quite funny.

Phil also used his skills to break into shops. One in particular was a newsagent at the end of the road where the family lived in Kilburn. In the early hours of the morning, Phil would climb onto the roof of the shop and break in through the ceiling by taking out tiles. He would fill a bag with boxes of cigarettes, cigarette papers, lighters, chewing gum and maybe some sweets if there was room left. He would sell this hoard in exchange for drugs, and he and Paula would be overjoyed with their run of luck. Life would be on the up when there was extra cash coming in; and Veronica would usually benefit too, having her share of the ill-gotten gum and sweets.

When she overheard her parents talking about the burglary, her dad swore her to secrecy.

He told Veronica not to arouse suspicion when she went to the shop by staring at the gaping hole in the ceiling. Phil burgled the same shop a few times over the course of a few weeks, which caused the shopkeeper great distress. Veronica would go in to buy tea bags or biscuits and overhear the shopkeeper telling other customers how it had impacted on his business. Phil didn't see any harm though, and to help clear his conscience he told himself that the shop keeper would claim it back on insurance anyway. He saw himself as a real-life Robin Hood, and told Veronica that he would take from the rich and give to the poor. Veronica thought her dad was really cool.

Phil and Paula would also search empty houses, looking for valuables left behind by previous tenants. They didn't see it as wrong or harmful as either the owners were no longer there, or they were the vacant properties of the deceased. Council workers would have eventually gone in to prepare the homes for new tenants anyway, so to them, it was just like collecting rubbish.

Well that's how they justified what they were doing; in fact they were looking for anything valuable to sell for drugs.

Veronica remembered a time when she was about five years old; they were walking through a house with missing floorboards, it was cold, dark and smelled of damp. She thought she was involved in a mystery game; it was very intriguing for her. As her parents led her upstairs, where there were some missing steps, a broken board gave way and Veronica's foot went through. She yelped and her dad told her to be quiet. She was very scared after that, frightened to put another foot wrong. It was then that she realised how dangerous the mystery game was, so it wasn't so exciting from then on. Her parents found money stashed under the bed and in clothes. They found jewellery that seemed very old; bracelets with garnets, gold rings with rubies and sapphires and other unusual items. Veronica was excited because she loved the pretty jewels and pleaded with her parents to keep something. There was an old tin box full of foreign coins too, Francs, Pesetas and more, which fascinated Veronica. This box of coins was to become very important and valuable to Veronica, as a prop in the imaginary games that occupied her mind.

The going out on burglaries proved to be fruitful, Veronica even ended up acquiring her own share of the haul. She would take great pleasure in playing with the many necklaces and bracelets her parents found.

One evening when Veronica was around six years old, her parents went out hunting for empty houses, but decided to leave Veronica at home in bed.

They lived in a ground floor one bedroom council flat at the time; where Veronica slept in a single bed in the same room as her parents. She was used to sharing a room with them and would sleep quite deeply, even when they were being loud, talking and smoking in the room.

On this night however, Veronica experienced a nightmare. She was being chased by a monster and no matter how fast she ran, she didn't seem to get very far. She was running through woods in the dark and she could hear the snarling and howling of a werewolf catching up behind her. Veronica screamed and woke up in a state, her heart was pounding through her chest and she struggled to catch her breath. Tears streamed down her cheeks as she tried to make sense of it all.

Though she knew it was just a bad dream, she was too scared to close her eyes and go back to sleep, in case the monster came back. The room was dark and quiet, she called for her mum, but there was no answer. Veronica felt worried; she got out of bed and turned on the light. She called her mum again and went out into the hall.

"Mummy where are you?" Still there was no reply. She called for her dad, again there was no answer. She searched the lounge, but there was no sign of her parents, she looked in the toilet and bathroom, still no sign. Veronica realised that she was home alone. This made her even more frightened, she cried and cried and ran back to her bed, sobbing herself to sleep.

The next morning when Veronica awoke, her parents were back in the bed opposite her. She roused her mum and told her that she had woken up in the night and realised she was alone. Her mum told her they'd had to go out for a little while, and left Veronica soundly sleeping as they didn't want to disturb her. Her mum said they'd asked their neighbour Don, who lived in the flat upstairs, to keep an ear open for Veronica. "We didn't leave you alone," said Veronica's mum.

But Veronica didn't see it this way; she didn't even know the neighbour upstairs. Why didn't Don come to settle her when she was crying with fear, she wondered? That evening was to affect Veronica for a long time, as she didn't feel safe when she went to bed.

She kept having nightmares of a monster chasing her, and she worried that if she went to sleep her parents would leave her.

When she was around seven years old, Veronica's parents took her to burgle the local Pine Furniture shop in West Hampstead. Philip was adept at picking locks, so soon found his way into the shop's basement. He'd arranged for a van to be waiting just around the corner; and Veronica found this all very amusing, as it was a step up from her usual burglary experiences of old houses and flats. Everything here was brand new and unused. Veronica enjoyed walking around the shop eyeing up all the beautiful pine furniture. She found a bed and got into it, pretending it was hers, she had never seen such beautiful furniture before; and felt like a princess lying in that bed!

It was late in the evening but there were still people around outside. Veronica remembered having to be quiet, but wondered about how obvious her dad would be carrying huge pieces of furniture out of the shop and into the van outside. If anyone spotted them though, they would probably assume they were the shop's staff or owners.

Philip also found a large envelope full of money stashed underneath some furniture. They could have just taken that and left, but they didn't. They filled the van to the brim before they went.

Veronica's lounge was like living in a furniture shop for many days afterwards, there was hardly any space to get around the room. Philip and Paula sold items to people they knew, or exchanged them for drugs. Their haul had been a success, and Veronica was so happy with the new furniture left in her home that she felt like this was the beginning of bigger and better things to come. Unfortunately though, it didn't last.

CHAPTER 9

A Fix

Veronica's childhood had been exciting at times, but also lonely and anxious. She often felt a sense of despair and carried a lot of responsibility for herself, her parents and younger siblings. In fact thinking back, she knows she unwittingly made it possible for her parents to carry on their lifestyle by being so useful and dependable. She had seen things a little girl shouldn't see and had experiences that were unusual and disturbing.

Her parents would go into another room to use their drugs, leaving Veronica for hours; she could hear the noises they were making - not all their trips were pleasant - and she was quite used to their blood and vomit. One afternoon in particular, Veronica was told to play in the lounge, and stay there until her parents said that she could leave the room.

Veronica knew what they were going to do, as she had got used to the routine. But it wasn't nice for her, she got very bored having to wait and wait, for what seemed like an eternity before being allowed to roam freely around the house again. She would pass the time by using her imagination, she loved singing and dancing; and imagined she had an audience watching her. In her mind the room was a theatre packed full of admirers, who had all come to see Veronica perform.

Meanwhile her parents were next door in the kitchen preparing a fix. Veronica had seen her mum take a belt from her dressing gown to use as a tourniquet and get a spoon and lighter. She could hear them discussing how much they should have; followed by their voices becoming very slow, slurred and croaky. She knew then, that her parents were effectively in another world.

Veronica tried not to worry, distracting herself by returning to the theatrical performance for her waiting audience. She twirled around the room singing as she went, her audience clapping and cheering, but she was sharply interrupted by her mother crying out her father's name in distress.

"Philip," Paula cried, "wake up, please wake up." There was no sound from Philip.

Paula's voice became louder and even more distressed; Veronica could hear her slapping Philip to wake him up, and she knew in her heart that something was seriously wrong.

She ran to the kitchen to see what was happening. Her dad was lying on the kitchen floor, his body was convulsing and shaking erratically, his eyes were closed. The tourniquet was still around his arm, but there was blood dripping from the side of it.

As Veronica started to scream for her dad, Paula turned around realising what her daughter had just witnessed. She told her to get out of the room and said, "Try not to worry; I don't want you to see this."

Veronica ran back to the lounge, her instinct was to open the window and scream for help, but she knew she would be in trouble if she did. She feared that her parents would be taken away by the police and she would not have a mum or dad anymore.

A few minutes later, her dad came round, but was very ill, he was dazed and confused, but at least he had stopped convulsing. Paula got him water and was crying.

"Phil you frightened me, I thought I had lost you." Veronica was still crying by the window, she had never been so scared and she had never seen her dad like this.

This was just one of many days though, when Veronica would have to sit and wait while her parents took their drugs. She didn't like it one bit, but could do nothing about it. She knew she could never speak a word of it to anyone, not even to her Nan, her cousins, or her teacher, no one. If she did, she knew the consequences. Her parents had sat her down and explained that she would be taken away and put into a care home with lots of other children without their families, and it was a sad and lonely place to be.

Veronica didn't like the idea of that, as she loved her parents so much she couldn't bear the thought of being apart from them.

CHAPTER 10

The Trial

After the raid when Police found heroin in Philip's home, he was charged with possessing class A drugs with the intention to supply, and this was the day in 1985 that the court would decide whether he was innocent, or guilty as charged. The trial had gone on for a few days and Veronica was very nervous.

She remembered the last time her dad went away and how lost her mum, Paula, was without him. That was only for six months, but seemed to go on forever, this time he could be sent down for many years.

Her dad had sat Veronica down and explained the consequences. It didn't bear thinking about.

Veronica could not even imagine the thought of her dad being sent to prison for that long.

She wondered how he would cope, being locked up all day every day for years. Tears filled her eyes whilst she was washing up some cups in the sink so she could make her mum and dad a lovely cup of tea before they left for court. She wondered too how her mum would cope without him, possibly for years. Her sister Ella was only a toddler, how would this affect her?

Veronica herself was only ten, how would she cope she wondered? She wiped her eyes and told herself that everything would work out fine in the end.

She imagined the judge banging his gavel to get the attention of the courtroom and proclaiming, "I find the defendant Philip Baker not guilty." Those words repeated themselves in Veronica's head, but despite her hopes, she knew they were just a fantasy.

She took her parents' tea upstairs to the bedroom on a tray, with a packet of her dad's favourite rich tea biscuits. She cuddled her dad and told him that she loved him more than anything in the world and wished him luck. They drank the tea and got ready for court.

Philip was dressed very smartly, wearing trousers and a proper shirt. It wasn't often that he dressed this way, usually preferring a T-shirt and jeans. Paula had dressed to impress too. Phil and Paula kissed their children goodbye, and set off for court. Veronica and her baby sister Ella were left with their Nan.

Veronica tried to forget about what was happening so played with her toys and watched television. The day dragged on and seemed like it would never end. She became increasingly agitated; and as daytime turned to early evening, Veronica asked her Nan, "When will Mum and Dad be back?"

Before Rose could answer, there was the sound of a key in the front door, and then Veronica's mum was coming up the stairs. Veronica ran to see if her dad was there too, but there was no sign of him. "Where's Dad?" she cried, already knowing inside; but hoping he was still outside.

Paula shook her head with disbelief, "I'm sorry babe," she said, "but Daddy's not coming home for a long time." Paula began to cry and Veronica burst into tears with her, she was so beside herself that she could hardly breathe. Paula went on to explain that the judge wanted to make an example of Philip, so he had been given nine years in total for his offences. In the end it was decided they would run concurrently rather than consecutively, which meant he was realistically looking at a stretch of three years. Paula said she thought that Philip was lucky he didn't get nine years, not that this made any of it any easier for Veronica, three years was a lifetime to her,

She cried so much her eyes were stinging and swollen; and she went to bed still crying, on a sopping wet pillow, snivelling herself to sleep.

Veronica's life changed as her childhood ended there and then, because suddenly she had to grow up and support her mum. In hindsight though, it was that which moulded her into becoming a responsible person; and she enjoyed a much closer connection with her mum. Though there were many difficulties and compromises at the time, looking back, Veronica now treasures those experiences.

CHAPTER 11

Whilst Philip's Away

The day after the trial, Veronica woke up in her mum's bed. This was to be the first of many where Veronica and little Ella would sleep in their mum's bed. Veronica found it hard accepting that her dad would be locked up for such a long time; Paula was also in shock. What would they do now? She had to toughen up and get on with it; Paula would have to be the one to keep it all together. She was on her own now, and had to look out for herself and the kids, she had her own expensive habit to pay for as well. Even though Paula was claiming benefits, her money couldn't stretch that far.

Life was becoming more difficult for Paula, not only did she have Veronica and Ella to fend for, but she realised with surprise that she was expecting again, and nearly five months gone. She was used to not having regular periods; this was part and parcel of having a habit, so hadn't suspected for a minute that she was pregnant again. Now with a newborn in tow as well, she would have to be really strong to sustain her lifestyle. She had to juggle the responsibilities of motherhood and routines such as getting Veronica off to school, seeing to Ella who was three years old, going to nursery and dealing with a newborn baby. Paula also had to be on hand day and night, to supply the demands of her punters.

Veronica remembers meeting strangers up the road with her mum, to supply drugs for cash.

She didn't know them well enough to invite them round to the flat, so she would meet them by the tube station and go off for a walk. When no one was around, Paula would hand over the heroin wrapped tightly in cling film. She found herself in some precarious situations, having to meet some seriously hardened types of male drug dealers, she could have been ripped off at any moment; and she would learn the hard way over the following three years to not trust anyone.

Veronica was very inquisitive and would listen to everything that was said. Paula would tell her off for being nosey but Veronica didn't want to be kept in the dark about anything, because she believed it was her duty to protect her mum now; and if anything went wrong, she would do the right thing.

Paula lived a risky life, which took a lot out of her; and she soon came to depend on Veronica for support. She became Paula's right arm. Veronica would bag up the dirty washing and take it to the Launderette, play there whilst waiting for the washing to finish, or do some shopping at the local supermarket whilst the washing was drying. When she returned to the launderette she would fold all the clothes and put them into Paula's baby buggy; and return home with the shopping as well. Though she felt extremely protective of her mum, Veronica also felt hard done by at times, especially during her early teens when she craved more freedom to hang out with friends. Instead, to enable Paula to tend to her punters, Veronica would have to carry out chores like washing up, vacuuming, cooking or taking care of her sisters. Then if it was not too late, she could go out for a couple of hours afterwards; which was her time to be a normal teenager with her friends. Even then she could not behave naturally though, as she had to remain guarded about her family's circumstances.

CHAPTER 12

Libby

Libby was Paula's best friend for a long time. She had a soft, gentle nature, was artistic and very good at drawing. She also loved antiques, especially old jewellery which she collected.

Libby came to England in her early twenties and soon met Bill, an English man who became her boyfriend. They lived together in a two bedroom flat just off the Harrow Road in North West London. They both experimented with drugs and alcohol, eventually becoming heroin addicts.

Libby had graduated in Czechoslovakia and came to London to find work. She'd always wanted children and she loved animals. Bill knew Phil and came round to see him when Veronica was around six or seven years old. He took to Veronica and offered to take her home to meet Libby and stay there overnight. Veronica was very willing to go, as she got quite bored at times. Veronica had nobody of her age to play with, so she was just as happy to go off with her parents' friends, in fact anyone who showed interest.

Libby enjoyed playing with Veronica, and would give her a huge wooden box filled with every coloured pencil you could imagine. Veronica would happily draw for hours, creating mosaic and paisley patterns in all colours. Libby would make Veronica muesli and fruit for breakfast, Veronica couldn't get enough of the attention.

Libby came to be a very special friend to Paula and an aunty figure to Veronica. In the following years when Ella came along, she became much attached to Libby too.

Phil and Paula would spend many afternoons and evenings around Libby's place smoking heroin and socialising. Sometimes Philip would get out his guitar and play some covers, whilst Libby would sing along with her beautiful voice.

As the years rolled by, Bill and Libby split up. Libby ended up alone whilst Bill met another addict, Claudia, who became the mother of his child. Libby suffered silently with depression and would drown her sorrows with alcohol and drugs. Despite this, she was a very loyal, trusting friend and ally to Paula; and she would be the only one of her friends to not end up in bed with Philip.

When Philip went to prison in 1985, Libby spent more time with Paula and the kids, often taking Veronica and Ella off for the day or two, to give Paula some time to sort out her dealings.

Veronica always enjoyed staying with Libby. Libby had an Alsatian bitch called Sapphire, which had grown up with Veronica's dog Lennon, who was a male cross Alsatian and Labrador. Libby would take the kids and dogs to Hampstead Heath and Primrose Hill for long walks. It is on times like these, that Veronica looks back with happiness.

In November 1986, Veronica and a friend went to West Hampstead tube station, where they spent hours asking people for a penny for the Guy. Lennon, who was about 5 years old at the time, followed them. Although Lennon did have a collar, he was never on a lead. He was a very street wise dog; and punters of Phil and Paula would report spotting him miles away from the family home, but Lennon always made his way back at the end of the day.

Veronica remembered a man with a bitch on heat walking into the tube station and Lennon trying to mount her. The man had asked Veronica to control Lennon and keep him back, which she did, but moments later after the man had gone, she let Lennon go and carried on her business of collecting for Guy Fawkes. Lennon didn't come home that evening, and Veronica would never see him again.

Veronica had an emotional break down over Lennon; she would wake in the night screaming for him. He had become her best friend, she loved him very much; and the thought of not knowing where he was or if he was still alive, tortured Veronica for months.

Paula would traipse down to Battersea Dogs' Home twice a week for weeks, searching for Lennon and posting notices up on trees all over Kilburn and the surrounding areas.

People would phone to say they had spotted him, and Veronica would rush off with Libby scouring streets and parks to find him, but to no avail. Lennon's disappearance was a complete mystery that Veronica had no choice but to accept.

Life was hard for her then, her dad had gone down for a long stretch in prison the year before and now she had lost her dog. Libby however was a tower of strength to Paula and the kids and would be on hand at a moment's notice. In fact Libby would be the one to look after Veronica and Ella when Paula went into labour on the 28th of March 1986 to give birth to Paulette.

Sadly, Libby died from hepatitis C and sclerosis of the liver in December 1994.

Every Christmas, she would go back to Czechoslovakia for a month to visit family.

Paula had found out that Libby had contracted hepatitis C only a few months before she died.

Libby's stomach was severely swollen, other punters and acquaintances that came to score at the family home would enquire if Libby was pregnant, but there was no possibility, as Libby was in her late forties or early fifties at this stage. Libby played the disease down to Paula probably because she didn't want to worry her.

That year, Ella had called Libby on Christmas Eve to wish her a Merry Christmas. Libby could hardly speak and told Ella she loved her and that she was sorry she had to go because she was ill with the flu.

Paula was very busy packing to go with Phil and the kids to his brother's in Hampshire; and by the time they got back in the New Year, Paula assumed that Libby had gone back home.

It would take another month before Paula found out from a mutual friend that Libby had died alone in hospital over Christmas. She had been cremated without a funeral, and her remains had been sent back to Czechoslovakia. Her dog Sapphire had been left behind howling in Libby's flat for days before someone got in and called the RSPCA, then she had been put down too. Libby's house had been ransacked and her jewels stolen.

Her family back home received nothing, other than her ashes.

CHAPTER 13

Philip's Prison Pals

Phil knew how to play the system whilst he was in Prison, drugs were good currency; and he continued to enjoy the advantages that being able to supply them bought for him. He made sure that he was well looked after during his time in various prisons. When he did his three year stretch, Phil had two good mates in prison, Dave and George.

Dave was from Uxbridge and was around 5 years younger than Phil and Paula.

He listened to musicians like Depeche Mode and Spandau Ballet and was very much into the British New Romantic movement. He liked the iconic Queen, Pink Floyd, Hendrix and Bob Marley too. During his time in prison he had sported pink spiked hair and become known by all the inmates as Pinky. Dave was particularly happy wearing eye liner.

In contrast, George was a big guy, covered in tattoos and with a shaven head; he was a man not to mess with. George came from the east end of London and was well known in his area. He had done some pretty ruthless things, allegedly even murder, but he was solid friends with Phil and became Phil's muscle. No one in the nick messed with George, and that meant Phil was pretty much looked out for. Although Philip had a temper of his own and had lost time for fighting inmates who had jumped queues for slopping out and such like, Philip did not care. He wasn't going to be intimidated by anyone, but with people like George around, Philip could keep his head down and get on with his sentence.

Although there were strict regulations for prison visits, and all visitors were searched before entering the visiting compound, Paula managed to hide heroin wrapped in condoms under her tongue. She would pass this to Philip when they kissed and he would swallow it down with a nice cup of tea during their visit. It would become available to trade a day or two later.

Being a regular supplier of drugs gave Philip a lot of power inside. He lived well, as he had the means to acquire everything else he needed. Tea, coffee, sugar, tobacco, cigarette papers, gum, you name it, Philip had it. Inmates would swap their supplies for a line of heroin, and that made Philip rich in prison.

All the prisoners had specific employment roles within the prison, which gave them a wage as well as a bargaining tool. An inmate working in the kitchen had access to extra food which he would use to barter for tobacco and such like. Philip became part of a supply ring; and as long as Paula kept the goods coming in, Philip could maintain a bearable existence inside.

Dave finished his sentence a year earlier than Philip and contacted Paula when he got outside.

Having been a self-employed plumber, Dave landed on his feet. He was married to a beautiful woman six years younger, by the name of Anna. She was from a well to do working class family that had supported her and Dave well.

He started up his own plumbing business when he came out of prison in 1986 and would often visit Paula to be supplied with heroin, which he had also got his young wife Anna into.

Dave would often chauffeur Paula and the kids to Suffolk to visit Phil in High Point prison.

This was a far cry, for Paula, from the usual trek of getting on the Tube with two kids, heavily pregnant, then waiting for a coach at Liverpool street station.

Paula would repay Dave in kind, and so Dave and Paula became firm friends.

Initially, Dave was a clever business man but as the years rolled by, the drugs took a bigger hold and his business suffered. Although he had a couple of employees who often covered for him, they eventually took advantage of him. Dave's wife ended up drifting apart from Dave, having had an affair, and deciding to get clean. Anna had taken a lot of abuse from Dave; when he was high on drugs he would call her fat and slap her. She walked out on him in 1991 never to return.

Heart broken and beside himself, Dave spent two years licking his wounds before meeting a woman twelve years younger. That only lasted a year and then in 1996 he met a fifteen year old girl and got her into heroin. She wanted to become a lap dancer and Dave encouraged it.

Phil and Paula saw less of Dave as he was living in Uxbridge again, and had found other more local suppliers. In 1999 Dave's picture was released in the Daily Mirror as a missing person's enquiry. It would take a further two years for Phil and Paula to discover that Dave's body had been found in a shallow grave in Epping Forest. At the time of writing, no one has yet been brought to justice for his murder and it remains a mystery.

When George was released from prison some months after Philip, he too became one of the many punters of the Baker household. He was a regular for many years, coming around to purchase heroin, sometimes two to three times per week. Veronica never really took much notice of George personally; to her he was just another punter. George had a very deep rough voice, he looked and sounded like a hard man, which in fact he was. He had done some pretty nasty things; and although this was evident in his mannerisms, he was always fond of kids. He was a doting dad and would often express this when talking about his own children.

Veronica knew little about George, but he was always very polite to her and always showed a keen interest in what she was doing at school, college or work.

As the years went on, George became quite ill with emphysema, but would still come round to get his heroin. To him the horse had bolted and it was too late to change. He would struggle to breathe and would sometimes bring an oxygen bottle in with him. Veronica felt sorry for George, but couldn't understand why he would still sit smoking cigarettes and heroin, chasing it on foil.

CHAPTER 14

Living with Addicts

Phil and Paula spent years abusing their bodies with drugs. Heroin had taken hold of Phil at the young age of thirteen, but Paula had not touched it until she was in her early twenties. Although she met Phil at sixteen, she vowed to never touch the drug, and gave Phil numerous ultimatums to 'give up or ship out'.

In the early years of their marriage, Paula would be alone for days with Veronica whilst Phil was out gigging with his band. He would party and get high and not come home for days at a time. Paula hated it, she knew that Phil was taking a lot of drugs, but she knew that when she first got with him. She had hoped that Phil would change; she hoped that he would come off them for her and his daughter Veronica. Paula spent hours in the kitchen preparing wholesome vegetarian meals for Phil, but he never returned home to eat them, so they ended up in the bin.

During those first few years Paula often felt isolated, despairing of Phil's drug abuse.

Phil would be out enjoying himself whilst she was stuck indoors with Veronica, who was often ill with pneumonia and in and out of hospital. As time went by, Phil made Paula feel as though she was missing out. She loved him and just wanted him to be with her more, but the drugs had a huge hold over Phil, and eventually it was to take a hold of Paula too. She later confessed to Veronica that she grew weak and thought that if you can't beat them join them and ended up getting into the drugs.

Paula hated it that Phil spent time around other women on drugs, whilst she was alone at home with Veronica waiting for his return. Paula became lonely and worried that Phil may end up going off with another woman, so she decided to join him; and quickly became as dependant as he was. Hence Veronica was often left alone in a room for hours whilst her parents and their friends would be gouching out all over the show.

Veronica found this part of her life was very tedious and worrying. She instinctively knew they were doing wrong and potentially harming themselves. She would creep up to the room they were in to see what everyone was doing because there would be complete silence, for what seemed an eternity to Veronica as a six year old.

She would become thirsty and hungry and didn't know if it was okay to interrupt them or not, as they had told her to stay out of the room they were in, until she was told otherwise.

Veronica would worry about whether her parents would wake from their drug induced sleep, or remain in a coma forever. When she stood to the side of the kitchen to peek around the door, she could see her parents spaced out with their bodies slumped over the kitchen table or slowly drifting off in their chair. There was no expression in their faces as all of the muscles had completely relaxed, and their mouths were turned down. Veronica didn't like seeing them like this, it frightened her and she often got so frustrated she would just call out to make them jump. Her dad would leap out of his skin and shout at her, but Veronica would insist that she was hungry and didn't want to be alone anymore.

Veronica would be told to go to her room and wait to be called. She would get into bed, though often it was daylight outside, but it may as well have been bed time; and Veronica would cry and cry until she cried herself to sleep.

Her parents never appreciated the impact their drug abuse had on Veronica. In fact the drugs didn't just abuse them, they abused Veronica too; and she felt they made her existence literally just that, an existence. Veronica found that living with addicts was very trying, it was so difficult to be patient with them because they always made promises they couldn't keep. She remembers her mum and dad offering to take her to the local swimming baths when she was about six years old. Veronica got very excited at the idea like any normal child would and wanted to go right there and then. She was told to be patient and that they would go soon, but as the day wore on, her mum and dad got completely out of it on the drugs. They couldn't function without regular doses of heroin as they were so heavily addicted. Veronica asked again about when they would be going swimming, and eventually she was told that it was too late and the swimming baths had closed, so they would have to go the next day. Sometimes this kind of situation would go on for a few days and Veronica would end up getting so frustrated and disappointed that she learned to take what they said with a pinch of salt. Veronica would have to amuse herself, but it was a very boring environment to be in; and there were days when she didn't even leave the house. Having learned from experience, Veronica became cautious about letting herself feel excited about any of her parents' promises.

Veronica remembers her tenth Birthday, she was at school and her mum had promised to collect her to take her straight to the clothes shop and toy shop, to buy her presents. She remembers feeling excited at school that day, but deep down she had a niggling feeling that they wouldn't go; and that she would be given an excuse of some kind. Veronica tried really hard to stop herself from feeling excited as she knew that if they didn't go, she would be so heart-broken, but in the end her mum did take her shopping; and Veronica got some lovely clothes for her birthday. She was very surprised and happy at this outcome, but sadly it wasn't consistent. More often than not there would be a change of plan, and she would end up feeling let down. As the years went by, Veronica trained herself to expect the worst, so that she didn't feel so let down and disappointed. This and her other experiences affected her emotionally. Veronica suffered with depression whilst growing up, but didn't realise what it was until she became old enough to understand. She also endured panic attacks on and off for years, the slightest thing would set them off. They were rooted in the worry she had as a child about waking up and finding her parents dead, as she'd seen the state her dad was in that time he was convulsing after a bad fix. Neither did she feel secure, because she'd had the experience of being left alone at home that night when she was five. Home didn't really feel like a safe haven for her either. She didn't feel safe after having had the front door broken down with sledge hammers, and police charging through shouting on many occasions. She became alarmed if she heard a noise outside at night and would jump out of bed and be at the window scouring the street below. Often the noises outside were just coming from people passing by, but she had adrenaline running through her body, expecting it to be the police or robbers. Without meaning to, Veronica had learned to be continuously on edge.

Her parents were very paranoid. One of the downfalls of drug addiction and their experience of police raids she supposed, but the effects spilled out onto her too. She listened intently to everything that happened and everything they told her. They openly shared their views on their addiction and how the outside world perceived them. They spoke of how society portrayed them as dirty, thieving and untrusting, when in fact they were very well kept and hygienic. Veronica was always well dressed and well bathed. Though in earlier years she remembers being hungry and living on porridge for a week or so, there was generally food available, they just ate late. So Veronica grew up with a rather large chip on her shoulder, believing that the outside world was the enemy. They didn't understand us, she thought, they were against normal people like Mum and Dad who had just been unfortunate to have become involved with drugs. Veronica didn't think they were the stereotypical drug addict family; her parents had an illness that they couldn't control, they were victims of the heroin that had taken hold of them. They needed help but couldn't get the right solution.

Paula went to drug clinics whilst Phil was in prison. She talked to Veronica about how their methods of trying to get addicts clean were useless. Paula would become miserable and despair of herself. Veronica grew up feeling very protective of her parents, she put them on a pedestal; and if anyone ever spoke ill of them then they would feel her wrath! Veronica knew her parents loved her because they always kissed and cuddled as a family. Phil and Paula were always very affectionate with her and her sisters, and with each other. But she can remember her dad hitting her mum at times, when she was young. Veronica would be sent to her room but she could hear him shouting and hitting her. She would hear her mum cry; it put the fear of God into her, to the point where she would wet herself. She wanted to stop him and save her mum, but on one occasion when Veronica screamed out, her dad threatened to hit her. This was when Phil and Paula were still quite young and obviously had a horrible addiction to live with.

As Veronica became a young adult, she also become aware of her dad's infidelity. He had slept with numerous other women over the years. Veronica was too young to remember some, but she has vivid memories of her parents falling out when she was around five or six years old. Her mum walked out and took Veronica with her to her dad's best friend's house, where they ended up staying the night. Paula had slept with Phil's best mate to get back at him for sleeping with another woman. Veronica remembers her dad crying and pleading with her mum to forgive him and not to leave him, it really shook him up. Veronica remembers crying and feeling sorry for her dad.

49

As Veronica got older and more able to understand her dad's behaviour, she could recognise when he was being shifty and sly. When she was fifteen, she discovered him having another affair with one of their punters. She didn't know how to break the news to her mum, but Paula suspected them of her own accord, and confided her fears to Veronica. She more or less confirmed it for her, as she had witnessed her dad sneaking round to the woman's house; returning drunk and smelling of whisky which he didn't usually drink, after being gone for hours. Veronica was furious as this woman had befriended her as well as her mum. Phil even took her away on the family boat and slept with her whilst Veronica's first boyfriend and cousins were also on board. Veronica hated her dad for this; she felt that he wanted to hurt her as well as her mum. He had no respect for any of his family but Paula forgave him. He did it again with another friend of her mum's when Veronica was twenty two. Veronica told him she hated him, and meant it. She took her mum away to Zante for two weeks to get some time to think. They knew that he continued to see the woman whilst they were away, as Veronica's sisters also caught him out. When Veronica learned that her dad had no remorse for his actions, her relationship with him completely changed from then on. She knew she had to get away from his verbal abuse and mood swings and live her own life. He thought he was the superior being in the house but she realised that he wasn't. Veronica saw him in a true light and he knew it, which is why she clashed with him for years after.

CHAPTER 15

Things Change When Phil Leaves Prison

In the time that Philip was in prison, Veronica changed a lot.

She was just a kid when her dad went inside, but she had to grow up overnight and take responsibility for herself and support her mum and little sisters. She had nearly lost her mum too when an inmate acquaintance of Philip had set up a deal where Paula would visit this man in prison and pass him heroin via a kiss. Unfortunately for this inmate and Paula, the prison officers had suspected their visit and watched them closely. When the prisoner left the visiting quarters, he was searched and the prison officers found the drugs. To save himself from further repercussions, he gave the officers information about Paula. Police watched her address for a few days before they barged their way in, breaking the front door down. Paula panicked, but realised that the officers couldn't search Veronica without her permission, so she gave her a small plastic bag with drugs in and told her to put them in the front of her knickers. Veronica knew and understood perfectly well what she was doing, this was a matter of survival and Veronica knew that her mum would be taken to prison if she didn't help her.

Paula packed some clothes for the kids and sent Veronica off to a friend, with the drugs and money on her. Paula was taken away by police to be strip searched, questioned and charged at the local police station, but she was released that same evening.

Veronica learnt to keep her cool in these situations; it became second nature to be on guard constantly, as life could change at any moment.

During Philip's stretch of almost three years, Veronica went from being a little girl to being a teenager nearing her 14th birthday. She had gone through puberty and started her periods at the age of twelve; she had finished primary school and had been to 2 secondary schools, suffering a year of constant bullying at the second. As far as Veronica was concerned, she was a young woman now, but when her dad came home from prison, he still treated her like the ten year old kid he had left behind.

Veronica had started to become interested in boys and wanted to be out with her friends until 9pm, which was what she had become accustomed to with her mum. Veronica would be on hand to help out with shopping, laundry, house chores and babysitting, then Paula would reward her with some pocket money and a few hours out with her friends. Often, Veronica had been allowed to bring a girlfriend back to stay the night, even on school nights. Her friends loved it because they felt a sense of freedom at Veronica's house.

The same wasn't true for Veronica though, as she would end up having to entertain her little sisters whilst her mum was seeing to punters in the lounge. But never the less, Veronica and her mum had become used to life without Philip, well Veronica had anyway!

She had forgotten what it was like to have a man around the house taking charge and throwing his orders around. Veronica didn't like it. Philip didn't like the fact that Veronica had an opinion and quickly brought her down by putting her in her place. Veronica got quite emotional about this. She would sob for ages in her pillow and say to herself, "Who does he think he is, he hasn't been here for all this time and now he thinks he owns the place!"

Veronica was aware that her mum had kept the dealing going not just to subsidise both their habits, but also to save money for Philip's return, so that they could do work to their yacht, which was by now very weathered and in need of some care. Veronica thought about how she had supported her mum all that time, and now her dad was talking down to her like she was a little child. Philip could see that Veronica didn't like it, so did it even more, that's how it seemed to Veronica anyway. He told her she wasn't allowed out past 8pm and teased Veronica about having a boyfriend. Veronica didn't have a boyfriend, but still her dad insisted, teased her and belittled her about it. He would say things like: "So you think you are a big woman now do you? And what are you gonna do when a boy takes advantage of you? These teenage boys want more than a kiss."

Veronica was totally embarrassed. Why was he saying these things? All she wanted to do was meet her best friend Nicki. Veronica had a crush on a local teenager but that was all, it never materialised even into a kiss, but her dad was adamant that she was up to something.

Paula tried to step in and stick up for Veronica, but was shouted down immediately by Philip. He would say, "She doesn't like it that Daddy is home now to put her in her place. She has got too big for her boots and it's your fault Paula for allowing it." Veronica wanted her dad to see that she wasn't just a kid anymore, she didn't like him belittling her, but he was the boss and that was that.

CHAPTER 16

The Stabbing 18th October 1992

It was Sunday morning and Veronica and her family were all fast asleep in bed.

Veronica was eighteen at the time and had been out drinking the night before with Natalie, one of her best friends who lived across the road. Ella came running into the bedroom that Veronica shared with both her sisters.

Veronica was fast asleep in the bottom bunk bed when Ella woke her up shaking her animatedly. "Veronica wake up," Ella cried, "Lou Lou is on the phone and wants to talk to you." Veronica barely opened her eyes grabbing the phone in confusion.

Lou Lou was a mouthy tomboy teenager who lived in the housing estate across the road.

Veronica had experienced problems with a whole gang of youths from this estate for years.

A few of them went to the same school as Veronica but didn't know her personally.

Veronica never liked the youths as they were always hanging around the streets, up to mischief and starting fights. The gang of girls always taunted Veronica whenever she was out and about, minding her own business, but Veronica tried hard to keep her head down and avoid trouble with the girls. Lou Lou was a younger member of the gang who used to do a lot of dirty work and trouble making for the older gang members. She used to ride about everywhere on her BMX bike terrorising anyone she could. She often rode past Veronica sneaking up quietly behind her hitting her in the back and riding off quickly to get away. Veronica wanted to punch Lou Lou so much, and Veronica's day would soon come.

Lou Lou did her habitual sneaking up on her bike behind Veronica, but this time Veronica knew she was there and pounced on Lou Lou, yanking her off her bike. Veronica got the girl by the neck and shook her angrily.

"You think you are smart picking on people but you are not, one of these days you are going to get the shit beaten out of you, now leave me alone you fucking bitch."

Lou Lou was scared. Veronica had put her in her place. Finally the trouble maker had got a taste of her own medicine and Veronica was feeling happy about this, it had been a long time coming as Lou Lou had terrorised many innocent girls and boys. Unfortunately this was to become the beginning of a series of events that would change Veronica and her family's life forever.

"Hello?" Veronica said.

"You fucking slag, we are coming to get you." Lou Lou shouted down the phone.

"Why don't you get a life?" Veronica slammed the phone down.

Veronica asked Ella how she came to be on the phone to Lou Lou. "How did she get our number Ella?" Ella told her that she'd been talking to her friend who lived down the road, her friend's older sister was mates with Lou Lou, and when Lou Lou realised her friend's little sister was talking to Veronica's sister she grabbed the phone, telling Ella to put Veronica on the phone. Veronica went back to sleep shrugging it off.

Five minutes later the doorbell rang, followed by another ring and another. Veronica leapt out of bed feeling hungover from the night before. She ran upstairs to the lounge and opened the window to see who was down at the door. Lou Lou was standing there with a large group of youths. One was known as Steve, he had been labouring on a maisonette a few doors away from Veronica and her family's maisonette. Veronica didn't know him but he had tried to chat her up, harassing her on her way to work a few days before. Veronica wasn't interested in him, her neighbour Raffy knew him and that he had two girlfriends already on the go. He informed Veronica of the girls' names, so when Steve continued to harass Veronica again on her way to work, she told him she knew he had these two girlfriends; and would tell them what he was up to if he didn't leave her alone. Steve was dumbfounded, how could Veronica know so much about him? She was pleased with herself and continued on her way to work, minding her own business.

Somehow Steve had come to know Lou Lou and the gang from the estate, and they had all hatched a plan to cause trouble at Veronica's door.

Steve shouted at Veronica calling her a whore. Two girls, one of whom was his girlfriend Jackie, started to threaten Veronica. "Get your ass down here whore, I'm going to kick your head in."

There were lads all around, eighteen to twenty years of age jeering and shouting and banging on the front door. Lou Lou continued, "You better come down here bitch or we are gonna kick the door in." Ella and Paulette were now hanging out the window witnessing the torments.

Ella ran up to her parents' bedroom shouting to her dad for help. Phil had been fast asleep, he leapt out of bed grabbing his jeans and running to the living room window to see what was happening. Veronica had already explained to her dad about Steve harassing her to go out with him a few days earlier in the street, and Phil was pleased with Veronica's way of handling him. Now, however, there was a mounting crowd of youths hurling abuse and kicking the door in. A few of them had knives, Steve did too. Phil panicked, he ran downstairs to fight the youths, there was no way they were going to come in his home and attack his family, over his dead body, he thought to himself. Before Veronica knew it, her dad was in the street having a fight. Steve came running towards Phil drop kicking him as he went. Veronica feared for her family's life, she couldn't believe what was happening. These youths had knives and were young and agile compared to her dad who was stick thin and now in his late thirties. Veronica knew there was an air rifle hidden behind one of the units in the lounge; she grabbed it and pointed it out of the window at the lads. She was scared that one of them would kill her dad. She screamed at the youths, "If any of you hurt him you will get this in the head." With that, a few of the lads ran off.

Neighbours and passers-by were gathering in the street and watching from their windows.

As Steve flew at Phil drop kicking him, they both tumbled to the ground. Veronica's view of them was hindered by a skip that the men were behind. Veronica couldn't tell if her dad was okay, she started screaming for her dad. Just then, Phil stood up dragging Steve with him.

Veronica's initial reaction was relief because her dad was okay, but she soon realised that things were far from alright. Steve had a white t shirt on that was now completely covered in blood.

Phil was cradling him almost like a baby. Veronica looked on in shock and horror. "Veronica get a large towel quickly and get down here," Phil yelled. Veronica wasted no time and did what she was told. Paula took the young girls away from the window; they were crying and screaming hysterically, Paula was crying too.

"What the fuck has just happened?" Paula yelled, crying in disbelief. Veronica ran outside to assist her dad.

Phil told her to wrap the towel around Steve's neck and put pressure on the wound. He had a gaping hole in his neck and blood was spurting out everywhere like a fountain. Veronica stopped the blood and held the towel with pressure as her dad had explained. He screamed at Paula to throw down the car keys and ran to the car to start the engine.

Steve tried to hit Veronica, she told him to stop as she was trying to save his life.

Phil and Veronica ushered Steve into the front passenger seat of Paula's XR2 and Veronica sat behind him in the back, keeping the pressure on the wound. Steve continued to hurl abuse, threatening that he would come back and kill the family.

Phil told him to calm down for his own good and that he never meant to hurt him as bad as he did but that he had a knife and was threatening his girls. Phil drove so fast, it was like speeding on the motorway. The police raced past the XR2 heading in the direction of Veronica's home, not realising that they had just passed the 'fugitive'. Finally they reached the hospital and parked the car right outside A & E. Phil and Veronica ushered Steve into the hospital leaving the doctors to care for the thug.

Within a few moments the police were pounding into A & E with Steve's girlfriend Jackie and her friend in tow. Veronica knew that her dad would soon be charged. He did too, shocked and full of remorse for what had happened, he told Veronica to run home and check up on her mum and sisters, assuring Veronica that he would be okay. Veronica didn't want to leave him, she cried inconsolably. She couldn't believe it, her dad would go to prison again and it was all her fault. With that she walked out of the hospital and as she left, noticed two more police cars with their sirens and lights flashing, entering the car park. Veronica's heart was pounding through her chest, the adrenaline was rushing through every part of her body, she knew they had come for her dad.

Veronica calmly walked past the cars and out on to the road. As soon as she was out of their sight, she took to her heels. She had no money to get a bus or train and the hospital was some four to five miles from her home. Her feet barely touched the ground as Veronica ran faster than she had ever run, desperate to get to her mum and sisters quickly. By the time she reached her doorstep, she could barely breathe; gasping for air.

Outside the home, down the stairs and along the pavement there was water where there had been Steve's blood. Veronica rang the doorbell and her mum looked out from the window above.

A few moments later Paula opened the door, impatient to find out what had happened at the hospital. Veronica was crying hysterically as she explained that she had left her dad at the hospital in A & E, as he had told Veronica to return home. Veronica told her mum that the police had turned up as she walked out the hospital gate.

Paula began to cry, "I can't believe what's happened Veronica, I can't believe he stabbed the bloke, what was he thinking?" Paula shook her head in disbelief at the events that had unfolded on what should have been a normal quiet relaxing Sunday morning. Veronica reminded her mum that they were all under siege by a gang of youths.

Paula hadn't seen the lads wielding knives at Phil, as she wasn't at the window and was trying to get the girls to shut the window and come away. "They were kicking the door in Mum; they were threatening all of us," Veronica continued. Veronica felt that she was to blame for the whole ordeal, she hated herself. She thought about how she told Lou Lou to get a life when she grabbed her off her bike only a couple of weeks before. Suddenly Veronica was filled with regret. She told herself that if she had just ignored Lou Lou then none of this would have happened; now her dad was going to jail, possibly for life, and it was all her doing.

Paula told Veronica that she had managed to hide all the money and get the drugs out of the house before the police turned up. She had run across the road to a neighbour who was also a regular punter, to hide the drugs as she suspected the police would raid the house once they had done a radio check on Phil's record.

The police turned up within a minute of Paula returning to the house. They questioned Paula who just said she didn't see anything and refused to give any information. They left after speaking to a couple of bystanders and neighbours in the street, before turning on their sirens, then racing off in the direction of the hospital.

Paula prepared buckets of water and went outside to scrub the floor and remove the blood from her doorsteps. "What is Dad gonna do?" Veronica asked her mum. "He was fast asleep and woke up to this mess, now he is probably being charged."

Veronica continued to cry uncontrollably. Paula said, "He is gonna get sick without his gear, he hadn't even had his usual morning dose."

"Poor Dad," Veronica replied, "give some to me Mum and I will get it to him, quickly before they take him from the hospital."

Paula agreed and went over the road to get the stash. She returned with some heroin wrapped thickly and tightly in cling film and a condom.

Veronica stashed the heroin in her knickers and ran like the wind back towards the hospital.

Her heart was beating hard out of her chest but she stopped just around the corner to catch her breath and compose herself, before entering the hospital.

Veronica walked into the A & E department where she had left her dad less than an hour ago.

There was no sign of him or any police. Veronica walked up to the reception desk and asked where her dad was, explaining that he had brought a stab victim in by the name of Steve. The receptionist told her that her dad had been charged and taken in handcuffs by the police to the local police station.

Veronica's fears were confirmed; she ran out of the hospital and headed for the police station.

When she arrived, she walked in and asked to see her dad. The officer at the desk took her details and sent Veronica to an interview room where she was told to stay. Steve's girlfriend Jackie and her mate, another girl of similar age, were in the same room. The girls started shouting at Veronica calling her dad a nutter. They said that he had been charged with attempted murder and would be put away for life.

Veronica burst into tears, her head was pounding from the stress of the whole ordeal and she felt sick and dizzy. Veronica told the girls that they were the ones who had started all the trouble for no good reason and there were no doubt witnesses who would come forward for her dad's defence. It was later revealed by a policeman that had Phil not got Steve to hospital when he did; and if Veronica had not held the wound in the neck tightly with a towel, Steve would have definitely died. It was revealed that he was given 8 pints of blood on the operating table, but luckily there was no damage to any vital organs.

Veronica pleaded with the officer to allow her to see her dad. She explained that they had been fast asleep in bed when they woke to the threats and commotion outside. Veronica told the officer that her dad was no murderer and was in shock. The officer wanted a statement, but Veronica refused until she was given a few moments with her dad to make sure he was okay. The officer went out of the room which was now locked; he returned a moment later agreeing to let Veronica see her dad. On the way to the holding cell she asked the officer if she could go for a pee, she told him she had practically wet herself through the whole ordeal.

The officer could see Veronica was beside herself and led her to a toilet, where she quickly removed the heroin from her knickers and placed it under her tongue.

Veronica didn't even take a moment to think about what she was doing.

This was a matter of urgency, this was a matter of survival, it was her fault her dad was in this mess. The least she could do was make sure he didn't get sick.

Veronica composed herself and walked out of the toilet. The officer led her along a cold corridor and into a holding cell where her dad was sitting white as a sheet and looking shell shocked. Veronica ran into her dad's arms in tears. "Dad I'm so sorry," she cried.

"It's alright babe," he replied, "I was protecting my family, what man wouldn't do that?"

The officer told Veronica she had 2 minutes and walked out of the cell, locking them both in.

Veronica wasted no time and cuddled her dad whispering in his ear that she had gear in her mouth for him. Tears streamed down his face, "Baby, you didn't have to do that," he replied.

"Of course I did Dad; I have to protect you too." He kissed her on the lips and Veronica pushed the heroin into his mouth, kissing him on the lips after. Relief swept over his face even though he was pale and weary.

"Dad I'm going to help you," Veronica continued, "I'm going to make up some notices and stick them through people's doors and pin them along the trees, to ask any witnesses to come forward in your defence." The officer's keys jangled in the lock of the cell door, and he came to lead Veronica into another room to get her statement.

"I love you so much Dad," she said as she was taken away.

"I love you too baby, more than you'll ever know."

CHAPTER 17

Being Bullied

Veronica had suffered bullying on and off, during her whole childhood.

It started when she was very young, even before she went to primary school.

Veronica had been born with a lazy eye, the doctors wanted to strengthen it by making her wear a patch over her other one, but Veronica really struggled with the patch.

She lived in a block of flats at the Oval South London, where there were many young families with lots of children who played outside in the courtyard. Veronica was teased by them, many of whom were older than her; they found it amusing to torment her every time she came out to play. They called her four eyes and told her she was ugly and scrawny. They chanted things like flea bag and would gather around her, pushing and pulling her hair. Veronica would run back indoors in floods of tears, but Phil wasn't having any of it. Many of the children who tormented her were from the gypsy community who were living in flats on the ground floor. Phil gave Veronica a hammer and told her that if the children approached her, to chase them with it.

Veronica felt empowered with the hammer in her hand and determined to get the bullies back.

Before long, the kids were back to torment Veronica as she tried to play. Veronica waved the hammer ferociously at them chasing them around the courtyard as they fled inside their homes.

Veronica went back in and told her dad what she had done, all happy and proud of herself.

Phil patted her on the head and told her well done, you taught the bullies a lesson.

Within a few minutes though, there was loud banging on their front door. Phil opened it, with the hammer still in his hand. There were all the parents gathered around the front of their flat, shouting and arguing with Phil. Veronica remembers him telling them, "Serves them right for being bullies." He then threatened to do the same to the parents if they didn't fuck off from his doorstep and keep their brats away from his daughter in future. From that day on, the kids kept their distance and Veronica was left in peace to play and skip in the courtyard.

As the family moved around, Veronica endured more bullying. It wasn't a constant theme, but on and off she experienced bouts of contention with other kids from school, or around the area she lived in. When Veronica was five, they moved to Kilburn, living in council temporary accommodation in Loveridge Road, before being given permanent housing in Maygrove Road.

Paula found a nice primary school which Veronica liked. During those early years at school however, Veronica spent lots of time in hospital with pneumonia and missed out on a lot of her schooling because of it. This made going back to school difficult, as Veronica had missed out on lots of topics that the other children had been taught.

On top of this, Veronica had trouble with her sight and struggled with learning to read and write, she would get upset and feel inadequate because she wasn't as bright as the other kids. They had settled and already formed groups of friends, whilst Veronica missed out on this early bonding and found herself being left out. Though she tried hard to be accepted, there were times when she felt so left out that she just didn't want to go to school and would plead with her mum not to send her. As time went by, Veronica accepted her situation and adjusted to life in and out of school. There were a couple of girls who Veronica befriended around the age of nine, who lived in the estate opposite, but those friendships fizzled out as the girls found other friends. The other girls that lived on this estate didn't know Veronica, but took a dislike to her for no apparent reason. When they walked past her in the street they would shout slag or ugly bitch, Veronica learnt to ignore their taunts, but they didn't let up for years.

Veronica had a close friend called Jenni. She lived about ten minutes away from her, but quite near their school. She was in Veronica's class all the way through primary and secondary schools. They would meet up with their bikes after school and play in the local park. Jenni was a quiet girl, whose mother and father were from Ireland. She had a strict upbringing and her parents were very protective of her. Jenni would have dinner at an early time compared with Veronica. It would be on the table at around 5pm at Jenni's house, which made Veronica envious as her dinner, nine times out of ten, would be around 9pm or sometimes even later.

Veronica became more accepted and liked by other kids at primary school as she became older and the bouts of pneumonia ceased, so she spent more time at school.

Secondary school was much the same, only there were a few kids from the estate opposite Veronica's house who also went to the school. Veronica kept her distance and didn't suffer much at school because those kids were in higher years. Out of school though, it became a problem.

There was a family similar to Veronica's that lived on the estate. The parents were heroin addicts and dealers, and their children also attended Veronica's secondary school. One daughter was in the same year but a different class. Veronica could get on with the girl but never trusted her to get too friendly, as she had a reputation for being a big mouth; and Veronica didn't need any more trouble in her life. This girl would eventually tire of Veronica however, and decide to spread nasty rumours around the school. When Philip spent three years in prison for dealing, she told everyone that he was in prison for raping Veronica. This made life particularly unbearable for a time, as kids would torment Veronica, teasing her and calling her dirty. In the end, the rumours stopped and the bullies got fed up and moved on to other victims.

The group of girls from this estate would still taunt Veronica from time to time, but she learned to ignore them. It was this same group of bullies though, who provoked the situation that lead to Veronica's dad stabbing Steve on the 18th of October 1992.

CHAPTER 18

Life with an Attempted Murder Charge Hanging in the Balance

After giving the police a statement, Veronica was allowed to leave the station and go home to her mum and sisters. The walk home seemed to take forever and Veronica wondered how she had managed to get back and forth so quickly earlier that day, when she ran for dear life.

Now that her dad had been charged and was being held at Hampstead police station, Veronica was bewildered. She was in a daze and shocked at the circumstances she had found herself in all day. The night before, she had been in a pub with her friends having a laugh and getting drunk, now her life had fallen apart; again!

Eventually Veronica reached her home and she was eager to see her mum and have a cuddle.

Paula came to the door looking exhausted and worried; she hugged Veronica and shut the door. Veronica burst into tears, telling her mum what had happened but explained that she had successfully passed the drugs to her dad. Paula looked a little relieved to know that Phil would be okay until the next visit. Paula had cleaned the house from top to bottom, trying to keep herself occupied throughout the day, whilst Phil and Veronica were in the police station.

Veronica couldn't sleep that night, she tossed and turned and cried on and off inconsolably. She felt that she was to blame for everything that had happened. Paula told Veronica to try not to worry; she told her that they would try to get Phil bailed one way or another.

The next few weeks were hard going. Phil was moved to Pentonville Prison, where he waited on remand for his case to come up. In the meantime Paula had to continue the dealing and visit Phil, making sure he was well looked after. Veronica also visited her dad in-between, taking him clothes and trainers, his Sony Discman and CDs.

The week after the stabbing, upon her return from the prison, Veronica was walking back home from the tube station when suddenly out of nowhere, Steve appeared. He was stomping fast towards Veronica, he had a neck brace on but his wounds didn't stop him coming back to intimidate and cause trouble. Veronica's heart pounded through her chest, adrenaline rushed through her making her feel queasy and scared. There was nowhere to run as he was too close for comfort. Veronica tried to ignore him as he was walking towards her, but he walked right into her path gobbing into her hair as he passed, calling her a cunt and threatening that she would be next. Veronica ran as fast as she could to her doorstep tripping up as she ran, fearing for her life.

Veronica rang the doorbell and Paula let her in, Veronica was hysterical. She told her mum what had happened and that Steve had told her she was next. Paula decided to call the police; she didn't want to take any chances.

The police turned up a couple of hours later and took a statement from Veronica but they didn't really seem that bothered by the threats and said there wasn't anything that could be done other than to have a word with the suspect.

Phil spent around three to four weeks in prison, until finally his mum, Emily, was able to stand surety to get him released on bail. Part of the bail conditions were that Phil was not allowed back home and would have to stay elsewhere. Dave, his friend from prison, lived alone in Hounslow. He had separated from his wife and had a lodger living with him and a spare room available. Phil moved in and Paula would visit him there; often staying over with the kids, leaving Veronica alone at the flat whilst they stayed at Dave's.

Veronica didn't mind the freedom of being alone but one night, she went to the local newsagent to get some chocolate. Whilst she was in the shop, a group of girls from the estate had spotted her, they came in and crowded her; Veronica was helpless as there were so many in the gang. One of the girls grabbed her by the throat and got her up over the sweets counter, banging her head against it whilst threatening her. The girl punched Veronica in the eye, and then the girls fled the shop. Veronica was in pieces. The shop keeper was a small man who feared the gang himself, so he hid below the counter when the girls attacked.

Veronica ran back home and called her parents on their mobile to tell them what had happened.

Paula told Veronica to call the police and report the incident. Veronica did, but again the police didn't seem interested. A few days later when Paula and the girls were back home, the gang put fireworks through their letterbox. The police were informed, but again they said there was nothing they could do. It seemed to Veronica that they were turning a blind eye because they were aware that her dad had stabbed a lad. The local newspapers printed the story, interviewing Steve and Lou Lou, who were treated like the victims. They told the reporter that they had come to the 'Baker house' to make peace; but were set upon for no reason.

Phil decided enough was enough; he couldn't go on living apart from his wife and children and leaving them in such danger. The gang was getting away with their attack on Veronica, as the shop keeper wouldn't give a statement. He was scared of repercussions, and the police were turning a blind eye to them putting fireworks through the door. What would the gang do next? Phil and Paula asked themselves.

Paula went to the housing department of the council to explain what was happening and to see if she could get a transfer, but the council didn't want to know and said there was nothing they could do. With that, Phil decided to find rented accommodation and the first place he found was a 3-bed mid terrace house in Edmonton. Phil called and set up a viewing. They went to look at the property the following day and within a couple of weeks the family had moved in.

Veronica fell into a deep depression; she didn't know anyone in Edmonton and couldn't drive.

The bus ride back to Kilburn took an hour and a half, longer than it took to get to Hampshire on the train to see her cousins. So Veronica felt like she was living at the end of the world, and that her life had come tumbling down.

The family council home back in Kilburn sat empty for a few months. Paula got worried that someone would notice and the council would find the property empty and claim it back. Paula had been there for 12 years with Phil and the girls, she had hoped that one day the council would upgrade them to a three-bedroom property, but with three daughters, the chances were slim. Nonetheless she didn't want to lose the council property because these thugs had turned her family's life upside down. Paula and Phil decided to rent the property out, they wanted someone to just look after the property until the trial was over and the family knew their fate and could move on from there. They weren't interested in making any money from the flat; they just wanted the bills to be covered. Their friend Abbie, who lived opposite, had a brother in law who needed a place to stay.

Abbie had been a regular punter over the years and her daughter Natalie was one of Veronica's closest friends. Abbie's brother in law turned out to be Don, who had been Phil and Paula's neighbour when they lived in Loveridge Road. He was the very same guy that Phil and Paula had left keeping an ear out for Veronica, when she was very young. Phil and Paula didn't really know him, but it was a small world and they decided to let him look after the flat.

Life in Edmonton was bleak for Veronica. The punters still came, even though some had to travel out of their way. For Phil and Paula, everyday life remained much the same, but for Veronica she felt completely isolated. She quickly learned who her real friends were as many could not be bothered to travel the distance to visit her.

Within a few months though, Veronica had her nineteenth birthday; and her parents bought her a little mini to help her get on the road. Veronica loved the car and couldn't wait to get out for some lessons with her dad. The fact that she lived so far from her friends gave Veronica the incentive to learn to drive. Without a job she couldn't afford lessons, but her dad had offered to take her out on the road. Veronica enjoyed having lessons with him because he would let her drive to Kilburn to pick up her friend Natalie to stay overnight.

Natalie was very envious of Veronica's new car, but Phil told Natalie that Veronica had been a very dutiful daughter and deserved the gift. The car cheered Veronica up no end, and took her mind off the trial. The date was set for July 1993 and the case was being heard at Wood Green Crown Court. Veronica became more nervous as the day drew nearer; she was worried that her dad's past with drugs abuse, dealing and GBH charges would go against him. Everything looked bleak and the family had planned and prepared for the worst outcome.

Veronica had bouts of panic attacks and had succumbed to smoking marijuana with her friend Natalie. She felt happy smoking when she was around her friends, as they could help her escape her life at home and the reality of the approaching trial, but when she was smoking marijuana at home, her mind would get carried away with worry; and she would soon get herself deep into a panic attack and scare herself senseless.

A week before the court case, Veronica's friends had arranged a night out in a pub in Hampstead Heath. Veronica was feeling fretful and didn't feel up for going out, but Natalie harassed Veronica to go along, assuring her it would take her mind off the trial.

Veronica gave in as she usually did to Natalie's whims, and went along feeling like a spare part and not really being interested in the conversations between the girls at the pub.

Veronica drank orange juice as there was no way she could consider getting drunk with her dad up in court for attempted murder the following day. Natalie and the others had planned to go to Tenerife on holiday and had originally agreed to wait for the verdict of Veronica's dad's trial, as if he was found not guilty, Veronica had saved enough money to go as well. Behind Veronica's back the girls became impatient and decided to go without her, they had booked flights for the same day that the trial was starting. Veronica was disappointed, more in her friend Natalie than the others. Veronica thought that Natalie understood Veronica's circumstances more than any of the others, after all, her mum was an addict too and she and her family had witnessed the stabbing.

Natalie had known Veronica since they were five years old but it obviously wasn't important to Natalie to hold out for her friend, and going with the others was ultimately more important.

The girls wanted to have a celebratory drink and say farewell to their friends. Veronica found herself on a completely different wave length and felt out of place around the girls in the pub.

Although she was standing amongst the usual huge crowd of young adults outside the Wells pub in Hampstead, where everyone was happily chatting away, laughing and joking, Veronica felt vulnerable and nervous. She started to feel short of breath and dizzy. She tried to fight her way through the crowd looking for Natalie who had found some other friends she was chatting to. Veronica grabbed Natalie's arm in a panic as she felt herself fainting and needed help. "Natalie can we leave please, I feel really unwell."

Natalie snapped at Veronica, thinking she was trying to spoil her night and was just attention seeking. Veronica felt the world spinning around her and suddenly the noises of all the people chatting around her became one loud noise that seemed to drown Veronica out from being heard. By now she could barely speak and everything started to go dark.

"Natalie," she cried, "please help me I'm fainting."

"I'm saying goodbye, what's wrong with you? Wait a minute," Natalie snapped again. Veronica could not hold herself up and fell to the ground banging her head on the kerb as she went. Veronica fell in the direction of Natalie but she moved out of the way watching in disbelief as Veronica collapsed to the floor.

Veronica could hear Natalie screaming for someone to get help and to get Veronica a drink but Veronica was too weak to talk. Veronica felt as though she was in a tunnel and the crowds of people were outside the tunnel calling to her. She couldn't respond and just wanted to sleep. Veronica felt exhausted; she couldn't even wink let alone lift a limb. Natalie slapped Veronica a few times in the face but still Veronica had no energy to respond.

A few minutes later a young lad came to help. He lifted Veronica's head and poured a tiny amount of water on her lips and put some on her face, stroking her face as he wet her. Slowly Veronica began to come round but she was still very weak.

"Veronica, have you eaten today?" he asked. Veronica realised that she hadn't eaten a thing all day. She shook her head.

Someone else had called an ambulance, but Veronica thought that she couldn't possibly end up in a hospital with her dad up in court the next day. She tried hard to pull herself together. The lad known as Martin gave Natalie some money and told her to run to McDonald's to get her a burger, some fries and a milk shake.

A few minutes later, Natalie returned with the food.

Martin carried Veronica across the road and found her a bench to sit on. Natalie gave Veronica the burger and Veronica ate like she had never eaten before. Veronica wouldn't usually want a 'McDonalds', but this was the best food she had ever tasted!

As her energy began to come back, an ambulance pulled up across the road outside the pub.

Veronica told Martin she couldn't go to the hospital as her dad was in court. She pleaded with him to help her hide so that they didn't take her. He helped Veronica to her feet and they walked around the corner hiding until the ambulance left. Once Veronica had finished her food, she felt so much better. She couldn't understand why she had fainted as she had not had any alcohol but Martin explained that her sugar levels must have been really low and with the stress getting to her, it sent her over the edge. Natalie was sorry for not helping Veronica sooner and listening to her but

Veronica realised that Natalie was more interested in her holiday than Veronica's feelings. Veronica got a taxi home to Edmonton and the girls left the next day for their holiday.

CHAPTER 19

The Trial

Veronica barely slept all night, she tossed and turned and got up for the loo continuously, feeling nervous, agitated and emotional. She cried at the thought of her dad being imprisoned for life.

Eventually she fell asleep in a puddle of tears and woke up sharply to the sound of her alarm clock and the realisation that the day had finally come.

Veronica got up and checked that her parents were also awake. Phil and Paula were up and in the bathroom getting ready for the first day of the trial. Veronica helped them with ironing her dad's shirt and making some breakfast. Ella and Paulette got up to get ready for school, and the family had one last group hug before Phil and Paula set off for the court.

Veronica waited by the phone all day, hoping to get a call from her mum to let her know what was happening. Finally Paula called, she told Veronica that they were on their way home and would fill her in on the details once they got there.

Feeling a little relieved that Phil was at least coming home for another night, Veronica ran to the kitchen to put the kettle on for her parents. Twenty minutes later they arrived, Phil was looking tired and stressed, so was Paula. They both went up to the bedroom to get some gear (heroin) and foil. They came back down to the lounge and prepared their smoke. Veronica made the coffee and brought it into the lounge. "What happened?" Veronica asked.

Paula replied, "The judge introduced the case to the jury and then your dad had to confirm his name etc. to the prosecution. Then he had to swear an oath and was questioned by the prosecution and the defence solicitors."

"Were you nervous Dad?" Veronica asked.

"I was quite nervous yeah, but at the same time confident because I am there to defend my name." Phil replied. "I told them how it was, how I was in my bed asleep minding my own business on a Sunday morning; and got woken up to threats at my door." Veronica nodded in agreement.

"That's exactly how it was," she said.

Phil told Veronica how Steve turned up in court looking like he just fell out of bed, wearing jeans that were hanging off him with his boxer shorts exposed and the crutch of the trousers down by his knees. He walked with a cocky swagger as if he was something cool, and when asked to stand in the witness box to confirm his name and details, he stood there chewing gum. Then he told the court room that he had heard that Veronica Baker was causing trouble for his friend Lou Lou and wanted to call round to the Baker's house to make peace, when a crazed man ran out and stabbed him for no good reason.

Veronica shook her head in disbelief. How could he say that, she thought?

Phil continued: "Then they called his girlfriend Jackie; they made Steve leave the courtroom because he was winking and nodding at Jackie trying to influence what she was saying. The judge cottoned on to him and had him removed. Jackie fell apart, she contradicted her statement and my solicitor made mincemeat of her story."

"That's good then isn't it Dad?"

"Well hopefully the jury will see him for the lying cheating pig he is," Phil replied. Then Phil was questioned and cross-examined. The prosecution tried to intimidate Phil into admitting that he had tried to kill Steve in a moment of sheer rage and that the attack was premeditated.

Phil didn't buckle, he responded, "If that was the case, then why was I only half dressed? Because I had just woken up to commotion and youths kicking in my door and threatening to kill my daughters. I didn't go out looking for a fight; they threatened me and my family. If my intention was to kill the man then why did I make every attempt to save him after?" Phil felt relieved this day was done, he was tired and hungry.

Veronica helped to get dinner ready and also felt relieved that her dad had done all he could.

CHAPTER 20

The Trial, Day Two

Veronica's alarm went off, she couldn't believe it was that time already, she had slept better than the night before; the initial fear of facing court had subsided and the news that Steve's girlfriend had fallen apart giving evidence had made Veronica feel a little more relaxed. Nevertheless she felt anxious.

Phil and Paula set off for their second day in court, and Veronica got her sisters to school then made her way home to be on standby near the phone. The day dragged on, and Veronica tried all sorts to occupy her mind. She played her guitar and tried to compose a song, but the words just wouldn't come. She cleaned the house from top to bottom, which was a great way to pass the time, but there was still half a day to get through.

Veronica collected her sisters from school and returned home to wait for news. Eventually Paula called to tell Veronica that they were on their way home.

Veronica was relieved her dad was free for another night, but anxious to hear how they had got on in court. Veronica would be called soon to give her evidence, and she worried that she would feel intimidated by the cross examiner if he tried to tie her up in knots.

A little while later her parents came through the door. Veronica greeted them with a cup of tea and sat beside them in the lounge to hear of the day's events.

"What happened today then?" Veronica asked.

"Today Steve was questioned some more," her dad said. "He was asked to confirm that he was in the NW6 area on the 18th of October 1992. He happily replied yes. The defence barrister read out a curfew that was implemented by another court that stated he wasn't allowed in the area of NW6 until further notice, as he was charged with ABH against a 10 year old boy. The jury sighed in unison. Steve lost it and got angry, he actually spat in the barrister's face to the horror of the jury. That pleased me no end because he showed his true colours."

Veronica was excited by this news. "That's great Dad, surely the jury will find you not guilty now."

Philip replied, "Who knows, it depends on how it all pans out. When the prosecution showed the horrific wounds to the jury, you should have seen their faces; I don't think that went down well."

"What about me Dad, when am I going to be called?" Veronica asked.

"Not yet, my solicitor is holding out to see how the case unfolds, he knows what you've been through with the bullying and the anxiety it's caused, he will only call you if it's absolutely necessary; and we still have our independent witness to be called yet."

Veronica felt a little relieved. She hoped that she wouldn't have to come face to face with the evil thug, but by the same token she would do whatever it takes to help free her dad of the awful charges against him.

The family enjoyed a meal and cuddled up together watching TV. Veronica still felt uneasy at the thought of the jury looking at the pictures of Steve's wounds. Veronica had seen these herself and they were pretty horrible. She wished her dad hadn't stabbed him, but in her heart she knew it could have easily have been her dad who'd got hurt; and he may not have been here to live this nightmare.

CHAPTER 21

The Trial, Day Three

The family was up early; Veronica got the girls off to school and returned home to wait again for news. The day dragged, and Veronica didn't get a lunch time call from her parents to update her on the progress in court. This made her extremely anxious, so much so that she sat by the phone all day and bit her nails to the quick, worrying.

After collecting her sisters from school, Veronica returned home and continued to sit by the phone and pace up and down in every room of the house. It was 5pm and still Veronica had heard nothing. Her heart sank and she began to cry. "They have found him guilty," she thought to herself. "Mum hasn't called because it's bad news."

Veronica wondered how they would cope without Phil again for what would be a lifetime.

It seemed surreal, but it was an almost inevitable reality. The prosecution would bring up Phil's past convictions and the jury would see him in a different light.

Just at that moment the phone rang, it was Veronica's dad. As soon as Veronica heard his voice, she knew in her heart the news was bad. "Hello Dad," she said meekly.

"Hi Vronx, they let me make one phone call...... I'm sorry babe."

Veronica burst into tears, crying inconsolably as she told her dad she loved him. There was a silence at the other end. "Are you there Dad?" Veronica asked as she snivelled. The silence seemed to last forever.

"Only joking!" her dad replied. "I'm free and we're on our way home, so get the kettle on."

"Dad, you scared me, how could you do that?" Phil laughed, as this was typical of him and his sense of humour.

Veronica's tears turned to screams of joy; she ran to her sisters and told them the news.

They danced all over the house chanting, "Dad is free, Dad is free!"

Half an hour later, Phil and Paula came through the front door with huge smiles and relief written across their faces. The family had a huge group hug. Veronica and the girls kissed their mum and dad continuously with joy.

"What happened then?" Veronica asked.

"Can you make us a tea?" Phil asked, "then I will tell you all about it."

Veronica went to the kitchen and made the tea as quickly as she could, she was eager to hear the news of the events that unfolded in court that day. She smiled and thought, "No more Steve taking up my thoughts, no more worrying that Dad will be taken away, now we are free to make plans to sail around the world and I can make plans to get on with my life."

Veronica brought the tea on a tray to her parents in the lounge; she sat down and said, "Tell me all about it."

"The independent witness gave evidence. She told how she was walking her dogs along Maygrove Road when she spotted a gang of youths shouting and kicking in the front door of the Baker household. She said some had knives and were threatening one of the girls inside the house. She told how a man came to the window with no top on and told the youths to fuck off, but they continued to hurl abuse and a lad now known as Steve was kicking the front door of the property, to attempt to get inside. A few moments later, the topless man emerged from the flat and was in the street. Steve ran at the topless man and drop kicked him to the ground. The men were punching and kicking when suddenly there was a pool of blood in the road and it became apparent that Steve had been stabbed. The other youths quickly disappeared running in the direction of the estate opposite, leaving Steve and his girlfriend Jackie screaming in the street." Paula said.

The independent witness had said, "The lad had intimidated the household and then attacked Philip Baker. The girls inside the house were petrified and crying." The witness then told the court room that Philip Baker had acted in self-defence and was quite rightly concerned for the safety of his daughters.

Paula continued, "The independent witness told it like it was, and the jury had already seen Steve in the real light when he spat in the barrister's face. After the witness gave evidence, the jury went out to deliberate their verdict. It was nerve racking," Paula exclaimed. "They didn't take long to reach their decision but it felt like an eternity. That's why we didn't call you earlier Veronica; we just couldn't do a thing until we knew."

"Oh my God Mum," said Veronica, "you must have been shaking with fear, I have been all day, I've been to the toilet constantly and haven't been able to eat. I've cried all day worrying. Then when Dad called to say he was allowed one phone call my heart sank, and I felt the world literally stop right there!"

"Ha ha ha, I know that was naughty of me, but I couldn't help it," Phil laughed.

"Dad, how could you do that, it wasn't funny at all?" Veronica said.

"It was mean," Paula agreed, "he has a strange sense of humour sometimes."

It did not matter anyway because Phil was free and so was the family. This awful ordeal had caused them to move from the area that they had known for many years. Veronica had endured bullying, and misrepresented reports of the family had been published all over the local papers. It had taken its toll; their lives had been turned upside down with an attempted murder charge hanging in the balance. Now that was all in the past, they were free to begin a new chapter in their lives.

Phil and Paula celebrated the following day, by inviting over some of their punters for a celebratory chase.

CHAPTER 22

The Yacht Nova

Though Veronica had resolved to leave home, there was a chance that her dream could come true and things could change, before she left.

Phil's mum Emily died of stomach cancer in 1997, at the age of 76. Phil's share of the inheritance was almost £50,000 which he decided to spend on a new yacht. He had searched the internet and found one for sale in Turkey that caught his eye. Soon he and Paula were on a flight to Turkey to inspect the yacht which was moored in Gocek. They left their drug dealing business in the hands of Theresa, one of Paula's friends who was over from Mexico for a while, and Veronica stayed at home to take care of her sisters.

Theresa was a very loyal friend to Phil and Paula, who had been introduced by mutual friends back in the early 1980s. She was a lively feminist hippy, who had studied hard and travelled to many countries. She too had a heroin habit and would score from Phil and Paula regularly.

Some months after being introduced to Phil and Paula, she left for India with her boyfriend Graham. They travelled for a year together before splitting up in Mexico. Theresa went on to meet a native Latin American guy called Julio in Mexico City, where they shacked up together and had two daughters, Lisa and Tina. Theresa returned to the UK in 1986 with Lisa then two years old whilst she was heavily pregnant with Tina. She just turned up at Paula's one day on the off chance she was at home. Paula couldn't believe it, having not seen Theresa in years and assuming that she would never see her again.

Theresa explained that she had come home as her mum was poorly, and that she had managed to get a flat from a housing association in Islington.

Soon after, Theresa gave birth to Tina and spent a great deal of time around Paula and the kids.

It didn't take long for Theresa to resume her drug taking and she learnt to make a living from it herself, scoring for other punters and adding her mark up to it.

Theresa claimed benefits and made the most of adult education and free courses that she could attend. As the years passed she depended more on Lisa to help out, and like Veronica, Lisa had to grow up quickly and help with chores and looking after her younger sister.

Theresa and Paula had become firm friends. Theresa would look after Veronica and her sisters when she was available, and Paula would look after Lisa and her sister too. Together they became almost like a tag team. Paula felt safe leaving the kids with Theresa and vice versa. This gave them a little more freedom when they had to go and meet new punters, or if Paula had to score from her supplier.

Often they would take the kids out together to the park, or cook up a nice meal and eat together.

Lisa and Tina became close friends with Ella and Paulette; they were similar in age and had a lot in common.

Theresa also had a lot of time for Veronica. She had taken an interest in Veronica's school work and would always encourage Veronica with her subjects and help with her homework. Veronica loved this about Theresa and really looked up to her.

When Veronica took her GCSEs Theresa was one of the few people to really help out. Veronica particularly enjoyed her English classes and geography, and as Theresa was very well travelled, she was of real benefit to her.

The yacht which Phil and Paula went to see was called Nova; she was fifty five feet and had been built in America. The previous owners were well to do English business people, who had sailed her three quarters of the way around the world, but decided to cut short their trip to pursue family and business plans, their last port of call was in Turkey. They had employed a South African couple to skipper the yacht at times when they had to return home for family business, they loved their job and had grown quite attached to yacht Nova.

When Phil and Paula flew out to Turkey to view the boat and take her out for a sail, the South African skipper was in charge of overseeing the details. They planned a day trip around the coastal bays to see how well Phil and Paula could handle the vessel. This all went swimmingly well as far as Phil and Paula were concerned, and so they returned to the UK to sort out the financial paper work to conclude the purchase.

In the meantime, the South Africans had reported back to their employers, that they suspected Phil and Paula were heroin addicts. They had spotted deep blue tracks in Paula's arms, which Phil and Paula both had from their prolific use of needles during the early eighties. Phil was very aware of his and always wore long sleeved shirts rolled up to three quarter length to hide them. He and Paula were very ashamed of this aspect of their lives.

Although they were still addicts, they were more circumspect about their use now, especially when around people outside of their circle. Phil had reinvented himself over the years. He had constantly rubbed shoulders with wealthy business people during the time he owned his yacht Soland and made plenty of friendships. He went out sailing with them and would carry out plumbing jobs and fix the engines on their yachts, so he became quite popular in South Sea Portsmouth, and was well known for being a daredevil at sea.

He would go out sailing in gale force winds when others would not even attempt it. Being very witty and intelligent, Phil had come a long way from the junkie he had been back then.

Now he had to defend his corner, how dare these busybody South Africans accuse him and his wife of such atrocities?

The sellers of yacht Nova telephoned Phil with the accusations; Phil was horrified, but quick to respond. He told them that Paula had been in a car accident where she'd lost a lot of blood and needed transfusions. He said she had spent months in hospital recovering, not just from the accident but from many infections; and that all the treatment had been the reason for the tracks in her arms. He then went on to attack the skippers by saying they shouldn't accuse people of such nasty things when they don't even know them.

The sellers apologised to Phil and the sale duly went ahead. Phil kept up this facade with the sellers for months afterwards though, maybe he had a point to prove.

So within a few weeks, Phil and Paula were owners of the yacht Nova; and Phil made plans to sail her back to the UK. Veronica was very excited because this was the start of a new life for her parents and sisters.

Deep down Veronica knew that the time had come for her to live her own life, but she was desperate to see her dad fulfil his dream of sailing around the world with Paula and the kids, bidding farewell to the life of drugs and dealing. She had waited her whole life for this moment and it was quite literally unbelievable and overwhelming.

Before she knew it, she was flying out to Gocek with her parents, her Uncle Michael and her dad's friend Ben. This was to be an unforgettable journey with its highs and lows, but seemed at times just like a romantic piece in a story book, of how two people who had become embroiled in a life of drugs had finally managed to free themselves.

Meanwhile, Theresa was on hand to help out again. She looked after Ella and Paulette as well as the dealing for Phil and Paula. They paid her well for seeing to their business and the children, which gave Theresa the chance to save enough funds to return to Mexico City with her children; and be with her beloved Julio.

Theresa played Mum to Ella and Paulette for over a month, whilst Phil, Paula and Veronica, sailed back towards the UK.

CHAPTER 23

The New-Found Crew of Yacht Nova

It was in July 1997 that Phil and Paula became the proud owners of the yacht Nova, and prepared to embark on the biggest voyage of their lives. Their previous experience at the helm was nearly ten years sailing a thirty-foot yacht around parts of the UK, mainly in and around The Solent; and now they were taking on a vessel nearly twice that size and sailing her through unknown territory.

Paula had her reservations, she wasn't very confident as she knew this wasn't going to be easy.

Nonetheless she had been pushed by Phil, and his determination knew no bounds.

They decided to take Veronica and leave the other two girls with Theresa back in the UK. Veronica being the eldest would be able to help in many ways. Although her experience of handling boats was zero, as she had never taken to sailing and had actually found it a chore rather than an interest, Phil knew she could take care of cooking, washing up, cleaning on board and helping out with night watches. She would learn other things along the way.

As well as taking Veronica, Phil decided to take his brother Michael and his friend Ben, who was a year younger than Veronica but had already sailed back and forth to the Caribbean with his dad on a seventeen foot boat.

Ben had many survival skills and could also fish, which appealed to Phil; and he had struck up a good friendship with Ben over the previous few years. Veronica had been in a brief relationship with Ben, which had ended six months before the voyage, she was therefore a bit apprehensive about being on board the yacht for days or weeks at a time with him. Veronica worried that Ben may try to resume the relationship as it was she who had called it off. Ben smoked a lot of Marijuana, and although

Veronica also smoked some, she knew one day things would change; this was just a passing phase and drugs were never going to get the better of her. Ben however, had a very addictive personality and Veronica realised this, he was also a dreamer. It seemed to Veronica that he was someone who would float along in life, going where there was least resistance, or wherever there was an offer of a free ride. He was a free-spirited individual and although Veronica found this endearing, it wasn't attractive enough for her to want a serious relationship with Ben.

So here they were, Phil, Paula, Michael, Veronica and Ben, the new-found crew of the yacht Nova. When this crew boarded their plane to Turkey, they were all feeling excited about the adventure that was about to unfold; and they were all tired when they arrived at Dalaman Airport just after midnight. Two taxis were called for the drive to Gocek Marina where the yacht was moored.

When they arrived, Phil ushered everyone together, and they made their way to a block of apartments opposite the marina. It was agreed that they should go straight to bed, as they needed an early rise to unpack their belongings on board the boat, to prepare for setting sail.

The next morning Veronica woke up to the sound of clanging bells and Turkish music. She opened the curtains and was almost blinded by the sun. It had been an uncomfortable night for her as it was so hot and muggy, and there was no air conditioning in the room. She scrambled through her bags to get some clean clothes and found her toiletries. Though she was desperate for a drink, Veronica felt mainly in need of a quick shower, to freshen up from the night of sweating. She got dressed after her shower and ventured out to her parents' room a few doors down the corridor.

To Veronica's surprise Phil was already up and ready, he took everyone to the breakfast cafe on the roof terrace, where they all had a lovely English breakfast. The views from the roof top were amazing. Veronica could see all the boats moored along the pontoons below, and the vast green mountains embracing each end of the bay, it was truly breath taking. Veronica felt happy that her parents were embarking on this life changing experience, her dad had spoken about sailing around the world for years, but although his intentions were good the drugs had always come first. Neither of them could function without their regular doses of heroin. Things always got done at a slower pace than the average person would manage, which was one of the most frustrating aspects of

Phil and Paula's life style that Veronica would have to accept and be patient with. Nevertheless, she pinched herself! Was this really happening, she thought? It was all she had ever dreamed of. Her mum and dad were finally saying farewell to heroin and living a healthy normal life. Not just living a mundane normal life either, oh no, they were taking on the seas and oceans to conquer the globe. What an amazing accomplishment that would be.

When they'd finished their breakfasts, Phil led everyone down to the Marina, then onto the pontoons towards his yacht Nova. When they reached her, Veronica was mesmerised by the sheer size of the vessel.

"It's huge," she exclaimed to her mum and dad in excitement. She jumped aboard and inspected every inch.

After a good look around, everyone had jobs to carry out. Phil had to get fuel for the engine and fill up the water tanks, whilst Veronica unpacked the bags of clothes and put them into the cupboards on board. Then once the chores were all complete, it was time for some fun!

The water in the Marina was crystal clear just like out at sea, which pleasantly surprised Veronica as it was a far cry from the murky water in South Sea Marina back in Portsmouth.

Here in Turkey, you were not allowed to foul the waters at all or you faced the risk of having your boat confiscated. You had to be a certain distance off shore before you could flush your toilet, which pleased Veronica no end, as this meant she could safely dive over board.

Her fat uncle Michael was the first to dive in. Veronica found it amusing as he did a belly flop, but she was quick to join him. Ben soon followed too, but Phil and Paula stayed on board having more serious things on their mind.

After a nice swim to cool down from the sweltering heat, they dried off and got back to the business of getting the show on the road; or the boat out to sea in this case!

Phil went into the engine room and got Michael to start her up. Phil was tinkering about in the engine room for ages as he'd spotted a few things that needed replacing, such as rivets, bolts and the like. They were relatively minor, but he wanted to make sure he had some spares just in case.

He sent Veronica and Ben off to the local marine shop to find the parts, but it was proving difficult to explain what they wanted, as the locals didn't speak English; and they certainly didn't understand Turkish. Ben even drew diagrams of the parts they needed, but this was to no avail.

In the end, Veronica and Ben scoured the streets looking for hardware shops and builders merchants to try to find the parts. This went on for a few days, which gave Phil time to discover that there were other minor issues with a couple of the sails, which needed stitching. It took around four days for all of the problems to be solved and for Phil to be happy to set off.

He'd found that the best place to stock up on food supplies was at a huge supermarket in Fethiye, which was not far from Gocek along the coast, so they untied the lines and set off to go shopping.

Phil and Paula eased into handling their new craft, she was completely different to Soland in many ways, but they just needed a little time and experience to adjust to her. They did well, and a couple of hours later they arrived at Fethiye. Ben was up in the bow, ready to fend off and jump onto the pontoon with the lines. Veronica was in the stern with Michael and was quick to jump off to do her bit too. She had never shown any interest in sailing previously, so now she was eager to demonstrate initiative and to pick up as much knowledge as she could, to be of service to her parents and everyone else on board.

Once Nova was safely secured to the pontoon, they all set off to discover the harbour and shops. They found an ancient ruin not far from there, which Veronica and her mum were eager to explore. They ran back to the boat to fetch Paula's camera so they could take some photographs. Paula had studied a short photography course from home as she enjoyed taking pictures, and Veronica liked taking photos too, particularly of pretty places she had visited. This was their only chance of getting some pictures of the ruin, as Phil only wanted to stay in Fethiye one night before setting sail. They rushed back with the camera and snapped away, happy to have found such an ancient place. It was hard to figure out exactly what the ruin was, but it looked like a mini amphitheatre. The exploration came to an abrupt end as night was descending and they had to get directions to the supermarket, so they could stock up on food supplies.

Eventually after a long walk, Veronica and her mum found the supermarket and set about buying enough food to feed everyone for a week.

Phil had worked out that the first leg of the journey would be from Fethiye to Malta. The reason they would not stop off at any of the Greek Islands was because Nova, being an American built boat, was subject to non-EU tax laws. If Phil and Paula were to stop in Greece, they would have to pay VAT on the purchase price of Nova at a rate of 20%, but Malta was a tax-free haven, which would allow a pit stop to refuel, fill the tanks and replenish food stocks for the next leg of the journey. It was Phil's plan to stop later at one of the Spanish Islands and pay the lesser rate of VAT which was 15%.

Four trips to the supermarket later, the yacht Nova was full to the brim with food and drink supplies. There were bags and cardboard boxes with plenty of fresh vegetables, fruit, eggs and meat; and some canned foods. Some of this was bought by chance, as everything was labelled in Turkish, so a lot was chosen by the pictures to guess what the contents were. Some of the tins were spot on but others they got completely wrong.

The crew would have to be disciplined with their food and water supplies on board. It was imperative to be fair with the treats and to be considerate at all times with other members of the crew. Unfortunately there was one individual who would prove to be greedy and very inconsiderate, which would become a bone of contention for the others on board; and would cause bad feeling and heated arguments during the voyage.

CHAPTER 24

Setting Sail

Once all of the shopping had been stowed away, it was time to cast off.

Veronica was a little sad to be saying goodbye to Turkey, she wished they had more time to discover the country, but her dad was determined to get back to the UK before the weather turned. He knew it would be tough sailing through the Bay of Biscay if it got too late in the season, so off they set in the dark of night, under engine power.

That first night was very exciting for everyone on board. There was a sense of team work and everyone was jovial. Phil took the helm for the initial 5-6 hours, handing over to Paula whilst he took a short toilet break and had something to eat. Veronica prepared a stew with chicken, potatoes and vegetables; and then she got her head down for a sleep. She didn't find it easy though, as the sound of the engine was very loud. She was also very excited, which made it more difficult to drop off. Eventually Veronica fell asleep, and then did not wake again until early morning. When she woke up, her uncle Michael was at the helm and her parents were fast asleep in the aft cabin. Veronica was mesmerised by the vastness of the sea that surrounded them. On the starboard side she could just about make out land in the distance, which was the island of Rhodes. Veronica had been to a few Greek islands for holidays in the past and really wished that they could stop to explore them, but she accepted that the higher rate of VAT would have to be paid, which was too costly an option.

Whilst taking this all in, Veronica felt a huge sense of pride. Her memory flashed back to the time her dad was convulsing on the floor after a bad fix of heroin. She thought about how scared she was of nearly losing him that day; yet now, here she was aboard a fifty five foot yacht, sailing through the Mediterranean with her parents, who were drug free!

It almost felt worth all the pain and anxiety to be standing there with a light, hot, breeze against her skin, the sun burning down upon her back and the beauty of being out there with her parents. The only thing missing was her sisters.

Veronica enjoyed this day immensely, everyone took turns in steering Nova, and the crew were making good headway under engine power; covering nearly 100 nautical miles in that first day.

The sailing honeymoon would be short lived though, as things were destined to take a turn for the worse. The next morning was a different story, they had motored into a storm and the seas quickly turned from a deep blue colour, to a choppy grey. The boat rocked back and forth and from side to side. Veronica felt very sick; she was dizzy and couldn't get comfortable. She hadn't anticipated seasickness and found it quite unbearable. The grey skies and choppy sea lasted all day and night but in the end she adjusted to it. To add to the difficulties of the weather, the engine broke down, so the only way to continue was under sail.

By day three, the weather improved and the sun continued to beat down, the boat was steady now and Veronica could sunbathe on deck. She wondered how brown she would be by the time they returned home, which made her happy.

Veronica felt inspired, so she took out her dad's Ovation guitar and strummed away. She began composing s song which went like this:

Miles away
That's where I want to stay forever
I'm in a back seat from reality
Miles away
I've lost track of time turned off my receiver
Where the world can't get on top of me
Fed up with society
And all its conformity I need some peace of mind
We all need a break sometimes
Caught up in the rat race
Feeling like I'm no place
A break from this monotony
Would do the world of good for me
Miles away
That's where

I want to stay forever
I'm in a back seat from reality
Miles away
I've lost track of time turned off my receiver
Where the world can't get on top of me
I'm day dreaming by the sea
As the waves wash over me
For the first time in a long time
I can hear my own heartbeat
There's not a single cloud in sight
As I wake up in the sun light
I feel like an innocent child
Happy free yes I can breathe.

By day six though, everyone was getting impatient to get to land. They were still over two hundred miles away from Malta and had lost a lot of miles as they had no engine power. The winds had dropped considerably, and Phil wasn't used to sailing with no winds, so it was taking a lot longer than they'd anticipated reaching the harbour. Everyone was starting to feel anxious and tetchy as the water supplies were running low and the food was also running out.

Phil and Paula had already had a huge row the night before, as Philip was taking out his frustration on her. Michael had tried to step in and stick up for Paula, but ended up being threatened with being thrown overboard if he didn't keep his mouth shut!

Veronica and Ben had started to fall out too, as he had used more than his share of water for a wash, which left Veronica with very little.

Then there was Michael. He had been eating more than his share of the treats, which Veronica was not happy about, and complained to her parents about his lack of consideration.

No one knew exactly how much longer it would take to get to Malta, as Nova had lost headway and was slowly drifting backwards. There was no sight of land anywhere and the water was so calm you could drop just a pebble into it and cause a huge ripple effect.

The vessel was in the Southern Ionian Sea where the water was four thousand meters deep. Everyone was hot and bothered and there was no way of cooling off, apart from diving into the sea. Phil told Ben and Veronica to jump in, but Veronica was nervous. She had never been in water so deep and was afraid of what lay beneath. The water was so dark, due to its depth, that she couldn't see what was below. Phil teased Veronica calling her a baby, but Ben dived in. He had no care in the world and swam around happily. Veronica looked on with envy as Ben was obviously feeling a lot cooler.

Philip had found a bodyboard that had been left behind by the previous owners of Nova. He gave it to Veronica and told her to go for it. He said, "What are you worried about, there are no sharks in this part of the ocean?" So with that, Veronica trusted her dad and leapt in. She was very nervous still and kept half her body on the bodyboard just in case, but was happy to be feeling cooler. Paula grabbed her camera and took some photos of Veronica and Ben. It was so calm that the only ripples in the water for miles around were those caused by the movement of the boat, and by Veronica and Ben swimming around it.

CHAPTER 25

Water Water Everywhere!

After their much needed cool down, Ben and Veronica swam back to the yacht and climbed on board. They dried off and were allowed a cup of fresh water to wash private parts, to avoid salt water sores. Veronica was annoyed that she wasn't able to shower, but was feeling much more content after having a swim.

"How much longer is it going to be before we reach land?" She asked her dad. He couldn't be sure exactly, but worked it out to be roughly another two or three days. Veronica had a look at the food supplies and was disappointed by the empty cupboards.

The fresh foods were all consumed and all that was left was tinned cans of sardines, beans, new potatoes, tomatoes, carrots, tuna, ham and some pasta, but not a lot else.

The milk and juice had run out a few days before, and all they had now was tea bags, coffee, some bottles of drinking water and dried powdered milk.

Veronica and Paula worked out what meals they could muster up from what was left, and although a few meals could be managed, they wouldn't be exciting and the portions would be small. Phil made a distress call on the radio, he made up a poem about the engine breaking down and drifting. It started like this:

'Water water everywhere
Not a drop to drink!'

The Captain of a huge cargo ship that had come from Japan and was heading for Rotterdam heard Phil's plea for assistance. This Captain felt sorry for Captain Phil and his crew, so decided to turn his ship around and come over a hundred miles out of his way to help.

As the ship became visible on the horizon, everyone on board Nova was taken aback by the size of it; panic began to take over as they quickly ran out on deck and tied all of the fenders along the port side. When the ship came alongside, Veronica's heart was in her mouth, as she thought this vessel could wipe them out in an instant if her dad didn't handle Nova correctly.

Michael, Ben and Veronica were in the bows to fend off. It was so risky and frightening for everyone on board Nova, who were novices at sea, fending off a fast-moving hull that was causing a lot of displacement and movement in the water, making it a tricky operation. The top of Nova's mast didn't even reach the ship's deck level, they were like a speck of a vessel compared to this ship; one false move could have cost them dearly, but the crew of the ship worked hard to bring their vessel to a reasonable halt.

Their crew consisted of people from different countries from Japan to Italy, who were all waving, cheering and clapping. The crew of Nova could hardly believe it; they had managed to come alongside a huge ship in the middle of the Southern Ionian Sea and worked together to make sure no damage was done.

The Captain gave Phil instructions on the radio that his crew would throw down some lines to tie alongside. Ben and Veronica caught these and tied one line to the bow and the other to the stern, to prevent their boat from drifting back and forth.

Then the Captain ordered his crew to throw down a water hose, and asked Phil to open Nova's water tanks and fill her up. Phil and his crew were so happy, especially Veronica who was desperate for a shower.

As the huge hose tumbled down, Veronica caught it and ran to open the tank under her dad's orders. At that point she decided to drench her dad and sprayed him completely with the hose.

He retaliated with another hose that he had caught and drenched Veronica. This amused the crew on board the ship, who were all laughing.

Once the tanks were full and the hoses had been handed back, the Captain sent down a line with a huge plastic container of chicken curry and another with boiled rice. They also sent two huge packs with cans of coke. Phil attached a bottle of whisky and a £50 pound note to say thank you.

The Captain explained that he had encountered a similar experience himself many years before, whilst out sailing in a similar vessel with his family. He said that though their ship was on a tight schedule, he just couldn't ignore Phil's Mayday and liked the poem.

Everyone on the ship, and on the yacht Nova, clapped and cheered. That day was like Xmas, the crew of Nova could not have asked for more.

Phil thanked the Captain, then Veronica, Ben and Michael untied the lines and fended off whilst Phil and Paula worked to steer Nova safely away from the ship. Once they were at a safe distance, Veronica ran to get the camera and snapped some shots of the ship and its crew waving goodbye.

Everyone on board Nova was ecstatic, the curry would see them through a couple of meals and the water would keep everyone going. Veronica couldn't resist a shower; she thought it was well deserved after all their efforts!

CHAPTER 26

Land at Last!

All on board Nova were very much content after receiving food from the Captain and crew of the cargo ship. Phil was a hero for making his distress call, and everyone joked about the poem he had made up. The chicken curry was very tasty, and there was so much of it that everyone had plenty for lunch, with lots left over for dinner too. Veronica was much more relaxed and proud of her dad's efforts; she took out her dad's guitar and strummed some songs, she even felt inspired to write another song.

The sun continued to shine and the sky was a beautiful turquoise, there were no clouds in sight at all. After such a successful day, everyone retired for an early night apart from Michael who was on night shift. Veronica and Ben had 4 hours until it was their turn for the night watch.

Veronica had got used to getting by on intervals of 4 hours of sleep. She looked forward to waking up and doing the night watches and would count the shooting stars until there were too many to keep track of. She had never seen so many in all of her life let alone in one night.

Venus shone very brightly out in the Southern Ionian, and the constellations were very clearly visible from out in the sea, as there were no street lights polluting the skies visibility. It was quite literally breathtaking, and watching the deep red sun come up over the sea's horizon first thing was out of this world.

Knowing they were nearing the end of the first leg made everyone feel relaxed and excited.

Philip continued to check his position with his maps and instruments, and then in the distance ahead, a speck of land could be seen. It was the Italian Island of Sicily. Nova had been at sea for ten days; Phil had estimated the journey from Fethiye to Malta to be roughly 5 days but hadn't anticipated the engine failure and winds dropping so considerably.

Everyone got very excited at the sight of land. It had been over a week since they had set eyes on it. Crete was the last island Nova had passed and now at last the first leg was nearly over.

It seemed to take forever to pass Sicily, at one point Veronica was convinced Nova was not making any headway, but it was her eagerness to reach land and impatience that took over.

By the time they were in sight of Malta and coming into port at Valletta harbour it was getting dark. The coast guard had to be contacted via Nova's radio. Phil was informed that the customs officer was off duty until the morning, so Nova would have to tie alongside a buoy until then.

Everyone was devastated as they had been so eager to get off Nova and touch land again.

Phil explained to the coastguard that the crew of Nova were hungry and had no food supplies as they had been at sea for 10 days.

A skipper from another yacht in Valletta harbour heard the conversation over the radio and asked Phil if he could get some supplies for the crew and bring them out on a dingy.

Phil accepted the offer and within the hour the dingy appeared through the darkness.

The gentleman had brought chocolates and cigarettes also.

The crew of Nova invited the man on board and everyone had some wine and beers to celebrate.

Phil reimbursed the gentleman and he set off back towards the harbour on his dingy.

The next morning everyone woke early and eager to get to land, it seemed like a never-ending waiting game as they waited for the customs officer to give Phil the go ahead to come through the harbour. It was a difficult exercise as there was no engine power but luckily the vessel got in safely. Initially, only Phil was allowed to step off Nova on to the harbour pontoon, where there were a couple of customs officers waiting to greet him. Phil had to take all of the crew's passports, and a member of customs came on board to do a brief search. They were given the all clear and everyone was then allowed to step off the boat.

The crew clapped and applauded each other for the efforts of getting Nova safely to Malta. Hurray - and Phil and Paula had not touched heroin in 10 days! Veronica was so proud of her parents.

CHAPTER 27

Discovering Valletta and Mdina

After relaxing for a couple of days, Veronica's parents decided that Paula would fly back to the UK to get the kids and check up on the dealing. They had left Theresa looking after Ella and Paulette, as they had been worried about taking them on the first leg with no experience of handling Nova. Now that they were feeling more confident, they wanted the children to join in the experience of sailing back to the UK. Paula needed to pick up some forgotten essentials and get some more money and methadone. When Paula booked her ticket, Michael also took the opportunity to go back home. He needed a break from Phil and was missing his home cooked meals and wife Kelly.

Ben had met an Australian couple who had a yacht moored opposite Nova in the next pontoon. Phil had got talking to them and discovered that they wanted someone to help with night watches, who could handle a boat. They offered to pay Ben a few hundred pounds to help them sail from Malta to Majorca, and then they would pay for his return flight as well. Ben asked Phil if it was okay, and Phil said he was happy for Ben to go.

That afternoon Ben and the Aussie couple set off for Majorca, and then a couple of hours later, Paula and Michael left for the airport to catch their flight back to the UK. It was very quiet on board Nova with only Phil and Veronica. Phil had got talking to a few of the local Maltese people who had yachts in the harbour. One in particular was a very wealthy family man who had taken an interest in Phil. He was intrigued by Phil's story of being a hard-working English man with his own plumbing business back in the UK, and how he had got into yachting and fishing from a young age and managed to buy his second yacht in Turkey, which he and his family were all attempting to sail back to the UK. Phil bought two "Di Blasi" folding mopeds from the guy, that were perfect to have on board as they would fold up into a bag which was easy to stow away; and they were great to get around on when in port. This Maltese guy wanted to show Phil and Veronica around Malta, he was very proud of his country and of his family. Veronica struck up a conversation with one of his daughters and soon she was whisked off her feet and shown around Valletta town.

Veronica and Phil were told about a beautiful ancient city called Mdina, so they decided to take a taxi to have a look. Veronica was mesmerised by how old and well preserved it was. The medieval town seemed to go on and on, with winding streets full of cobbles. It was very tranquil and illuminated by many street lamps. On the other hand there was a lot of noticeable destruction left over from bombings during the Second World War. Phil told Veronica that his dad was stationed in Malta as a medic during the war to help with the wounded. This was a poignant moment for Phil as he had lost his dad to lung cancer when he was just six years old.

They found a nice restaurant to have a meal, which was a highlight of the time spent in Malta; and what Veronica most appreciated was that she had spent some quality time there with her dad. She was very proud that her dad had managed to manoeuvre Nova so well, considering she was almost twice the size of their previous yacht; and that he had achieved this at the same time as kicking his lifelong heroin habit. Veronica felt as though she was finally getting to know her dad, her real dad, not the person who was high on heroin every day.

Phil had opened up to Veronica about how ashamed he was of his past and the life he had led, fuelled by drug abuse. He confided in Veronica that he had let his family down and wanted to give his children a wholesome life, to teach them about the wonders of the world by sailing around it with them. He felt terrible for letting Ella and Paulette's education slip as they had missed a lot of time at school. He thought he had not given them enough quality time and attention, so he wanted to do something positive about that.

Veronica understood exactly what Phil was talking about and felt sad for Ella and Paulette. Veronica did not consider what she had lost out on; she at least had studied for her GCSEs, albeit at the last hour, and gained enough to get her to college. Ella and Paulette had suffered bullying at school, as had Veronica, but unlike her they refused to go to school and ended up smoking marijuana from a young age.

Phil had to get back to the job of getting Nova's engine fixed and was given details of a reputable marine engineer who lived locally. The following few days were focused on getting Nova ready for her next journey. Ben returned from his trip seven days later, having flown back to the UK before getting another flight to Malta. Both flights had been paid for by the Aussies, as well as them having paid him generously for his services. Ben was full of spirit and very happy to be back on yacht Nova, he had enjoyed his trip aboard the Aussie's boat, but found conversations difficult as he didn't know the people. He was relieved to be back with his mate Phil and to be getting ready for the next leg.

Paula and the kids arrived the following day; Veronica was very pleased to see her younger sisters. She thought they deserved the experience of sailing on Nova with drug free parents too.

Veronica wondered if her mum had remained good during her week-long return to their dealing reality in London. Paula was adamant that she had stayed off the drugs, but Veronica wasn't wholly confident that she had. She wanted to believe her mum, but knew that the temptation could have been too strong. Nevertheless Veronica was pleased that the whole family was together at last, and Michael rejoined them the following day.

Nova was ship shape and fully crewed again, and everyone on board was eager to get going. Phil decided to take Paula, Veronica and the kids to Mdina first, to show them some of the beauty and history of Malta before they left. Then after a couple of blissful days, the crew decided they would get an early night and make a start for Majorca the following day. The next morning everyone got up quite early in readiness for the busy day ahead. Suddenly they became aware that people were congregating on the pontoons talking hysterically. Phil went to find out what was happening, boats all over the harbour had lowered their flags to half-mast. Princess Diana had been confirmed dead in a French hospital after being involved in a car crash in Paris. The feeling was surreal; no one could quite believe it, what a shock. Up until then, everyone had felt so happy about the impending trip, now everyone was in complete shock and horrified to hear that Princess Diana had died. Phil immediately lowered his flag in respect for the royal family and their loss. It couldn't be true everyone on board argued, it must be a hoax. The whole morning was taken over by mixed emotions whilst calls were made to the UK to confirm the news. No one felt able to switch off and concentrate on the job at hand, as the senseless loss was totally indescribable. But they all had to overcome their shock and get on with getting Nova safely out of Valletta harbour. It was a very sombre day.

CHAPTER 28

Mini Tornadoes at Dawn

Once Nova was safely out of Valletta harbour, Phil followed the coast and found a small, picturesque bay where he and Paula thought it would be a good idea to drop anchor for a few hours. Ben and Veronica were in awe of the pretty cove that lay ahead; Ben asked if he could dive in and Phil was happy for everyone to swim, or relax and chill out.

Phil and Paula seemed sensitive to the water, maybe it was part and parcel of coming off heroin, but they made no attempt to swim. Ben and Veronica however wasted no time, Veronica was happy to dive in, as though the water was deep, she could see what lay beneath the surface.

Splash went Ben, splash followed Veronica; they enjoyed diving off the coach roof doing all sorts of somersaults. Veronica even stood on Ben's shoulders as they dived in together, they were having such fun. Ben decided to swim ashore; Veronica was impressed with how quickly he got there, almost in a flash. She wasn't interested in joining him though, as there was nothing apart from a tiny beach and lots of rocks. Veronica was worried that she might cut her feet, so she stayed behind on the boat.

An hour later, Ben returned pleased with his little expedition. Veronica had showered, and Ben hosed off above deck. Paula prepared a light lunch and then Phil raised Nova's anchor and they set off again. Once Nova was safely away from land, Phil was able to set a straight course on auto helm; and his crew members were able to sit back and relax once again.

They were still dazed and shocked by the news of Diana's death. It didn't make sense, how could someone so worldly famous and supposedly protected by the best of bodyguards, have come to such a fatal end? Everyone on board discussed the possibility of a conspiracy.

As time passed, they all began to adjust to being at sea again and being confined to a small space. Veronica had gone to the starboard deck, where she was deep in thought, taking in the surrounding view. Nova was moving at a reasonable speed under engine power, as Veronica gazed out at the vastness around her. Then in the blink of an eye she spotted a small group of fish leaping out of the water, she screamed with joy! Just beneath the surface she could make out a larger fish, it was a tuna which was chasing the smaller fish. The flying fish were jumping for their lives. Phil was below deck when he heard Veronica's scream and came running up to the deck in a panic, tripping up the stairs, whacking his shins along the way.

"For fuck's sake," he shouted, seeing that Veronica was okay and just excited like a child, pointing at the flying fish. "I thought something was wrong, you fucking idiot, why did you scream like that? I thought someone had gone overboard!"

Veronica felt embarrassed and hurt that her dad was calling her an idiot. Phil lost his temper a lot and often put Veronica down. He did it to Paula and the other kids too, but Veronica was sensitive and took everything seriously. Phil made her feel very inadequate; she was always trying to please her dad and just wanted him to be proud of her, but no matter how hard she tried, it rarely seemed enough.

"Sorry Dad, I just got excited, it made me jump too. I've never seen anything like that, it's amazing," Veronica replied, but Phil was not impressed with her 'over the top' behaviour.

The day went on and everyone took their turn at the helm, keeping to the course that Phil had set. The next day was more of the same, until a school of around twenty bottle nosed dolphins appeared, swimming alongside Nova's bow. They leapt out of the water, twisting and somersaulting as they swam, everyone on board was mesmerised by the sheer beauty of these mammals as they moved so gracefully through the water.

Veronica and Ben wished they could swim amongst them, but Nova was under engine power and moving too quickly, so it wasn't safe to dive in; and these mammals were wild.

Nonetheless, the experience was exquisite. The dolphins had come of their own accord to visit Nova and her crew, everyone felt very lucky.

As the day wore on, the sun disappeared behind some clouds; and the clear blue sky and tranquil sea that had been Nova's backdrop all day rapidly deteriorated as the skies turned grey and dark. Everyone felt a little chillier as the wind picked up, Nova was heading into a storm and there was no way around it. Phil and Paula were on watch until 4am and steered Nova through the first part of the storm, but it wasn't anything they hadn't experienced in the past. They had dealt with gale force eights on many occasions when sailing Soland through the Solent and had even got caught on a sandbank in a horrible storm, when they had to be rescued by the RNLI's lifeboat, so this was comparatively easy for them, but soon it was time for Ben and Veronica's watch. Phil woke Veronica and Ben and went below deck for a much-needed sleep.

Gone was the calm turquoise sea, the water was choppy and grey, the wind was blowing quite hard and it was raining. Unlike Soland that had an enclosed wheelhouse, Nova's cockpit was open to the elements; she had obviously been built for a warmer climate.

Ben and Veronica put on some waterproofs and continued the watch. As dawn broke, the storm worsened and they could see mini tornados on the horizon ahead. Veronica panicked, she ran below to the aft cabin where her parents were asleep and hurriedly tapped her dad to wake him.

Phil came up on deck and scoured the horizon, he double checked Nova's course and position, and told Ben to re set the course slightly to steer around the tornado. He then returned to his bed, confident that Ben was a competent sailor and more than capable of dealing with the storm. Veronica however, wasn't as confident. She had seen tornados on the television destroying towns across America and killing many people. Her heart pounded at the sight of the tornado ahead, but Ben kept calm, he reset Nova's position and steered away from it. Five minutes later they saw another tornado on the horizon ahead. Veronica shouted to Ben to steer Nova away yet again; but as he did, there was another then another. Nova seemed to be going round in circles, constantly trying to avoid the tornados for what seemed like forever. The ordeal was stressful and exhausting. Eventually after a couple of hours of dodging and circling, the tornados began to dissipate; and Nova finally got through the worst of the storm. Everyone else on board had slept like babies through this event, but Ben and Veronica were completely shattered and desperately in need of a rest. Phil found the whole experience quite amusing, he didn't let little things like mini tornados get to him.

CHAPTER 29

Reaching Majorca

After a well-deserved rest which recharged her after the long night watch, Veronica was feeling more refreshed. She woke with the sun beaming into her eyes through the hatch beside her and sat up to see if the skies had cleared. Veronica was pleased to observe that they were back to an amazingly clear turquoise colour and felt instantly relieved. Nova was sailing smoothly through the Mediterranean Sea and everyone on board was feeling cheerful, as they were over half way through the second leg. Phil noticed some land in the distance; he checked their position and deduced that it was Algeria. Just then a conversation started on the radio, an English guy was talking about an ordeal that he and his ship mate had just experienced sailing along the coastline there. He explained that some Algerians had come alongside their yacht with guns and ordered them off. They were petrified and had been held captive for a few days until being released without their yacht or any papers. They eventually found where their boat had been taken and managed to get back on board without being seen. The Algerians had taken everything and had ransacked the yacht. They motored out of the port fleeing for their lives without their documents or any money. The Algerians had chased them, but gave up once the English were a certain distance offshore, as there was little they could do. Luckily the men had escaped relatively unscathed, having been shaken up and a little bruised from their attack. Phil was horrified at the conversation taking place between the English skipper and a coastguard from one of the Spanish Islands. The skipper wanted to warn other boats of the danger, to prevent them being attacked too. Phil altered Nova's course immediately to ensure greater distance from Algeria's coast line. Veronica felt full of fear, the same fear that had engulfed her when she was eight years old, being tied up by the French drug addicts who had ransacked her home years before. It wasn't a nice feeling, the adrenaline rushed through her as she tried hard to remain calm and gain mental control of her emotions. Phil steered Nova safely away and they continued in peace towards Majorca.

The rest of the trip remained tranquil, and everyone enjoyed plenty of sunshine and lovely home cooking on board. On the fifth day, Majorca came rapidly into view and everyone was relieved to be another leg closer to getting safely home. As Phil piloted Nova into Palma's harbour, the sight of land again was very welcoming. Veronica was eager to get an ice cream, as she had been dreaming of having a mint chocolate chip cornet since leaving Fethiye in Turkey. She had been disappointed to discover that they didn't sell that flavour in Malta, but had pistachio instead, so now she had her fingers crossed that she would find one in Majorca.

There was an ancient monastery towering over the Marina, its gothic looking steeples were visually striking; and Veronica was amazed by its ancient beauty. The Marina was full to the brim with yachts of all sizes, but they found a berth and Veronica couldn't wait to tie Nova's lines and go exploring. She looked forward to another adventure with her drug free parents and sisters.

CHAPTER 30

Exploring Majorca

When Nova arrived in Palma, Phil and Paula had a lot of paper work to fill in. This was the first European port of call since her circumnavigation began when she set sail from Florida with her previous owners.

Phil and Paula were now liable to pay 15% Value Added Tax on the purchase price of Nova, which was unfortunate but had to be done. Once her crew's papers had been checked by customs, everyone was free to step onto dry land and explore Palma.

Ella and Paulette couldn't wait to get to a shop and get a well-deserved ice cream and some sweets. This was their first experience of sailing abroad as they had previously only been at sea for a day or two in the Solent. The girls had been very well behaved so Paula was more than happy to treat them. Veronica set off with her mum and the girls to explore the locality. They invited Ben to join them but he was more interested in staying on board Nova smoking and listening to music. Veronica found Ben boring, she couldn't understand why he didn't want to explore the town, but Phil reminded her that Ben had already been to Palma the week before.

Paula, Veronica and the girls set off, leaving Phil and Michael to go and find some supermarkets to replenish the food on board Nova.

The two fold-up mopeds that Phil had purchased in Malta, were very useful for getting around. Phil thought they were a good buy, as they would pay for themselves eventually in savings from car hire and taxi fares. They were indeed very useful in Palma, as Phil and Michael were able to go some distance to a decent hypermarket and pick up the necessary groceries without it costing too much. The petrol was very cheap too.

Paula, Veronica and the girls had found the streets bustling with all types of shops and stalls.

They sold alcohol, food, and arts and crafts. Dream catchers were on display at every other stall which was something the girls particularly liked. They found a huge McDonalds which pleased Ella and Paulette no end, as this was their favourite fast food. Veronica however wasn't so impressed. She hated burgers, preferring salads and fresh sandwiches for lunch. She was pleasantly surprised though, to find that McDonalds in Palma was a little different to back home. Here they sold fresh salads with chicken and ham. The salads were very well prepared so Veronica was happy to eat there after all.

The family enjoyed three weeks of scouring the streets of Palma and sunbathing by the port, using one of the port hotel's facilities and outdoor pool. The girls had lots of fun in the pool and Veronica was very happy to assist in looking after them whilst Phil and Paula had some quality time together on Nova.

September was a few days away and the girls were due back at school. Paula also needed to get back to the dealing as Theresa had been overseeing things for weeks, and she had her own obligations too. Phil decided that he, Michael and Ben would be able to proceed with the next leg without them, and as Veronica was needed to assist Paula, her time on Nova was coming to an end. Veronica felt quite sad as she had had the time of her life with her family. She didn't want it to end: for the first time in her life her parents were free from drugs and seemed happy and relaxed. A far cry from the mundane reality of their habits back home in London. Veronica didn't miss the punters calling round every day and intruding into what should have been normal family life. The punters were always priority as that's what kept the money coming in and allowed the lifestyle that Phil, Paula and the girls had got used to.

Veronica however didn't want it. She hated the hold that the drugs had on her parents.

She thought that this trip through the Med aboard Nova was the start of a whole new beginning, and during the voyage it really was. But things were about to go back to the same old reality.

Paula and the girls packed their belongings and Paula went to a nearby travel agent to purchase one way tickets back to the UK.

Before Veronica knew it, it was time to leave. She was sad, but she didn't really want to be the only girl on board Nova. Phil could be quite harsh with his tongue and Veronica didn't want his stress to spill out onto her. If she wasn't in the firing line then he would find someone else to take it out on. Veronica wondered if her dad's temperament was part and parcel of coming off the drugs, but then again he was always like Jekyll and Hyde, even on the drugs.

Nevertheless, Veronica was very proud of her mum and dad. This had been an amazing experience that had opened her eyes to the real Phil and Paula: a 'Phil and Paula' who had actually had a dream and made it a reality. How many heroin addicts could do that?

Veronica thought her parents were amazingly strong to be able to give up a lifelong habit, whilst also taking on seas that they had no experience of. There were many sober people out there who had lived pretty normal lives, who wouldn't even have the guts to attempt sailing a 50 foot yacht through unknown territory, let alone battling heroin addiction to boot.

Veronica accepted that her part of this journey was over, so said goodbye to her dad and wished him luck with the rest of his voyage. Paula and Phil hugged and kissed for what seemed like ages, they knew it would be weeks before they would be together again. It was a sad moment, but one that filled Veronica with pride. They left for the airport in a cab.

CHAPTER 31

Arriving Home

Paula and the girls had a pretty simple journey home from Palma. The flight only took two hours and their luggage was light. They had taken minimal clothing as they were able to hand wash on board Nova. Paula hailed a cab outside Gatwick airport and an hour later they arrived back at their home in Edmonton, North London. Veronica suddenly felt down, as soon as they approached their road, the reality of life back in North London sank in. Veronica's guts twisted and turned, she knew in her heart that the dream had come to an end. She could tell by her mum's behaviour and her eagerness to get into the house, what she was about to do, but she told herself not to jump to conclusions. As soon as Paula stepped inside, Theresa was there to greet them. Immediately Theresa began to give Paula the rundown on all the dealing politics of what had occurred whilst the family was away. Veronica felt sick to her stomach at hearing the same old news. Paula told Veronica to put the kettle on and make a cuppa whilst she went upstairs to the bedroom with Theresa to sort things out. Veronica's heart sank again; she knew that her mum was sneaking off for a smoke.

Veronica put the kettle on then crept upstairs, quietly so that her mum and Theresa didn't hear her sneaking up behind them. She listened intently behind her mum's bedroom door to see what they were up to. Veronica heard Paula ask Theresa for the 'gear'. Then Veronica heard the rustling of the foil, followed a few moments later by the pitch in Paula's voice changing, so Veronica burst into the room. She caught Paula in the act, chasing heroin on foil as she had suspected. Veronica wished she could pack a bag and leave right there and then, but there was nowhere for her to go.

She shouted at Paula, "Mum, what are you doing?" Paula jumped out of her skin as she didn't want Veronica to see what she was doing.

"Mum I was so proud of you and now you have ruined everything. I knew that it was the first thing you would do when you got in the door, but I told myself not to doubt you, to have faith, to believe in you, but I was right. I bet you had gear when you came back for the kids from Malta didn't you?"

"No I didn't Veronica, I swear!" Paula replied.

"I don't believe you Mum, Dad has been out there all this time clean; and you couldn't do it could you? But you would lie and let me think you are clean and still get high behind my back, I'm telling Dad when I speak to him," Veronica said, then slammed the bedroom door and ran into her room crying.

Paula followed her and pleaded with Veronica not to tell her dad. "You will devastate him Veronica, you can't tell him please. I'm not going to get on it every day I promise, I'm gonna be clean by the time Dad gets home."

Veronica shook her head in disbelief. "I don't believe you Mum, you've broken my heart, I thought this was the beginning of a whole new life. How stupid of me to believe it! You will never come off for good, you are too weak and I can't go on hanging around waiting for you to do it. I'm gonna get my life together now, it's down to yourself." Paula said sorry and left Veronica alone in her room.

Veronica cried all night but the next day accepted the old way of life once again. In her heart though, she knew that she had to find her own way in the world, she didn't want to live that lifestyle with drug addicts around her continually bringing her down. This was the life her parents had chosen; this had never been Veronica's choice, all she had ever craved was normality, a life without drugs, without crime, without police busting through the house in the middle of the night. She wanted to work and build herself a peaceful way of life, free from paranoia. Veronica was tired of jumping up at the window because of strange noises outside, fearful that the police or gangsters would come pounding through the house. This was no longer the life for her and she would have to face hard facts. Her parents would never give up the drugs for her or for anyone, they would only ever do it for themselves.

Veronica was nearly twenty four years of age and had stayed living with her parents for way too long. She feared for her sisters, what would become of them when she left home?

She had always felt responsible for her sisters but at the end of the day, they were not her children. Veronica had a new vision; she would get a job and start saving for her new life.

She loved her parents dearly but they couldn't be depended on to make that final break, and Veronica realised this for the first time in her life. She was full of despair, but was now accepting that her parents' choices were their choices; and Veronica was entitled to make her own now.

CHAPTER 32

The Last Leg of Nova's
Voyage Home to the UK

Phil, Michael and Ben had sailed Nova from Palma to Gibraltar with ease.

The journey was shorter than the last two legs and they were much more confident and equipped for handling Nova. Michael flew back home from Gibraltar, he was missing his wife and family and Phil had assured Michael that he and Ben would manage Nova just fine without him.

Phil and Ben docked in Gibraltar for a few weeks before setting sail on their last leg through the Bay of Biscay. Gibraltar was an interesting place to Phil and Ben, where anything went. There were many travellers from all over Europe, busking and selling all sorts of artefacts.

Pipes of all colours and shapes were everywhere, so too was the sale of marijuana on the black market; readily available to anyone who wanted it.

Phil and Ben met other fellow yachtsmen and women in Gibraltar. The ones who puffed were cool to hang out with, so Phil and Ben were very relaxed there. With bundles of puff available, there was nothing rushing them, only of course the weather, which was changing. The temperature was dropping and the winds were fiercer, the sea was also becoming choppy, especially as November drew near.

Experienced yachtsmen and captains of huge ships dodged the Bay of Biscay in November but Phil wasn't at all worried, he took everything in his stride. Phil had his own clock that the world and all therein would have to accept. Phil rushed for no one, ever; the sea would have to wait for Phil! Even his own mum said on many occasions, that her son would be late for his own funeral.

After their extended stay in Gibraltar, it was finally time to get sober and get Nova back on her way. Phil and Ben set sail in the first week of November, and the weather had turned. The winds were high and the skies were grey, but as far as Phil was concerned, if he got Nova's position right the wind would be right on their tail, enabling them to get home sooner.

The first few days at sea were wet and choppy, but it was nothing that Phil hadn't been used to when sailing Soland through the Solent. The difference now was they had a much larger vessel, with an open cockpit. They took it in turns to get their waterproofs.

As they sailed towards the Bay of Biscay, they could see on the horizon that the weather was worsening. The skies had turned from a deep grey to quite a black colour, it was almost as dark as night. The waves were huge, some higher than houses and coming from all angles. Phil realised that he had taken on more than he was prepared for; he had under estimated the weather patterns in the Bay of Biscay, so here they were, battling gales of force ten and over; and there was no way out as they were right in the midst of a storm. The boat was swaying from side to side and her bow was literally leaping out of the water by some considerable height. Phil had tied the camcorder to Nova's mast and left it on record, to show Paula and the kids how bad the storm was when they got home. Phil found the whole experience thrilling, he was shouting with joy like a complete lunatic. He embraced the storm and the rough sea, he felt at one in this situation, the boat was keeling so far on its side, it was nearly in the water. At this point Phil and Ben decided there was nothing they could do other than to set Nova a course using the auto helm, and batten down below deck to try and get dry, as they were completely soaked through. The gale outside continued to beat Nova's hull and decks, whilst Phil and Ben attempted to cook dinner.

They managed it successfully and decided to play a game of Scrabble to kill some time and take their mind off the storm. Scrabble became a new game which they renamed 'Scribble' as they had re-written the rules, deciding that making up their own new words was much more fun. Of course the marijuana had some influence no doubt, and the men both laughed hysterically at each other's new invented words. This became a great theme that would keep them both happily entertained for the remainder of their journey, and somehow kept them sane through a most terrifying experience.

A couple of days later, the winds dropped and the sea became calmer. Phil checked their position, England was in sight and their journey was nearing its end. The men cheered and patted each other on the back for they were proud of what they had come through. There had been a few scary moments where they really wondered if they would get home alive, or at least in one piece.

When later they sailed into South Sea Marina, the skippers of other yachts there were cheering and clapping as Nova came into dock. Phil was the talk of the Marina for months to come.

Apparently there had been a write up in the local paper about his journey and his sheer guts to take on the Bay of Biscay with one fellow crew member on a fifty foot yacht in the month of November. Phil was practically a hero in the eyes of his fellow skipper friends.

Veronica drove Paula to South Sea to pick her dad and Ben up and bring them back to North London. She was immensely proud of her dad and his determination, but deep down she knew, once her dad was back in Edmonton, the dream would be over.

CHAPTER 33

Life Back in the Real World

Phil was on a real high after his trip through the Bay of Biscay.

He told everyone from his entire family to the punters that were still coming through the family door about it. This high would gradually be replaced by a massive low.

Phil soon realised that Paula had been weak and quickly joined her in having regular doses of heroin again. This was no surprise to Veronica, but she was disappointed.

She had remained slightly hopeful that he would be strong and encourage Paula to be good, but in the end he joined her.

Ella and Paulette were aware of everything that was going on but seemed to not let it upset them. They accepted their parents' addiction a lot more easily than Veronica could. They didn't seem to be bothered by it; and continued to catch up with their friends on their return, letting everything go over their heads. They were free to be kids, because Veronica had been there to take the brunt of the reality of life with addict parents. She had, in essence, been a surrogate mum to Ella and Paulette when needed; and if Phil or Paula were ever busted again, Veronica was now old enough to take care of her sisters and they knew that. Veronica was there to shield her sisters from many of the harsh realities that she had faced as a young child, but Ella and Paulette were oblivious to this. There were many experiences that Veronica had not even spoken about to her sisters, they were too young to understand; and anyway things were different now. Phil and Paula had stopped using needles when Ella was born; they were much more composed these days.

Life back in Edmonton with Phil safely home from his voyage was quickly getting back to normal. The same old punters came calling for their regular doses; and Veronica soon slipped back into the routine of being on hand to open the door, make tea, help clean the house and look after her sisters when needed. In between, Veronica would pack a bag and go and stay with her best friend Jenni for a night here or there to escape; and then Veronica found a job waitressing in London's West End. She worked night shifts in Piccadilly Circus at the London's sports café, serving well-to-do business men and sports fanatics. Veronica could make up to £150 in tips serving one large table but it had its downside, as sometimes when the restaurant was extremely busy, a table of guests would walk out without paying; and this would be deducted from Veronica's wages.

Waitressing from 5pm till 4am was hard going, sometimes Veronica would return home to north London, have 3-4 hours' sleep and be back at work for 11am for a day shift. The job quickly took its toll on her, but the night shifts paid well with tips; and Veronica was determined to save for her future.

Phil had told Veronica to decide what she wanted to do with her life. He told her that he and Paula were selling everything up to move onto Nova with the kids. They would then set sail for a circumnavigation, which he offered Veronica the opportunity to join, but there were many conditions. He told her that she must be on hand at any moment to look after the girls, and that she would have to be a team member in all preparations etc. Phil expected Veronica to give up the idea of a job and her social life, to be on hand at his say so. This did not appeal to Veronica one bit, she couldn't bear the thought of having no escape from the clutches of her parents' lifestyle; and although Phil convinced himself that he was going around the world, Veronica knew that the drugs would again slow him down; and she would be waiting and waiting whilst getting impatient. She told her dad her feelings and explained that she wanted her own life. His reaction was quite spiteful, he told Veronica that if she wasn't going to be part of the family team then she would need to hurry up and figure out where she was going to live. He told her that life in the real world was hard, and without a sufficient income it would be miserable for Veronica trying to find her way alone in the world. He made Veronica feel like she couldn't do it, that she wasn't strong enough to cope. Veronica sank into a depressive state, feeling confused and unsure.

In the meantime, she continued to work and squirrel her money away into a savings account.

When Phil's mum, Veronica's Nan, passed away the previous year, she had left her nine grandchildren £2000 each in her will. Veronica had put this into an ISA account, deciding to build on it for her deposit on a flat and a ticket to a new life of freedom. Still doubting herself and feeling depressed at life back in Edmonton living around the usual punters coming in and out of the house, Veronica noticed that her dad's attitude was increasingly changing towards her. He started to treat her like an outsider and made her feel inadequate. He and Paula would go down to the boat and leave Veronica in charge of her sisters. Ella was now fifteen and had a boyfriend; Paulette was twelve but hanging out with Ella and her friends, so she had the attitude of a fifteen year old too. Ella and Paulette had been experimenting with marijuana for some time; Veronica was horrified when she discovered what the girls were up to. She confided in her mum and was again shocked to learn that her mum already knew and was even accepting of the girls' behaviour. Paula would even turn a blind eye and let Ella pinch bits of Phil's stash.

When Phil was out or on the boat, the girls would congregate with their schoolmates in their room and take it in turns to smoke joints and prepare makeshift bongs with plastic coke bottles.

At the time, Veronica smoked marijuana herself, but tried not to let it take over her life. She had already had periods of smoking it all day, and found it had had a large impact on her mood and confidence.

Veronica was disappointed that the girls were now doing the same at a young age; she hadn't started smoking it until she was nearly nineteen years old. Paulette was only twelve, not even a teenager, and Veronica was astonished that her mum had accepted this. She argued with her mum but was told, "How can I preach to them when I'm an addict myself and I did drugs at their age. I don't like it, but if I'm too strict they will only do it behind my back out in the streets, where they could get nicked. At least here, they are not out getting into all sorts of trouble." Veronica understood where her mum was coming from but didn't agree.

When Phil and Paula were down at the boat and Veronica was left responsible for the home, the girls would continue their antics, having no respect for Veronica at all. Ella was even sneaking her boyfriend and his mates into the house during the night when Veronica was asleep. When Veronica caught her out, they ended up having a fight as Ella had been completely rude, swearing at Veronica in front of her mates. Veronica slapped Ella in the face and Ella ran out of the house threatening to not come back. Veronica felt trapped as her dad was unaware of the girls' behaviour; Paula kept it from him as she knew he would go ballistic and even hit them and was concerned that she would be blamed if all was revealed. This worried Veronica no end, but there was nothing she could do, her life at home was becoming increasingly uncomfortable.

One weekend when her mum and dad were away in Portsmouth, Veronica was home alone. A few punters called the landline to find out when Phil was due back as they were in need of some heroin. A couple of hours later, her dad called her from his mobile and explained that they were running late getting home. He told Veronica to get the heroin stashed in a boot in the cloakroom and the electronic scales in the kitchen, and weigh an eighth for one of their punters, George. He told her to use a piece of cardboard from a cigarette packet to carefully scoop the powder from the bag and put it on the scales. Veronica told her dad that she didn't want to do it and pleaded with him not to ask her. She felt bad saying no to him, as she always wanted to help her parents out, but this was a step too far. How could he ask this of her she thought, but his response was nasty. He told her to shut up and that as long as she was living under his roof then she must do what he told her. He asked her if she thought her £40 per week keep was sufficient for all of the food and water and heating she consumed living at home. He told her that it wasn't and if she didn't like the rules, then she should hurry up and fuck off.

Veronica couldn't believe it, she was dumbfounded, she felt used and abused. She was his daughter, she had been dutiful all her life, how could he treat her like this?

Against her will, Veronica did as she was told, but as she weighed the powdered drug, her hands shook uncontrollably with fear. She was frightened of spilling it everywhere and in the end she did, it was all over her jeans and the floor. Veronica cried to herself as she tried to clear up the mess she had made.

From this day on, Veronica questioned her parents love. Did they really love me? She asked herself over and over. How could they if they are prepared to put me at risk?

If the police had burst into the house at that moment, Veronica would have been caught in the act of supplying class A drugs and she would have gone down for it. How could her parents really love her, knowing how much she hated the drugs, and then making her deal for them?

From this moment on there was no doubt in her mind that she needed to get away.

A little later when George came round to buy drugs again, Veronica led him into the dining room and made him a cup of tea whilst he waited for Paula to come downstairs and serve him. He asked Veronica why she was still hanging around living at home. She told him that she just wanted her mum and dad to give up the drugs, and that she believed everything they had promised her about getting enough money to sail around the world, so they could start a new life.

George told Veronica that she should stop wasting her own life waiting around for something that may never happen. This shocked her because she had become quite depressed and unhappy with her life around her parents, but didn't know anything else. Her dad would always tell her how hard the real world was out there and how she wouldn't earn enough money to live, let alone pay rent. Veronica confided in George that she didn't feel confident enough to move out, as she didn't think she could cope. George told Veronica that she was more than capable, as he had watched her looking after her parents and sisters all those years.

Veronica told George that she loved them dearly and it broke her heart that they hadn't stopped the drugs and the dealing. She told him that was all she ever wanted, and now she realised that it wasn't going to happen.

"They will never stop for no one; if they can't do it for themselves then they certainly won't stop for you." George said.

Veronica told him that she was ready to leave home, but she was scared. She told him that she was scared of living alone in a bedsit with barely any money left after her bills were paid, but at the same time she was tired of living at home. She told George that she was thinking of travelling first, before getting tied down by the bills. She told him she didn't feel confident at venturing out on her own, as her dad had made her feel inadequate.

"Don't be silly, a clever girl like you could do anything you put your mind to; and you are young. Don't waste your life mopping up after them; life is passing you by." George replied.

Veronica couldn't believe it; she had never had such a deep conversation with George on any subject, let alone something so close to her heart. If anyone knew about the reality of drugs and being an addict, he did, being one himself. George was very sick and struggled to breathe when he spoke. The doctors had told him to quit smoking but of course he hadn't, and now he had an oxygen bottle with him when he came around to score. His life was all but over and he knew it, "What are you waiting for girl? Get out there and do it, it's your life and you are letting it pass you by, hanging around for them."

CHAPTER 34

Theresa

Paula's long-time friend and punter Theresa, was planning to return to Mexico.

Theresa knew and understood that Veronica was ready to go out into the world and find her own way and thought backpacking was a good idea for Veronica's confidence.

She offered Veronica the opportunity to join her on her trip to Mexico City. Veronica had other friends who had been travelling all over Central and Southern America and had come back with some amazing pictures and stories. She quite liked the idea of visiting the Mayan ruins and spending time on the Caribbean Coast in the Yucatan.

Theresa encouraged Veronica and educated her on how to travel successfully on her own. The thought of travelling alone in a foreign country petrified her, but Theresa helped Veronica get equipped with a lonely planet guide and travel essentials. Veronica had a vision once again!

She told herself, if I can travel alone through Mexico and come back in one piece, then I can do anything!

When she discussed her plans with her dad, he wasn't happy. He told her, "I will give you a week and you will be wanting to come back home. How are you gonna cope with facing the reality of the third world people that are poor and living on the streets? You won't last five minutes."

Veronica explained that she wanted to find herself, and that when she came home she would be ready to move out. Her dad thought the whole idea was stupid.

He said angrily, "What do you think you are gonna find when you get there? You take the same shit with you. Find yourself? If you don't know who you are by now you never will," he scoffed. Veronica was emotional;

she went up to her room and cried. She told herself that she was going to prove him wrong, and most importantly, prove herself.

The next day she arranged to meet Theresa, and they went to purchase their tickets. Veronica's was an open return for up to one year. Theresa told her that if she stayed in well-known hostels then her money would go quite far. Veronica wished she had a boyfriend that she could travel with, but unfortunately all the guys Veronica had been in relationships with up to this point in time, were wasters. Veronica bought a large rucksack and began to pack. She had two weeks until her flight and so made preparations to tie up her loose ends. Her dad told her, "If you think we are gonna hang around waiting for you to come back, you're mistaken. Make sure your belongings are packed up ready to go, because by the time you come back we will be leaving for our circumnavigation." Veronica felt sad, as she realised that although she wanted this change, things were definitely never going to be the same again.

Paula understood that Veronica was desperate to get away from her dad. She had confided in her mum before, that her feelings towards her dad had changed; she thought he was a bully. Ever since his last affair with Orla, another punter and friend of Paula, Veronica had seen through her dad. He didn't respect her mum, he didn't respect his kids, and he didn't even respect himself. Veronica loved him but didn't like him; and although she had been proud of his achievements when sailing Nova home, he was still the same old bully and womaniser underneath.

Now that Veronica felt ready, the conversation with George came back to her. When he'd said that it's your life and you are letting it pass you by, hanging around for them, those words were the catalyst for a whole new Veronica. George had clarified everything for her and she now had no doubt at all, Mexico couldn't come quickly enough.

CHAPTER 35

Leaving for Mexico, August 1998

Veronica had been busy preparing for the trip of her life; and as the day of her departure drew nearer, she became increasingly nervous. She kept asking herself, "What if this is a big mistake, what if my dad is right and I hate it out there?" She was worried that she would have wasted all her hard-earned money on a whim. Veronica was good at doubting herself, this is what she did best, but something else was emerging inside her; a brave and confident side to her character that was slowly but surely showing itself. She knew she couldn't continue living the way she had for the rest of her life, as her parents' decisions and life style had a massive impact on her emotional bearings. She had become stuck and felt like she was in a rut. Even if Mexico turned out to be the worst experience ever, at least it would be different; at least she would be miles away from her parents and their drugs. She would be free to breathe, and experience a part of the world for herself without the responsibilities that dragged her down at home.

Suddenly Veronica felt determined, and a sense of optimism pushed the negative thoughts away.

She arranged a farewell get together with her best friends Niki and Jenni. The girls came round to Veronica's the night before her departure, to wish her well and say their goodbyes. To Veronica it felt like a final goodbye, like she was never going to see her friends again.

Veronica's eyes filled with tears, she loved her friends Niki and Jenni. She had grown up with the girls and gone through so much of her adolescence with them, they knew Veronica inside out.

They had witnessed the tears time and time again, when Veronica despaired of her parents' drug abuse. There were times when Veronica would have lost the plot, if it hadn't been for her loyal friends Jenni and

Niki. They always managed to distract her from her worrying; and get her out of the house to play in the park, cycling and playing games.

As teenagers their attention turned to boys, fashion and music. The girls would hang out together listening to their favourite music, sharing their 'Just Seventeen' magazines, trying out the new rage hairstyles with one another; and talking about the boys they fancied.

The young women reminisced the night away 'til Veronica said goodbye and went to bed. Life would have changed by the time she came home and this was it now, time to move on.

Her rucksack was huge; Veronica wondered how the hell she was going to get around Mexico with it on her back. She packed it and unpacked it, took things out and put things back. "Have I got too much," she wondered to herself, but then she was going to Mexico City first with Theresa, so she could leave stuff there if needed.

The following day, Veronica was up early. She had her breakfast and a quick bath, then packed her last bits and pieces, making sure she had her lonely planet guide at the ready, along with her passport, pesos and camera.

Paula was up too, as she was driving Veronica to Theresa's house to leave for Heathrow airport.

Veronica was very excited, but also sad to be leaving her mum and sisters. Veronica idolised Paula, more than Paula knew. Veronica wished she could whisk her away and take her with her, but she knew it could never happen. Paula had Ella and Paulette to look out for and most of all Phil. He demanded more attention from Paula than all three girls put together, he couldn't function without Paula. She had to get him up every day and make sure he had his breakfast ready in bed, his clothes clean and ironed ready to put on, his bath run ready to get in; and so on.

Phil would not get up without his Weetabix and coffee in bed, followed by a smoke.

Phil didn't like Paula to be too far away from his beck and call. If Paula ran the girls to school in the car, Phil would remain in bed until she returned to make his breakfast, unless Veronica was there to sort him out. Paula couldn't do anything without him; and although she encouraged this by happily adhering to his wishes, sometimes it was stifling for her. When the family went to Kefalonia in May 1997 Phil spent most of his days in bed sleeping. Veronica would take the girls out to get breakfast at a local taverna and then return to the apartment to see if her dad was awake.

More often than not, he would still be in bed, either asleep or listening to music and smoking. Veronica would get the girls to grab their towels and head out down the road to the beach, where they would spend hours sunbathing and swimming before Phil and Paula joined them. Paula had to be by Phil's side.

A few times towards the end of the holiday she went with her daughters to get breakfast, and Veronica insisted that her mum join her and the girls at the beach. Paula did a couple of times and really enjoyed the sunshine, but Phil wasn't happy waking up to find no one at his side. Paula had accepted Phil and his lazy habits; and she joined him too, often spending all hours of the night smoking heroin in bed, watching TV. It was quite normal for Phil to be awake past 6am.

As the years rolled by, Paula wasn't comfortable with this lifestyle anymore, she wanted to get clean and live a normal healthy existence. She confided this to Veronica, but Phil would never change his habits and Paula grew weaker as time went by, she just succumbed to her lot and accepted it. Veronica felt sad for all these reasons, but she had to find her own path.

Veronica kissed her sisters and dad goodbye, then Paula and Veronica drove off in the direction of Theresa's. When they arrived, Lisa and Tara, Theresa's children, were frantically running around grabbing their last items of clothing and such like. Paula chatted with Theresa, asking questions about the trip, then five minutes later the taxi arrived and it was time to go.

Paula waited for Theresa, her girls and Veronica to load up the taxi with their luggage and then gave Veronica a huge hug and kiss. Paula had tears in her eyes and suddenly looked bewildered.

Veronica got in the taxi and waved down the road at her mum as they drove away. She burst into tears as she realised her mum was crying, and Veronica knew at that point the impact her leaving would have on her mum.

CHAPTER 36

Mexico City

After arriving at Heathrow airport with Theresa and the girls, Veronica began to feel nervous.

"What if I hate Mexico?" She thought, "What if I can't handle it out there?"

Then they were called to check in their bags, "This is it now," Veronica thought. "There is no turning back!" Within an hour, they were through customs and waiting in the departure lounge. Veronica could see their waiting British Airways Jumbo Jet through the window, she was mesmerised by its size. As they were called to board, she excitedly rummaged through her hand bag to grasp her camera. When they got outside, Veronica asked Theresa to take a picture of her standing beside the plane. At that moment she felt filled with pride, she had been through a lot of soul searching to reach this point; and now her moment had finally arrived.

They boarded the plane, stowed their hand luggage and got seated.

The flight seemed never ending to Veronica, she had never been on a long-haul flight before and was eager to get there. She had mixed feelings of excitement and apprehension, yet the journey dragged and dragged on, 'til eventually after nearly twelve hours, the plane started its descent for landing.

Veronica looked out of the window scanning the land below. The city was vast and looked like it was in the shape of a bowl. There was thick smog all around, and it was very cloudy and dusty looking. Lots of the buildings looked like they had fallen into disrepair with pieces missing, but they were painted in many bright colours. Some looked in such bad shape that she thought they needed pulling down or boarding up, but people lived in them, they were their homes.

As the plane came to a halt, the people on board collected their hand luggage and queued to get off the plane. Veronica felt anxious, she was going to be staying with Theresa in the suburbs of Mexico City, at the home of her boyfriend's brother, she didn't know what to expect.

Theresa had told her that Alejandro was a well-known respected builder in Mexico City and he had worked hard to build his own house on a plot he had bought. Although they had come from poor backgrounds, Alejandro and his wife had worked hard to get out of the rut and make a better life for their daughter who was 8 years old.

Theresa and Veronica waited to collect their bags and then went to the arrivals area, where Theresa's boyfriend, the father of Lisa and Tara, was waiting with his brother Alejandro to greet them. They were typical dark-skinned and black haired Mexicans, who Veronica thought had an Aztec look about them. She was mesmerised, it felt like an immediate culture shock, she was a light-skinned, light haired girl surrounded by Mexicans. She felt like an outsider and this made her feel quite uneasy.

Veronica waited until Theresa had kissed Julio and the family, to be introduced.

They all hugged Veronica very warmly and spoke very fast in Latin Spanish. Veronica didn't have a clue what the family were saying and needed Theresa to interpret everything.

Veronica decided right then that she would need to learn as much of the language as possible to survive her time in Mexico. This was going to be a huge challenge for her, but then her whole life had been full of challenges, so this was nothing new.

CHAPTER 37

Staying at Alejandro's

Having been introduced to the family, Veronica was then ushered out of the airport into a car park, where Alejandro's truck was parked. The men loaded the bags into the back of the truck and Theresa, Veronica and the girls got in. As they drove off through the city streets Veronica was shocked by the poverty on nearly every street corner they passed. Children were begging for money, they looked miserable, dressed poorly and in need of a wash. The sight of poor children really disturbed Veronica, she felt so sorry for them. They drove past some busy markets selling everything from spices to clothes and watches, where Mexican men were haggling for the right price. Before long they were heading away from the city into the suburbs.

They came to a large house that was gated all around the front. Alejandro unlocked the gates and drove the truck around the back of the yard, where he parked. Veronica was tired and hungry and full of nerves. She hadn't really thought about how she would feel fitting in with strangers, or about the language barrier that would also make settling in difficult. Veronica felt like a spare part, but looked to Theresa for support.

Inside the house, Veronica was shown the room where she would sleep. It was a small room with a tiled floor and a single bed with blankets and a sheet. At that point Veronica felt quite home sick and missed her family. As she put her bags away, she wondered if her dad was right after all. Having seen the poverty-stricken children begging in the streets, she thought back to her dad's words: "I will give you a week and you will come running home, you will not cope out there and you will be disappointed."

Veronica went downstairs to the family lounge, and Theresa introduced Veronica to Alejandro's wife and daughter. They all became engrossed in discussion which Veronica could not understand, though she tried to read what was being said, by watching their body language and facial expressions intently. Theresa would interpret pieces of their conversation, but Veronica soon got lost and couldn't keep up.

Lisa was sitting in the corner of the room gazing at the floor and looking sad, Veronica put her arm around her and asked her if she was okay. Lisa wasn't happy at all to be in Mexico; and just wished she could go back home to the UK and her school, to be with her friends.

Veronica reassured Lisa that she would be fine, though it would take some time to get used to a new way of life, but Lisa was insistent that she would not get used to life in Mexico, that it wasn't the life for her.

Alejandro's wife had been busy cooking in the kitchen. She had made a chicken and cactus stew.

As the family sat down at the table in the dining room, Veronica looked at the bowl of stew and felt very disappointed. "This looks like washing up water," she thought, but had to make the effort to eat it and look like she was enjoying the meal. The chicken in the stew had bones and skin, all still attached. Theresa could see that Veronica was not entirely happy as she was struggling to pick the meat from the bones.

"Just eat what you can Veronica," Theresa told her.

"I'm just very tired," Veronica replied, hoping that was enough to get her away from the table and the awful stew she could not stomach. Lisa and Veronica both went upstairs to bed.

As Veronica lay in the dark room alone, she thought of her mum waving her off outside Theresa's house in London; and remembered the tears streaming down her face. Veronica cried until she fell asleep.

CHAPTER 38

Alejandro's House

The next day Veronica woke up aching and feeling hazy. The mattress she had slept on was quite thin, so she had not had the best night's sleep and was suffering from an aching back. As she sat up, she realised that she was thousands of miles away from her home and family; and felt a little upset, wondering if she really was up to the challenge of travelling through Mexico alone.

She got dressed and found the family bathroom to use the loo. When she finished, she wandered downstairs to find Theresa, who was going through her travelling bags to show Alejandro's wife some of the things she'd brought with her. There were pots and pans, stationery, towels and blankets. She had also brought Julio a keyboard as a present. The women were in deep conversation and Veronica could not make out the words in Spanish, as they spoke so fast.

Veronica felt bewildered and deflated. "I can't even communicate with people," she thought. "Maybe I should have gone to America or Australia; at least I wouldn't have had the language barrier."

Veronica sat down on the sofa next to Theresa. A few minutes later, Theresa asked Veronica if she'd slept okay, and enquired if she wanted some breakfast. Veronica was feeling a bit weak as she had barely eaten since leaving London. Alejandro's wife went into the kitchen and started cooking some eggs. Veronica could smell them and was pleased to be getting a normal meal for breakfast, or so she thought. Ten minutes later the table was set and Theresa asked Veronica to be seated. Alejandro's wife brought in a bowl of scrambled eggs, along with a round container filled with corn tortillas. But the eggs had a homemade salsa mixed in, with onions and chillies. Veronica felt disappointed, she'd hoped she was getting plain eggs, but tucked in anyway, as she was starving. The chillies burnt her mouth, but she still wolfed down a fair share of the meal as she was so ravenous. She got used to the taste of salsa and chillies in the end and quite enjoyed her breakfast. Theresa told Veronica that she was going to stay with Julio in the city for the night, and that they had some important things to discuss.

She told Veronica that she was leaving Lisa and Tina with Alejandro and his wife, and that she wanted Veronica to stay too. "It will be good for you to get to know the family, and with me gone, you will make more effort to communicate and learn a bit of Spanish," she reasoned.

Veronica felt quite uncomfortable with the idea of Theresa leaving, especially as they had only just arrived. She had come out to do her own thing and wanted to get to the heart of the city to get her bearings and make plans. She told Theresa that she would be happy to leave for the city with her, and asked if she could be dropped at a good hotel, from where she could make her own way. Theresa really wanted Veronica to look after the children though, as both Alejandro and his wife worked during the day. She told her that it was only for one day, so Veronica reluctantly agreed; and within a couple of hours Theresa and Julio were gone, Alejandro's wife went to work, and Veronica was left in the house alone with Lisa and Tara.

Veronica and Lisa decided to practice Veronica's very basic knowledge of Spanish and work on some more words. Lisa's cousin had a chalk board in the dining room, and Lisa began to write basic words in Spanish with their meanings in English. Lisa taught Veronica how to count, she already knew how to count to ten, but Lisa taught her the numbers twenty, thirty, forty, fifty etc. up to one hundred. This would help Veronica a great deal when shopping and buying tickets for her bus journeys through Mexico. Lisa taught Veronica how to ask the time; how to ask for the toilet; for somewhere to eat etc. Veronica practiced over and over until it bored Lisa to tears, but Veronica was now feeling pretty excited. Lisa got upset during the day and told Veronica that she didn't feel comfortable around her Mexican family either. She said she wished she could have stayed with her Aunty in England and continue with her schooling in the UK. Although Lisa was only twelve years old, she was quite mature in her outlook.

Like Veronica, she had grown up fast and had to be dependable for her mum. Theresa had struggled with heroin addiction for years, even before she had Lisa and Tara. She would score from Phil and Paula and supply a few of her acquaintances to help pay for her own supply, and give her some extra money. Life was hard being a single mum on benefits; and Theresa was determined to get her English and Spanish degrees under her belt, as she wanted to teach in Mexico City. Lisa had to help a lot around the house and look after her younger sister, as well as keeping up with her schoolwork. Theresa had put the girls in a Saturday school to learn Spanish from a young age, the downside for Lisa, like Veronica, was that she never had enough time just to be free and be a kid. Veronica took Lisa under her wing, she felt protective of her as she realised that she too was vulnerable. The girls spent the rest of the day playing outside in the back yard, while Veronica decided to get her head into her lonely planet guide. She read about the Mayans and the ancient Mayan calendar; she learned about their magnificent ruins dotted all over Mexico and Central America and about the Aztec peoples of Mexico. She read about the Spanish leader Cortez, who invaded Mexico in the 1500s. Veronica was captivated by this historical country and decided that she must visit as many of the sites of the ruins as possible. She would begin by visiting a few of the museums in the city; and Chapultepec Zoo, which was situated in Chapultepec Park, the largest city park in the world.

For the first time since landing in Mexico, Veronica felt excited and positive about finding her feet. All she needed was to get to a reasonable hotel in the centre of the city, from where she could find her way. She had her planet guide and this would be her bible.

As day turned to evening, Alejandro and his wife returned home; dinner was cooked and Veronica sat down with the family to eat. After a meal of stuffed chillies, rice and chicken, the girls retired to bed for an early night, still quite jet lagged from the day before.

CHAPTER 39

Waiting for Theresa's Return

When she woke up the next morning, Veronica was feeling a bit more confident about her visit to Mexico. She had learned a bit of the lingo, thanks to Lisa, which had made a huge difference to Veronica's mood. She was feeling full of energy, bright-eyed and bushy-tailed, as she had a shower and got dressed. She went downstairs for breakfast and said good morning to the family in Spanish, "Buenos Dias Lisa y Tina," to which Lisa responded, "Buenos Dias Veronica."

There was no sign of Alejandro or his wife as they were at work.

Veronica got her lonely planet guide and went outside in the back yard to read it in the fresh air and sunshine. It was winter time in Mexico, which was a disappointment to Veronica, as it was pretty cool in the city and surrounding areas; she'd thought it would be hot like in Cancun.

As she sat on a plastic chair in the yard and began to read her guide, Lisa and Tina screamed, "Look at that scorpion on the floor by your feet Veronica." Veronica jumped to her feet, feeling scared as she scanned the floor beneath her chair. There it was, walking sideways across the ground with its tail in the air.

"Wow," Veronica exclaimed, "I've never seen a wild scorpion in my life!" Amazed by it, the girls gathered around watching it move.

"I wonder if its sting is poisonous," Lisa asked.

"I'm not sure," Veronica replied, "but I know if it stings, it is supposed to be really painful." The girls held the planet guide and carefully guided the scorpion onto the book and put it outside of the yard. Then they played every game they could think of, until they became bored.

"What time is Mum coming back?" Lisa asked Veronica.

"I have no idea Lisa, your mum didn't say, she just said they were going for the night and would be back today."

The day wore on and Alejandro's wife returned with some shopping. A little later Alejandro returned from work and the girls all asked when Theresa would be back.

As evening was fast approaching, Veronica was feeling increasingly agitated and fed up with being stuck within the four walls of Alejandro's home. She didn't feel safe walking around outside, as the area was like a huge waste land with houses plotted here and there, and children and stray dogs roaming the streets.

Alejandro had come down from having a shower and getting changed, he spoke to Lisa in Spanish, which Lisa interpreted to Veronica. "He says my mum is staying another night with my dad, she is sorry but had to sort some things out today and won't be back 'til tomorrow now."

Veronica felt angry and used. "I think your mum is out of order Lisa, she has dumped us here and gone off gallivanting with your dad. They should have taken you kids with them. I didn't come out here to play babysitter, I came to go travelling and I feel like I'm imprisoned here, it's boring and frustrating and as she said it was only one night, I accepted, but she is abusing the situation." Lisa cried, "I didn't even want to come here to live, I want to go home. I don't even know my dad, he is just a stranger."

"I know honey, but you will get to know him and things will get better, it takes time that's all," Veronica replied.

"How can I get to know him when they just dumped us here and disappeared?"

"I know, I'm upset with them too," said Veronica, "don't worry, once they get back things will fall into place."

The next morning was the same. The girls were alone again and had to amuse themselves. It wasn't like there was any English television to watch to help pass the time, but the girls improvised and played games like I-Spy. Lisa taught Veronica some more Spanish and they practised together. The day passed again and Veronica was feeling quite frustrated with Theresa; she thought to herself, "I'm going to blow when she gets back, she is taking the piss out of me.'"

Eventually around 8pm Theresa and Julio came through the door like everything was hunky dory. Veronica snapped, "Where the hell have you been Theresa?" Theresa explained that she and Julio needed some quality time to catch up after being apart for over ten years, to get their bearings and to sort some things out. "So you've been shagging each other's brains out for two days while we've been stuck here feeling like aliens in a house that's not ours, and with people I've never met in my life and that your daughters do not know either. It's your duty to ease them in and make them feel secure Theresa, not just piss off and think of yourself. I didn't come out to be plonked here and be your babysitter; you know I've done that my whole life with my own sisters. I am not staying here another moment. Get me a taxi please, I have found a hotel in my guide that will put me in an ideal spot to do what I came here for. I want to go to the Monte Carlo Hotel in Mexico City please. I can't believe you just dumped us like that, your poor daughters don't know what to think. Lisa doesn't even want to be here and after going off like you did, I don't blame her, what a joke."

Tina was okay as she was playing with her Mexican cousin who had been back sometime from school. They communicated pretty well and seemed to hit it off, but Lisa was on another wavelength. She became upset, Lisa wasn't into playing with dollies, she was more like a little teenager, and she clung to Veronica. "I don't want you to go Veronica, please don't leave me here," she begged.

CHAPTER 40

At Julio's Sister's Place

Theresa apologised, but Veronica was still emotional, she also felt Lisa's pain and started to cry.

"This is a bit of a culture shock for me Theresa, we barely landed and you disappeared on us. Lisa is at a very difficult age as she is going through puberty as well, she needs your support. I need to get my independence, and as long as I'm stuck here, it's not going to happen. Please send for a taxi."

"Please Veronica don't be so hasty, I'm sorry for upsetting you and I didn't realise, but I wanted you to get to know the family out here, to ease you in and to show you around also."

"That's fine Theresa," Veronica said, more calmly, "But I need my own space, so I would appreciate it if you could arrange for me to be dropped at the hotel."

Theresa agreed, but asked Veronica to spend one more day with the family and stay at Julio's sister's place in Mexico City. "Lisa can go with you so at least you will have each other for company and communication. It would be lovely for us all to have dinner with them, and you can go on the underground and visit the Basilica de Nuestra Señora de Guadalupe." (Our Lady of Guadalupe, a monastery at a sacred site in Mexico City.)

Veronica replied that she also wanted to visit a few museums in the city, before heading off to some of the sites around Mexico where the ancient Mayan ruins stood, such as Chichen Itza and Tulum, which were situated in the Yucatan. Veronica had come to Mexico with a thirty-day tourist visa, so she needed Theresa to assist her in getting an extension. Theresa agreed to take her to the immigration office the following day, if Veronica stayed on a little longer to get her bearings. Veronica agreed, after all, she had a one year open ticket so her priority was to sort out extending her visa.

Theresa kept her word, and the family soon set off for the city. Veronica shook hands with Alejandro and thanked him for his and his wife's hospitality. When they arrived at Julio's sister's house in the city, Veronica was stunned by how small it was. She was expecting a house, but it was more like a room, if you could even call it a room. From the outside there was a window and a small door. The window was covered with a wrought iron grate, and when they went inside, Veronica was taken aback at how tiny the place was. The room was a compact lounge diner with a kitchenette on the side, at the end of which there was a door frame with a curtain; and beyond that was a toilet with a shower head in the corner.

Back inside the lounge diner, there was a three seater settee and a small table with four chairs. Above the table was a mezzanine type floor with a ladder to the side. The mezzanine floor was where the family slept. Once up there, you had to crawl to the sleeping area as there wasn't enough height to walk. Mum, Dad and their kids all slept up on this floor. There were thin mattresses with blankets for beds, and a thin partition wall to separate the parents' and children's sleeping areas. Veronica could not believe how a whole family could live so happily and comfortably in such a small confined area. Like Alejandro, the family were very welcoming, and Veronica realised that she had no choice but to try and fit in. She knew she would soon have her independence and so made the most of the time she had left with Lisa, to whom she had now become quite attached.

The next morning Veronica woke up, and for a second or so, thought she was back home in her bed in England. It took a few moments for her to get her bearings and realise that once again, she was in a strange place with people she didn't know.

Veronica was feeling quite homesick; she particularly missed her mum and sisters.

She rubbed her eyes and looked out of the window. Beyond the net curtains Veronica could see the sun beaming along the narrow street and could hear some women outside who were having a conversation in Latin Spanish. They were quite loud and spoke very fast; and though she tried to tune in, Veronica couldn't make out a single word.

Lisa was still sleeping beside her, but soon turned over and opened her eyes. Veronica wished Lisa a good morning as she sat up rubbing her eyes and yawning. Lisa looked disappointed when she realised where she was. "I dreamt I was back in England," Lisa said.

"I thought I was back home too for a moment as I woke up," Veronica replied.

"It's so strange being here with people we don't know, isn't it?" Lisa said.

"Yes," Veronica agreed, "I guess it's the same for you Lisa, even though these people are your relatives."

"I don't know them, they are different to me, it's nothing like life in London is it? They are very behind out here, look how they live. I know Mum doesn't have much back home, but we have a house way bigger than this and I miss all my friends and school, I just don't want to be here Veronica. Why did Mum bring us here after all these years? I'm a stranger to this part of my family," Lisa said.

"I know it must be very difficult for you Lisa," Veronica answered, "you will adjust in time and get to know all of your family. They seem very sweet, I'm sure you will grow close to your cousins and you will make new friends once you start school."

"Their life is so different out here though, my dad is lazy; he sits about waiting for the women to attend to everything. My mum is constantly licking his backside, what's happened to her? She isn't like that back home. She is normally independent, but here it's like she is acting all needy around my dad like she wants to please him."

"She must love him Lisa," Veronica replied. "But she hasn't seen him for over ten years; and she has had sex with other men since she saw my dad all them years ago, so how can she still be in love with him?" Lisa asked.

Veronica didn't have an answer, she told Lisa that she would have to make an effort to get to know her dad and his family, as she was about to make a new life here whether she liked it or not; and she would only make life harder for herself if she didn't try to adapt.

Lisa wasn't convinced. "I don't like my dad, he expects the women to do everything; and my mum has changed since we arrived. She doesn't even care about us because she just ran off with my dad and left us alone. If he wanted us, he would have taken us with them. If he wanted to know me, he would try to get to know me; but he thinks I'm just a stroppy selfish kid because I heard him say that to Mum."

"Oh I didn't know that," Veronica replied. "I'm going to tell my mum to send me back to England. I would rather live with my Aunty in London than stay here with Mum. It's not what I want, I know I'm just a kid but I've lived my life in London and now I'm expected to live like a Mexican out here. I'm not, and I never will be, whether mum likes it or not."

Veronica felt bad for Lisa. Theresa had not really made a good start by dumping the girls at Alejandro's but what could she do? Tina on the other hand, accepted the situation quite well and adjusted more easily than Lisa. Tina blended in naturally and played with the younger children. She was happy to speak fluent Spanish, whereas Lisa could, but didn't want to.

Theresa left the girls with Julio's sister and family for the night while she returned to Julio's. A lot of work was needed on his property as there was only one room for sleeping, loose floorboards all over the place, and no running water in the toilet or kitchen. Theresa had agreed to return in the morning and take the girls on the metro to the heart of the city, to the immigration office, to help Veronica get a six-month visa. The girls got up, got dressed, used the toilet and brushed their teeth. Julio's sister made them breakfast, and to their delight, there was a choice of cereal; Veronica was pleased to have some cornflakes. After breakfast Theresa returned and took the girls to the metro station. It was just like the London Underground, but the streets of Mexico City were like something out of the past. Many streets were falling apart with houses boarded up and the roads full of gaping holes. It was dangerous but this was how they lived. They got to the station and waited at the platform. The train came and the girls got on, Veronica was impressed with how smart the trains were. They were actually faster and smarter looking than the tube trains in London, the technology seemed to be more up to date. Theresa told Veronica that they had one of the best metro services in the world. Veronica was surprised, because the people lived in shoe boxes yet they had all this technology, it seemed so contradictory, but Veronica just sat back and took it all in.

When they arrived at their destination, they had to walk for about ten minutes to reach the immigration offices. As they walked from one block to another, Veronica realised that this part of the city was much smarter; and even resembled parts of Central London with grand hotels and buildings. There were cafés which had internet access, and mobile phone shops that sold everything you would need for a phone. There were pharmacies that put ours back home to shame, and banks on every street corner. The banks all had armed guards outside. The cash points were inside and there would be an armed guard to see you in, one by one; and to stand watch. Again this was a shock to Veronica who had never seen anything like this. "If only they had this back in London," she said to Theresa.

"There wouldn't be so much robbery would there?" Theresa agreed.

"There is just as much crime, if not more out here though; people are poorer and more desperate than back home." Just then, they walked past a beggar, he was a young boy who had lost his legs. He was lying chest down, strapped to a wooden skate board, and used his arms to manoeuvre himself. He looked very young, younger than Lisa and Tina, his face was dirty and his hair a mess. He was holding a plastic cup with coins inside and had a piece of cardboard with a message strapped to his back. He was chanting, "Peso por favor."

Veronica was devastated at the sight of this young boy. "Theresa that's awful," she said.

"I know, but they don't have any choice, that's how it is out here. There is no social security or NHS like we have in the UK. Poor people just don't get anything, so if they are disabled they can't get work and are forced to beg."

Veronica couldn't take it in. The sight of this boy would become a lasting picture in her mind of the harsh reality of life in Mexico City for many people. She burst into tears, "I want to go home Theresa," she cried. "I don't think I can handle this." The culture shock hit her right there and then; and if she could have clicked her fingers like Dorothy, she would have been back home with her family. This made Veronica realise just how lucky she was, at home she had her creature comforts, television, good quality food when she wanted it; and opportunities to strive for a good life. Here in Mexico it was quite different. If you were poor, you had nothing at all and no support services to turn to either. It was really a third world existence, and Veronica was thrown right into the middle of it.

They soon arrived at the immigration offices, which reminded Veronica of the benefits office back home that she had sat queuing in for hours. It had a similar feel; there were Mexican families all around the building sitting on stools, or on the floor when there were no seats available. Theresa went to a window where a woman wearing an immigration badge was waiting to see Veronica's papers. She asked

Theresa a million and one questions, and Veronica had to prove that she had over £1000 to keep her in Mexico for the time required.

Once the visa was approved, Veronica felt relieved. Theresa told the girls that they would meet Julio for lunch in a Cantina a few blocks from where they were.

Veronica still felt shell shocked after seeing the young disabled boy begging. "Can I buy a phone card to call home Theresa?" Veronica asked. "I would like to let my mum and dad know we are okay, I haven't spoken to them since leaving the UK."

"Yes," Theresa replied, and they went to a news agent to buy a £10 phone card.

Feeling eager, Veronica scanned the streets looking for a pay phone. Eventually they found one and Theresa told Veronica to dial the country code before the area code.

The dialling tone was strange compared to a phone line in the UK. Veronica waited impatiently for the phone to answer, then just as she was about to hang up, she heard her mum's voice answer, "Hello." Adrenaline and excitement ran through Veronica's veins.

"Mum," she cried.

"Veronica is that you?" Paula answered. "Yes, Mum I love you; I miss you so much it hurts."

"Oh I've been worried about you Veronica, we didn't know whether you got there okay or not, why didn't you ring sooner?"

"I couldn't Mum," Veronica replied, "Theresa sent me to her bloke's brother's house outside Mexico City and me and the girls were left there for two days whilst Theresa went off with Julio."

Theresa was listening outside and didn't look too impressed with what Veronica was saying.

"That's out of order," Paula replied. "What she just dumped you off in a strange house and left you?"

"Yeah but I'm okay now, I'm in the city and I'm about to go to a hotel called Monte Carlo in the city centre. I'll be close to all amenities there and I will be able to get my bearings before I go off on my own."

"Please be careful Veronica, me and Dad are worried about you."

"I know, there is a lot of poverty out here Mum, I just saw a boy with no legs strapped face down to a skate board begging. It was horrible Mum. Right now, I just want to come home." Veronica burst into tears.

Paula told her to calm down. "You will be okay, just be street wise and be careful; if you really don't fit in once you've given it a chance, you've got an open ticket, so just book a flight and come home. But you've got to give it a chance. You worked hard for this and saved a lot of money."

"I know," Veronica replied. A Mexican woman's voice came over the phone counting down the last minute of the call. "Mum my credit is going; I love you all, tell Dad, Ella and Paulette I love them and miss them. Once I get going, I will call you and let you know where I am going etc. Love you so much."

"Love you honey," Paula replied. The line went dead, and Veronica was left standing in floods of tears.

Theresa put her arm around her and patted her on the shoulder. "Come on Vronx, you are stronger than this, you'll be fine."

"I know, it's just I'm so far away from all of my family, I've never been this far from my mum and sisters. The culture shock is a bit much to bear today, since seeing that poor boy. I've never seen anything like that, it's so upsetting Theresa."

"I know," she replied, "but you get used to it, you have to, you will see it more and more during your time here and you will harden to it."

"I don't want to harden to it Theresa, that would mean that I would stop caring," Veronica replied.

"No, you never stop caring Veronica, but you accept that there is little you can do. It's their existence. You can make a difference by giving a peso. At least you know they can eat then or get a drink. You can make a difference just by doing that, but you can't give to everyone so you have to harden to it."

Veronica understood the logic behind what Theresa was saying and wiped her tears.

"Come on," Theresa said, "let's go to the Cantina for some lunch; and then I will take all you girls to the Zoo, how about that?" Veronica cheered up immediately. Lisa and Tina were excited too and began to skip along the road. This was the first time Veronica had seen Lisa smile since they arrived.

After walking some blocks down, they came to a Cantina. Inside were lots of Mexican men seated at individual tables, stuffing their faces with paella, tortillas and soup. Theresa and the girls queued for a plate and then for the food. Veronica was disappointed at the choice available, but chose paella. They paid for their food and sat down where Julio was already waiting and eating. Veronica realised that she had shell fish in her paella, with their shells still attached. This was something she was not used to, so she picked out all of the shells and put them on the side of her plate. Julio asked her if she wanted them. Theresa translated and Veronica said no. Julio took the shell fish and picked them apart to eat them. Lisa looked on, disgusted at her dad.

After the meal, they said goodbye to Julio. Theresa made arrangements to meet him later, and the girls walked back to the metro station to get a train to the Zoo.

Chapultepec was a vast and beautiful area, Theresa explained that Mexico was the only country to have a Zoo where pandas had successfully mated and produced offspring. Veronica was impressed. The gardens were beautiful, full of exotic plants and flowers that she had never seen. The area of land the animals had to freely roam in was quite vast compared with the relatively small confined areas at London Zoo. In Veronica's mind, this was what you called a Zoo!

Veronica was very pleased to see the pandas, but unfortunately they had decided to fall asleep with their legs up against the viewing window and their bums pressed up against it.

Veronica and the girls laughed hysterically, it was like the pandas were saying, "You can have a look at our bums." After a long day, they all returned to Julio's sister's place. Theresa asked Veronica if she would stay one more night there. She told Veronica that she may as well save her money for her travels, but although Veronica could see the practical side of what Theresa was saying, her independence was just as important.

Veronica agreed to stay a couple of more nights however, and Theresa arranged for her 18 year old niece to take Veronica to the monastery the following day. Lisa wanted to stay with Veronica, but Tina wanted to be with her mum and dad. So Lisa stayed with Veronica, and at least the girls had each other for company.

CHAPTER 41

Staying with Julio's Sister

Veronica and Lisa visited the monastery the following day with Lisa's cousin.

On their way back they got caught in a severe thunder storm. Veronica and Lisa found it very amusing as they had never witnessed a tropical rainstorm like this before.

The gutters were not equipped for the heavy rain that fell and before long the streets were swimming with water and the girls were wading their way to get through them.

Veronica had a pair of sandals on, so her feet were soaked and so too were her cotton trousers.

By the time they made it back to Julio's sister's house, the girls were sopping wet.

They were sent to get changed into something dry and given a cloth dampened with tequila and patted across the forehead to prevent a cold. Veronica found this amusing as she had never heard of this remedy. They were given a hot dinner of meat, vegetables and tortillas, then Lisa and Veronica settled down for an early night.

The next day Veronica went with the family to Julio's mum's house. She lived just north of Polanco, in another part of the city, so the family had to take the metro to get there.

Julio's mum was in her seventies and had brought up many children and grandchildren. Her house was also very small but she did not have a mezzanine floor as a bedroom, she had an extra room, albeit tiny. There were two single beds in the room; whilst the sofa in the lounge, also pulled out into a bed. There was a tiny bathroom with fitted shower, but Julio's mum had a tiled wall and floor which made the bathroom like a wet room with a toilet.

Veronica started to feel more settled around the family. Everyone seemed to like her and asked many questions, which had to be interpreted by Theresa or Lisa.

Lisa and Tina wanted to play out as there was a park across the road. Veronica fancied some fresh air too and offered to take the girls with their Mexican cousin. On their way, they passed a huge Corona factory called the Cerveceria Modelo plant. The barley hops could be smelt all around the area. It was a very strong smell and the girls found it to be quite overbearing, to the point where they were feeling sick after a while. The smell was still very potent in the park, where the girls played for well over an hour on the swings and slides; with Veronica joining in to have a turn on the swings.

All the swinging and twirling on the roundabout whilst breathing in the fumes from the nearby factory, made them all feel quite queasy. The girls returned to Julio's mum's and had some lunch. Veronica was getting accustomed to eating chillies and found that she had built up an appetite for the local cuisine. Julio's mum made a tomato and vegetable soup with pasta and chilli. Veronica couldn't get enough of it and almost licked the bowl. When she asked for seconds, the family were impressed with her tolerance to chillies. Veronica felt very relaxed at this point; and even though the family didn't have a lot in the way of money and creature comforts, it was plain to see that they were very close and loving and knew how to enjoy life regardless of their daily struggles. The average wage for a Mexican was around £1.90 per day and so it was easy to see why they didn't have much, but they were very happy nonetheless. Veronica admired their upbeat personalities.

Mexicans enjoyed the simple things in life and they were very creative people. Many loved to paint and work as artisans, whilst others liked to play musical instruments, but everyone she had met so far had been very family orientated, who loved spending free time with one another. The Mexican people loved their food, which was at the centre of every gathering. Veronica appreciated this part of the Mexican lifestyle and thought about how much better off the people of the UK would be if they remembered the importance of these simple pleasures. Back home, it seemed people were motivated purely by money and greed. People had lost their true identity as they were more interested in what latest gadgets they acquired, such as computers and cars; or by what kind of property they would buy. Possessions as status symbols had been drummed into

144

society's consciousness by advertising and the media. The UK was becoming more like the US. In Mexico however, the simple things still counted the most; and family and friendships were more important.

Veronica felt that she was starting to understand more about herself and the longing she had inside to find her true self. It was like a feeling of belonging had been missing for her; whereas this was something that was quite tangible amongst the family that Veronica met in Mexico City.

CHAPTER 42

The Monte Carlo Hotel

Veronica spent one last night at Julio's sister's house, she was feeling more relaxed and confident about taking on Mexico City by herself. Lisa however was very attached to Veronica and didn't want her to leave. Lisa told Veronica that she wished she could stay with her in the hotel. Veronica quite liked the idea of having Lisa for company; and as she didn't yet have a school to go to, wondered if Theresa would be happy for Lisa to accompany her. So the girls asked Theresa, and she asked Julio. Lisa didn't think it had anything to do with Julio. "Why is she asking him?" Lisa exclaimed. "He is a stranger, he may be my biological father but he has never taken responsibility for me or Tina. Where was he all the years when Mum struggled alone in London? Here, carrying on like a bachelor. Now Mum thinks he has a right to tell me what I can or cannot do, it's ridiculous."

Veronica agreed and understood Lisa, but kept her opinion to herself. Veronica couldn't get involved as it was up to Theresa to deal with Lisa's situation and make the decisions for her. Theresa spoke with Julio and they both agreed to let Lisa stay at the hotel with Veronica.

Lisa was very excited and so too was Veronica. The next morning the family got up and had breakfast as usual, Veronica packed her things and Alejandro arrived with Julio in his truck to take the girls to the hotel. Veronica was nervous but really excited; Lisa couldn't wait to get away from her new found Mexican family. The whole experience was overbearing for her and she was looking forward to having some freedom with Veronica.

Veronica didn't mind taking Lisa all over the city sight-seeing; in fact Lisa had been helping Veronica learn a bit of the lingo which Veronica had already begun to use in communicating with the locals.

The girls were dropped at the hotel and Veronica was amazed at how big their room was. It was fit for a queen and at £4 per night, it was worth every penny. They were staying in the heart of the city, right near lots of amenities such as bars, cantinas, restaurants, clubs and a few patisseries; at least they wouldn't go hungry. Soon after being dropped at the hotel, Veronica decided to visit the National Museum of Anthropology. Her lonely planet guide had all of the city's road markings, and Veronica could easily find the museum as it was so many blocks away from the hotel, well within walking distance. Lisa was very excited and couldn't wait to go. Veronica told her, "This will be a great way to get to know your dad's homeland. You will learn lots about the history of its people by the time we've visited all these museums." Veronica laughed. Lisa agreed, maybe she would understand the culture of her new-found family better too. The girls stopped at a shop and bought some bottled water; and a sandwich from a nearby deli. They walked for miles through bustling busy streets. The taxis in Mexico City were all green and white Volkswagen beetle cars, which Veronica found hilarious, as they were so small. With Mexican families being so huge, Veronica thought they would have had mini bus taxis. The girls soon found the museum and gushed at all of the historical delights. Veronica was amazed to learn of the Mayan calendar and that its end date was 21st December 2012. Some believed that some catastrophic event would take place and the world would come to an end on this date.

It was truly inspiring to learn of these Mayan people that walked these parts of the world thousands of years ago, who had the skill to build such beautiful pyramids in magnificent cities. Some like Palenque had conduits built underground to supply the inhabitants with water: their plumbing was quite extraordinary. Lisa and Veronica had a memorable day together and snapped away happily taking photos of the displays and each other.

The walk back to the hotel seemed a lot longer than the journey to the museum, but the girls had been on their feet all day. When they reached their hotel, they collapsed into bed and fell asleep.

Veronica felt a new sense of independence; and her confidence was growing, slowly but surely.

CHAPTER 43

Mexico City

Veronica and Lisa spent a few days touring all of the city's museums. Veronica had taken so many photos that she wondered how many more films she would need to get, as she travelled around Mexico. Lisa had enjoyed the luxury of the hotel room and the freedom she had with Veronica. She really wanted to go travelling as well. "I want to visit some of those sights with you Veronica," said Lisa. "It would be lovely if you could come along; we make a good pair Lisa."

"I've enjoyed your company, you are quite mature for a twelve year old and you've taught me loads of Spanish which has really helped me to get around. I don't know what I would do without that. It costs money to travel around Mexico though and I don't think your mum would be able to afford it. You also need to adjust to life here with the family," Veronica replied.

"I don't want to Veronica, I want to go back to London and be with my friends," Lisa replied. "Tina is younger than me and has cousins her age; she is enjoying it here but not me. I don't like my dad; he wasn't even interested in me."

"Well I can only ask your mum Lisa, but don't get your hopes up; they will be looking to get you into school."

The girls were meeting Theresa for lunch later, so they made the most of the morning by looking around the local shops. The patisserie over the road had lots of wonderful cakes; it was so cheap compared with prices back home that the girls bought more than they could eat, as the choice was almost too much. Lisa had complained of tummy pains for a couple of days, Veronica put it down to change in diet but when they got back to the hotel room and Lisa went for a pee, she discovered blood in her knickers and came out in a panic showing Veronica.

Veronica realised it was her first period which explained a lot of her moodiness and stroppy behaviour towards her mum and Julio. Veronica had some sanitary towels and gave one to Lisa.

She also had some paracetamol and gave Lisa a tablet as she was old enough to take one.

"Welcome to womanhood little lady!" Veronica said. Lisa wasn't impressed, but Veronica told her she would need to keep really clean whilst on her period; and to change her towels regularly as it could be unhygienic if she didn't. Veronica gave Lisa a hug as she became a little tearful. Veronica remembered twelve years earlier when she began her period and the shock she felt, so she understood Lisa's feelings and felt sorry for her having to deal with all those horrid changes to her body and mind as well as having to adjust to a new life with a new culture.

Theresa turned up later than expected. As they left for lunch in a nearby cantina, Lisa told her mum that she had started her period. "Right well I better get you some pads then, you'll be okay." Lisa looked at her mum astonished that that was all she had to say. Veronica wasn't impressed either, she expected Theresa to give her daughter a great big hug and reassure her, but it wasn't forthcoming. Veronica realised that Theresa was quite a hardy kind of woman, a 'no nonsense, no fuss' kind of girl! But this was her daughter, her firstborn; and she was having her first ever period at the mere age of twelve. Veronica felt sorry for Lisa but realised that her being there for Lisa was also a Godsend. Veronica asked Theresa if Lisa could go travelling around the Yucatan with her for a couple of weeks.

"I don't mind taking her off your hands, it would give Lisa an insight into her other family's past; and seeing the wonders of this country may inspire her to adjust here. It gives you and Julio time to adjust to each other as well, as Tina has just automatically fitted in which is really nice."

"I have some money I can give her, probably enough to get her around the Yucatan with you anyway. I will run it by Julio and see what he says and let you know," Theresa promised.

"Great," said Veronica, "I'm thinking about going in the next couple of days Theresa, we've done all there is to do here in the city. I really want to start with Merida, as that's the place to buy handmade hammocks. I need to get a couple and then I can easily make my way to Chichen Itza and Tulum from there."

The girls went to their local cantina for lunch as planned and then returned to the hotel.

Theresa went back home to Julio and arranged to meet the girls later. When she returned, she had spoken to Julio about Lisa travelling with Veronica and he had agreed to let her go. Theresa had reassured him that Veronica was a very sensible young woman, who was very streetwise.

Veronica and Lisa were jumping for joy at the news. Veronica felt even more excited about going off travelling, as Lisa spoke very fluent Spanish. Theresa arranged to pack Lisa's things and bring them round the following day. She told them that the buses ran regularly to Merida; and she would take the girls to the bus station the following evening, as it was a twenty two hour journey through Mexico, so would be better to travel overnight. The girls jumped for joy when Theresa left. Veronica was happy to have company with her on her first mission through Mexico.

The next evening Theresa and Julio met the girls, Veronica settled her hotel bill and they set off on the metro to the bus station. Once there, Veronica was amazed by how big it was. There were hundreds of buses and dozens of routes out of the city. Their bus was due to leave, so the girls said their goodbyes to Theresa and Julio. Theresa gave Veronica a phone card and asked her to call Alejandro's number the following day once they had arrived at their hotel, to let them know they had got there safely.

The group all hugged and kissed each other, and Veronica and Lisa boarded their bus.

For Veronica it was a massive step. They were travelling a huge distance over Mexico through the night; and then once they arrived at their destination, it was down to the girls to look after themselves and each other. "This is going to be a marvellous experience," Veronica told Lisa. "We are going to the Caribbean side of the country where the weather is hot and humid, so we can soak up the sun and have fun, just like on a holiday."

CHAPTER 44

The Road to Merida

After a few hours on the bus, the girls' excitement turned to boredom. The seats were not the most comfortable either, especially for such a long journey. They tried lying across two seats to get comfy and tried to get a nap, but the driver drove the bus erratically, throwing his passengers all over the place, which made it difficult for them to relax. Eventually they fell asleep for a couple of hours, then woke up as the driver was shouting for people to get off at the stop.

The coach had pulled in for a pit stop to refuel and for passengers to buy snacks and use the toilets in a nearby cantina. They were in the middle of nowhere in pitch black darkness.

The girls had been aboard the bus over five hours and were hungry and tired. The cantina was in a roadside hut, it was a family run business where they sold Mexican wraps and cold drinks, such as Coke and Fanta. The girls were relieved to be eating and grabbed some crisps and bottled water as well for the continuing journey.

They were on a country road and the sound of bugs could be heard all around. After a thirty minute break everyone was ushered back to board the bus for departure. The girls soon got comfortable enough to fall asleep. Sometime later, Veronica woke up to the bus driver throwing the bus around a sharp bend. Her rucksack which was on the floor in front of her, had been thrown to the other end of the bus and back again. Veronica leapt out of her seat to retrieve the bag, but as she picked it up and sat back down with it, she realised her rucksack was soaked at the bottom. The strong smell of urine suddenly hit her senses and Veronica threw her bag down in disgust. There was a drunken Mexican man a few rows up, in front of the girls. Veronica looked down and could see that the urine was trailing from his seat to hers, along the floor of the bus. She became extremely angry and felt so hot tempered that she 'blew.' She stood up and began shouting at the drunken man, calling him a disgusting pig. She flew into a rage as her trousers were also covered in his urine. The man had fallen asleep drunk and wet himself. Veronica could not believe her luck. Of all things to happen, she ended up with a tramp's urine all over her and her bag of clothes. Veronica had got a couple of carrier bags with the crisps and drinks she had bought; and had one in her rucksack with photographic film in. She emptied her bag and transferred her clothes quickly to the carrier bags before the urine soaked through, and cleaned her hands with an antiseptic hand wash that she had. Once she had moved her clothes, she removed her cotton trousers. Luckily Veronica had a pair of leggings on underneath. She folded up the urine sodden trousers and put them into the urine covered rucksack. Lisa was half asleep and unaware of Veronica's grief, until she woke her to move to seats which were further away from the tramp. Angry, tired and fed up with being on the bus, Veronica sighed and said, "This journey feels like it's never going to end." But the girls closed their eyes again and fell back to sleep. Sometime later they woke up as they pulled into another bus terminal.

Dazed and confused, the girls wiped their eyes. They had been on the bus for eleven hours and it was nearly 7am. Veronica felt dirty and wanted a bed. The driver told everybody to get off the bus as it was stopping for half an hour.

The girls found some toilets and had a wash in the sink and brushed their teeth. They had just enough time to grab an egg and chilli roll for breakfast, before boarding their bus for departure.

Some new passengers joined them; and among them was a group of young Mexicans, who made conversation with the girls. They were university students who were going on a short vacation to Merida and were visiting Chichen Itza and Uxmal like Veronica and Lisa. Veronica enjoyed practising her Spanish with their new-found friends. Lisa asked them where they were staying in Merida, it turned out that they were staying at the same hotel; Veronica and Lisa were very pleased. The Mexican group of three young women and one young man, asked the girls to join them on their trip to see the sites. Veronica told Lisa that it would be a good idea to tag along as they were sure to get their bus prices and admission tickets at the normal price, whereas if they went alone, there was a good chance that they would get ripped off, as Veronica was quite obviously a western tourist.

The remainder of the bus journey wasn't as tedious now that the girls had made friends. As they got closer to the Yucatan, the weather changed dramatically, becoming very hot and humid. The weather in the city had been much cooler. The roads went from being highways, to dusty dirt roads through jungle-like foliage. They could see pretty birds flying by; and when they got off at a pit stop to refuel and use the toilet facilities, the humidity took the girls breath away. They went into the toilets and stripped off, exchanging their jumpers, jackets and leggings for shorts and vests.

The journey was nearing its end, as they only had a few more hours to go. The girls got some lunch and tagged along with their New Mexican friends, then they boarded the bus for the last part of the journey.

Lisa and Veronica were getting very excited. The sun was shining, the sky was clear blue; and there were Mayan people in the streets. The women wore bright white dresses with colourful embroidered flowers. The men wore long shirts with collarless necks and embroidery along the chest area. The Mayan people had dark skin and wide bridged noses. Their faces were almost flat, similar to those of oriental people. They were distinctly different to the Mexican people Veronica had seen in the city.

Finally they arrived in Merida at around 8pm. The girls couldn't wait to get off the bus. Veronica grabbed her lonely planet guide and found the street maps, to figure out where they were and where they had to go, to find their hotel. The walk was only a short distance, and the girls were very pleased when they found the hotel and realised it had a lovely outdoor swimming pool. Once they got their keys for the room, they dropped their bags, changed into their swimming costumes and literally ran to the pool jumping in with joy.

CHAPTER 45

Merida and Chichen Itza

Veronica and Lisa's room in Merida was modern and comfortable with a TV. They spent their first evening swimming in the hotel's pool and playing around, then they found a restaurant and had chicken fajitas for dinner, which Veronica really enjoyed.

On their walk back to the hotel, they spotted a small museum and decided to visit the next day.

When the girls woke the following morning, the sun was glaring through the curtains, almost blinding them. Lisa was very excited and woke Veronica, begging to go for another swim in the pool. Veronica felt quite relaxed for the first time since arriving in Mexico, there was no rush after all, so she agreed; and decided to spend some of the day chilling by the pool. She thought they could enjoy the pool for most of the early part of the day and then venture out in the afternoon to explore the town and look at the shops and stalls selling artisan items and clothes. In Merida you could buy handmade hammocks, leather sandals, jewellery; and ornaments made from clay and porcelain.

Lisa and Veronica thoroughly enjoyed the pool and the sunshine. In some ways it reminded Veronica of being in the Mediterranean, with her family on the yacht Nova.

The sun beat down so hard that she could feel her skin burning, but at that moment in time, Veronica felt like she was in paradise. This moment could last forever she thought to herself. For the first time since arriving in Mexico, Veronica felt proud and pleased with herself for coming so far in such a short time. Most of all, she felt free from the worries of her parents' drug addiction and dealing. Here she could finally breathe a sigh of relief. She was over five thousand miles from home and its everyday annoyances of drug abuse. She could allow her soul to grow and to be free, away from the emotional restrictions of watching her parents abuse themselves day after day, year after year. It had taken a huge toll on Veronica, her well-being, and her perspective on life. She knew it wasn't her reality, the one in which she wanted to live; and the only way she would ever realise her own reality was to make a decisive break away from her parents and their negative lifestyle.

Finally, after all her struggles, both mental and physical, Veronica was here in a Mexican paradise. She was in control of her own destiny for the first time ever, without restraints or burdens to hold her back. The feeling of immense freedom washed over her, she had even felt held back when she arrived at Alejandro's; but here she was, on the other side of Mexico from Theresa and Julio's family, and also responsible for a twelve year old child and her welfare.

The girls headed out in the afternoon to go shopping. Veronica used the street maps in her guide book to figure out where to go. They were mesmerised by the huge amount of choice. There were beautiful handmade leather bags and sandals, Veronica found a pair of sandals that she thought her mum would like and bought them for her. Then they found the famous hammock stalls, there were so many to choose from. Veronica wanted to buy a hammock for her parents to use on their yacht Nova. She could visualise them somewhere, moored out in the Caribbean with the hammock above deck tied to the mast. That image brought a smile to Veronica's face, it has to be done, she thought, and found a double hammock that was fit for two.

Veronica paid for the hammock and the girls ventured on. After spending most of the afternoon rummaging through the stalls and trying out the local cantinas, the girls headed back for the hotel. On their way back, they stopped at the small local museum to take a look. All of the information was in Spanish so Lisa interpreted for Veronica. They found the museum to be quite informative, giving information about the history of Merida and its population. There were also a few artefacts which the girls took pictures of. Once they had been right round the museum, they continued their way back to the hotel.

Veronica and Lisa were ready to head out to the archaeological sites of the Yucatan, so needed to find their way back to the bus station to book tickets for an excursion to Chichen Itza. Veronica had seen many pictures of the site and couldn't wait to visit.

The girls agreed to drop their shopping back at the hotel and then take a short walk to the bus station where there was a tourist information centre. At the hotel they bumped into their new found Mexican friends, who they had met on the bus trip down to Merida. They were also planning to visit Chichen Itza the following day and agreed to go along with the girls to purchase their tickets.

The bus journey was only a couple of hours to Chichen Itza, 'a breeze' the girls thought, based on what they had endured coming from Mexico City.

At the ticket office, they were able to book an early morning bus ride for the following day.

Veronica was ecstatic, she had dreamed of this moment from the minute she booked her flight to Mexico. The girls headed back to their hotel to have a cool-off and some fun in the pool.

Veronica was beginning to get a tan. Her hair was also becoming bleached at the ends by the sun.

The weather in Merida exceeded 34 degrees and was a far cry from the cooler weather back in the city let alone the weather back home in the UK. The girls enjoyed the pool and a meal out in the town, after which they retired for an early night, to prepare for their day trip in the morning, as they had to be up early to catch their bus.

Next morning they took with them some bananas and drinks for their breakfast and headed for the bus station. Downstairs in the hotel reception were their Mexican friends, they all grouped together and set off. The bus was quite small, hot and stuffy, so Lisa and Veronica were dripping with sweat after only a few minutes, and wondered how they would survive the two hour journey without air conditioning.

The route took them along highways and through some areas of deep jungle; Veronica thought the journey was breath taking. As they approached Chichen Itza, the girls could see many buses lining up with tourists queuing in line towards a large straw hut. The site was gated and had boarding surrounding its perimeters, so it was difficult to tell at this point what the site looked like. The girls and their friends joined the other tourists queuing at the entrance. Once inside they were given maps; they had to walk along paths to designated areas, with huts providing toilets and snack bars along the way. Eventually they came to the main ruins of Chichen Itza.

Veronica could not believe the size of the temple. The steps leading up were very steep and approximately 2 to 3 times the depth of a normal step. They began to climb; there were chains along the side of the steps to hold on to, but after climbing only about six steps, Veronica felt a little out of breath!

"Oh my God Lisa, this isn't going to be easy," she said, but Lisa wasn't feeling very energetic, having only had five hours' sleep, and was now wondering what she had let herself in for. Veronica however was very excited and determined to get to the top. "Come on Lisa, this is a mission to be proud of," she told her. "Imagine the view once we reach the top."

The girls took around twenty minutes to get to the top, stopping every so often to catch their breath. Once at the peak, the view was even more astonishing than Veronica expected. From the top you could see the horizon all around. There was a thick carpet of dark green jungle as far as the eye could see; and there were other peaks of temples dotted around, protruding from the foliage.

"Wow!" Veronica remarked, "Lisa this is so incredibly beautiful. Have you ever seen anything like this?" Lisa had her mouth wide open in amazement. She was lost for words. The girls took it in turns to take photos of the views around them and of each other. They made their descent to the bottom of the temple and continued along the paths to view other parts of the archaeological site.

Inside some of the temples there were parts like underground caves. The girls were a little nervous whilst almost crawling through some of the tiny areas. "The Mayans must have been really short people," Veronica called out to Lisa, trying to duck through a small underground tunnel which led to an ancient tomb. It was quite cold inside, which was a nice relief from the sweltering heat above. Just then, the Mexican friends rejoined the girls. It was clear that one of them was feeling uneasy about being in a dark confined space. Yelping and screaming the girl was quite on edge. Just then the sound of a snake could be heard, making a very distinctive rattling sound.

"Ah!" the girl cried, "animale animale, vamanos, vamanos." Everybody panicked and darted back outside the temple. Lisa and Veronica felt startled, they hadn't realised that there were snakes in this part of the world. They had to be more cautious from then on and were more alert as they continued their way around the site.

The girls had climbed every single temple and examined every single artefact that was available to view. Veronica had taken a whole roll of photos, and at the end of their excursion the girls were shattered and hungry. They returned to their hotel by early evening and headed straight for the nearest restaurant for dinner. An early night was had; and the girls 'high fived' each other, for a successful trip was now under their belts.

CHAPTER 46

Uxmal

Veronica was fascinated by the Mayan people's history and impressed by their ancient civilisation. Lisa began to take an interest too and was very happy to be on such an important journey of discovery with Veronica. It was quite an adventure for Lisa, which was helpful in taking her mind off the anxiety she felt about fitting into the new culture that her mum had forced upon her.

Having seen Chichen Itza, Veronica wanted to see Uxmal, which was another archaeological site where the temples were very different in style, so the girls walked back to the bus station to book tickets for an excursion the following day; and then enjoyed the sun by the pool once again.

Next morning they were up early to catch the bus. When they got there, they found their way around, climbing every temple they came to. The steps were just as steep as at Chichen Itza's temples and they were taken aback when they spotted a tarantula by Veronica's foot. Lisa screamed, but Veronica was mesmerised by the size of the spider and its long hair. She usually hated spiders, but out in the wild Veronica wasn't bothered by this one; and stopped to take a photo of it.

The day was as long and as hot as ever, and the temples were steep to climb and very tiring. The girls liked being in the shade of the jungle, but they were very concerned about the insects there and the possibility of finding snakes. They had seen many iguanas of various sizes in the Yucatan, but so far no snakes. Veronica loved the sound of the jungle, but didn't enjoy being eaten alive by Mosquitoes and gnats. They covered their exposed skin with repellents, in the hope that they would not be bitten. Veronica and Lisa enjoyed a long hard day of trekking before returning by bus to Merida once again. They felt completely shattered when they got back, so retired for an early night.

Veronica felt 'at one' with herself and her ability to find her way around such a vast country, with a language barrier to boot. It was very handy having Lisa around to interpret, but Veronica knew that eventually she would be travelling alone, so would need to learn more Spanish to empower herself.

Aside from that though, Veronica was pleased with her progress; and also with her sense of peace. She had a feeling of equilibrium within herself, a feeling that she had never truly known before. All of her life so far, she had felt fear, panic, paranoia and worry, but all that began to melt away. Veronica was beginning to find 'Veronica' and this person was becoming someone very different to the Veronica she had been up until now.

There was nothing to be afraid of, no reason to panic; and therefore nothing to worry about.

She missed her parents and her sisters very much, but at the same time appreciated her time alone. She had time to think about what Veronica wanted from life and where she wanted to go.

Right now Veronica was happy just plodding along, trekking around Mexico, taking in all of the sights, the sounds and smells of a completely different culture. She realised that this had woken up the spirit within her; and Veronica felt very optimistic, confident and happy at last.

CHAPTER 47

Coba & Tulum

Veronica and Lisa visited a smaller archaeological site at Coba, en route to Tulum, where they met an Australian couple who were also travelling through the Yucatan; and got chatting.

They asked Veronica if they wanted to hook up and share a cabana in Tulum if it was a cheaper option. They said they were happy to go along with the idea if it meant they could save some money.

Veronica was excited about heading for Tulum, she was impressed by the pictures she had seen in her guide which showed it was right on the Caribbean coast of the Yucatan peninsula, far from civilisation. The area was like paradise, untouched by man's concrete jungle and an idyllic place to be.

The bus journey to Tulum from Merida via Coba was arduous though, and the girls found the sweltering heat without air conditioning or clean toilets hard going, but they knew the sacrifice would be worth the outcome. They had really enjoyed their exciting adventure so far, discovering the ancient civilisations of Mexico and how mankind's ancestors had lived then.

This part of Mexico was truly breath taking with its scenery, tropical plants and wild life. The girls were awe inspired and determined to see all that they could; and so their journey moved on, as they drove for hours through dense jungle to get to the Caribbean coast.

When they eventually arrived, the girls and their Australian acquaintances were dropped at a tiny bus stop along a wide-open dirt road. There were a few shops nearby, but then there was nothing for what seemed like miles. The girls asked the driver for directions because they could see no signs. They were told they had a long walk, as they were going to the middle of nowhere.

The lonely planet guide had information on the cabanas there, and the rough price to sleep in one, but no pictures to show them what to expect. The walk took more than an hour, but with new companions to talk to, the journey seemed to go much quicker. Once they arrived, they could not believe what they had found. There was a huge straw hut with a reception desk, and a guy with long black hair, dressed in a Mayan tunic. He welcomed the girls and the Australians to Tulum and asked how long they were staying. Veronica told him they needed a cabana for a few days and asked the price of a double and that of a quadruple. As it turned out to be a bit cheaper to share with the Australians, they all agreed to have one cabana between them.

Everyone was eager to get some rest after their long day travelling, so they followed the young Mayan through the back of the hut, where it opened out onto the Caribbean Sea. They were on a long stretch of beach that had the silkiest of white sand they had ever set eyes on, and fifty yards down the beach was the bright turquoise sea. The girls immediately felt overwhelmed with excitement. Suddenly their weary eyes were wide open and they were more eager to dip their toes in the water, than to go to sleep. The Mayan man led them along the beach and showed them the men's and ladies outside showers, which were separate huts with cubicles inside. They were pretty basic but sufficient enough to do the job.

There was a large sink with running cold water to do hand laundry, which pleased Veronica as some of her clothes were in need of a wash.

The man then ushered everyone onwards to their cabana. The floor inside the hut was of sand, just as outside; and there were four single camp beds with mosquito nets tied up above them.

Veronica gulped and her heart sank, she loved the idea of staying on the beach and in the hut, but there were no creature comforts whatsoever; and the bed was like a hard canvas hammock.

They thanked the man then put their rucksacks down on the sandy floor.

Lisa and Veronica were eager to go and explore, but the Australian couple were more interested in resting up, so the girls left their bags and wandered off. Veronica kept her bum bag, where she kept the money and passports, with her to be on the safe side, as they didn't know this couple from Adam and they could be anybody.

The girls explored the camp and discovered there were many Americans and Europeans staying in groups of all sizes around barbecues and bonfires. They felt quite at home in a sense, as all of these people were on a mission just like them.

The girls were ecstatic, the water was so blue it was almost too perfect, they dipped their toes and were surprised at how warm it was. Neither of them had ever felt sea water so warm before.

Veronica had travelled in some parts of the Mediterranean where the sea was very clear and beautiful, but nowhere near as hot as this, it was almost unbelievable.

They were in their element. This was by far the prettiest place on earth they had ever seen.

Veronica asked Lisa, "Do you realise how lucky we are Lisa? This is just amazing."

They soon felt very relaxed but also very hungry as they had not eaten since early afternoon and darkness was soon approaching.

There was a restaurant in the main hut by the entrance to the cabanas. They could smell the cooking of meats and potatoes and followed their noses to see what was on offer. When they got there, they were disappointed to discover the extortionate prices though. To eat a meal each was equivalent to around £20 which was way too much for their budget.

Veronica had brought a tiny gas stove with her, so suggested to Lisa, "Why don't we walk back to the cabana and ask the Aussies if they want to chip in for some groceries and walk back to that shop beside the bus stop. I know it's real far but there is no other way we can afford to eat here. I should have thought of that when the bus pulled up outside! We can cook a few bits for a meal tonight and some breakfast tomorrow." Lisa thought it was a good idea so they headed back to the cabana to see the couple. They agreed that the price of the food was ridiculously expensive.

It seemed that although they were in very basic accommodation, the owners were really making huge profits on the food. Travellers were stuck between a rock and a hard place if they had no option, but Veronica however did, and so the Aussie couple were happy to walk back to the shop a few miles down the road with them to buy some food. The walk back to the shop seemed to take even longer than reaching the cabana had earlier that day, as everyone was feeling very weary; but when they got there they eagerly looked for things they could cook. Veronica found packs of tortillas, limes, bananas, fresh cheese, tomatoes, onions, peppers, garlic, cooking lard and cans of tuna. She could at least make quesadillas with either just cheese or with tuna. There were also tins of ham, which was useful as there was nowhere cold to store their food.

The girls also grabbed bottles of fresh water, as the drinks on site were very expensive.

It was dark by the time they were ready to walk back. The sky was pitch black, with only the stars to illuminate the night. Fortunately the girls had torches to help them find their way through the jungle-fringed dirt tracks, but they could not take their eyes off of the bright stars above.

Veronica had spent many a night stargazing out at sea aboard their yacht Nova, sailing through the Mediterranean, and had seen many shooting stars there; but the sky was very different here and there were constellations that she had not seen before. Veronica stared and stared so much that she nearly tripped over some branches in the road. Eventually she spotted a shooting star that zoomed across the sky, Veronica shouted for joy like a child.

"This whole journey is a complete discovery of just how wonderful this world really is," Veronica exclaimed. "I couldn't think of a nicer place to be right now and I feel so lucky to be here."

Veronica was nearly wiped out with fatigue by the time they reached their site, as their shopping seemed heavier with every step they took, but her work was by no means complete.

She got the cooking utensils out of her tray and began to cut the onions and peppers on a small plate that came with her camping stove. Using a wooden chair as a work surface, Veronica continuously cut using her basic utensils. It wasn't as easy as she'd hoped, but they were so hungry that giving up was not an option.

Veronica lit the gas under her stove and put her pan on with some lard in it, then as it began to sizzle she dropped the onions and peppers in; and when they'd cooked she added the garlic and tomatoes.

Everyone fancied the cheese that night, which made cooking easier and there would still be ham and tuna left for the morning. Then she poured the contents of the pan into a bowl, before putting more lard in the pan to fry the tortillas. Once the tortilla was slightly crisp on one side, she flipped it over adding some of the cooked veg and cheese. The smell was amazing, everyone was eager to eat it. Veronica finished off the tortilla with a squeeze of lime, these fruits were a big part of the Mexican diet and

Veronica had acquired a taste for them. They were known to be good as a natural anti septic, which was useful in the given environment.

Veronica cooked the tortillas one by one and offered them to the Aussies and Lisa before lastly cooking for herself with what was left. Everyone thoroughly enjoyed them, but left Veronica to do the washing up at the outside sink, before she could return to the cabana for a much-needed rest.

CHAPTER 48

Waking Up in Tulum

Veronica woke up in a pool of sweat, her hair was soaked right through and her mouth was so dry that her lips were virtually stuck together. She tried to swallow saliva in her mouth but there was barely any to swallow and instead her throat felt like there were razors inside. As she attempted to sit up, her neck began to hurt. She had obviously fallen asleep in an awkward position.

Veronica looked around and could see Lisa still sleeping nearby, and the Australian couple opposite were still asleep in their camp beds too. It felt like there was no air inside the cabana, and Veronica could feel the sweltering heat outside being absorbed into the hut. She crawled out of bed and stood up to stretch her limbs. She found a bottle of water beside the chair she had used to cook on the night before and picked it up to pour some into a cup. The water felt hot, Veronica had not anticipated this but drank the water anyway as she was so thirsty.

Lisa heard Veronica shuffling around, finding her clothes and toothbrush. Lisa sat up also in a pool of sweat. She stretched her arms out wide and yawned, "I'm so hot."

"Tell me about it," Veronica replied. "I'm going to the showers to get clean and fresh, then I will come back and get breakfast going for you," Veronica said.

"Can I come, I need a shower too, I'm covered in sweat." Lisa asked.

"Ok, come on then, get some fresh clothes," replied Veronica.

The girls got dressed, took their clothes, toiletries and towels from their bags and headed out to the showers. When they got there, they found a small queue gathering outside. The girls got in line and waited their turn. After a cool shower the girls returned to the cabana for some breakfast. The Aussie couple were up and about and ready for breakfast too.

Veronica got her gas stove and found a bench outside on the beach to prepare food. She lit the gas and began to lightly fry some tortillas. Lisa and the Aussies fancied banana and lime, Veronica joined them for banana tortillas which were very tasty, to her surprise.

After breakfast the girls said goodbye to the couple and headed off for the Mayan ruins which were situated 1.5 kilometres down the beach from the cabanas. It was early Sunday morning and archaeological sites offered free entry on Sundays, which was an added bonus for the girls as they were on a tight budget. Theresa had only given enough money for Lisa to live comfortably for two weeks and no more, but by Veronica's calculations they could stretch the money to nearly three weeks and get more sights under their belts. Off they set toward the Mayan ruins.

Once again the girls were taken away by the sheer beauty of their surroundings. Here, not only were the temples striking to look at but their location was out of this world. Veronica thought to herself that back home in England, she could never imagine Mexico being so beautiful.

Although the pictures gave a clear view of its vast beauty, they certainly could not do it true justice. The girls ran around the temples like excited children snapping happily away with their cameras, and Veronica asked someone to take a photo of her and Lisa.

Out of all of the Mayan ruins Veronica Intended to visit, Tulum was top of the list because of its location. Veronica kissed Lisa and told her, "Well done Lisa, you have been an amazing travel companion and I think we have got on very well together don't you?"

"Yeah," Lisa replied, "I've had so much fun, I'm so glad you let me come with you, it's been so amazing."

The girls continued to walk around exploring the site for a couple of hours and saw loads of iguanas sunbathing on the steps of the temples. Lisa and Veronica were feeling extremely hot and lethargic, it was only 10:00 am and yet the sun was hotter than any midday sun they had ever experienced back home. Wiping the sweat from their brow they started their descent and made their way back to the cabanas. "Why don't we go for a nice swim in the sea when we get back?" Veronica suggested. Lisa agreed, so when they got back they grabbed their swim suits and ran down the beach and into the sea splashing each other along the way.

After a nice swim Lisa felt tired and decided to head back to the cabana for a nap.

Veronica was more alert after cooling off in the sea and wanted to stay out a little Longer.

She happily floated in the water for what seemed like forever, taking in her surroundings and feeling relaxed. As she headed out of the water to make her way back to the cabana, she heard an almighty scream. Veronica recognised the tone immediately and knew it was Lisa. She ran in a panic to see what the matter was, when suddenly Lisa bolted back down the beach towards Veronica in a hysterical state.

"What's wrong Lisa?" Veronica shouted.

"There's a snake in the cabana, it's in my bag, I'm lucky it didn't bite me," she said.

"Where are the Australians?" Veronica asked.

"I don't know, their stuff is still in the cabana so they can't be far," Lisa replied.

"Don't go back in there Lisa until they are back, I bet that guy will know what to do, they have snakes and all sorts in Australia."

Ten minutes later the Australians showed up and they managed to get rid of the snake. Lisa went back into the hut and had a sleep.

The girls enjoyed the day chilling, swimming and cooking together. The next day, the Australian couple announced they were leaving for another part of the Yucatan.

The girls were surprised but having seen what they had come to see, were in agreement that it was time to move on. Veronica decided to pack and leave too for Playa del Carmen. They were excited, another place, another experience to be had.

Veronica wanted to go to Cozumel Island as they had a reef there which was great for snorkelling and diving. Jacques Cousteau had discovered the beauty of Cozumel's reef in 1961 and declared it one of the best scuba diving areas in the world. Veronica wanted to sample Cozumel for herself, so the girls paid their bill for the cabana and made their way back to the bus stop. The Australians were heading in another direction and said their goodbyes and boarded another bus.

Veronica and Lisa were feeling extremely positive and happy with the events and experiences of the past week. They had become very adept at travelling and they knew it.

CHAPTER 49

Playa Del Carmen

The bus to Playa del Carmen took no time at all, in little more than an hour the girls were back in civilisation. They were still on the beautiful Caribbean coast of the Yucatan though, which was the most picturesque stretch of Mexico so far.

Playa Del Carmen was a densely built up area with many streets, shops, hotels, petrol stations, supermarkets, hostels, bars and much more. It had a very retro feel to it and there were travellers from all around the world. Some had settled to set up shops selling handmade arts and crafts, which gave the area a very unique feel. It was hard to believe that the comparative isolation of Tulum lay just an hour along the coast. They got off at the main bus station and then headed towards some cheap hostels that Veronica had seen in her guide book. The one they found was clean but basic, yet it was just right for what the girls needed. They were within a two minute walk of the beach and close to all the necessary shops, restaurants and bars.

Veronica unpacked some of her things in their room and counted her money. She kept a regular check on what she had, as they were on a tight budget. Veronica didn't have any bank cards with her as she'd had trouble with her debit card in the Monte Carlo hotel in Mexico City. All she had was cash; and she didn't want to travel all over Mexico with all of her money, so she took what she needed for her trip with Lisa and left the rest with Theresa back in the city.

Veronica was initially confused, as there were about 300 pesos missing from the pouch in her bag. The last check she made was before leaving the cabana in Tulum; then she had left her bag with the Australians whilst she and Lisa collected their laundry from the line.

Veronica thought back to the day's events and counting her money in the cabana. She always counted and re-counted two to three times.

Veronica had done this in Tulum so she was sure there was money missing, and 300 pesos was a lot to the girls.

"The Australians must have gone through my bag," Veronica said.

"That's terrible," Lisa replied.

"We can't leave anything to chance from now on, you can't trust anyone," Veronica said. "How disgusting of them, I have a child with me as well, some people have no morals. Well that's shaved our budget a bit; we may as well have had our own cabana after all," Veronica sighed. "Oh well, let's put it down to experience, but how disappointing."

The girls quickly settled in to their new environment and headed out to explore once more.

The beach was beautiful and the sea a clear turquoise, so they decided to have a swim, racing each other to get in. They felt immediately relieved, as although the water was quite warm, it was cooling compared to the sweltering heat they had endured all day. The girls chatted happily in the sea, discussing their plans for tomorrow and deciding to try SCUBA diving in Cozumel Island. The ferry ran there every hour from a jetty just a stone's throw down the beach from their accommodation, so they went to find out what times it departed and booked tickets for the following morning. Then they spent the evening eating in a Mexican cantina ten minutes' walk away from the beach front. As Playa del Carmen was full of tourists it was very pricy to eat there, but Veronica had learnt quickly that by walking just ten minutes out of the tourist zone, they could save a fortune.

The girls managed to find a quiet local cantina that served fajitas at a fraction of the price charged near their hostel. They enjoyed their meal so much they decided to go back there for dinner the following day, after their excursion across to Cozumel. They headed back to their room to get an early night as they were very tired from all of the walking they had done.

The next morning they got to the ferry pier nice and early, arriving fifteen minutes before departure. They were fully loaded with swimwear already on under their shorts and tops, and they carried fruit, water and towels; they also had their sunscreen and tickets and were eager to go! The ferry departed on time and the girls headed up on deck to take pictures.

The journey to Cozumel Island took forty five minutes, then when they arrived they were directed to the nearby diving school.

They went inside and waited at a shop counter for assistance. A few minutes later a stocky Mexican guy appeared from a back room behind the counter. He spoke mainly Spanish with some broken English. Lisa explained that they wanted to learn to dive. The man agreed and told Lisa the price. He said the girls would first practice in shallow water nearby before heading out to deeper waters, to which they agreed. He took the girls out the back of the shop to another room, where he had his diving equipment. He gave them each an air cylinder and a mask to carry. Then he gave them regulators to breathe through and rummaged through some fins, asking what shoe size the girls were. Once he found the correct sizes he asked the girls to try them on and then took them outside to a concrete quay with steps leading into the water. The instructor told the girls to put their fins on and demonstrated how to walk sideways, so as not to trip over.

At first the water was shallow, only reaching the girls' waists. The instructor showed them how to put on their masks, spitting into his and wiping the saliva around the glass, explaining that it acted as a barrier and helped prevent the mask from steaming up.

They followed suit and adjusted their masks over their faces. Then they attached the breathing apparatus and the instructor showed them how to equalize the pressure in their ears.

As they descended into the water the girls felt a little panicked, the sea became darker and colder as they went deeper. They saw some big fish in all shapes and colours swimming by and Veronica was amazed how pretty they were.

As they got deeper, Veronica felt a sharp piercing in her ear and the pain was unbearable. She began to get really upset and tried to signal to the instructor that she was in trouble.

He continued to take Lisa further down but Veronica couldn't bear it as her ear was killing her.

Veronica began writhing around in the water to get their attention and began to ascend to the surface. The instructor and Lisa realised something was wrong and followed.

When they reached the surface they took their mouth pieces out and Veronica told the instructor and Lisa that her ear had popped and the pain was unbearable. The instructor was angry and said they hadn't gone deep enough for that to happen but Veronica assured him that she was in agony. He told her that she couldn't have followed his instructions on equalizing, as if she had then there would have been no problem. Veronica found the language barrier a little difficult in this situation, as although Lisa was interpreting, some of it was guess work for her.

Anyway, Veronica was sure she followed the instructions, but she knew there was something wrong as her ear was piercing with pain and she couldn't unblock it. The instructor told her to get out of the sea and offered to continue with Lisa. Lisa didn't want to go without Veronica as she didn't entirely feel comfortable with the instructor being that he was a stranger, so the girls both got out and got changed. Veronica was really disappointed and felt like she had let Lisa down.

Lisa assured Veronica that she wasn't all that bothered about the dive and what they had seen was still fascinating. Veronica was worried about her ear, the pain continued as they made their way back on the ferry to Playa del Carmen, so she decided to go back to their room for a lie down.

The trip so far had been one pleasant experience after another, there was bound to be the odd bad one, so Veronica accepted it as one of those things.

The next day, the girls spent the day on the beach, but Veronica couldn't swim as her ear was still in pain. It hadn't eased at all, so they found a pharmacy and Veronica got some pain relief.

The pharmacist had a look at Veronica's ear and explained to Lisa that there was blood inside and that the ear drum may have been burst. Veronica wasn't happy about it, but then again what could she do? She wasn't going to let it spoil her trip, so the girls decided to pack up and leave for Palenque the next day.

CHAPTER 50

Palenque

The bus to Palenque took twelve long, hot and bumpy hours. Palenque was situated in the heart of the Campeche jungle and had some magnificent Mayan ruins. The girls tried to sleep as much as they could and get as comfortable as possible, but the journey was exhausting nonetheless. They were happy to get to the hostel and get their heads down for the night, even though they missed their evening meal. The next morning, they wandered down the road looking for a place to eat; and found a lovely restaurant which served beautiful fresh coffee and wonderful fruit salads. They were ravenous and had plenty of fruit and yogurt, followed by eggs. On their way back to the hostel the girls passed a hut that had meat hanging from its roof, including two pig's heads which attracted lots of flies.

The girls looked in horror, "That's disgusting," they both exclaimed at the same time. As they walked past the hut they came to an old lady sitting at a table on a small terrace, who stared at them with a look of evil. She muttered something in Mexican and then spat at Veronica, hitting her right in the side of her face. Veronica was in complete shock. "What the fuck is she doing?" Veronica shouted. Lisa told her that the woman had called her a white foreigner. Veronica wanted to go back and spit at the woman but wisely left, in case of more trouble.

It made Veronica feel dirty and very upset that a complete stranger would feel the need to attack her like that. She hadn't done anything wrong and was minding her own business. Maybe the woman was a drunk. "What an evil cow," Veronica said to Lisa.

When she got back to the hostel, Veronica washed her face. The room was more like a cell, with a tiled floor, two single metal beds with a mattress that wasn't even an inch thick, and grey itchy blankets. The toilet was very basic, with a hand-held shower head in the corner which just about worked; the doors had metal gratings alongside them, reminiscent of a police cell. Veronica wanted to spend as little time as possible there, they had stayed in much better rooms; even the sandy floored cabana beat this. They went back out to find where to get the bus to the Mayan ruins; then headed straight there.

The site was pretty close to the town; in fact it was only 6 kilometres away. Once there, the girls paid their entrance fees and set off through the jungle to roam the site.

The temples were very different again in style to those at Chichen Itza, Uxmal, Tulum and Coba.

These temples had very intricate carvings; and the tallest of all of them was the Templo de Las Inscripcions, which housed a tomb of the Mayan leader Pakal, who reigned for 68 years until his death around 683 CE.

Lisa and Veronica climbed deep down into the pyramid to discover the tomb. It was very dark and eerie inside. The tomb was huge and the lid looked like it was slightly open. The girls shrieked as they took photos, impressed with themselves for being so brave!

After exploring the other nearby temples, they headed through the jungle to find a hidden waterfall which they had to cross a drawbridge to reach. The girls felt like they were on the set of Raiders of The Lost Ark! They had to take a long trek through the jungle to find it, and climb down steep ancient steps that were carpeted with foliage. When they finally reached the bottom, there was a beautiful water fall, with a shallow rock pool surrounding it where people were cooling off. The girls were so excited and just wanted to take pictures.

There was a small crowd of young tourists building up as they, like the girls, were waiting to take their turn in getting a full view of the waterfall to take pictures.

Once Veronica and Lisa were able to get up close, Veronica noticed graffiti all across the rocks where the water fell. Her heart sank, one moment she was in complete awe of the scenery around her and then in an instant that feeling was replaced with shock and disappointment, that people could be so thoughtless and reckless to scribble their names across rocks that had lain hidden and untouched for over a thousand years. At that very moment Veronica felt ashamed, almost guilty even, as if she had destroyed that waterfall.

The girls made the most of their time cooling off and then headed back up the steep jungle steps, stopping occasionally to catch their breath and take in the scenery.

Veronica was up ahead of Lisa and stopped to take a photograph of her. As she called to Lisa to strike a pose, Lisa screeched with fear pointing towards Veronica's feet. Veronica looked down, but couldn't see what Lisa was screaming about. Then Lisa said, "Look to your left, be careful Veronica it's a huge snake." With that, Veronica caught the pattern of the enormous snake beside her. It was draped across maybe half a dozen steps, and each step was a large stride for Veronica to climb. Veronica froze with fear and scanned the foliage filled steps above her, to see if she could find the snake's head. It seemed to have veered off left into the jungle, so Veronica shouted to Lisa to run for her life and they both ran up the steps past the rest of the snake's body. The girls didn't say a word until they had cleared the snake, then they let out an almighty scream. Their hearts were pounding through their chests. "Oh my god Lisa, I have never seen anything like that in my entire life, not even on television." The snake was a kind of grey and black in colour and must have been about 8 feet in length. At its thickest, the body was wider than Veronica's thigh.

The girls reached the top of the hill and headed for the archaeological site's exit. When they reached it, they saw signs warning them about the different species of snakes in the area. The snake the girls had crossed paths with, was a Chiapas Boa. They felt lucky to be alive and could not believe what they had just experienced. What if they had crossed paths a few moments earlier? Was the snake there when they had come down the hill previously, when looking for the water fall? What if it had bitten one of us, they wondered, how would we have coped? Are they poisonous? Veronica realised that she was still very naive; wandering around the jungle without a care in the world, they had very nearly become a snake's lunch. But then again, they had been lucky enough to come out unscathed and alive to tell the tale! The girls returned by bus to their hostel and had a shower; they were exhausted and dirty from sweating all day. Then they went to the local restaurant for a quiet meal and returned for a much-needed early night.

The following day, they would be heading out through Chiapas towards Agua Azul and Misol Ha, to explore the amazing cascades and waterfalls.

CHAPTER 51

Agua Azul and Misol Ha

The girls got up early as usual for another day of exploration; they were getting used to the long bus rides and walking for miles in the sweltering heat. Veronica and Lisa were very proud of what they had achieved so far together. They took the rough with the smooth and Veronica was very surprised by the mature head on Lisa's shoulders. She often forgot that Lisa was only twelve. Lisa didn't act like a typical kid, she was already like a young woman and she enjoyed exploring as much as Veronica.

The girls had seen pictures of Agua Azul and Misol Ha in their local restaurant in Palenque, where they had their breakfasts and dinners. The journey was a winding one, going through dense jungle covered mountains. When the girls entered Agua Azul, the sheer beauty of the cascades took their breath away, it was even better than the pictures they had seen.

They followed a trail with other tourists, trekking upstream along a path that wound up through the cascades, they stopped every so often to take pictures. The cascades were over two kilometres long; and it was very difficult at times to climb over the stones along the way, as they were very slimy and slippery from the green algae that had formed over them. The girls slipped and tumbled and bruised their legs and bottoms as they went, but it had them in stitches of laughter because they were so happy and overwhelmed to be in such a remote and beautiful location. "Lisa, this country is absolutely spectacular. You are a lucky girl to have family out here. I hope you make the most of them when you get back to the city," Veronica said.

Lisa agreed that it was very beautiful in Mexico but she still wasn't so sure about the family and living there. She loved England with its pop culture and fashion. Mexicans were far from fashionable in her opinion, but Veronica found the whole experience emotionally liberating and mentally educating. In fact it was like being in an outdoor classroom.

The insects were huge, which Veronica didn't particularly like, but some of them were amazing to look at. A bright green cricket had somehow found its way into Veronica's rucksack during their walk through the ruins at Palenque; and when she reached inside for her bottle of water, she grabbed the insect without realising it was there, until it flew up into her face causing her to scream and jump out of her skin. They had seen wild pigs in the jungle, something Veronica had never imagined back home, yet somehow found the sight of them in the jungle to be quite hilarious. They saw bright red centipedes crawling on the jungle floor; and the strangest looking birds, that would sit on top of the ruins with their wings spread out, as if they were sunbathing. Added to this was the huge snake that they had encountered in Palenque and the tarantula which accompanied the girls in a temple at Uxmal. Veronica couldn't put a price on what this experience meant to her; and not just for its educational value, but also for the spiritual one.

Veronica felt empowered; and had a growing sense of confidence, trusting her ability to look after herself and Lisa in unknown territory. She remembered her dad's pre-departure lecture about hating the trip and running back home within a week.

She smiled to herself because she had proved him wrong and proven to herself that she could achieve whatever she set her mind to. As long as she had self-belief and perseverance, she would do just fine. Veronica missed her mum and sisters a lot; and although she loved and respected her dad, she didn't miss his mood swings and the lectures. Here Veronica could reinvent herself. Veronica in Mexico was a completely different character to the Veronica she had left back home with her parents.

When the trek through Agua Azul was finished, the tour guides took them to another site called Misol Ha, which was the tallest waterfall in Mexico. It looked like a scene from a Tarzan movie.

Lisa and Veronica gasped at the beauty of the waterfall, they were able to walk right behind it and take pictures. The girls took turns in using the camera.

The day had been another success, and another treasure of Mexico had been explored by them.

They returned to their hostel again for an early night; and would enjoy one last day, relaxing by the hostel before returning by bus to Mexico City.

They were running out of funds; and as Veronica had paid for Lisa to stay on another week with her, they had been travelling for nearly three weeks now and hadn't been in contact with Theresa since staying in Playa del Carmen. Veronica and Lisa were happy with their achievements and pleased that they had looked after each other so well and got on like two peas in a pod. "I've loved travelling with you Lisa, it's been just brilliant, every minute of it; and I've seen so much in this short time that we've been travelling. I just don't want it to end, but the money is nearly gone now so we must get back to the city," Veronica said sadly. Lisa agreed, but was also sad that their explorations were coming to an end.

"I wish I could come with you on your next voyage Veronica," Lisa said.

"I know honey, but you have to knuckle down and get to school and make an effort to get to know all of your new family. You promised your mum that when you went home you would make a go of it and really try Lisa. Your mum has been good letting you go all these miles across Mexico with me. Now you need to show her how appreciative you are." Lisa nodded and agreed she would try hard to fit in on their return. "Lisa you may just get to like it, just don't worry, it will all work out I'm sure."

The girls continued to enjoy their last day in Palenque town, then boarded the bus for Mexico City the following day. The journey back was long and monotonous, they found it extremely uncomfortable and boring, but they knew it had to be done. They arrived at the bus station in the city the following morning and made their way to the metro station. They had a few stops to go to get to Julio's house and a ten minute walk from the metro line.

Theresa wasn't expecting the girls and was still in bed when they arrived. Veronica was shocked at the sight of Julio's place. It was a run-down old building that had holes in the stairs, and the walls and ceiling were badly cracked. Julio had one large room with dusty floor boards and a small kitchen, which had an old stove and sink in it with a tiny table and four stools.

There was no running water in the kitchen, and you had to walk downstairs to a small outside yard with a cold water tap. The bathroom consisted of just a toilet which couldn't be flushed as it hadn't been plumbed in. There was no bath or shower, just a drain in the corner of the room to have strip washes. Veronica was horrified that Theresa would drag her kids out to Mexico to live like that. What on earth was she thinking? Veronica thought to herself.

Julio had many years to make his house a home, but he had done nothing; and lived like a bachelor. He was an artist who painted pictures and sold them for a living. He made good money for a Mexican, so there was no reason why he could not have tried to get his house in order, especially when he knew for at least a couple of years that Theresa was saving up to come over with their children. His brother Alejandro was a builder, why hadn't he helped Julio prepare the house for the girls at the very least? Theresa made excuses and apologised for the state of the place. She told Veronica that was why she didn't want her coming to stay at Julio's when they first arrived; she hadn't wanted to put that on Veronica. At Julio's, Lisa would sleep on air beds on the floor. Theresa offered Veronica one of them for a few days until she was ready to go off on her next adventure, this time solo. Veronica wasn't happy about the lack of comfort, but had to make do if she were to make her money stretch.

She asked Theresa to take her shopping for essentials, and she bought some groceries to contribute whilst staying with the family.

CHAPTER 52

Oaxaca

Theresa was intrigued to hear about the girls' experience of travelling together through the Yucatan and Campeche. She was very proud of Veronica and Lisa for doing so well, and impressed that Veronica had paced themselves with the money they had and taken advantage of the free entry to museums and temples on a Sunday. Theresa was very excited by the girls' stories, as it took her back to her travelling days during the eighties with Graham.

Veronica felt a lot more relaxed in the city now, having become surer of herself and her ability to get around. She spent a further couple of days with Julio's family getting to know everyone a little bit more, then when it was time for her to move on, Veronica packed up her small rucksack, counted what money she had left and took enough to last her approximately three weeks. She wanted to try out the Pacific coast of Mexico, stopping at Oaxaca first.

Theresa had told her that there were a lot of indigenous people living there, and many artisans and museums. When she arrived at Oaxaca bus station, Veronica asked one of the staff for directions to a nearby hostel. It took her ten minutes to walk to her destination and when she arrived it was dark and late. The accommodation was very cheap and when Veronica agreed the price the man led her to her room.

They climbed some rickety iron stairs within the building which looked more akin to a prison block. When they reached the floor, the corridor was narrow with wrought iron shutters and doors behind them. The man pointed to Veronica's room, opened the shutter and turned on the light. The man said good night and left Veronica the key.

The room was just like a cell. The floor was concrete with no carpet or mats, the walls were brick that had been painted white. The bed was an old metal frame with the thinnest mattress that Veronica had ever seen.

There were no creature comforts at all, one pillow, a sheet and a rough itchy blanket. Veronica sat on the bed feeling a bit deflated. This was her first night alone in Mexico and she felt very lonely and isolated. It was around 10pm and Veronica had not had a proper meal since leaving Mexico City. There were no fast food places here and it was too dangerous for her to be walking the streets of Oaxaca so late alone, looking for somewhere to eat. Veronica had a bottle of water which would at least keep her hydrated until the morning, or so she thought! She went to bed, but couldn't sleep. She could hear the clanking of other shutters from nearby rooms and the jangling of keys and the owner's deep voice as he was showing other occupants to their rooms. There was no air conditioning which made it very hot and stifling, so Veronica tossed and turned all night, sweating and waking dehydrated, in need of water. Her little bottle didn't last her long at all and the remainder of the night was pretty unbearable. Veronica got up at around half past seven, had a wash in the basin in her room, got dressed and went out to explore and find a place to eat. She found a cantina down the road, where she had a typical Mexican breakfast of frijoles, scrambled eggs and maze tortillas. She was ravenous and couldn't eat quickly enough. Then she spent the day walking through the streets of Oaxaca exploring the shops and the articles the artisans had for sale. She bought a few small items to take home, then made her way back to the room with some drinks and snacks to have at hand. She lay down and fell asleep for what must have been hours, waking up in a pool of sweat feeling worse than before. When she looked outside and realised it was pitch black and nearly seven in the evening, she jumped up and got dressed to go out for some food. Veronica had missed her meals the day before, so it was important that she got her dinner. Veronica went back to the local cantina she had found that morning and had a light meal.

Aside from the many shops in the area, there wasn't much that interested Veronica in Oaxaca, so she decided to move on to Puerto Escondido the following morning.

It was another long, arduous bus journey, with many winding roads that seemed to go on forever, winding upwards through the dense forested mountains and then slowly winding down the other side towards the beautiful Pacific coast. Veronica was pleasantly surprised by the beauty of Puerto Escondido and wondered what adventures she would have there.

CHAPTER 53

Puerto Escondido

Veronica's excitement continued, she had found a lovely apartment with a pool in her guide book, not far from the beach. It was quite expensive but offered Veronica all her creature comforts for a little while. She spent that afternoon swimming in the pool before setting off down the beach to see what was happening in Escondido. It didn't take her long to get chatting to other fellow travellers and before long Veronica felt very relaxed. They told her about the Cabanas which were basic but cheap and allowed Veronica to stretch her budget further. She hit it off with one woman in particular, an Aussie girl called Sophie, who played guitar and wrote her own songs. Veronica and Sophie sang songs by all-time greats such as Bob Marley and Eric Clapton and soon realised they had a fair bit in common. Sophie said she had had a pretty normal upbringing, apart from realising in her early teens that her older sister was a heroin addict. The girls went off for a long walk along the beach, swapping stories of their knowledge of drug abuse and heartache at having to stand back and watch their loved ones self-abuse as they were growing up. They talked about the emotional torture they endured in coming to terms with the fact they could do nothing to change the situation. For the first time ever, Veronica didn't feel alone and odd. She had found someone who knew exactly how she felt.

Veronica shared a song she had started to write whilst on board the yacht Nova the previous year, about her parents.

Just one more hit
And that is it,
You say.
Just one more hit
Will take the pain away.

If you choose to stay in bed
And waste your days away,
I can't stop you getting out of your head
And I won't stand in your way.
La la la la la laaaaa
Waste your days away
La la la la la laaaaa
Waste your days away
La la la la la laaaaa

Another day another deal is fixed,
From society you hide your dirty tricks.
And through it all you've found yourself in such corruption,
Knee deep in self-destruction.
What ever happened to the high?
La la la la la laaaaa
Waste the days away
La la la la la laaaaa
Waste the days away
La la la la la laaaaa
La la la la la laaaaa.
Chasing the dragon
In the back of a wagon,
In a side road out of view.
You don't want it anymore
But you know you've got to score,
The drugs have got the better of you.
And all the while it's only you who has been wasted,
It makes you so frustrated
Because you don't know what to do.
All those promises you made
You know you couldn't keep.
I believed in you,
But deep down knew,
That you were just too weak.
All those years have passed you by,
And things are much the same,
You deny;

And justify
But it's the same old game.
Yes it's the same old game.
Yeah it's the same old game.
La la la la la laaaaa
Waste the days away.

Sophie thought she had endured hard times with her sister, but after hearing about Veronica's life with the difficulties of her parents' addiction, she soon realised it wasn't so bad.

This meeting of minds was to be another turning point for Veronica and her future.

Sophie had endured the promises and lies just like Veronica; and had unwittingly helped her sister to maintain her habit, as opposed to actually helping her to come off, which was all Sophie wanted. In the end, Sophie turned her back on her sister as she couldn't cope with being used anymore. Her sister had stolen from her numerous times and Sophie had just let it go, as she felt sorry for her situation. Heroin addiction is like an illness; its victims cannot control their urges. Both girls knew this too well and it had had a massive emotional impact on them.

Sophie and Veronica felt like they had known each other forever and yet they had only met a few hours before. They spent the next couple of days happily exchanging life experiences whilst Sophie strummed her guitar and sang so beautifully, that Veronica felt she had met a soul sister!

Sophie felt exactly the same, as the girls soon realised their musical backgrounds and influences were also very similar. They harmonised their vocals for hours, dreaming of a musical future together. Veronica was in her element!

CHAPTER 54

The Final Excursion

Veronica and Sophie hung around together for a while until Sophie had to head back to return to Australia for family reasons. Veronica wasn't quite ready to end her adventures yet and decided to travel the Pacific coast a little, to visit Angel and Zipolite. The name meant 'beach of death' as it was famous for its huge waves and was a meeting point for keen surfers from all over the world. Zipolite was also known as a hippy retreat, rife with drugs. This did not phase Veronica one bit, why would it? There was nothing she hadn't seen and nothing could shock her, as long as she didn't get mixed up with these folk she would be fine.

When she got there she found that everyone was smoking pot. There were some old American hippies who looked as though they had been there for years. Their skin was all dark and shrivelled like leather from too much sun exposure, and they were so stoned they couldn't string a sentence together. Veronica thought it was sad that people way past middle age were living like that. She thought about her parents, at least they hadn't let go of themselves like this and they actually had dreams to travel the world, taking her sisters with them. They were a far cry from these shrivelled old hippies who seemed to have got stuck here.

Veronica spent her first day in Zipolite on the beach with some new found English friends.

A man called Philip was heading back to Mexico City the following day as his journey was nearing its end, and Veronica decided to join him and head back to Theresa's. She felt it was time to return to base and work out her next mission, so the following day, Veronica and Philip boarded the bus together. It made a nice change to have company en route Veronica thought, it made the 16 hour trip a lot less boring.

CHAPTER 55

Returning Home from Mexico,
23rd December 1998

Veronica had experienced an amazing time in Mexico, she felt she had a new sense of identity.

Veronica was a changed young woman, the essence of her personality remained the same but she was a lot more confidant and sure of herself. Veronica had seen how native Mexicans lived, and literally walked in their shoes when staying with Theresa, Julio and his family.

Although very clued up regarding the drugs culture in London, Veronica was very naive regarding the new culture she had found in Mexico. The way of life there was completely different, in many ways more simple yet in others, much more complex.

The Mexican people didn't have all of the typical luxuries that British people took for granted.

Wages for instance were a world apart. Veronica could live quite comfortably within her money, but soon learned to drop her standards so that her money could stretch further.

She had visited near enough every Mayan site and many of the Aztec sites too. She had crossed the border via river into Guatemala and travelled through the Peten Rainforest, visiting the famous ruins at Tikal, sharing her breakfast at the peak of these ancient ruins with wild raccoons.

She had driven by bus through Belize and back to Mexico with only an Austrian back packer she had met along the way, for company. She had run from one hurricane on the pacific coast only to end up stuck on the Yucatan coast of Playa del Carmen as hurricane Mitch was headed her way. Stuck there for two weeks due to flooded roads, Veronica had at times been very frightened and lonely. She had been on rowing boats through mangrove fringed rivers, had swum in the notoriously rough surfer's paradise, Zipolite beach of death; visited the picturesque ruins at Tulum and suffered food poisoning alone in a cabana in Escondido.

These experiences were both beautiful and enduring, and Veronica would not have changed any aspect of them. In fact they had shaped her into a more confident, happy person, who believed that whatever she put her mind to, with determination, she could overcome and achieve. Veronica felt ready to return home to the UK.

She was determined to continue her journey, her exploration of life, and make her own way in the world. For the first time ever, she wasn't afraid of what the future had in store because it was all part of the journey; and Veronica had finally realised this. Determined to get her own place to live on her return, Veronica was ready. She had missed her family, her mum, dad and sisters very much and couldn't wait for their reunion, but Veronica also felt apprehensive.

She wondered what kind of reception she would encounter on her return, as her dad had not been a bit pleased with her going off at a time when he wanted her to commit to him and his plan for the final trip on yacht Nova. Veronica knew she had to break away from it, she was getting too dragged down by it all and wanted to distance herself from it. She was 24 years of age and had felt at times that she had put her plans on hold to support her parents. Now it was time for her to find her own way, and Veronica felt excited to be going home.

CHAPTER 56

Back in the UK

After a long flight, Veronica was feeling excited about seeing her dad at the airport.

She had visions of running into his arms and hugging him tight. She loved her dad despite his lifestyle, and she had missed him. She collected her luggage and walked through to the departure lounge where she surveyed the area looking for her dad, but couldn't see him anywhere. She waited for around fifteen minutes, but still there was no sign of him. Veronica was sure he would be there, so continued to wait sitting on her bag. After what seemed like ages there was still no sign of him, so she found a pay phone and called home. Veronica's mum answered, "Hi Babe, it's lovely to hear your voice," she said.

Veronica asked her mum if her dad was on his way to pick her up. Her mum told her they'd asked Dave to pick her up as he lived near the airport, and he wanted to come and score, which would save her dad the journey. Veronica's heart sank. Paula gave Veronica Dave's mobile number to find out where he was, but as she said goodbye to her mum, she heard Dave's voice calling her from behind.

Veronica turned to see him. Dave was looking completely out of his head, Veronica was crying inside, how disappointing to be met by Dave, who was high on heroin. This wasn't what Veronica had been expecting. Dave was chatting away about the traffic he'd been stuck in to get to the airport but Veronica wasn't listening. Then Dave started going on about his work and all of his problems, this was typical of him. Whenever he was high he had a tendency to babble on, but all Veronica wanted was some peace and quiet after her long journey. She had barely slept on the flight and was exhausted.

They got into Dave's car, he had a Ford Probe. Dave had bought it with the intention of pulling the young ladies. Veronica thought it was a bad attempt at a penis extension.

Dave had an eye for younger women, his ex-wife Anita had been several years younger. She met Dave as a naive young woman and ended up joining him with drug abuse and addiction. Eventually after years of mental and physical bullying, she left him. Dave had been heartbroken for a few years, before meeting another woman who was much younger by fifteen years or so. She wasn't a pushover however and didn't fall into the trap of drug abuse. She left Dave after two years. Single again, Dave was always on the lookout. He had a smarmy way about him and often said things to Veronica that were way out of line for a friend of her father.

Years before, when Veronica was about fourteen, she was practicing her dancing with her best mate in the lounge at home. Dave had walked into the lounge when the girls were in a crab position and spurted, "I wish my missus could get into that position." Dave had been put in his place many a time by Phil for this, but he would soon forget the boundaries. Dave would say to Veronica, "When are you going to accept that you were meant for me and marry me?"

Veronica found his remarks grotesque and would reply, "As if I would marry someone old enough to be my dad, and an addict at that!" Now here she was after her expedition around Central America, sitting in Dave's Ford Probe.

Veronica drowned him out and thought of all the wonderful things she had seen and done.

As they got down the motorway Dave said, "I'm just gonna stop at mine for an hour as I'm waiting for someone to drop me some money as they want me to score some gear for them." Veronica couldn't believe it, what a homecoming! She sat in Dave's kitchen bored and tired, whilst Dave went on and on about himself and some young woman he'd met. Veronica wasn't interested and just wanted to get home. In the end, nearly three hours passed before Dave's friend showed up and they were on their way to Veronica's. Dave had spent ages gouching out and drooling on himself. Veronica was used to seeing him like this, but didn't enjoy being stuck in Hayes where he lived. Unfortunately she had no choice but to accept a lift, because she had no English money on her to get a train,

When they finally headed back on to the motorway, it was dark. Dave was still semi-gouching at the steering wheel and Veronica became worried.

"Dave watch out!" she yelled, as he was swerving from one lane to the next. Cars were beeping their horns at him and yelling abuse as they overtook. Dave apologised.

"You need to slow down and keep your eyes open Dave, or you can pull over and let me drive," Veronica said.

Dave laughed in his slurred, semi-conscious state. "You can't drive this," he replied. "Well I would drive it far better than you in the state you're in," Veronica retorted. The journey seemed to go on forever, Veronica grabbed the steering wheel a couple of times but somehow they arrived safely. Veronica couldn't wait to get out of the car; she rang the doorbell and her sister Ella answered with a big cuddle.

"Wow!" said Ella, "You don't look like Veronica anymore, you are so brown and your hair is blonde!" Veronica laughed and hugged Ella tight.

Paulette was standing behind Ella waiting for her turn; Veronica grabbed her close and hugged her tight. "I've missed you so much you two," Veronica said, "How have you been?"

Just then Paula came out of the kitchen with a big smile on her face and rushed over to Veronica for a cuddle. Veronica felt relieved to have them back in her arms; she had missed them so much.

"Where's Dad?" Veronica asked her mum.

"He's upstairs in bed watching telly," she replied. Veronica went upstairs and flew at her dad for a hug.

After catching up and having some tea, Phil told Veronica that as she had been away such a long while, they had decided it wasn't fair to have her room sat empty, so had given it to Ella. "You decided you didn't want to commit to coming with us on the boat as a team and as a family, so now you have to decide what you are going to do. We are selling everything to move on to the boat, so you need to find somewhere to live ASAP. You can sleep in with Paulette, there's a mattress on the floor until you do."

Veronica couldn't believe it, she felt like she wasn't a member of the family anymore. She was being made to pay for choosing to do her own thing.

Ella was using Veronica's chest of drawers and music system that she had bought herself with her wages. Veronica had nowhere to put her belongings and had to live out of her bag. She wanted to cry. What am I going to do now she asked herself? She decided to get up early and go out job hunting. She would call on her friends to catch up and stay out of the way of the family. Then Veronica remembered it was Xmas Eve the next day, so job hunting would have to wait.

Veronica was so deflated by her homecoming and her reception that she turned in for an early night. She had gone from feeling excited to see her family, to being completely dumbfounded by them. As she lay on a mattress on the floor of her twelve year old baby sister's room, Veronica cried herself to sleep. She wondered why her parents had treated her so badly.

It was a shock; she had expected to receive a more welcoming return home. It was as if they couldn't be bothered with her because she had left them to get on with things for the past four months, it was like they had been angry and wanted to make her pay.

Lots of her friends had been travelling; some had gone for over a year. They had younger siblings too yet their parents hadn't given their room up, on the contrary their rooms were ready and waiting for their return. Veronica felt completely shut out, almost like an outsider.

As Xmas came and went, it was evident that Veronica's position within the family had changed.

Her dad quickly reverted to his ways of telling Veronica what she would have to do whilst living under the family roof, but made it clear that she would have to move out soon.

Veronica wanted this more than anything; the freedom to live her life by her own rules was what she was building up to anyway. It was why she had needed to experience a piece of the bigger world, to give her the confidence to let go of the life she had lived with her parents so far.

But the attitude of her parents, especially her dad, was quite disdainful.

"While you fucked off to swan around Mexico living the life of Riley, we've been here working hard to get our plans finalised for moving on to the boat. Don't think that you can swan back in and live here scot-free! You'd better sort somewhere to live and find a job, because we ain't gonna be here for much longer to look after you."

Veronica worried that she might not find a job in time. She started to feel guilty about her trip around Mexico, maybe her dad was right, and maybe she was selfish. Veronica felt very low, it was the worst Xmas and New Year it had ever been.

Her dad reminded her on several occasions to get a job, but the timing was bad. Veronica wished she had stayed in Mexico for the Christmas holiday; she could have spent it in Escondido quite happily, living on a shoe string. But here she was living around her dad's drugs and nitpicking: January couldn't come quickly enough.

CHAPTER 57

Moving Out

The moment the holiday period was over, Veronica was out job hunting.

She made a point of catching up with friends, so she could stay out of the way of her family. Being in the house got her down. It was tough not having her own private space, sharing with her sister was proving difficult, so Veronica stayed away all day.

A few weeks passed before Veronica was called for an interview. The job was working as a postal clerk at the North Middlesex hospital. It wasn't the kind of job that Veronica would have normally applied for, but a job was a job; and as long as she could pay for a room somewhere, she didn't care. Veronica sold herself well at the interview and was offered the position. She was so happy that she went home to tell her parents, they also seemed happy enough that she had got a job. Veronica was really pleased, now she had a reason to get up and go out every day; and she would only have to go home for her evening meal and sleep.

After a couple of weeks working, Veronica was settling into her new role. She sorted bags of mail and delivered it to all departments and wards. It was a laborious job and Veronica knew that she wouldn't be happy there forever, but it was better than having nothing and being dictated to by her dad every day. Money was freedom no matter how small, and Veronica had learnt this a long time ago. With money you had options, it could change your life and it was going to work for Veronica by hook or by crook.

Veronica called a couple of rooms local to the hospital that were up for rent, but they had already gone. She searched the local papers during her breaks, circling potential rooms to view.

A few days later, as she was out on one of her hospital post rounds, Veronica bumped into a guy who was painting on one of the trust board floors. He stood up and moved to the side to allow Veronica to pass by with her trolley full of mail. "There you go darling," he said as she walked past.

"Thank you," Veronica replied. The next day, she saw the painter again. This time, he saw her coming from another building and stood for ages holding a door open for her. Veronica went red. She thought it was funny that this guy was holding a door open across a street for her!

This was more than a gentleman; he had a look in his eye. Veronica knew he was flirting with her but tried to ignore it. There was something about him that was sweet, but he was a thick set stocky guy and looked very muscly. This wasn't the type of guy that Veronica went for, so she tried to not give eye contact and continue with her business. The painter wasn't letting Veronica get away that easily though and followed her on her rounds asking questions. Veronica blushed as he asked her out for a date.

"I don't even know you," she replied.

"Well come out and get to know me," he said.

"No," Veronica replied, "I am not looking for a relationship at the moment."

"Why not, are you already in one?" the painter asked. "Kind of," Veronica said, but she was lying. She had been seeing a young man before she travelled to Mexico, but it was nothing serious and she hadn't been back in touch since her return.

"My name is Rae," the painter replied. "Have a think about it and let me know."

Veronica blushed again. She started to feel slightly attracted to him but she couldn't figure out why, he was a good-looking man but he just wasn't the type she had gone for in the past. He was older than she was, but she wasn't sure how much older exactly. He had a look about him that told Veronica there was more to him than first impressions could tell, but Veronica couldn't put her finger on it.

Over the following few weeks, Rae persisted in asking Veronica out until she gave in and went for a drink. She knew he had been married and had gone through a messy divorce after his ex-wife had cheated on him and taken his two children away. He had been fighting a custody battle and had won a joint custody order for his children. He was about to give back to his ex-wife the marital home, a council property the couple had shared for nearly ten years, based on the agreement that she would give him joint custody of the children. Rae didn't care about the home or the contents he had worked so hard to pay for over the years. All he wanted was to have his children as much as possible, and he was prepared to walk away from everything and start again. Veronica was blown away by this man. How many fathers would go through all of this and fight so hard for their children? She realised what a special man he was. They went on a few dates and Veronica very quickly fell for him; before she knew it, she was all gooey eyed and on cloud nine. So was Rae, he hadn't felt this way for a very long time, in fact he had never been so happy and the couple quickly decided to make a home together.

Rae introduced Veronica to his son and daughter, they all got on amazingly well, which annoyed his ex-wife, but they didn't let it stop them. Veronica's parents were not amused by the situation either, they worried that Veronica was rushing into a relationship too fast and getting involved with someone who had just got divorced with two children. It wasn't what they had imagined for her. Her dad told her, "You will never come first, as his children will always come before you, you know that don't you?"

But Veronica would have thought less of Rae if he didn't put his children first. In fact what her dad didn't realise is that this was one of the qualities that attracted her to him. She could see what a devoted parent he was and how loving and protective he was of his children. This was the kind of man that she would eventually want to have a family with, not some guy that didn't want to stick around or make sacrifices for a family life. Veronica felt safe in Rae's arms and felt she could sleep without fear of the police charging through the door and raiding her home.

Veronica stayed most nights with Rae for a few months, but when she did spend time at her parents' home, her dad was displeased with her. He said that she was treating the place like a hotel, dropping off her washing and picking up clean clothes before haring back off. Veronica felt like she couldn't win with her dad. What did he want? He told her to hurry up and find a place and move out, but then when she did, he didn't like it.

Veronica had been giving her mum £50 per week from her wages, even though she was staying with Rae and eating with him every night. In the end Rae asked, "Why are you giving them £50 out of your wages?" and suggested, "You can do your washing here; if we are going to live together you may as well start now."

With that, Veronica told her parents she needed every penny to contribute to living with Rae, he was looking for a rented flat but didn't have the deposit. Veronica had £2000 saved which her Nan had left her two years before in her will, so she decided to use it for their deposit on a fully furnished flat. They spent a couple of months buying cutlery, bedding and a few electronic essentials. Veronica was very excited, this was going to be her first home; and her first home with Rae and his two children who would be living with them half of the week. There were a lot of things to consider, but they were so happy and content together, it felt just right.

As the moving date drew near, Veronica went back to her parents' house to gather her belongings. She needed her pine chest of drawers and stereo that she had bought with money earned from a previous job, but because her sister Ella had been using them since moving into Veronica's room while she was in Mexico, Ella wasn't happy to give them back.

Veronica had told her mum weeks in advance that she would need them, but on the day she called to collect them, they weren't prepared. Veronica's mum got angry with her as Ella wanted to keep hold of them for longer. But Veronica had nowhere to put her clothes, she had been living out of bags since coming home from Mexico, so she put her foot down and told her mum that she was taking them. Her mum called her a cunt.

Rae stood with his mouth open in disbelief. He helped Veronica take the chest downstairs and out of the house into his car. When he got to the car he told Veronica, "I'm going to wait here while you get the last bits. I can't go back in there, I'm so angry and disgusted with the way your mum just treated you. How can she call her daughter a cunt?" he asked. "You don't talk to your children that way, even when they're adult, you will be better off out of there."

Veronica told him she was used to being called names like that, it was thrown around frequently, but Rae wasn't used to it and he refused to ever accept it as normal behaviour. Veronica was disappointed as she had wanted to leave on good terms, but sadly it wasn't to be.

CHAPTER 58

Becoming a Mother

After being together for three and a half years, Veronica and Rae decided to plan a family of their own. Veronica was 29 and feeling ready to settle down and have a baby.

Her sister Ella had just had a daughter, Helen, at the age of 19 with a lad of 18 years. The couple had been together 3 months when Ella became pregnant but by the time Helen came along, there were signs of strain in the young couples' relationship.

Ella, as young as she was, adapted to motherhood well. Veronica was really proud of her sister and elated at the arrival of baby Helen. She was beautiful and angelic looking, which made her proud Aunty Veronica feel doubly broody.

Veronica also wanted to get married, she had been engaged for two and a half years but Rae wanted to have their wedding abroad. He felt uncomfortable with Veronica's family being there because they never showed any interest in them or in his children, and it was obvious to Rae that they did not accept him. Veronica however still felt a sense of loyalty and loved her parents despite their behaviour, which only confused her. She told Rae that she wanted to get married at home in England so that her parents and her sisters could be there. Veronica was old fashioned at heart and didn't feel comfortable with the idea of running off to another country to tie the knot, with only Rae's two children at the ceremony.

Soon after deciding to start a family, Veronica became pregnant; Rae and the children were over the moon with excitement. This happy event also caused them to rethink the plans for their wedding. They had been saving to go abroad, but now that Veronica was pregnant, she would be too far gone to travel by the time they had enough money; so Rae agreed to have a simple registry office ceremony at home, followed by a short honeymoon abroad.

They set to work on their plans, Rae worked extra late to pay for the wedding, whilst Veronica also worked to pay for the honeymoon. Veronica was relieved that her family would be there to share her special day, and before long the couple were in a registry office exchanging their vows.

It was a very emotional day for them, it meant so much to Rae that he was tearful as he said his vows; he had wanted this day for four years. Veronica too was crying with joy, it was the happiest day of her life. Rae had treated her like a princess, showing his love and devotion to her from the moment they met. Veronica felt like the luckiest woman alive.

Veronica's dad sat in the front row beside her as she waited to be called up by the registrar. Phil leant across to Veronica and said in her ear, "Take your last breath as a Baker."

Veronica looked at Rae who was sat at her other side. He too had heard what her dad had said.

Veronica was already emotional and nervous, but her dad's words had made her feel even more anxious. She wondered what had motivated him to say this, but there wasn't time to take it all in as she and Rae were called to take their vows.

Rae's voice broke with emotion as he said his vows, which set Veronica off too.

Many of the family, including Veronica's mum and sisters, began to cry at the sight of the couple becoming emotional as they took their vows. It was evident that they meant every word of them and their love was plain to see.

After the ceremony they held their reception in a 'Harvester' where everyone had a 3 course lunch and drinks. The couple hadn't spent too much money on a lavish reception as they had wanted to have a honeymoon, but invited everyone back to their home for drinks.

It was a cold February day and they hadn't had many photos taken with the family after the wedding, so they arranged to have some more done in their garden.

Veronica's parents went home first, insisting they would return within the hour. But they didn't return until four or five hours later. By this time it was nearly dark outside and the newly-weds only managed to get two photos with their family.

Rae's parents had asked Veronica what had happened to her parents and why they had left so soon. Veronica was embarrassed and made excuses up for her mum and dad, but it was obvious that Rae's mum was disappointed by their absence. When they finally returned, it was evident that they had taken something. Veronica had known in her heart why her parents had done a disappearing act. They had done this her whole life, why would they stop now?

It didn't spoil Rae and Veronica's day however, and it turned out to be a wonderful day.

Veronica was proud to become Mrs Cook and loved her new name. Their honeymoon was an amazing experience, they had decided there was no place better than the Maldives and ended up on a lavish little island where they were made to feel like a King and Queen!

They were both blown away by the wonder of the clear turquoise sea and white sand, they spent every day snorkelling and exploring the underwater life. Certain fish seemed to like Veronica and even followed her! She wondered if she gave off some kind of signal because of her pregnancy as the fish swam in between her legs and got exceptionally close, which didn't seem to happen to Rae or anyone else. They didn't want to come home from their paradise island, but they had their future to plan and Jade and Charlie to come home to.

Over the next month, Veronica's mum became quite ill. She suffered severe pains in her lower right abdomen which became so bad that she was taken to the local hospital.

Paula was kept in for a couple of weeks as the doctors did tests to try to find out what was wrong. Veronica worked in the pathology department at the hospital her mum was staying in, so when it was her lunch hour she went straight up to the ward to visit her mum.

Veronica was really worried about her, Paula had suffered with constipation for years, something which was part and parcel of taking drugs, but could this cause more serious problems Veronica wondered? Years of prolonged constipation couldn't be good, she thought.

Paula looked thin and pale, Veronica asked her mum if the doctors were aware of her habit but she had told them nothing and didn't want them to know.

Veronica wondered how that could be possible, but unless they tested her for drugs, then how would they know? Paula was relying on Phil to bring her heroin. She would go to the patients' toilets and snort it up her nose, as smoking it was not an option in her new environment.

Veronica wondered how her mum would ever get better. How could she if she continued taking the drugs? But there was no point in going over this with her, it was all too obvious; she was stuck in a rut that she couldn't get out of.

While Paula was in the hospital, Ella had split with Helen's dad and was sleeping on the lounge floor on a mattress with Helen, at her mum's flat down the road. Phil was working full time as a plumber, so Ella was seeing to the household chores and looking after her dad and her 16 year old sister Paulette, whilst Paula was in hospital. Paulette had come down with a high temperature and flu like symptoms; within a few days it was evident it wasn't flu though.

Helen had also been unwell and unsettled, and they woke up one day to find her covered from head to toe in spots; she had chicken pox. Within a day Paulette was covered in spots as well and suffering terribly with fever.

Veronica had been in contact with them all; and worried about immunity for her unborn child.

She was sent to A & E for a blood test which revealed that Veronica had no immunity to chicken pox so she was given a vaccine injection in her buttocks. Luckily Veronica didn't become ill with it, but had to keep her distance from her sisters.

The doctors put Paula's illness down to an infection, but couldn't conclude anything in particular, so after a long course of antibiotics and drips, Paula was sent home.

Over the next few months, Veronica's pregnancy became difficult and she put on a lot of weight.

She had been skinny and underweight her whole life, weighing just 7.5 stone, which for a 5ft 6 inch lady was considered light, even though she had always eaten well most of the time.

Now she was 32 weeks pregnant and weighed nearly 12 stone. Her mum was worried about her because she had a lot of swelling everywhere. Her dad had said, "I can't believe how fat you are," which really upset Veronica and made her snap.

"I'm pregnant Dad not fat."

But Phil had never seen Veronica like this, in fact she didn't realise herself how big she'd become. People she knew at work would walk past her in the street not recognising her.

Eventually at 34 weeks Veronica had her usual check with the midwife where her blood pressure was checked and found to be sky high. She was told to go straight to A and E, where after hours of waiting she was put on the maternity ward after being diagnosed with pre-eclampsia.

Veronica was kept in hospital for 4 days whilst she was given medication and had to be kept under close observation. She had become easily agitated and stressed out over nothing, but had just put it down to being fed up and big. Veronica struggled to breathe as the baby was already creating pressure on her diaphragm, but she had such a lot of water retention around her body that even her head and face were swollen. The doctors told Veronica to take it easy, but warned that her pregnancy would be induced at some point because of the pre-eclampsia. Two and a half weeks later, she was sent back into hospital and induced, giving birth to a baby boy weighing 6lb 3oz.

The overwhelming feeling of protectiveness that washed over her when she held her son would change her forever. Her job now was to protect her son Ashley and to love and nurture him. She felt like the only woman in the world who had ever had a child! She felt so proud and special for succeeding in giving birth to her beautiful boy, and no one would ever come between them or the love that she had for her child. This would be the beginning of a whole new Veronica, in so many ways it was a positive thing. After all, she had only ever wanted a normal life with love and security and a family of her own. Now that she had that, something inside her began to question things. Her love for her child was so strong and immense, that on the flip side, it brought up issues that had until now remained hidden within her subconscious. Veronica started questioning all of the things that she had experienced as a child, that had made her feel vulnerable. She would never allow her son to feel that way, not as long as she had a breath in her body, but in contrast, she questioned her own parents' love for her.

CHAPTER 59

Uprooting and Leaving London

Veronica soon experienced the highs and lows of parenting, and Rae was reminded of how demanding it was having a baby. Veronica didn't have her mother to lean on as she was spending lots of time with Ella and Helen, who was 15 months old when Ashley was born. Ella had always stuck to her mum like glue and needed her support. Though Veronica was much older than Ella and more settled in life, there were times when she too could have done with her mother's support. Ashley cried a lot in the early months, he was breast fed, but as Veronica couldn't express her milk, she felt under a lot of pressure because Ashley never seemed to be content and wanted to be fed what seemed like every hour. Veronica was exhausted and so too was Rae.

They went through a difficult patch, snapping at each other and temporarily losing their closeness and understanding. Veronica felt vulnerable at times because she was no longer free to just walk away when the going got rough; she had a child to consider and also the wellbeing of her step children. Rae worked hard as a self-employed builder. He had spent the last few years building up his reputation as a rapid response engineer who could put his hands to most tasks.

The companies he worked for threw as much work his way as he could handle. He often worked 16 hour shifts with a long drive on top. Veronica would get upset that he had barely slept some weeks, but he was determined to get a better life for his family.

Veronica respected this about her husband and wanted the same things in life, but she wanted a happy medium between work and quality time. It wasn't unusual for Rae to be called out on a job whilst they were all in a cinema, so he'd have to leave Veronica with Jade and Charlie to watch the rest of the film without him.

As the years went by though, Rae's hard work would eventually pay off. He was offered the chance to work for a large supermarket chain, carrying out maintenance repairs to the stores, which meant employing people and setting up a company. Rae asked Veronica if she would help him do it. He needed her support as she had always looked after the household finances and was competent with handling business letters, invoicing and such like. They would have to get into some debt before they got paid, but it was a risk worth taking so they grabbed the opportunity with both hands.

At the same time, the couple had considered moving out of London. They had always talked about this but had no idea where, until Veronica's best friend from school moved to Kent and invited Veronica, Rae and the kids down for the day. Veronica loved it and wondered if it would be possible to get on the property ladder, as the houses were a lot cheaper in Kent than they were in London. They knew that they would have a better quality of life living away from the constant hustle and bustle of the city.

A lot of Rae's work was based in Kent, so it was an easy decision to make. Veronica's dad wasn't too pleased about the move though. He had never seen eye to eye with Rae and felt as though he was trying to take Veronica away from her family and everything she knew.

"How are you gonna feel when Rae is out for 16 hours a day and you are in Kent alone with Ashley, with no one to turn to?" he asked Veronica.

But Veronica had been alone in London even with her parents just down the road. She had become very close to Ella though, spending most days with her and Helen. If there was one thing Veronica would really miss, it was them, but she vowed to drive to London regularly every fortnight to spend the weekend with her family.

Her dad sniggered, "The novelty will soon wear off and we won't see you for dust." This upset Veronica as she had always been very committed to her family, but she was at a time in her life where she had to make decisions not just for her future but for her son.

Rae's daughter Jade was 15 years old and living with her mum full time. Living with two sets of rules had become difficult for Jade and so she decided to stay with her mum.

His son Charlie on the other hand, didn't like the school he went to and was particularly close to his dad. At 12 years of age, he decided he wanted to live full time with him and Veronica.

It didn't take long to find a suitable home and within a few months, they were moved in.

It was a massive life change, but one that instantly improved their lives. Veronica had always appreciated being in the countryside and being by the sea. They were close to many seaside towns, some only 20 minutes' drive away, so Veronica settled happily into her new life and wasn't missing London at all. She made her fortnightly journey to London as promised and stayed with Ella all weekend.

It was lovely, as they had lots to catch up on and the children were equally happy to see each other. Veronica went out of her way to cheer Ella up and get her out of the house for a spot of shopping, or a day out with the children. During half term, she would collect Ella and Helen and bring them back to Kent; she wanted to give her sister and niece a kind of holiday. Veronica would take them to the beach and treat the kids to seaside rides and ice cream.

Ella suffered with depression, primarily due to ending up on her own with Helen and being skint. Veronica knew this so she made it her mission to lighten her sister's mood.

As the months passed, Rae and Veronica's business blossomed and the money came rolling in.

Veronica was quickly able to pay off their debts and improve family life. She had always been generous with her family, even before she had a bit of money, but now she could actually help make a difference and this made Veronica happy.

Veronica wanted to go abroad for a holiday, but Rae was working full on and overseeing operatives who were now working on behalf of the couple's company. Rae felt it wasn't the time to have a break, but insisted instead that Veronica should treat her sister and Helen to a week away in Greece. Veronica was over the moon, as she loved spending time with her sister and felt a strong sense of responsibility for her and Helen. She couldn't wait to call Ella and give her the good news. Within weeks the girls were away and enjoying their time.

Veronica felt a sense of pride at being able to treat her sister and niece, but also felt bad for her youngest sister Paulette, who wasn't the least bit interested in joining her sisters with 'two young whingeing kids' as she put it. Veronica would later pay for Paulette to go on holiday to Spain with her boyfriend, instead.

It felt liberating to have enough money to be able to put a smile on her family members' faces, and Veronica would go on to lavish her sisters and parents with expensive gifts.

Her mum had unfortunately had her car stolen from outside her flat in Tottenham. The car had already been scratched and broken into on numerous occasions by local thugs, which made Veronica feel terrible. Her mum lived in a rundown, stinking tower block on the edge of Tottenham, where street crime and stabbings were a daily occurrence. Paula had also been attacked by an Afro-Caribbean man, who mugged her and ripped a gold belcher from her neck. She'd had it for years, it had a locket full of Phil's mum's hair; and she had died ten years earlier.

Veronica wanted nothing more than to get her parents out of London, but they showed no interest. At least, she could help by treating her mum to another car.

Veronica took a dividend out of the company with Rae's consent and looked around for a second-hand Ford Escort for her mum. This was the car she wanted and in no time Veronica and Rae found a nice clean, tidy one, and Veronica arranged for her mum to come by train to pick it up. Paula was speechless; she couldn't believe it and was almost unbelieving of what was happening. Veronica felt a little uncomfortable with this as she didn't want any gratification; she only wanted to cheer her mum up after the ordeal of having her car stolen.

She often asked her mum to complain about the attack to the council, as it had made her really depressed and scared to leave the flats once it was dark outside. Veronica really wished she was rich enough to buy her parents a nice little place in the country.

Phil had been self-employed working for a few companies during the years Veronica and Rae had been together. When Paula was waiting to be re-housed by the council, Phil was working in a boatyard in Portsmouth carrying out repairs on boats and rigging. He liked the work but there wasn't enough of it coming in to earn a good living, so Rae put in a word for him with his employer; and Phil got a full-time job as a plumber. This job would see Phil through for some years, all the while he was living with Paula in a bedsit and then in her flat in Tottenham.

Rae and Veronica started to improve their lifestyle with the everyday comforts and holidays that they had saved for, but Veronica's parents never seemed to be any better off. They were always complaining of being broke instead.

This annoyed and frustrated Veronica no end, as she and Rae worked all the hours to pay for the things they had, yet her parents never had anything new. They barely shopped for new clothes and spent no money on their flat, apart from buying the odd TV.

Phil was earning the same as Rae; and Paula was claiming housing benefits and income support, so they should have been financially better off, yet they weren't. Veronica knew deep down that it was the drugs, which was why they had nothing. All their income went on the drugs.

Veronica had found that difficult to accept all her life, but somehow seemed to struggle more with the reality of her parents' circumstances since leaving their environment and finding her own way. It was as if by not being faced with the drugs day in and day out, Veronica had blissfully forgotten that aspect of life. Her parents would go on about their van and car being broken into, every other week, it seemed. Veronica just thought they were going through a very unlucky patch, but Rae did not always believe the stories and tried to tell Veronica it was lies, but she would have none of it. Her parents wouldn't lie to her like that, she thought!

So as the business became more profitable and the couple earned more, Veronica lavished more on her family, naïvely believing that it would produce small miracles that would help to change her parents' life for the better. Veronica was in a dream world, almost identical to the one she had created whilst living around the drugs. But every now and then she would get a wake-up call, a slap in the face even, metaphorically speaking.

Veronica's dad had a split personality. She knew this only too well, but every now and then he would verbally pick on her out of the blue, with no warning. He would get a bee in his bonnet and put Veronica down. It used to upset her so much, as all she wanted was for her dad to love her and be nice to her.

CHAPTER 60

Devastating News, 2006

Veronica and Rae had been living in Kent for 4 months, the new business was taking off and Veronica had booked the holiday to take her sister Ella and the kids to Greece.

Veronica called her mum on the telephone one early July morning to see how she was. Veronica was very excited to be taking her sister and Helen away and shared this excitement with her mum.

"I've not been feeling very well Veronica."

"What's wrong Mum, do you have a bug or something?" Veronica asked, assuming it was something simple.

"No, it's not a bug," Paula replied. "If I tell you this, you must promise not to tell Ella or Paulette, I don't want to worry Ella as she is so looking forward to this holiday and I don't want to upset her."

Veronica's stomach sank; she knew at this point it was something serious. "Mum you are scaring me, what's wrong?" she asked.

Paula replied, "I had some blood tests through the clinic I get my methadone from. The tests came back positive for Hepatitis C. It's what Libby died from."

Veronica burst into tears, this could not be happening, this couldn't be true, not her little mum.

After all these years of agonising and praying for a happy ending, it couldn't be so. "Mum, it can't be, they got it wrong. Why Mum, what's going to happen?"

"I have to go on a waiting list for treatment. I have to have some tests to see if my liver is damaged and if so, how damaged it is. Do you remember when I ended up in hospital when you were heavily pregnant with Ashley?'' she continued, "well I think it was all down to my liver. I never told the doctors that I was an addict so they never tested for it as they didn't suspect. As the time went by, I just had a feeling. I had shared needles with Libby and Bob and all those people that ended up with hepatitis C, it was inevitable Vron, but I just lived in denial and hoped that I had somehow escaped it."

Veronica could feel her heart beating out of her chest, this was her worst nightmare, this was the thing she feared her whole life. She pinched herself as if to clarify that it wasn't a bad dream. Veronica's world collapsed there and then and she could barely breathe before the tears came flooding. "Mum can they cure it?" Veronica asked desperately.

"No babe, there is no cure for it, it is known as the silent killer because you can have it for years without any symptoms; and by the time the symptoms show, the liver is usually already sclerotic. There is a treatment called interferon which works in a similar way to cancer drugs. It's not a nice drug apparently but I will have to have it. It has been known to eradicate some strains of the Hep C virus, but it depends what strain I have and I need further tests to find out," Paula explained.

"Oh my God Mum, I can't believe this!" Veronica exclaimed.

"Also Veronica, there is a possibility that others have become infected by me. The virus can live in dried blood for up to three months, so if I bled shaving and dried myself on a towel and you came along and used that towel, or if I brushed my teeth and my gums bled and you used that brush after me and had an open wound or small cut, you could be infected by the virus, so you must get yourself tested. I am so sorry to tell you this Veronica and I feel so ashamed of myself, I wish I could turn back the clock. I would never live with myself if I infected my babies, I just couldn't cope with that. I pray to God that you girls are all okay, so please get yourself checked as soon as possible."

Veronica was dumbfounded, suddenly she thought of her son Ashley. If she had the virus then surely that meant that Ashley and Rae had it. How would she tell Rae?

Veronica felt frightened, this must be how her mum felt. "Mum, it will be alright, how could I have it? They tested me for everything when I was pregnant, even HIV, surely they would have tested for that?"

"I don't know honey, but you must do it just in case. I will not rest until I know my babies are okay. I don't give a shit about me, I got what I deserved, that's what happens when you dice with life, but you kids don't deserve this. Please keep it to yourself until you get back from Greece, Ella has had a terrible few years and I just want her to have a good time, I don't want to spoil her holiday."

Veronica agreed, the last thing she wanted was to upset her sister, but how was Ella going to take the news when they returned? Veronica wondered. What about Paulette, she was only 20 and was also in a sexual relationship. What if Paula had become infected before having the girls? What if they had the virus also?

All these questions were hard to bear, Veronica was in shock. All day she burst into tears and went into deep thought about the years gone by and the days when she was six years old and her parents were in the kitchen having a fix. It had come back to haunt her, there would never be any way of escaping her parents' past and their bad choices.

Veronica thought about how she was going to break the news to Rae and how he might take it.

Well, surely her dad would have to accept that Rae needed to know the truth behind Veronica's upbringing? Veronica had never let on to her parents that she had spilled the beans to Rae, but then again she hadn't denied his knowledge either, only ever giving vague answers to their questions when they asked what he knew. Veronica had always felt disloyal to them for opening up to Rae, but on the other hand she knew it was only fair and part of being true to herself and her husband. After all, she had never asked for the circumstance she had found herself in growing up, yet she seemed to have to pay the emotional and mental price. It was a constant struggle to feel accepted in society for her, to feel like 'a normal person'. She hadn't lived a normal life, but then again what was 'normal' anyway?

Rae returned home from work, Veronica had spent all afternoon crying which was obvious to Rae when he saw her swollen face. Ashley was playing with his Bob the Builder toys. Veronica had kept close to her son, constantly cuddling him for comfort. "What's wrong babe?" Rae asked.

"I don't know how to tell you this but my mum found out she has Hep C, it's a deadly virus that is contracted through sharing dirty needles amongst users. They told Mum she has probably had it for twenty five years or more and there is treatment but no cure. Also, there is a possibility that she could have infected others. I need to be tested babe."

Rae looked shocked; he couldn't believe what he was hearing. Veronica also felt responsible to him and their son. "Well you'd better ring the doctor now and get an emergency appointment," he said.

Veronica was shaking all over; she had adrenaline rushing through her which made her feel physically sick.

"Surely they would have tested for it when you were pregnant Vron, I'm sure you are fine babe, try not to panic," Rae said reassuringly.

"What about my little mum though?" Veronica asked, "She isn't fine, this could eventually kill her, this is what her lovely friend Libby died of."

"I know babe, it's horrible and I'm sorry for your mum but this is what happens when you mess about dicing with your life. Your parents knew what they were doing and it didn't stop them, what about you girls now? What if you have it? This isn't your fault yet you could be paying the price, and even if you are all clear, you will still pay the price because now you will have to see your mum suffer."

Veronica cried like a baby and fell into Rae's arms. Ashley came over to cuddle his mum, he was just 3 years old, "Mummy you okay? Don't cry Mummy," he said. Veronica wiped her tears and kissed Ashley.

"I'm sorry baby," she said, "Mummy is just a little upset, I will be okay honey."

Rae told her she had to be strong for her son and not worry. "It's pointless to worry until you know Vron, I'm sure you are all clear anyway, you haven't got it. But what I will say is how selfish of your parents to put you through this."

Veronica didn't want to hear this, she felt awful about her mum. To Veronica, her mum was just as innocent in all this, she had been dragged into the drugs by her dad all those years ago, he led her down this path and yet it would be her who paid the final price. What if her dad had the virus too? What would this mean for her sisters? How would they cope if both parents had it and eventually died from it? Veronica would need to be there to support her sisters.

Veronica had an overwhelming sense of guilt wash over her. How could she look after her sisters now she was all the way in Kent? She would need to do everything possible to maintain regular contact with her siblings and parents.

The following day, Veronica had a blood test at the local hospital, she would have to wait five to ten days for the result and the time was agonising. Veronica kept her promise to her mum and didn't tell Ella, but found it very hard not being able to openly express her feelings with her.

The result eventually came back negative; and Veronica was relieved, more for Rae and her son Ashley than for herself, but she had to call her mum and put her mind at rest. As the suspense had tortured Veronica for over a week, she knew her mum must have been in a worse position, as she had been the one who used the drugs.

"Mum I'm all clear, which means Ashley and Rae are too," Veronica said. "Thank God for that," Paula replied, "That's one worry off my mind, I just pray to God that the girls are clear too, I would never forgive myself if I have infected any of my babies Veronica. Right now I don't even care about myself."

Veronica would feel the same if she were in her mum's shoes but she didn't want her mum to feel this way, "Don't blame yourself Mum, it's not your fault, you were young and naive and got caught up in a bad situation. You didn't set out to hurt anyone, I know that. You are my lovely mum, you've always loved us and protected us the best way you could, don't beat yourself up Mum. You've got to try and get this treatment, and hopefully it will eradicate the virus. We've just got to stay strong Mum."

But inside, Veronica was crying. Inside she knew in her heart that this wasn't going to be a happy ending, but like her mum, she too would live in denial, because denial was bliss.

CHAPTER 61

Hepatitis C

Veronica and Rae worked very hard and their business continued to prosper. As their contract was only a verbal agreement, they made huge efforts to keep their main customer happy. Veronica's dad was becoming tired of the company he had worked for over the last couple of years, as he felt he was being taken advantage of. His hours were constantly long and his overtime was rarely paid properly, so Veronica felt sorry for him and asked Rae if they could give him a position as a maintenance operative, working on behalf of their company. There was a snag however, Phil had been provided with company vans up until this point and didn't have his own. The only way Rae could give him regular work, was if he could provide his own transport, but Phil needed a deposit to buy one on hire purchase. This was something he had never done before and didn't feel at ease about it. One thing was sure though, and that was that Phil's current position at the other company was looking bleaker by the minute.

They had started to lay operatives off; and were asking remaining staff to work for less pay, due to losing some of their contracts. There was no way that Phil could continue like this, it was bad enough that he wasn't getting his wages paid correctly or on time as it was. There was just one more thing Veronica and Rae could do to help, and that was to lend Phil some money for the deposit on a van. She would be able to deduct an agreed amount each month from his pay to reimburse the company. Veronica wished she could just give it to her dad, but it was early days for their business and Veronica wasn't even taking a wage herself. Phil accepted the financial help and was soon working alongside Rae, being sent to various stores to carry out maintenance. Veronica had convinced herself that her parents were no longer using drugs. Paula had been signed to a rehabilitation clinic for around four years. At the beginning, Phil was also signed up to the clinic, but had been struck off twice for repeatedly missing appointments and turning up late. In the end, Paula had made out that her habit was worse than it was, to obtain extra methadone to sustain both her and Phil's habit, unbeknown to the clinic.

Veronica knew that her mum was regularly checked, as she had accepted urine samples during her position as a medical laboratory assistant at the local hospital, from Paula's GP's surgery. This would be the clinic that eventually tested Paula for hepatitis C in 2006 when Veronica's dad first started to work for her and her husband Rae.

Paula had claimed benefits since Veronica moved out in 1999 and as the unemployment department began to crack down on long term benefit claimants, Paula was sent on a 'back to work' course through the Job Centre. She found it difficult at first, getting up early and getting out, but she soon adjusted and really enjoyed getting out of the flat and meeting new people. Paula was offered a position doing voluntary work, helping out at a local centre that took in second hand furniture to be fixed up and shipped out to those in desperate need.

She loved this job and told Veronica excitedly how it had given her a confidence boost. She also went on short courses subsidised by the benefits department, to try and gain new skills to help her get back into paid work. She told Veronica that she wanted nothing more than to have a nice little paid job, so that she could stop claiming. She wanted a little place of her own in the country, which she'd often visualised for herself and Phil in their later years.

She told Veronica that she wished Phil would give up the grand ideas of sailing his yacht around the world and accept that they were not getting any younger or any richer! She just wished he would sell the boat for whatever he could get and put the money towards a nice little place out of London somewhere, where she could spend time in her garden with her grandchildren.

Veronica was proud of her mum for putting in so much effort with the voluntary work and her courses. Paula learnt how to create spreadsheets and use various office computer tools.

"I hope you get a job Mum, I've not seen you smile like this for such a long time," Veronica told her.

Paula had become tired and bored of her lifestyle and the drugs. It did nothing for her anymore and all she wanted was a fresh start. She often confided this to Veronica.

Paula was also proud of her daughter's achievements, she would often tell her, "I love telling people about you and your business with Rae, you've come so far and I'm so proud of you Veronica." This made Veronica gleam from cheek to cheek, there was no better feeling in the world than making her mum happy.

Paula's new-found happiness and independence would however be short lived. Finding out she had hepatitis C certainly brought the reality of her life back down to earth with an almighty bang. Now Paula was on a long waiting list for a six-month course of medication called Interferon. It was an expensive drug to get on the NHS but Paula had no choice other than to wait.

Veronica cried herself to sleep night after night, week after week, worrying about her mother's future health prospects. Veronica knew this was what had killed Libby so unexpectedly all those years ago and wondered if this would happen to her mum. But Rae told her to stay positive saying, "Your mum looks relatively healthy, she's probably got another twenty years or so in her, don't panic Vron, you panic too much." Veronica would eventually shrug it off, agreeing that things would not come to that for her mum.

Phil worked for Rae, but in what seemed like no time at all, little discrepancies were showing up with his paperwork. Phil was charging for materials he had already bought previously on other jobs for other companies and putting it down as van stock. It started with small items like half a dozen screws, or particular plumbing bits and parts for a few pounds here and there, and then the van stock hit the roof with charges of up to £150 some weeks. Veronica did find this uncomfortable, as she knew this would be dead money for her and Rae's company. They couldn't claim VAT back on any of this as there were no receipts provided, but Veronica kept her mouth shut as she couldn't bring herself to question her father. Then it was becoming apparent that Philip was putting down early start times on the company time sheets, but Rae would be on site before Philip arrived. At the end of the week when all the operatives' time sheets were sent in, Rae would tell Veronica that some of Philip's start times were two to three hours out. He would put 7am for his start time, but Rae wouldn't see him arrive until after 9am.

Rae also felt uncomfortable with this knowledge and found it hard to broach the subject with Veronica as she would become very defensive of her father, not wanting to believe that he would try to rip off his own daughter, but in the end it became so blatant and obvious that there was no denying it. The big crunch came when Veronica and Rae took the children away on a family holiday. There were half a dozen operatives working for the couple at this stage, and they were in the final stages of carrying out a store rip out. Veronica had set up payments to go out to the engineers while they were away. She didn't feel entirely happy about this, but then again, how could they expect the guys to work past a month without any payment? By the time the couple came home, the operatives had already been paid. When Rae returned to site the following week, the store's surveyor called Rae for a meeting. She took him into the security office and played him some CCTV footage of the CIS operatives' daily entry into store compared to the paperwork with the operatives' times. Rae could not believe it. Every operative working on that site had lied about start and finish times to get extra pay. The worst culprit of all was Veronica's dad. He tried to excuse himself when questioned by telling Veronica if he had put 7am start, he would only charge until 5pm even though he stayed on site till 7pm to make his time up, but this didn't tally either. Rae didn't believe any of it, but decided to put it down to experience.

Rae and Veronica lost a total of £8,000 on that job, due to the times being fiddled, but Rae was not going to let this happen again. He decided to turn up to site unannounced and wait across the street in his father's car so no one would recognise him.

He often caught a couple of the guys out, but none more than Philip, so Rae decided to lay him off that job. Phil was furious and rang Veronica up demanding an explanation, but Veronica asked her dad to leave her out of it. Phil never respected this and continued to slag Rae off for months, even years to come.

Rae loved Veronica so much and could see she was extremely naive about her dad's behaviour, and was even manipulated by him. Phil would often call Veronica and go on about being her dad, and about Rae having no respect or loyalty to his father in law. Veronica was worn down by her father to the point where she would snap at Rae and take it out on him. Rae stood back and allowed Veronica to shower her parents with gifts, holidays, cars, furniture and money, he knew she desperately loved them and only wanted to help, but Rae had seen Phil's true colours and didn't like him at all. He could see that Phil would have been happy to have split the couple up so that he could continue to control and manipulate Veronica into giving and doing what he wanted.

All the while, Paula had been receiving treatment for her hep C virus. It was draining and very painful for her, she became increasingly tired and would sleep most of the day. This was a typical symptom of hep C anyway, but also a known side effect from the Interferon treatment.

Ella had come a long way over the past few years, ending up with a two-bedroom house in Edmonton, just a ten minute drive from her mum's. Veronica and Rae had helped Ella massively by furnishing her home and helping out with money here and there.

Paula loved nothing more than to spend time at Ella's in her garden with Helen. It was an escape from her flat and the reality of her virus. Ella relied on her mum for support with Helen; and Paula had also come to rely on Ella for support with her virus, accompanying her to hospital visits for appointments. Paula had discovered from tests and CT scans that her liver was already quite sclerotic and her spleen was also inflamed. The virus she had was a particularly aggressive one that was hard to treat. The consultant was worried about the amount of Interferon that Paula could handle, as she was particularly thin and underweight. It was like a catch 22 situation because one of the side effects of hepatitis C was weight loss. They had wanted Paula to gain weight prior to starting her treatment, but it was a losing battle for her as she became increasingly unwell. Two months into her harrowing treatment, Paula visited her GP. She was still using methadone and had to be regularly monitored. On this occasion she saw a different doctor to her usual one, who decided to give Paula the pneumonia vaccine. She thought nothing of it and went home and continued her daily interferon injections, which she had learnt to administer into her abdomen. As the days passed, she became very ill. It started with flu like symptoms and then pains in her chest. Eventually after a couple of weeks, she had become so ill and frail that she ended up in hospital.

Paula had pneumonia and was taken off the interferon drug immediately. It was made clear that if she had continued with Interferon whilst suffering pneumonia, she would have died. Her consultant decided that Paula was too weak and frail to start taking Interferon again and wanted to send her for more tests. She had a biopsy on her liver to determine the damage and various X-rays and scans to view the liver in more detail. Paula was tired and fed up with being prodded about; she hated every minute of it and just wished she could get her treatment. These tests and waiting lists for appointments had gone on for over two years already, but finally she was given her second chance at taking the interferon.

Again the consultant would only have her take a small dose because of her weight. Paula would depend heavily on Ella during the day as she would just sleep it away and couldn't remember a thing. It was increasingly frustrating for Ella, as she couldn't get a conversation out of her mother all day, but Ella understood the reasons behind it and tried to stay positive and supportive to her mum's needs. There were times however where Ella would forget and would end up arguing with her younger sister Paulette, which would erupt into a fight. Paula found this extremely upsetting and stressful. There were times when she would call Veronica to let off steam, and Veronica would be in complete shock at her sister's behaviour. It wasn't uncommon for Ella to lash out at their mother verbally and even physically. On one occasion she had thrown her mum out of her flat over an argument with Paulette. The sisters all had a temper, a temper that if left unchecked could easily erupt into rage. Paula had said that the girls had taken after their dad for this, but Ella's temper was the worst of all. She had been known to literally beat up Helen's dad when they were going through their split.

These were very difficult times for the girls, and for Phil and Paula, having to live with the reality of their choices and the consequences for Paula's health and potential life span.

They often asked the consultant, "What if the treatment doesn't work?" They were told that eventually the liver would stop working, but they could not determine how long that process would take as every patient is different. If the treatment doesn't work, then Paula would eventually need a liver transplant. Paula, Philip and the girls found the reality of this was very hard to accept.

Eventually Paula's six-month treatment came to an end in the summer of 2009. Some blood tests revealed that the virus was undetected, and a positive result was given that interferon had eradicated the hep C virus from Paula's blood stream. Veronica was pregnant with her second child at the time and the news couldn't have been more welcome.

Veronica's business was still doing well, and she had visions of helping her parents get out of London to start a new, healthier life.

CHAPTER 62

Veronica's Breakdown

Veronica and Rae achieved many things during the first four years of running their company. They bought their first home, something they had previously never thought they would accomplish. They travelled to many places around the world, taking their sons with them and being in a comfortable financial position to treat relatives to holidays as well.

They had bought cars they could only ever dream of before, and enjoyed a lavish lifestyle that was a far cry from the days when they had first met at the hospital in North London.

Veronica and Rae had given her dad work on two separate occasions during this time, but not only was his time keeping erratic, one of the surveyors had spotted Phil with a huge spliff in his mouth, as he was walking in the store's car park.

He complained to Rae about it and said it wasn't a great look for the company, operatives sporting spliffs on site and looking like they were on another planet. This shocked Rae immensely, as he took his business seriously. Although he knew that Philip was heavily addicted to marijuana, he never thought he would be so brazen as to walk around on site with it.

Rae rang Phil to discuss some other issues with work but Phil lost his temper and called Rae a cunt. He later called back to apologise, but Rae had had enough. He felt torn because he knew that if he sacked Phil then it would cause a huge row with Veronica, but he had put up with more than enough from someone who blatantly and shamelessly showed no respect for him or for his own daughter.

Unfortunately for Veronica, she still had not faced up to this, but these events would mark a turning point. Rae spoke to Veronica that evening and explained that he'd had enough with her dad taking liberties and being grossly disrespectful. Rae reminded Veronica of all the money they had given her parents over the years, and of the special treatment at work that had almost cost them their livelihood. If it had been any other surveyor that had spotted Phil with the spliff that day, the company would have been given its marching orders.

Veronica was completely disgusted with her dad's behaviour, and of course he denied the whole thing, but how else would the surveyor have known about her dad's addiction? Rae wasn't going to let anything ruin what he and Veronica had worked so hard for, he certainly wasn't going to let her dad do it, so Phil was given no more work; and from that moment on, every time Veronica spoke to her dad on the phone, he would take every opportunity to bring it up and blame Rae and her for his lack of income.

He would stir abuse between other fellow operatives that were still working for Rae, which had a negative impact on his relationships with them, causing more stress. He would constantly call Rae names down the phone to Veronica, making her feel like she had to avoid him wherever possible. Her dad told everyone that Rae had laid him off work on top of Xmas, yet it was really the first week of September!

Veronica and Rae had just moved to a bigger house as they were expecting another child. Rae had gutted the property and refurbished it within six weeks of purchase, whilst still running a busy maintenance company with Veronica. It had cost them an arm and a leg, but they had a beautiful large home at the end of it, by which time Veronica was nearly eight months pregnant. Veronica called her mum to have a chat, but her dad answered the phone. The niceties of conversation quickly gave way to her dad taking the opportunity of abusing Rae once more.

Veronica had had enough, she had put up with this for years. Her dad had even belittled Rae in front of their son Ashley when they were staying with Ella and he came round to see them, this however was the last straw. After everything the couple had been through together, after all of the support Rae had happily given to her parents and sisters, her dad still abused him this way. He called Rae a cunt again down the phone and said it with such disdainfulness it was obvious he despised Rae. How could he, after everything Rae had done for him? He was the father of her son, Ashley, and of their expected daughter, Sienna. He was an amazing father and husband too, how could her dad be so nasty?

Veronica had become impatient, she was heavily pregnant, notoriously moody, and in this state she wasn't scared of anything or anyone for that matter.

"How dare you call my husband a cunt, who do you think you are? What makes you think you have any right to disrespect my husband like that after everything he has done for you over the years, how dare you?" she screamed down the phone.

Philip was shocked by Veronica's sudden retaliation, but as far as she was concerned it was a long time overdue.

"How dare you speak to me like that?" her dad snarled, "You disrespectful bitch, blood obviously isn't thicker than water. You are the most selfish bitch I've ever known, everything is all about Veronica and Veronica's world! We did everything for you growing up, bought you a car, paid for your first holiday abroad and this is how you repay us."

Veronica could not believe what she was hearing, what planet was this man on? Veronica felt her blood boil, at that point in time she didn't care less if she never spoke to this man again.

"You may have bought me my first car and paid for my holiday abroad, but isn't that what you do for your kids? Why the fuck are you throwing it in my face? I would never chuck in Ashley's face all the things I'd given him, that's my duty as a parent to give him all I can in life. And as for selfish, ha! You are the most selfish person I have ever known. You need to take a long hard look in the mirror Dad, you can't even call yourself a dad, I would never put my kids through any of the shit you made us live through, so if anyone is a fucking cunt it's YOU!" And with that, Veronica slammed the phone down; she was shaking from head to toe.

Rae had come downstairs to see if she was okay and Veronica burst into tears. "I'm so sorry Rae for everything I've put you through, I'm so sorry for being so naive and stupid with my dad. I fucking hate him right now and I will never ever let him come between us ever again; and I will never let him get away with speaking ill of you."

Veronica cried on and off all night, it was to be the first part of a huge wake up call, a reality check for her that brought with it, tears, anger, shock, pain and confusion.

CHAPTER 63

Veronica's Breakdown, Part Two

Veronica kept her distance from her dad, only calling her mum on her mobile occasionally.

Paula wasn't happy with Veronica's outburst, it had upset her a lot, but Veronica told her mum it was nothing to do with her and only between her and her father.

Veronica did question both her parents' behaviour throughout her childhood and adolescence, but it was evident that her mum was full of remorse and regret. Paula had often apologised to Veronica for the things she had unfortunately witnessed due to her parents' drug addictions, but Phil had never shown any remorse at all. On the contrary, he had excused his behaviour by saying, "You were not abused or left hungry. You were always loved and had a roof over your head. You could have ended up in care, if we really didn't love you." But this still didn't excuse things in Veronica's view.

This seemed to become more evident in her dad's behaviour as the years passed by. He would often excuse his actions with such comments and he acted as if he had the right to treat his daughters any way he liked. If he woke up one day in a bad mood and started on them verbally or physically, he acted as if it was his right as the father and that he should be respected no matter what. Veronica had seen through this as she grew up and began to dislike her dad for it more and more, but her head and her heart were often at war with each other. The pity she felt for the miserable circumstances they were now living in, clashed with her opinion of her dad's personality. Veronica was beginning to realise that no matter what she did or didn't do, nothing would ever be good enough in her dad's eyes.

She decided to focus on her own life, her husband and her children. The business was at a very busy, stressful time in their lives, and Veronica worked throughout her pregnancy to help maintain their lifestyle.

Veronica did not enjoy much of this pregnancy, suffering with aches and pains throughout.

She had a lot of oedema and felt her blood pressure rocketing as little things seemed to get on top of her. The consultant she was under was meant to be monitoring Veronica closely for pre-eclampsia, as she had suffered this disorder when pregnant with Ashley, but it seemed to go unnoticed. Veronica begged to be induced at 38 weeks as she knew this was considered term and had Ashley induced at 37 weeks. She had struggled to sleep for weeks, the baby seemed to be constantly pressing on her bladder for what seemed like months; and a growth scan at 32 weeks confirmed the baby was already 7lb 3oz. Her pleas fell on deaf ears, and her consultant found no reason to induce Veronica early. Eventually at 41 weeks and 2 days, Veronica woke up to discover that her urine was a bright orange colour and she knew something was wrong.

After tests, it was revealed that Veronica did after all have pre-eclampsia, so was kept in and induced the following morning. To help keep the baby comfortable, Veronica was advised to have an epidural, which would also help to keep Veronica's blood pressure down as well.

The labour was very slow; the baby did not want to come. Eventually after 36 hours, the baby's heart rate was dropping, so the midwife decided to give a higher dose of the drug used to induce labour. Veronica was fed up and wondered why they had taken so long to do this. Now the baby was at risk, her cervix was still only 3cm dilated, Veronica felt frustrated. Finally after receiving more drugs through an intravenous drip, Veronica was fully dilated and baby's head was low down. She was told to push, and within an hour or so, Sienna was born.

When Sienna was finally pushed out, there was a sound like a 'pop' which made Veronica jump, but she just put it down to pushing a big baby. Veronica could not believe how big she was, she did not look like a new born baby at all, but she was beautiful; and Veronica and Rae were mesmerised by her.

The next day, Veronica was allowed to go home with Sienna, but over the following few weeks, Veronica suffered with pains below. She hadn't healed from the stitches, in fact they had come apart and Veronica had a terrible infection. During her midwife check, she was told to go home and practice her pelvic floor exercises, but Veronica had no control whatsoever; and every time she sneezed or coughed, she wet herself. The infection was also not getting any better despite Veronica being given antibiotics. She felt desperate for someone to just make her feel well, she was in a lot of pain and where her stitches had come apart, there was no perineum any more. Rae had a look at her and gasped.

This frightened Veronica because she knew that something wasn't right. She'd not had any problems at all after the birth of Ashley and had healed well. Rae tried to get some answers from the hospital where Veronica had given birth, but they shrugged it off by saying that she could have a procedure called vaginal fashioning at some point in the future. This meant going on a waiting list and going through the process of GP referral etcetera, but Veronica was in agony and couldn't live with the pain. Rae decided to take matters into his own hands and found a Gynaecologist in Harley Street and called them up.

They agreed to see Veronica promptly with a free consultation that week. When Veronica and Rae arrived they were greeted by a nurse who led them to a waiting room and gave them some forms to complete. Moments later, Veronica was called into the doctor's office. There she and Rae were introduced to Professor Dormby (pseudonym). After an examination, Professor Dormby told Veronica she had a prolapsed bladder and bowel due to muscle damage caused by the trauma of giving birth to a large baby.

He said she should never have been left to walk around in that state and that 1 in 3 women are left with similar issues after child birth by the NHS. Veronica also had another issue.

She had torn quite badly and the stitches had fallen apart leaving her with an open wound that was getting infected. Professor Dormby told her she needed plastic surgery called perineoplasty, to rebuild the perineum. This frightened Veronica, but the professor assured her that everything could be fixed; and as the surgery involved laser rather than a scalpel, there was less risk of infection and less scarring.

He told Veronica that her bladder and bowel were protruding into the vagina, and over time she would become incontinent and should expect to have no sexual life because of this. Veronica burst into tears, she knew in her heart all along that things were not right. Rae put his arm around her to comfort her and reassured her that everything would be okay. He asked the professor how much the surgery would cost and was quoted £5,000 for the procedure. He was told that the sooner Veronica had the surgery, the better for her. So Rae put down a deposit for a date, it would be less than two weeks later but Veronica just wanted to heal; and in the state she was in, this was not going to happen.

On the 19th March 2010 Veronica went into the Harley street clinic for the surgery.

She was shaking from head to toe, as the procedure was not well known across the medical industry; and information about it was minimal. Professor Dormby was the only surgeon in Europe to use the laser method for vaginal reconstruction surgery.

Veronica was shown to a changing room where she had to undress and put on a gown and paper knickers, she was asked to sign a consent form and then led into the theatre.

By this time, Veronica was shaking like a leaf. She prayed that she would be okay and that there would be no complications. She was introduced to an anaesthetist who put a line through her hand. She was told to relax and close her eyes and with that, Veronica was out.

When she came to, she was in another room with a couple of other women. The moment she woke, she felt tremendous pain in her vaginal area. Veronica cried loudly asking for help.

The nurse came by and Veronica asked her for pain relief. The nurse told her, she shouldn't feel any pain as she had been given strong pain relief but Veronica told her she was in agony.

She was told to wait ten minutes for the professor to assess her for more pain relief.

When he eventually came round to Veronica's bed, she told him she was still in a lot of pain.

He told her that the only thing that would help would be an injection into the area. Veronica just wanted the pain to go. Professor Dormby called for two nurses to assist him by holding Veronica's arms and legs down as he injected her in the vagina. She screamed at the top of her voice. This was the most personal and horrific experience of her life, but within a few moments, the area was numb. Veronica shut her eyes and fell asleep.

She was woken abruptly by a nurse checking her heart rate and blood pressure; then she was asked to sit up and start moving around. Veronica had a catheter due to the operation; she would need a catheter for 72 hours after surgery. She needed to get her circulation moving and to get ready to be discharged. Veronica was given a prescription of two types of antibiotics to stave off any possible infection, then sent home. She could barely walk, and having a catheter to go home with was a strange situation to be in. Three days later, she decided to see her GP to have the catheter removed. This saved time and money instead of going back to Harley Street, but Veronica could not urinate even though she felt desperate to go. By the following morning, she felt as though her bladder was going to burst and she was so frustrated by the fact that she could not seem to urinate, she cried.

Rae was concerned and told her to ring the Harley Street clinic for advice. The nurse there told Veronica that if she didn't urinate soon, she would be in big trouble; and told her to call an ambulance.

"Babe they said call an ambulance, I may end up with a bloomin' bag for the rest of my life if I don't urinate!" Veronica screamed to Rae.

Rae wasn't having any of it. He told Veronica, "You are not giving up that easy so get on the bloody loo and go will you Vron, it's mind over matter so just concentrate and tell your bladder to go."

Veronica sat for ages crying, Rae came in and held Veronica's hands and lifted her head up. "Babe, I don't want you to go to hospital, you have a seven week old daughter here who needs you, you have Ashley and Charlie that need you, I need you and the business needs you, you've always been determined, you've never given up in all the years we've been together so come on, you can do this."

Veronica imagined her bladder opening and the urine coming out, within a few minutes she was peeing and relieved. Rae was as white as a sheet with worry but as soon as Veronica urinated, the colour in his face quickly returned and his worried expression turned to relief. Veronica too was relieved, literally and emotionally.

This would be just one of many trials that Veronica endured throughout the following few months though. She was very slow to heal and she had an enduring infection despite being told that the laser would minimise this. Veronica was sutured through three layers of her skin, where her perineum had been rebuilt. Dissolvable stitches were not an option with this procedure and therefore Veronica's skin was healing on top of sutures, which meant they needed to naturally find their way out of the body.

Veronica found the whole experience scary and horrific. She could feel a deep pain like a pulling or bearing down sensation that would not go for around three weeks. Eventually, it was time to go back to Harley Street for her 4 week check-up.

When Veronica and Rae got there, they were greeted by Professor Dormby's secretary. She told the couple that unfortunately after Veronica's procedure, Professor Dormby had been suspended by the General Medical Council as he was under investigation for a complaint made by another patient for a procedure he had performed in 2006. Veronica's heart sank, at that point she felt like a complete freak. The pain and infections she had endured since her operation had worried her so much that she had imagined the worst possible scenarios of what state her insides were in. She was hoping that professor Dormby may have examined her to put her mind at ease, yet here she was being told he had been suspended by the GMC under investigation. Veronica was certain that he had messed her up internally and that she would suffer for the rest of her life. She couldn't believe it; they had paid the price to go to the best. Veronica never thought in a million years that she would receive any kind of private care at Harley Street, yet she found herself in the most unusual circumstances at a time when she was already very vulnerable.

The clinic had arranged for another Gynaecologist to step in and examine her, but it was evident that her fear would be too much to allow the doctor to perform an internal examination, so he was only able to examine the outer part of her vagina. Veronica sobbed uncontrollably as the doctor tried to determine her healing and concluded that there was evidence of infection which had hindered the healing process. Veronica was beside herself. The doctor prescribed another dose of antibiotics, this time in a cream that Veronica was instructed to syringe into her vagina. Again, Veronica found the whole experience too much to bear; she went home, sobbing all the way.

Rae felt helpless as to what to do to make Veronica feel okay; he too was shocked at the news of the professor's suspension, but told Veronica not to panic.

Veronica began to spiral into a deep depressive state. She felt like a freak and didn't even want to leave the house. She did not want to talk to anyone; she couldn't even bear to deal with her crying baby; Rae found it impossible.

Veronica would find it hard to fall asleep at night due to her intense pain. She would toss and turn and burst into tears; Veronica felt so low, she got every bug going. She got a terrible cold and woke up from coughing so much, that she thought she had torn herself below. She sat bolt upright screaming. Rae woke in a panic, confused and dazed. Veronica cried, "I think I've torn below where I coughed so hard."

"Don't be silly Vron of course you haven't," Rae replied, but Veronica wasn't having any of it and pleaded with Rae to check her out. She was okay after all, but the whole experience had made Veronica paranoid and edgy. She cried herself back to sleep.

During the next couple of weeks the pain persisted and Veronica became increasingly worried about what the professor had done to be suspended, and questioned what he might have done to her. The infection seemed to be worse not better, and Veronica could not sleep at all. In the end, she asked Rae's mum to go to A & E with her. Rae stayed to look after the kids whilst Veronica and Irene went. They sat in A & E for hours until eventually a doctor examined Veronica. He examined her using a cervix clamp, and Veronica found the whole ordeal particularly painful and stressful. He told Veronica that her vagina was very red and this was the same right up to the opening of the cervix. He said it looked like endometriosis and told her to stop using the antibiotic cream and pills that the Harley Street Gynaecologist had prescribed. He prescribed an entirely different antibiotic instead, Veronica was frustrated. How could she have endometriosis she thought? She'd never had this before, but she thought maybe all of the infections had led to it; and did what the doctor said.

She went home and took some pain relief that was also prescribed and went to bed.

Over the following few days, the pain got so bad, Veronica just wished she could go to sleep and not wake up. The next couple of weeks would see her going back and forth to A & E demanding morphine to help her sleep. At this point, she had never felt so low in her life.

The nurses and A & E staff treated Veronica like she was going crazy. She felt as though no one understood her and was just desperate for someone to find out why she was in so much pain and to stop it. But because she'd had a procedure that wasn't even recognised by the NHS, even the doctors were at a loss as to what to do. Eventually Veronica was sent to an NHS consultant called Dr Newman.

Veronica had been seen by a gynaecology nurse who had told Veronica that in her 25 years of experience and service in the gynie department, she had never seen a woman's parts the colour of a fire engine and decided to admit Veronica for pain relief.

Doctor Newman came and gave Veronica an examination. She had never had her parts scrutinised so much in her whole life, it put the absolute fear of God in her.

Dr Newman was a mild-mannered gentleman who could see how vulnerable Veronica was.

He assured her that he would find out what was wrong with her and get her treated correctly.

He took a swab from her, then doused the area in a fluid that contained the same ingredients used to numb the gums by dentists. Veronica felt immediate relief. For the first time in five months, Veronica felt human again and even managed to laugh.

Dr Newman explained that Veronica had consumed eleven doses of antibiotics since giving birth to her daughter. He tested for thrush and suspected this was the cause of all the pain.

He told her to stop the antibiotics that the A&E doctor had prescribed, and gave her a prescription for diclofen to take for a 4-week period instead. He had to wait for the lab result to confirm the diagnosis and told Veronica he would telephone her the next day to give her the result, before taking the medication. This thrush was going to be a stubborn one to fix he said. He too had never seen anything like it but assured Veronica that he would not let her down and would get her better.

He gave Veronica a bag full of large syringes with the fluid like meds he had used to douse her vagina to numb. He gave her a prescription for pain relief in tablet form and gave instructions on how to apply the meds.

"At last," Veronica sighed, "I will be able to sleep. I've been treated like a freak because of my procedure and told I have post-natal depression, but I don't. I am depressed because I'm in so much pain." Veronica thanked the consultant and went home.

Like he promised, the doctor called the next day to confirm that she did have severe thrush.

He explained that because she'd had it for a long time, it would be time consuming to get rid of it and that Veronica would have to be patient. She would need to take her medication for at least a month, but Veronica didn't care as long as she got rid of it.

Veronica had also seen a counsellor to help her deal with her anxiety and depression. She got the number from her GP surgery and booked an appointment. Her first session was very helpful.

The counsellor made Veronica feel relaxed and at ease. Very quickly he was able to establish Veronica's fears and help her to deal with the anxiety. Veronica booked to see the man weekly until she improved.

The following week, her session went equally well but it soon emerged that Veronica had dealt with so much in her life that the anxiety she suffered from the trauma of her birth to Sienna was a lot more deeply rooted. She began to open up to this therapist about her childhood and life with drug addict parents. He soon realised that Veronica had a lot of more complex issues to deal with, not just coping with the everyday pain she had been living with for months.

This therapy would be the start of a major life-changing transformation that would help Veronica come to terms with her past and her parents' choices and life style.

Veronica had become more distant towards her parents and sisters. It seemed they had no time for her and were only concerned with their own troubles. They never bothered to visit Veronica during her months of illness. On the contrary, when Veronica had called Ella one day in total agony and asked for her sister's help, her sister couldn't handle talking to her as she was busy having fun with her friends.

Veronica pleaded and cried down the phone to her sister. "Ella please can you come and help me with Sienna this weekend?" she asked, but Ella had already made plans to go out with friends. Veronica thought of all the times Ella was alone and depressed and Veronica wanted to be there to help Ella snap out of her moods. All the times she took her out with Helen, to cheer her up and spoil her with a meal whilst taking the kids out. Veronica had not needed anything from her family until now.

This was the time she felt low and so low she didn't care if she went to sleep and never woke up. Ella was not only too busy for Veronica, she seemed too busy to talk to Veronica, as she would rudely start talking to her friend who was around, sun bathing in Ella's garden with her. Veronica suddenly felt embarrassed to be crying and virtually begging to her sister, especially as it didn't seem to faze her.

"Veronica you need to sort yourself out, I think you have post-natal depression!" Veronica felt her heart sink. Her sister didn't understand and Veronica wasn't strong enough to try to explain. She said goodbye to her sister and cried in her pillow. *How could her life have come to this?* she thought, feeling sorry for herself. Veronica vowed that she would never ask anything of her sister again. She had never asked them for a thing since the day she and Rae had got together.

Veronica knew that her mum had hepatitis and although the doctors told her it was eradicated from her blood stream in summer 2009, she had found out six months later that the virus had not been eradicated after all, as it had come back with a vengeance.

Paula was now on the waiting list again for more treatment and more scans, so Veronica knew her mum had her own health issues to deal with, but she managed to see a lot of Ella and Veronica wished that her mum could have made more time for her too.

It was like this in the years Veronica lived in North London around the corner from them, so Veronica just learned to accept that things were never going to change, she was never going to have that kind of family closeness she had craved. It didn't matter how giving Veronica was with her love, her time or her money, it would never be enough to change things as she had subconsciously hoped for all her life; and now Veronica was beginning to see this.

CHAPTER 64

Moving On 2010-2011

With the support of her loving husband Rae and their children, Veronica grew stronger by the day.

Her health issues and breakdown had stripped her of her confidence but she had finally started to heal and her visits to a local counsellor had helped her finally face her demons from her past.

Veronica never realised that she carried so much guilt. This guilt was weighing her down to the point where in the end her health concerns had been one thing too much to bear, and had virtually sent her over the edge. Luckily the counsellor recognised this and helped Veronica by showing her mental exercises to let go of the fears of her past. She noticed that these changes were having a profound impact on her new family life as well. There were some negative side effects for some time, as the emotions she had buried for so many years were finally starting to be faced; and with this came fear, anger, emotion, regret and finally acceptance, letting go and the feeling of peace.

Veronica was very up and down for weeks whilst she processed and evaluated childhood experiences. This did not just affect her during her sessions but also profoundly around the home, Rae found her extremely touchy at times and unpredictable. Even Veronica herself had trouble accepting what she was going through. It was very cathartic for Veronica however; and as difficult as this process was, she was already feeling a lot lighter in herself and beginning to accept everything.

Veronica joined a local gym and attended regular exercise classes. She felt very uplifted and positive after attending a class and she soon became hooked. The gym classes soon overtook her life to the point where she would reschedule as much as she could to fit her classes in, and the more classes she did, the happier she felt. She noticed she was starting to lose the baby weight she had gained, and this in turn made her feel positive.

Within months, Veronica was feeling on top of the world and happier than she had felt in a long time.

The business was showing signs of strain as their main supplier had slashed the rates and had become exceptionally slow to pay. Veronica and Rae had been through such hard times over the years though, this was a mere blip to them and they believed they would surmount their troubles if they stayed determined and hard working as ever.

Veronica's relationship with her parents and sisters became more strained. She had decided to step back and concentrate on Rae and the children. Sienna was a full-on kind of baby, she had never slept all night in her cot, waking and crying on and off for hours. The unsettled nights soon took their toll on the couple. The strains of their company also seemed to become more difficult by the minute, and they were both feeling physically and mentally exhausted.

The last thing Veronica wanted to do was drive the kids down to London for the weekend.

It was unsettling for Sienna anyway, as staying with Ella meant three in a bed. Veronica had cut back her trips due to this but Ella and her parents acted like they weren't bothered anyway.

Veronica felt herself distancing from them, it wasn't something she had envisaged in the past, but it seemed to just naturally progress this way.

Veronica realised that it was she who had tried so hard to prevent this.

The minute Veronica stopped running, her relationships with them ground to a halt. She realised it had been one-way traffic and it wasn't fair. Yet her dad always had a way of making Veronica feel bad for the lack of contact.

When Veronica explained the difficulties she had with Sienna, he would shrug it off telling Veronica that she shouldn't bow to the whims of her kids, but they should learn and adapt to her. Veronica thought this was typical of her dad and selfish. There had been times where Veronica had been stuck in traffic on the A13 and Sienna had screamed for twenty minutes with nowhere for Veronica to pull over. Poor Ashley had found the ordeal so stressful it had driven him to tears. He too was growing tired of the repeated journeys, only to find himself waiting and waiting for his Nan and Granddad to turn up late at Ella's, when he was fed up and tired. He had endured this repeated routine for years; and when he did finally get his Granddad's attention, it was soon spoiled by Helen getting jealous and causing a scene.

Phil had almost encouraged this behaviour by pandering to Helen and pushing Ashley to one side. Ashley felt as though he wasn't good enough; and as he got older, he wanted to go less and less. Veronica felt terrible about this. In all the years she had run back and forth to her family, she had been in denial, but clearly Ashley wasn't and now it was time to take notice. Veronica was disappointed but what could she do? She was never going to change her family, they would never see things the way she did.

They too were in denial; and had spent the better part of their lives in denial about their habits, the drugs, their lifestyle and their relationships. Nothing would ever make them see sense and Veronica had finally seen the light of day. From now on, her priorities were her own little family; and her sisters and parents knew where she was if they wanted her.

CHAPTER 65

Worse News

Veronica hadn't been to stay with Ella for months, but Ella had busied herself with friends and socialising at weekends when Helen was at her dad's, or staying with Phil and Paula.

Ella had met a Greek guy called Petros, and she'd brought him down to meet Veronica and Rae on a couple of occasions. He seemed friendly enough, but it soon came to light that he had fathered three children by two different women; and two of the sons by the different women were a month apart in age. This sent alarm bells ringing in Veronica's head but when she asked Ella about this, she explained that Petros had split from his long-term girlfriend when he met the second woman, but when he realised that the long-term girlfriend was pregnant, he went back to patch things up not realising that the new girl had become pregnant too. Veronica thought he was a player and many of Ella's friends who knew Petros had told her he was a player too, but Ella didn't care. She had fallen for him literally overnight, and she liked the fact that he doted on all three of his children regardless of the circumstances. He was heavily into marijuana and dealing it too, but this didn't worry Ella, she had lived with worse so this was nothing to her.

Veronica had spoken to her mum and she had told Veronica that she and her dad were not keen on this new boyfriend of Ella's. They were worried that Ella was rushing into things too quickly and that she wasn't considering Helen who had shown an immediate dislike to the man.

Veronica thought they were right to feel guarded, but they had behaved in a similar way towards Rae. Perhaps they were never going to accept any guy their daughters chose to be with, but it wasn't their decision at the end of the day so they would just have to watch and see how things panned out.

Ella would call Veronica complaining that their parents were overreacting towards her affair with Petros. Ella told Veronica, "The trouble is they've been around me and Helen all these years that I've been on my own, it's like they don't want to see me get on. They like to be in control."

But Veronica could see it from both points of view and told Ella to just take things slowly and follow her heart.

Veronica also knew that her parents were very controlling; they had been with her, as with Ella. Even though Ella had left the parental home, they still spent lots of time around each other and in Ella's home, so it was as if nothing had changed apart from the fact that Ella had her own place and a child. The relationship dynamics remained the same as they had been when Ella lived at home. Ella had become more aware of this since meeting her new boyfriend, and it had brought out conflicts in her relationship with her parents.

Ella went round to her parents' flat less and less, which meant they saw Helen less, which upset them, especially Paula who doted on her granddaughter. Having Helen around was a lovely distraction for Paula, she loved spending time listening to her, playing with her and reading to her. Helen was extremely close to her Nanny Paula and would tell Ella, "I want my Nanny," whenever she got upset with her mum for any reason.

Paula had been a softie with her children and was now even more so with her granddaughter.

As young as she was, Helen knew how to wrap Nanny around her finger, but Paula didn't mind this one bit! In Paula's eyes, this was what being a grandparent was all about. She often said that it was a grandparent's right to spoil grandchildren, as they could hand them back and not have the horrible job of chastising them. But Paula and Phil were losing their grip on Ella, and Paula was missing Helen terribly.

Veronica called her mum one night to see how she was. Paula slept a lot throughout the day, not having much energy to do anything, and this was making her frustrated. She had also become very forgetful and her pains were getting increasingly stronger in her abdomen. She had been for another scan and was waiting to see the liver specialist consultant at the Kings College Hospital, to find out when she could expect more treatment for the hep C virus.

Paula told Veronica that she was getting very frustrated with it all, as she just wanted to get better. She told Veronica that she just wished she could feel normal again.

She said that the consultant was hesitant when asked about her forthcoming treatment.

She told Veronica that at her scan, the nurse had said her AFP levels were very high.

Paula had asked the nurse what alpha feta protein levels were tested for and the nurse had said it was a tumour marker, and that people infected with the hep C virus had fluctuating AFP levels. This was considered normal for people with hep C, but Paula's were very high. Veronica asked her mum what that meant. "I'm not sure but I'm frightened Veronica, that they won't give me the treatment," Paula said.

Veronica hated hearing this, it scared her but she wanted to keep her mum feeling positive and hopeful. Deep down, Veronica was very scared too but she told herself that things would be ok and that Paula would get the treatment she needed. After all, they had almost eradicated the virus before; surely with a higher dose they stood a better chance? Veronica held on to this and told her mum to stay positive.

Paula had a week until her appointment with the consultant and she tried hard to remain hopeful.

The week passed, but on the day of Paula's appointment Veronica had to attend a driver awareness course, as she'd been caught speeding. Veronica found it very difficult to pay attention as she couldn't stop thinking about her mum, she was impatient to get out of the training centre and get home. When Veronica finally left at around 4pm she checked her phone for messages. There were none, but Veronica felt very anxious. Rae told Veronica not to worry but something inside her almost knew that something wasn't right. She called her mum but there was no answer. She waited half an hour and tried again but still no answer. Eventually at around 6.30pm Veronica's phone rang. Instead of hearing her mum's voice at the end of the phone, she heard her sister Ella's. Her voice was serious. "Veronica," she said, "Mum has cancer."

With that, the world stopped. Veronica could hear nothing else around her; the surrounding noises of her household, the dog barking, her baby crying, Ashley playing, the television blaring; all became silent to her in an instant. There was a long pause at the end of the phone. Veronica called out her sister's name, "Ella," she shouted, "what do you mean she has cancer Ella? It can't be right Ella."

"Vron," Ella replied, "that's not all, it is terminal."

Veronica's heart was already pounding so hard she could hear it pulsing in her ears, adrenaline rushed through her and she could barely breathe. Veronica burst into tears, "No Ella, no Ella, no it can't be true, please tell me it's not true Ella."

Ella was crying, "I know Vron it's terrible, Mum and Dad are in shock Vron. Dad collapsed in the consultant's room, Mum had to pick him up Vron, little Mum, she is dying."

"Oh no Ella it can't be true, I thought they were going to make her better and give her more interferon. They almost eradicated the hep C, how could this happen?" Ella replied, "They said it's happened really quickly, they said there was no sign of cancer between January and March; those were the last tests she had before these. The AFP levels being high were an indicator of cancer. The scan showed that the tumour is quite large and is growing where all the main blood vessels are within her liver. If it had grown anywhere else in her liver they may have been able to cut it out, but because of where it is, they can't and that's why it's terminal."

Veronica couldn't take it all in, she'd known deep down that something was wrong all day, but she hadn't anticipated this. "I just can't believe it Ella, our little mum, it's not fair, why her?

"She doesn't deserve this."

"I know Vron, how are we all going to live without her? How is Dad going to live without her? She is his world Vron; they sat in the car for hours talking in the hospital car park because they were in shock Vron. They couldn't even bring themselves to ring you Vron, they are in bits, Mum is so scared."

Veronica was upset that they had told Ella but not her, but under the circumstances, she could see they were in too much shock. Veronica ran outside with her phone to the back of her garden and went into her summerhouse to cry. She didn't want the children to panic and to get upset, she didn't even want Ashley to know. Ella continued, "Vron we just have to pull together and be strong for them."

"How long have they given her, Ella?"

"Six to nine months with no treatment and up to two years with treatment."

237

"Oh my God Ella, I can't imagine life without our mum, all those times I took it for granted that I would see her, all those years I boasted that my mum was only 17 when she had me, which meant I would have her around forever, that we would grow old together. How wrong was I to think that! And all those years as a child when I panicked about them using drugs and dying from them. Well now she is and it's all because of heroin Ella, it's not fair Ella."

Veronica cried and howled like a baby. Ella too was crying down the phone. "I can't believe it Ella, it's like this is a bad dream and I am going to wake in a minute and realise that Mum is fine and on her way to getting her treatment."

"I know Vron, that's how I feel too, I wish it was a bad dream but it isn't."

"What about Paulette?" Veronica asked, "How is she going to cope without Mum? She relies on her so much."

"I don't know Vron, how any of us will cope, but Mum is going to have chemo to try and shrink the tumour and give her longer."

"Yes Ella you are right, if we keep her positive and take her mind off it as much as possible, that might help to keep her strong. We all need to look after her and Dad. Ella, I haven't spoken to Dad in weeks, we fell out, how am I going to sort this out?"

"Vron you just got to put it aside and make up, he's your dad and he loves you at the end of the day."

"I love him too Ella, we have issues and we clash but I still love him."

"I know you do Vron, we have all got to be strong for them now and be there for each other, I'm going to go now because Helen is calling me."

The sisters told each other they loved one another and said goodbye. Veronica spent the rest of the evening in bed. She told Ashley she wasn't feeling well and needed to lie down. Veronica spent the whole night in tears. All her life she had feared this; one or both of her parents dying prematurely because of drugs. She had created a make-believe world as a youngster, where she would imagine everything was rosy. This was the place she would go when things were worrying her or when her parents were out of it. Now her mum was actually going to die because of a dirty fix, it didn't kill her instantly from overdosing, but caused her to contract a deadly virus that would attack her liver for years and lead to cancer. Veronica thought of all those victims of heroin who had lost their lives to the drug. She had come to know them well throughout her childhood and adolescence, and now her mum was another victim. The hardest thing was that they would all suffer as they watched Paula deteriorate from a debilitating disease.

CHAPTER 66

Liver Cancer

The next couple of days were like torture for Veronica, she disliked her father so much that she didn't know how to maintain her relationship with him, to enable her to be close to her mum.

She loved her dad and felt terrible for what he was faced with, but it didn't change the person he was. Somehow Veronica would have to swallow her pride and deal with what was more important, her mum.

Ella had called to say that her parents were about to 'face time' call her. Veronica was dreading it, she didn't want to break down in front of them, she had been crying all night and all morning, her face was so swollen that she looked like she had been in a fight. The call came and Veronica answered. Her parents were lying in bed, their hair all messed up and their faces pale with shock, but Veronica scanned her mother's features and thought how beautiful she looked, despite her illness. To look at someone in this way, you would never know they had cancer. Veronica felt the emotion welling up inside her chest, she struggled so hard to hold it back but she couldn't cope. The tears fell so heavily that she just gave way. "I'm sorry," she said to her parents, "I tried not to, but I can't control it."

"It's all right babe," her dad replied, "that's all we've done ourselves."

Veronica looked at her Mother's eyes; she could see the fear in them and didn't know what to say. Nothing could make it better; nothing could give her hope now.

Until now, Veronica had been in denial, this was the kind of outcome for others, not her mum, but the truth was staring everyone in the face and it was unbearable and painful.

"I'm so sorry Mum, I love you so much, I just don't know what to say."

"There's nothing anyone can say or do," Paula replied. "Will you have treatment?" Veronica asked.

"Yes, if it means I have longer, I don't want to die," Paula replied. Veronica couldn't bear this, she wished she had a magic wand but she didn't. "I need to come and see you both, I need a hug, when can I come?"

Philip replied, "Whenever you want babe, just take your time when driving because I know how emotional you get." Veronica agreed, she said goodbye and got herself ready.

The whole world could have stopped and Veronica would not have noticed, she was so deep in thought and total shock. All she could think about was her mother's circumstances, it didn't even seem real. Veronica had a shower and got ready to drive to London. Rae stayed home to look after Ashley and Sienna.

Ashley suspected something was wrong because he knew his mother too well. Veronica's body language spoke volumes, and Ashley was too well tuned in for this to go unnoticed. "What's wrong Mum?" Ashley asked.

"Nothing boy, I'm just not feeling too good that's all, I feel a bit sick." Veronica hated fibbing to the children, but there was no way she could bring herself to tell Ashley. He was nearly nine, only a few weeks from his birthday.

"Why are you going to see your mum and dad without taking us?" Ashley asked.

"I had a falling out with granddad and I need to go and sort things out. I need to have some private time with him and Nanny; I will be back before you know it." Veronica hugged Ashley and told him she loved him; he went off happily to play in his room. Veronica wondered how she was going to keep the truth from him.

Her parents had also asked that the grandchildren be kept from knowing straight away, until they thought the time was right. Veronica kissed Rae and the children, then headed off in the car.

It took an hour to get to Ella's, which is where Veronica always went to visit her parents.

She hadn't been to their flat in Tottenham since Ashley was tiny. Veronica's mum didn't want her going there with Ashley, as she would say there was too much of Phil's diving equipment and fishing rods up the stairs and crammed in the rooms of the tiny two bedroom flat.

Paula hated living there and never really bothered to make it homely for that reason, so there was never enough room for Veronica to stay there. Paula desperately wanted to get out of the flat and have a nice house somewhere with a garden. Where she lived, on the border of Tottenham and Edmonton, was a rough estate with regular stabbings, which also made Veronica feel uneasy; she was better off driving to Ella's house, ten minutes down the road in Edmonton. Although it was in the same part of North London, Ella's house was tucked away in a quiet residential road, which made a difference.

The sisters hugged and cried, then Veronica went into the lounge and literally fell into her mum's arms. Then she hugged her dad, she whispered that she was sorry for falling out with him and that she loved him all the same. She said she would be around as much as possible to help the family and be strong for them all. The family didn't really talk much about the news, preferring to forget it and talk about the good times gone by, instead.

Ella and Paulette remembered the fun times they had as kids growing up on their yacht Nova.

They enjoyed their childhood, having spent most weekends in Southsea or sailing to Cowes. They had frolicked in the sea on a doughnut ring, which Phil would tow behind the speed boat, with Ella and Paulette bouncing along the waves in it, wearing life jackets. They had learned to fish, to row and sail too. Veronica didn't get that bug; she was more interested in hanging out with her friends back in London when she was a teenager. She did enjoy some aspects of this marine lifestyle though, particularly in the summer months when she loved being on a beach, she just didn't love sailing.

The family laughed and joked about these times and it was nice to reminisce, but Veronica's heart sank. She thought of all the good times she had missed out on, not through her parents' fault but just by the timing. If things had been like this in her childhood, she would have felt different, but Veronica was brought up with experiences like the time her dad was having a fit because of a dirty fix, the time they were all gagged and tied up, the times the police came crashing in destroying the family home. Veronica's childhood memories were a far cry from her sisters'; and now her mum was going to die after all, because of the drugs she had taken all those years ago, from a dirty fix.

Veronica welled up with tears and whilst she fought to hold them back, Ella was remembering the trip on yacht Nova around the Med. Veronica smiled, this was a happy time, this was a time she had been so, so proud of her parents. They had achieved so much in so little time and were seeing the beauty of the world in a new way too. They were so close to that happy ending then, how had it come to this now? Veronica cried, she couldn't hold it in any more.

CHAPTER 67

The Appointment

Paula had an appointment to see the liver specialist the following week.

As Paula's tumour was quite big, the doctors wanted to get her in for chemotherapy as soon as possible, but first she would need an appointment to discuss all of her options with the possible treatments and procedures. It was a lot to take in for everyone, but none more so than for Paula.

She had just found out that she was dying; she barely had time to get that thought around her head before she had to travel up to Kings College Hospital, to discuss chemotherapy.

Everything was happening so fast, too fast and it was terrifying.

Veronica was shaking like a leaf at just the thought of being in her mum's position, she wanted to be strong for her and she needed to be there to support her. Veronica took a deep breath and said, "I will go with you both to the hospital if you like. I will take you there and I will be there to support you both if you want me to?"

Paula looked at Phil; he said, "You've got such a lot on your plate babe, with Sienna and the business, we will be okay."

"I want to be there for you Dad, Rae can look after Sienna, I would much rather be with you to help support you both Dad, it's not going to be easy I know, but also there may be questions that you may forget to ask, that I may think of. You know what it's like when you are emotional, everything leaves your mind," Veronica replied.

Paula agreed and said that she would feel better if Veronica came along. "Are you sure you don't mind babe?" Paula asked.

"Of course not Mum, you mean the world to me and I want to be there for you as much as I possibly can."

"Okay babe, thank you, it means a lot," Paula said. Veronica kissed and hugged her mum tight.

"I love you so much Mum, you don't know how much."

"I know you do babe," Paula replied, as she played with Veronica's hair whilst her head was snuggled into her mother's arms. Veronica wanted to cry inside but she held it in. She knew she couldn't fall apart; it wouldn't be fair on her mother and the rest of the family.

The following week, Veronica got up early and drove back to London to pick up her parents.

She met them at Ella's and then drove through London to Kings College Hospital.

The journey took a long time, it was midday and the traffic was thick and it took some time to find parking, but eventually they arrived at the Hepatology Department where Paula was shown to an area to be weighed. Then she was sent to a room to have bloods taken and the family were directed to a waiting room. In this room there were many patients with liver problems. Some looked like alcoholics as they had the typical bright red face and stank of alcohol, and there were people who looked thin and jaundiced; and some had swollen tummies.

Paula told Veronica, "I first came here with Ella a couple of years ago. Looking at these patients, I knew that this would be my fate." Veronica hugged her mum close. There was nothing she could say to her mum to reassure her. For the first time, Veronica had no words of comfort; all she could do was to tell her she loved her. It was a very unnerving environment to be in. Many of these people were dead people walking, there was no denying it, the reality was staring them right in the face. This would soon be Paula's fate and no one, not even Veronica, could change that.

They sat in silence, trying to switch off from the sights of jaundiced patients with swollen stomachs; patients who had lost their hair, whose bones were jutting out everywhere due to weight loss. Veronica found it a horrifying experience, but she had to keep calm and not show this fear to her mum who was sitting beside her, shaking like a leaf.

Eventually after what seemed an eternity, a lady doctor appeared calling out her mother's name.

They all got up and followed the doctor into her office. "Hello, my name is Lillian," she said to Veronica, "Please sit down. Hello Pauline, your consultant explained that you have a tumour that is 5cm in diameter roughly, growing in the region where there are major blood vessels in the liver, this is where the blood is supplied and unfortunately this is why we

245

are unable to operate and remove this tumour. We are able to give you some chemotherapy and we believe that the best chance of stunting the growth of this tumour would be to use a localised form of chemotherapy known as chemoembolization. This entails using a cannula to insert some beads to shut off the tumour from the blood supply. Then we will inject the chemo drug through the cannula which will deliver it directly to the liver and tumour as opposed to it being injected through a vein and circulating around your blood stream.

"The benefit of chemo embolization is that more of the powerful drug gets to the area where it is required, and the beads help to keep the drug in that area for longer and shut off the oxygen which is needed for tumours to grow. The down side to this procedure is that the chemo drug will not circulate freely within the body, so if there are signs of cancer anywhere else, those areas will not get treated. But at this stage we really need to shrink this one."

The information was brutally blunt and a lot for everyone to take in. Paula looked dazed, so did Philip. Veronica felt like her heart was going to bleed; the pain in her chest was unbearable. How could this be happening to her little mum she thought? Although she had been a drug addict for most of her life and a drug dealer with her husband over the years, she was pretty innocent at heart. Veronica always saw this element of her mum's personality, there was an almost childlike innocence about Paula which Veronica loved. Her childlike innocence was plain to see in this room, she was like a lost soul and Veronica couldn't do a thing to change it.

"Why can't Mum have a transplant?" Veronica asked Lillian. "Because patients with cancer do not survive going through the ordeal of a transplant. The cancer has usually spread by the time the patients receive the donor liver. It makes them more poorly than with just cancer and the survival rates were none, so we stopped doing it," Lillian explained.

"Ok, so what about taking a piece of healthy liver from someone who is compatible to Mum and growing it? They can grow a full-size liver in the lab in a matter of weeks can't they?" Veronica asked.

"Yes," said Lillian, "but we are around ten years off from having the funding to carry out these treatments, and they are still in the early stages of research."

Veronica couldn't believe it; she didn't want to believe it. There had to be something they could do to save her mum. She couldn't accept it and instead insisted that if they gave Paula treatment to prolong her life, then new treatments may be available to her mum later that may save her. Veronica wanted her mum to stay positive, but Paula was in another place completely. She was the one facing her death, the reality of being no more. She was alone in this, only she could come to terms in her own way. Everyone else though, decided not to accept it, it was their way of coping; and Veronica would not talk about death around her mum.

Lillian gave the family directions for the Palliative care department. Everyone thanked Lillian for her time; and the family were given a date for Paula's chemo on the 30th of May, which was only a few weeks away. Veronica tried to keep her parents focused. "You've got to look after yourself Mum and eat plenty of all the right things. You need vitamins to keep your strength up too." Paula agreed. They eventually found the Palliative care information centre in another part of the hospital. The department was shut, but a security officer allowed them inside to get some leaflets. All of the information was clearly labelled into sections relating to different types of cancers and services. Whilst Veronica and Philip picked leaflets relating to Paula's illness, Paula had gone to another section and was busy reading. Veronica walked over to her mother to see what she was reading; Paula had picked up an information booklet about lung cancer and emphysema. Veronica looked confused.

"Why are you looking at those leaflets Mum?"

"Because I'm worried about your dad," she replied. "I know he's definitely got something wrong with him and I think he's got emphysema. I don't think he had Hep C, he's never had any symptoms and he was shown to have immunity when tested years ago. He's had a nasty cough for ages though, a smokers' cough that he has never really been able to shift. I wouldn't be at all surprised if he's got emphysema. What will he do when I'm no longer here?" she asked her daughter. "Who will look after him then?"

"Don't worry Mum, I know, but we are here for you right now. We need to look after you." But Paula didn't even seem that interested, it was a very sad day.

Here was Paula facing the reality of looking at death, and she was more concerned for her husband and what would happen to him when she was no longer around. Veronica found it all a bit overwhelming and just wanted to break down and cry, but with all her might she held it in and kept a brave face for her mum. Veronica wondered what would happen to her dad when her mum was gone too. She knew that she would have to try and look after him with her sisters, but would it be enough? He couldn't function without Paula. How would he survive?

They grabbed as many leaflets as they could and made their way back to the car. The journey was long, the traffic was heavy as always; and it was two hours before they reached north London. It had been a long day, but Veronica still had to make the drive back to Kent, where her two year old daughter and eight year old son were waiting for her return.

Veronica was shattered and emotionally worn out.

CHAPTER 68

Facing Reality

The family vowed to stick together and be brave for Paula. Veronica wanted to be around as much as she could, but living in Kent with a business to run and two children to look after, meant that life was already hectic for Veronica and Rae. She was determined to be with her mum as much as she possibly could though.

Paula was scheduled to have chemoembolization in less than three weeks, which was going to be a tough treatment for her to endure. Veronica asked Rae if she could book a caravan in Kent for a weekend, to give her parents and sisters some time out. She wanted to give Paula a little fresh air and change of scene away from her dingy flat in Tottenham. Maybe a little break would do her the world of good, Paula rarely got away from the flat and Veronica knew how much her mum hated living there.

Rae agreed that it was a good idea, and told Veronica to do whatever she wanted for her mum.

Veronica felt so thankful to have such an understanding husband. Despite the long-standing difficulties in the relationship between Rae and Veronica's parents, he still remained understanding and knew how much Veronica needed to help them. Paula had also always wanted to go on the London Eye. Phil and Paula had often spoken about going one day, but just never got round to it. Veronica thought this would be a nice distraction for Paula too.

Rae kindly went online and booked tickets for Veronica's parents, her sisters, her niece Helen; and their own children Ashley and Sienna. Rae did not want to go along, Veronica understood his reasons; he told her to have quality family time.

Veronica liaised with her mum to make sure she had no appointments; and then the following weekend, she got up early and drove to North

London to meet her parents and sisters. They all got the train down to Central London. Sienna hadn't spent much time with her grandparents and she found the whole experience exciting. Philip made a huge effort to entertain Sienna, making her laugh throughout the day.

Paula thoroughly enjoyed the London Eye. She knew London like the back of her hand and pointed out particular places where she and Phil had lived and grown up. Paula also pointed out Battersea power station, which brought back memories for Veronica, of trekking down there on the underground with her mum, Ella and Paulette in the pram, to look for their dog Lennon, when he had disappeared. Veronica welled up inside and wanted to cry, but she had to stay strong for her mum, dad and sisters. Falling apart wasn't an option and after all, they were here to have some time out, to forget and enjoy the moment.

Veronica encouraged the children to have a look at the sights. They could see the Houses of Parliament and Big Ben. Ashley had learnt about Guy Fawkes and his attempt at blowing them up; it was fascinating for him to see them from the top of the Eye.

The family took some pictures and then asked another passenger to take some photos of them all together. It was a proud moment for Veronica, but one that was also tinged with sadness. It wasn't often that her family did this kind of thing, it made a nice change for everyone to be there together and all for Paula. Why hadn't they done this many times before now? Veronica wondered. But it was pointless wondering and what mattered was they were here now.

The ride came to an end and it was time to exit the wheel. Veronica went to find directions for the boat she had booked for lunch. Eventually they found it and climbed on board. They were taken to their table; Paula looked pale and tired when she sat down and Veronica wondered if all the travelling and queuing had been too much for her. She asked her mum if she was okay. Paula said she was feeling a bit tired but was okay. They all chatted and enjoyed the experience of having their lunch on board a boat, and Veronica asked the waiter to take a family photo.

Her sisters were making the most of the experience, enjoying the food and drink. Veronica was glad that her family enjoyed the day, but the pain of knowing her mum's fate was always present. Everyone avoided the subject; it wasn't possible to discuss it even if they had wanted to. Helen and Ashley had no idea and were happy and carefree as ever. Sienna was also happy playing with her mini mouse, with granddad entertaining her.

It was soon time to leave and head back to North London. The journey was pretty straightforward, although there were many stairs to climb in the underground. It was quite a tiring day for everyone, but most of all for Paula who was ready to go to bed upon their return to Edmonton. Paula had a smile on her face though and thanked Veronica for an unforgettable day.

Veronica kissed her mum, dad and sister Paulette, goodbye, then headed back to Ella's where she had left her car. She kissed Ella and Helen and made her way home.

The day had been lovely; and although very tiring, one that was memorable for all of the family and most importantly for Veronica's mum.

Finally after all the years she had said she wanted to visit the London Eye, Paula had done it; and they had all done it as a family, together.

CHAPTER 69

Chemoembolization

The following week went by quite quickly. Veronica was working from home, being as busy as ever. Her weekly paperwork had become very laborious and tedious since Masterstores had asked all contractors to complete extra forms to invoice them for works carried out. One invoice could have as many as a dozen sheets of paperwork to it, and some days Veronica would complete five invoices for their company. As the invoicing was only one aspect of her work, Veronica was kept very busy. She welcomed it as a major distraction from the worry of her mother's up and coming treatment though, but it was never far from her mind.

Paula was due to have her chemoembolization on Wednesday 30th May. Veronica wanted to be there for her parents, she worried about how her dad would cope alone without Paula by his side. Apart from his time spent in prison and time away on the boat, Phil had not spent a night apart from Paula in years. Veronica had offered to drop her responsibilities at home to assist them in any way, but Philip told her that she had a lot on her plate and that they would cope, so Veronica agreed just to be on standby for them.

Wednesday came and Paula set off to Kings College Hospital to have her treatment, but their car broke down on the way. Paula couldn't believe it, of all the times for this to happen, it had to happen when she was due at hospital for chemotherapy. Veronica was at home in Kent texting her mum. Paula sent her a message saying, "Can you believe it, we've broken down." Veronica felt panicked, what if her mum got to hospital late and missed her appointment, would she lose out on having chemo? Phil and Paula had to wait for Ella and Petros to drive through London and pick them up. Veronica couldn't believe what was happening, it was almost surreal. Eventually they got to the hospital and Paula was shown to a private room, the chemoembolization therapy was due to take place in the morning. Paula had some blood tests that evening to prepare her for theatre, and the consultant came to her bed and explained the procedure and the affects.

Veronica rang her mum and arranged to bring her home when she was discharged. She offered to drive to Edmonton first to pick up her dad and then drive to the hospital to collect Paula.

Paula's procedure was successfully completed and the consultant phoned Philip to explain what had happened. They had managed the procedure well; the beads were in place around the tumour to block off its blood supply and hold the drug there for long enough to do its work. It would take around two weeks to shrink the tumour and then further tests would be done to check the results. It was all a matter of time, a waiting game; and no one knew what effect this would have on Paula. She was told that she may or may not lose her hair, some people did and others didn't.

She was told that she may lose weight and that as one of the effects of chemotherapy was sickness, she was prescribed anti sickness tablets. Paula had been suffering severe pains caused by the cancer and liver disease, so she was prescribed morphine as well.

On the second day after surgery, Paula was allowed to go home. Veronica got up early and drove to London to pick up her dad. She called Rae en route, on the hands free. He was very moody with Veronica on the phone, so she asked him what his problem was, and was it because she was leaving him to cope with Sienna.

He snapped in response to her, "There are bigger things concerning me right now, like being dumped by Masterstores!" Veronica was shocked, what did he mean, why was he behaving like this when she had so much on her mind?

"What do you mean, being dumped by Masterstores?" she asked.

"I've sent you the email that I've just received from Masterstores," Rae replied. "You know they got us to drop our rates again and tender again, well we've lost it and they are giving us one month's notice. Our contract comes to an end next month."

Veronica was silent, her heart sank. What on earth would they do now with no income, no job and a mortgage of £1700 per month to pay? There was no way they could get another contract like that any time soon. Veronica was angry, not just with Masterstores, but with Rae for his timing in delivering the news. He knew what she was already facing, her mum was dying and she was collecting her from her chemotherapy treatment in hospital.

"Did you fucking have to tell me now?" Veronica shouted down the phone.

"Well you asked me what was wrong so I told you," he replied, "you wanted to know." But Veronica couldn't believe his insensitivity and his selfishness.

"Well," she said, "I couldn't give a fuck right now what happens, because all I'm concerned for at this time is my mum, you selfish arsehole," she continued. "Typical of you this is, I really didn't need this today of all days!" and she slammed the phone down.

Veronica burst into tears, the Gods had it in for her, she thought. It wasn't enough to deal with the reality of her mum dying, now she faced losing her job and possibly her home if they didn't find some other income promptly.

Veronica was parked outside her parent's block of flats waiting for her dad to come down.

She was sobbing uncontrollably, fearful of the future, then she wiped her eyes, "Fuck Masterstores," she thought, they had been a nightmare to work for during the past few years. They had brought nothing but headache and stress. All that mattered to Veronica was her little mum and spending every moment she could with her. Phil knocked on the car door and Veronica let him in.

"What's the matter Vronx?" her dad asked.

"Oh nothing, I'm alright."

"No you're not babe," he said, "I know you better than you think, and your face says it all, what's the matter?"

"Rae has just told me we've lost Masterstores. They got us to drop our rates even though we already did that two years ago. We had a contract for three years but they have a clause that allows them to dump us any time they like; and a company has come in way cheaper than us and thousands of others, so they are getting rid of 3000 companies including us, with one month's notice."

Phil's face looked shocked, "Are you joking Vronx?"

"No Dad, I'm not, I don't know what we will do now, we will have to sell everything quickly before we lose it all. Everything we've worked so hard for these past 8 years."

"They are bastards," said Phil. "You are just another number to them, replaceable!"

"I know Dad, part of me is relieved because I've hated the last few years working with them and the pressures, but part of me is scared because I don't know how we will cope and I really didn't need this right now!"

"I know babe, I bet Rae is gutted, but he's a grafter and he's never let you down, something will show up, he's got his fingers in a few pies."

Veronica agreed, she didn't want to think about it, all she wanted to focus on was her mum, so they agreed not to talk about it anymore and to focus instead on Paula.

The journey through London was arduous and boring again, but eventually they arrived at Kings College Hospital. Veronica thought it was a very eerie place; and she didn't like being where there were lots of poorly people, many of whom were on their last legs. Eventually they arrived at the ward where Paula was staying. Veronica couldn't wait to give her mum a kiss and a hug. "How are you my beautiful mum?" Veronica asked.

Paula smiled and chuckled, "All the better for seeing you two," she replied. Veronica was surprised at how spritely her mum appeared to be. She was dressed and ready to leave, she had colour in her cheeks and a presence of optimism. Veronica felt relieved by this; her mum after all was a fighter. She may have been a small person but she had fight in her, and Veronica remembered the struggles her mum endured when she was alone and coping with three young children whilst Philip was in prison.

For the first time since receiving Paula's bad news, Veronica felt hopeful that her mum would get through this and prove the doctors wrong. "Mum you look amazing, you wouldn't know you've undergone chemo, you really wouldn't," Veronica said.

"Ah thanks babe, I don't feel too bad actually. The procedure was quite uncomfortable and not very nice but I feel okay today."

"That's great news Mum, let's get you home and get you comfy. We need to feed you up with lots of wholesome foods to keep your energy up, so you can fight this thing hey."

Paula smiled and agreed. They got Paula's clothes and belongings packed and waited for the doctor to discharge her. She was given a concoction of drugs to take home and an appointment to return within a couple of weeks. The journey back to north London was longer still, traffic was so heavy that for periods of up to ten minutes, the car barely moved a few feet. They had been in the car for over an hour when Paula asked, "Can we stop for a drink?"

"Yeah of course," Veronica replied. Everyone was in need of a drink, particularly Paula whose mouth was really dry, so they stopped at the next petrol station and Philip went in to get some drinks.

Veronica sat in the back of the car to give her mum a hug. "You are so brave Mum," said Veronica.

"Oh I don't know about that babe," Paula replied, "I just don't have any choice do I?"

Veronica agreed but said, "I wouldn't be as brave as you Mum."

They spoke about death, and Paula said she was frightened to die. Veronica said, "I don't think it's as bad as we expect. It's a natural thing like being born isn't it? I think it's a peaceful thing and when it happens it's just natural."

Paula smiled at Veronica, she stroked her daughter's face and said, "You always know the right things to say, and you have a positive way of looking at even the worst things."

"I don't know what it is Mum," Veronica replied, "maybe it's because I was such a sick child and had to grow up fast, but I always felt like I was different. I always felt I wasn't the same as everyone else, I looked at life differently and I've always been so emotional. I never felt like I belonged here on this earth, I know it probably sounds stupid, but it's true, I always felt like I never quite fit in with people. I often thought that there was a better world than this and when I die that's where I will go. I want you to know that Mum, because there is a better world than this for all of us."

Paula replied, "I am an atheist; I believe we die and that is it."

"No Mum, you are wrong," Veronica said, "I wish you believed me, there is a beautiful world much better than this. I don't know how I know that, I've always sensed an afterlife, not that I've seen spirits or even talked to them, but I know they exist and I know there is more to life than just here and now."

"Well if there is, I'm gonna come back and haunt you!" Paula chuckled; and Veronica burst into laughter. Mother and daughter were literally giggling like children in the back of the car.

Veronica fought to catch her breath she laughed so much, "Mum do you mean that? Please, I want you to, because I am not afraid. You know that don't you?"

"I promise," Paula replied, "I will let you know."

The women cuddled and kissed and laughed some more. "You will see I was right, and I've never let you down have I Mum?" Veronica said.

"No babe, you haven't."

Veronica let her dad drive the car, whilst she cuddled her mum in the back. Paula started to look tired and fell asleep, still cuddling her daughter.

CHAPTER 70

Paula's 56th Birthday

The last two weeks had taken their toll on Paula. The drugs in her liver had affected her energy level, leaving her feeling even more tired than she was before. They also made her hair fall out in clumps, which was very distressing. Paula had suffered from thin hair for years anyway, but now she was losing it all, waking up to find piles of hair on her pillow.

Ella had chosen a couple of head scarves for her to wear when she went out, but Paula didn't feel like going out as she was constantly tired and in pain. It was evident to see she was feeling very down in the dumps.

Veronica drove to Ella's where her mum and dad were staying, for Paula's 56th Birthday. Ella had offered to help her dad take care of her mum; she had plenty of room and a spare double bed she had been given by Veronica a couple of years ago.

Ella was doing a good job of cooking regular meals for her mum and dad and helping Paula keep on top of her medication, such as her anti sickness drugs and pain relief.

Veronica took Ella shopping to buy food and a birthday cake for Paula's birthday tea.

They prepared a lovely meal and set some candles out on the cake. It was quite emotional for everyone, they were all very aware that this could be Paula's last birthday, but that wasn't spoken about as they all wanted to make the most of this precious day and spoil their mum with lots of fuss and attention.

Ella put some music on in the living room where everyone was sitting, and they all started to sing along to Bob Marley. When Ella, Veronica, Paulette and the children got up to dance, Paula brightened up immediately. She sat up smiling and clapping, singing along to Bob Marley's album, Legend. The girls all danced like they were at a party and Paula loved every minute of it. She clapped throughout, smiling and singing with her daughters whilst watching her grandchildren dance. Sienna was wiggling her hips from side to side and clapping along too.

Paula thoroughly enjoyed herself, but it wasn't long before pain interrupted her moments of fun and left her feeling exhausted. It was a constant reminder of the painful truth that the whole family had to face.

It was soon time for Veronica to make her way back to Kent, as there wasn't enough room for her and her children to stay at Ella's, along with her parents. Sienna was starting to become restless, grumpy and tired anyway, so Veronica kissed her family goodbye and headed back home.

Her mum was now feeling the full effects of her Chemoembolization; the pain was still very intense and difficult to manage. Paula had to be careful with the pain relief she took though, particularly morphine, because it was too much for her liver to withstand. It could cause a build-up of toxins in her body which her liver couldn't filter out, as it was not receiving its normal flow of oxygen because of the micro beads strategically placed around the tumour. The accumulation affected her brain and her memory, causing Paula to be incoherent for days, which was very distressing for her and her family.

Even the grandchildren were aware that their Nan's illness wasn't just a bug, but Veronica and Ella were not ready to discuss Paula's cancer with the children just yet. They wanted to remain hopeful and tried desperately to keep up morale.

CHAPTER 71

North Middlesex Hospital

Paula had developed a swollen tummy, it looked like she was pregnant and her stomach was hard like a rock to touch. This was extremely uncomfortable for her and made walking even more unbearable and painful. She couldn't get comfortable in bed either, tossing and turning and getting up and pacing around, to try to ease the pain. It was really frustrating for her family having to watch Paula suffer like this and not be able to do anything to help her.

She had gone off her food too, as she constantly felt sick. The anti-sickness drugs didn't seem to do enough, and she had developed mouth ulcers which made eating particularly painful.

Everyone tried so hard to keep Paula feeling positive, but it was difficult with so many negative aspects that she had to deal with on a daily basis.

A few days after Paula's birthday she had gone to sleep in the morning, and when Philip tried waking her, he could not get any sense from her. She was confused and mumbled nonsensical words. Philip was frightened because he had never seen his wife like this, he couldn't get her to listen to him or take her medication, she was completely out of it and didn't even know who she was or who Philip was. Paula would burst into tears with frustration and become very argumentative and difficult to handle, she would get out of bed and start talking about something that didn't make sense and Philip found it unbearable as he would be awake night after night with Paula suffering. In the end, he called for an ambulance and Paula was sent to the local hospital in North London, where she was put on a ward with other cancer patients.

One lady in a bed opposite was dying from breast cancer, another lady next to Paula had ovarian cancer, but Paula wasn't even aware that she was in a hospital bed as she had been incoherent for a few days. The doctors fed her a drip with antibiotics as they tested her blood and inserted a catheter. Veronica had driven back to the hospital to be by her mother's side; she could not believe the environment her mum was in, surrounded by terminally ill patients. She wondered how her mum would feel when she woke up and realised where she was.

Just then Paula opened her eyes. "Oh thank God you are here," she said looking relieved to see her daughter sat beside her. "Where's Dad?"

"He's at home having a bath and getting ready to come and see you Mum," Veronica replied. "He has been by your side Mum all night, but they kicked him out at 11pm last night and he's exhausted."

"How did I get here Vron?" Paula asked, "I don't remember coming here, I just remember going to bed at home. The next thing, I woke up here and someone in another room over there was crying really loud and calling for help, it frightened me. What's wrong, why am I here?"

"We are not sure Mum, you went to sleep like you said, a few days ago, and you've been incoherent and confused ever since. Dad woke you and couldn't get you to do anything for yourself, you wouldn't take your pills or eat; and you've been really confused. They think it's a build-up of all the toxins that your liver isn't getting rid of," Veronica told her mum.

Paula looked fed up. "Why does this have to happen to me? Why can't I just feel okay for a few days? I've had one thing after another since the chemo; I thought it was going to help me."

Veronica wished she could tell her something positive, but she couldn't and she wasn't going to lie, but the truth was still difficult to discuss. Veronica stayed by her mother's side and tried to distract her attention by giving her a newspaper to read and talking about Sienna and Ashley, but the day was wearing on and it was getting late.

It was nearly 4pm and there was still no sign of Philip. Ella had turned up to visit her mum and brought Helen along which cheered her up no end.

"Where's Dad, Ella?" Veronica asked, "He said he was getting ready hours ago."

"Oh he's gone to get some food for Mum, you know, some fresh sandwiches and that. He's gone to Tesco to pick up some bits and then he will be here."

Veronica had spoken to her dad two hours ago and he was leaving to go to the supermarket then. It was only a ten minute drive away from the hospital so what was taking him so long? But in her heart, Veronica knew what her dad was like and she knew what he was up to. She thought about her mum's distress at him not being there, which made her feel angry.

She understood that it was intolerable for anyone to be dealing with what he was faced with, but in all of the years that he and Paula had been together, this was the time she needed him the most. She needed him to be strong and support her, and to make her feel at ease, but Phil would use his drugs as a way of escape and a way of denial.

Unfortunately though, the drugs had a negative impact on Phil's personality, which reared its ugly head from time to time. It wasn't just Paula who would suffer this, Veronica, Ella and Paulette would all suffer too.

Paula needed to go to the toilet so Veronica offered to go with her mum; she hadn't been for a few days since having her catheter removed. Veronica helped with the drip and held her mum's arm. She went into the toilet with her to help get her comfortable and to make sure she didn't fall. Veronica was worried that her mum was still unsteady on her feet and not completely back to herself. Paula's urine was extremely dark, like a deep orange colour, which shocked both Paula and Veronica, but Veronica tried to remain calm for her mum. "It's probably normal Mum, you've been given plasma too and wouldn't that affect the colour of your urine?" Veronica said trying to get her mum to find a logical reason for it. "Do you want me to call the nurse and ask?" Paula agreed. "Don't flush the toilet Mum, so we can show her," Veronica said as she helped her mum to straighten herself out and wash her hands, then she went outside to call a nurse.

It took a while to get someone's attention, but eventually one of the nurses came and took a look at the urine. She told Paula not to worry and sent her back to bed, then she flushed the toilet. Veronica and Paula felt confused as they hadn't been given an explanation, "We will ask your consultant Mum, we will ring Lillian and see what she says."

Paula was so upset and fed up; Veronica just didn't have enough words of comfort for her mum, which made it all the more difficult. When Veronica helped her mum back to bed, Helen wanted to cuddle up to her Nan. She had spent a lot of time with Paula during her ten years. Nanny Paula was like a surrogate mother to Helen and they had a very close relationship. Paula had a very soft approach to parenting and would proverbially cover Helen up in cotton wool whenever she thought Ella was being hard on her. This had made Helen particularly clingy to her

Nan. Helen didn't like seeing her Nan so unwell and was quite upset about it.

Paula stroked Helen's hair and told her not to worry and that Nanny would be home and well soon.

She gave her a kiss and Helen smiled as if Nanny had made everything better in just one sentence.

Eventually Philip turned up with a couple of bags of food containing fresh sandwiches and pasta salads he had brought for Paula. She was relieved to have her husband by her side. "What took you so long?" Paula asked.

"I had a bath and had to sort a few bills out," he said. "Then I drove to Sainsbury's to get you some food." Veronica stayed a little longer to catch up with her dad and then left to make her way back to Kent.

Veronica and Rae's business life had taken a turn for the worse. Finding out that they had lost their contract with Masterstores supermarkets with a little over a month's notice was a huge shock. They racked their brains as to how they would make money and pay their mortgage.

Their house had been up for sale for almost a year. They had turned down a few offers previously, hoping to get a better offer eventually, but now it was time to take what they could get. They had a few viewings and an offer was made and accepted. They both crossed their fingers that the sale would go through before they ran out of work and money. This was a very stressful time for them and Veronica feared that they would lose their home if they didn't sell in time, losing everything they had worked so hard for. In the meantime, Paula had been sent back home to rest and was told to keep taking her medication.

CHAPTER 72

Ella's Wedding

Although they'd only been together a matter of months, Ella and Petros had decided to get married. Ella wanted her mum to be at her wedding; and though Veronica thought it was all a bit rushed and too soon after Paula's chemotherapy, she understood her sister's determination to have her mum there for her big day. As the occasion drew nearer though, Paula's condition got worse. She had lost most of her hair and a lot of weight, so she looked extremely gaunt and bony.

It was heartbreaking to see such a beautiful woman fading away so fast before everyone's eyes, but nothing could bring home the reality of how terminal her illness was, more than her daughter's big day.

Ella had engaged a friend, who was a beauty therapist, to do her makeup; and she had another friend doing her and Paulette's hair. Rae had offered the use of their Range Rover as a wedding car to take the couple to and from the registry office, whilst Veronica would use her smaller car to drive herself and the kids to London for the wedding. They dressed up the wedding car with a bow to make it look authentic.

When they arrived at Ella's house, it was full of Ella's closest school friends and family.

Veronica found her sister upstairs in the bedroom, having her hair done and makeup applied. Her mum was there too, sitting on the bed having her makeup done.

Paula was wearing a head scarf to hide her hair loss, and a pair of jeans. Veronica noticed how tiny Paula's jeans were, and how thin her legs looked. Her mum had always been very slim for most of her life, but never this thin.

The makeup artist had done a wonderful job, but there was no disguising Paula's gaunt face.

Veronica welled up with emotion; she tried so hard to hold her tears back, but the sudden burst of emotion was unexpected and uncontrollable. Veronica turned away trying to hide the tears from her mum, but Paula was very in tune with her daughters' behaviour and knew when they were upset. "What's wrong Veronica?" Paula asked.

"I'm alright Mum," Veronica answered. "It's just a little emotional, Ella getting married and all," but Paula knew that wasn't the reason her daughter was getting upset.

Ella looked stunning. She was heavily pregnant and looked radiant. She looked amazing in her dress, and her hair had been styled beautifully. Veronica was mesmerised by her sister's appearance, and Helen looked equally pretty with her matching dress. Veronica went downstairs to wait for the women to finish getting ready. She was feeling extremely emotional after seeing her mum looking so frail. Veronica hadn't seen her mum all week, and she had deteriorated quite a bit and lost so much weight in such a short time, that it was a complete shock.

Veronica's dad was downstairs; he was looking equally thin and pale. His face appeared gaunt; and if it hadn't been for his full head of hair, it would have been hard to tell which parent was sick, as they both looked painfully thin and withdrawn. Veronica sat deep in thought.

It was Ella's wedding day, which by rights should have been a happy joyous day for all of the family, but it was tainted by the reality of Paula's terminal illness.

Veronica wondered if her mum was well enough to manage the day ahead, but Paula was determined not to give in to her pain and let her daughter down. Cancer had ripped the family's hearts apart when they lost Phil's mum to cancer in 1997, but although it was a heartbreaking time, it was easier for Veronica to accept as her Nan was 76 years old.

Veronica felt that her mum was being cheated. She was only just 56 and had so much to live for.

The women soon came downstairs and everyone made their way to their cars, to go to the registry office which was a ten minute drive away.

Veronica wasn't happy about her sister marrying Petros. It had been revealed that he was involved with skunk farms in and around the area. Setting up single mums with the equipment and plants, he would keep a regular check on their growth and give the women, who were mostly on state benefits, a cut of the profits for housing his stock. Veronica found this exploitation of vulnerable women disgusting. How had Ella come to accept his behaviour, surely she wanted better from a man? But it was plain to see that she was happy to settle for someone who was like her dad and mimicked his antics. Like her mum, she too would accept the dark side of life and settle for living life on the edge.

Didn't she want more for her daughter Helen and her unborn child, Veronica wondered? Clearly not, she wanted the money and all its trappings, but she wasn't too concerned about how she got it. Her attitude was that she wasn't doing anything wrong it was only a bit of skunk. Veronica thought it was selfish of her, she obviously hadn't considered the risks involved. What if the police found out, what if they arrested Ella? Worse still, what if one of the local drug gangs got wind of what Petros was doing? People in gangs had no consideration for life, let alone anything else. They could turn up at any moment armed with knives or guns, those thugs thought nothing of stabbing someone. What if they hurt the children? Ella obviously thought they were untouchable. Veronica feared for Helen and what she would now face on a daily basis in her new life, with Petros as her stepdad.

He was claiming sickness benefits for back problems too, yet he was ducking and diving and selling large amounts of skunk. Veronica couldn't believe that Ella was rushing into marriage with him but it was her life, for her to live. All Veronica could do was to be there and go along with her sister's wishes. If she had said anything negative towards Ella and her plan to marry, she would have been accused of being nasty, so she tried hard to keep her opinions to herself and pretend that she was happy for her sister.

They arrived at the registry office to find that the number of guests was growing rapidly.

Petros was Greek and had a huge family and many friends, who all turned up to the ceremony.

Veronica and Rae were surprised by how many people were there; so many that there were not enough chairs, so people were standing up, crammed into the back of the room.

Veronica had been under the impression that the ceremony was going to be a quiet, low key private affair with only immediate family and a handful of friends, especially with Paula being so frail. Instead, it was as if Paula's terminal illness was put on show for all and sundry to see, which made Veronica feel quite angry. Her poor mum was sitting up at the front near her daughter, looking lost and as if she'd been put on the spot. Her dad looked dumbfounded by the number of strangers in the room too.

After making their vows, the newly-weds went outside for some wedding pictures. Everyone took photos, and Veronica welled up again looking at her mum standing next to Ella and Helen.

The bitter truth was evident right there. It was an awful contrast to see Paula with her head scarf and bony body, next to Ella with her huge bump looking swell in her cream dress, with gorgeous little Helen on her other side. It really was too much for Veronica to bear, but she held in her emotions with all her might, not wanting to upset anyone else around her. Helen and Ashley were still oblivious to their nanny's fate.

Petros's family and friends were constantly staring at Paula which made her feel on edge. Veronica just wanted to cover her up in cotton wool and carry her away but she couldn't; and Paula would have to endure a long day and evening surrounded by strangers, pretending to have a good time when really she was in pain and just wanted to go to her bed.

Everyone moved on to the reception, which was a ten minute drive away, where the dinner and disco went on for hours. The tables in the venue were laid out so that the married couple, their parents and children were at the top table, whilst everyone else sat around other tables.

Paula was seated facing everyone, she couldn't hide away at all; and it was soon clear to see that Paula was struggling. She was falling asleep on her chair snuggled into her husband's arms, looking frail and sick. Veronica went over to her parents to ask if they wanted her to take Mum home, but Paula was determined to see out her daughter's wedding reception.

Paula had experienced episodes of confusion over the last few weeks, which the health professionals explained were due to her liver not functioning properly, so that the build-up of toxins in her body affected her brain. Paula became quite incoherent at the reception, and Veronica pleaded with her dad to take her home. "It's too much for her dad, she got through the wedding ceremony and the dinner, it's too much for her now, look at her, she needs to be in bed," but her dad insisted that Paula wanted to sit it out a while longer. Veronica went back to her table to join Rae, Jade, Charlie and the kids.

The music started to get louder and people began to dance. Everyone tried so hard to enjoy it for Ella, but it was so difficult with Paula being so ill; and she was getting worse not better. It was nearly nine o clock at night before Rae and Veronica persuaded Philip to take his wife home to bed. Rae offered to drive them and Veronica helped get her mum into the back of the car. She wrapped her up in Sienna's blankets which were in the boot, as Paula was shivering. Veronica got into the back of the car and sat beside her mum for a few minutes whilst everyone was saying goodbye to her dad. She cradled her mum's head and rubbed her back and arms trying to warm her up, and Rae put the heating on to full blast. "You are a good girl," Paula told Veronica.

"Why?" Veronica asked.

"You are always thinking of others, you are always looking after me. You are an angel."

Veronica smiled at her mum and told her she was the most precious woman in the world to her and that she needed looking after. She told her dad to take her straight to the hospital in the morning if her mum was still getting confused. He promised he would and Veronica kissed both her parents goodbye and told them she loved them.

Rae set off in the direction of their flat and Veronica went back inside to the reception.

Veronica had a little dance with her sisters. Paulette was quite drunk by this time and was starting to get loud and show herself up. She was struggling with coming to terms with her mum's illness too, but she masked it, determined to get as drunk as possible. Veronica had found the whole day extremely emotional. Not only was it horrifying watching her frail mum being put on show for Petros's entire family and friends to see, but Veronica was very disappointed that her sister had chosen such a partner for life.

Veronica kissed her sisters and cousins goodbye and made her way home back to Kent.

CHAPTER 73

King's College Hospital

The next day, Veronica called her dad to see how her mum was. He said she wasn't any better and that all she had done was sleep. He said that he couldn't get much sense out of Paula and she was refusing to eat. Veronica asked if he was taking her back to the hospital to make sure she was okay. He said he would get ready and take her in the afternoon if she didn't perk up.

Veronica had a lot to do. Sienna was being a handful to look after, having numerous crying fits throughout the day, which was exhausting for Veronica and her family.

Sienna would scream for over an hour if she didn't get what she wanted; and there was no way of talking her out of it, as this only made things worse. The whole family had to endure her crying episodes which would completely take over everything going on within the family home.

Veronica blamed herself; she wondered if by being a busy working mum, this had somehow had a negative impact on Sienna. Veronica did struggle with having to juggle her work duties and that of being mum to Sienna. Ashley however was much more settled, he was an easy-going boy, much more laid back and easy to please.

Veronica was wrapping up the last bits of invoicing and paperwork for Masterstores. She wondered how they would cope once that income ran out. Since living in Kent, they had known no other way of earning, but somehow, some way, they would need to find other work.

Veronica called her dad later that evening to see how things were with her mum, as she hadn't heard anything. Her dad was half asleep and said he'd been up all the night before and that day with Paula, seeing to her needs and he was exhausted.

Veronica asked if he had called the hospital to find out if Paula's confusion and non-coherence was anything to worry about. He said he hadn't as he had fallen asleep but he would in the morning if Paula hadn't improved. Veronica let her dad get back to resting and agreed to call the next day. She was worried though, Paula had looked so ill at Ella's wedding and she had deteriorated rapidly since having chemotherapy. Veronica was eager to know the outcome of her mum's chemoembolization and it was frustrating having to wait for the results. The family wanted Paula to have the best possible chance at keeping her tumour at bay but they were all in the dark, not knowing if the treatment had worked and even wondered if having the treatment was a mistake. The worry was intense and there was no let up for Paula, who seemed to be suffering more pain since having her chemo.

Veronica and Rae also had a holiday to Mexico coming up in just under a week. The holiday had been booked the previous year, before finding out about Paula's terminal illness and losing their contract with Masterstores. They were booked to stay in a 5-star all-inclusive resort in Playa del Carmen for two weeks with the children. Rae told Veronica that this may be their last chance of a nice holiday for some time to come, but she didn't feel good about going on a holiday whilst her mum was dying. Rae insisted that the stress they had been under dealing with her mum's illness, losing their business and selling their home, was a lot to bear on anyone's shoulders. The holiday was already paid for and it was a chance for the children to have some fun and new experiences too. Veronica agreed but still didn't want to leave her mum.

Veronica found it hard getting through to her dad on the telephone over the next few days. The phone would just ring and eventually go to answer phone. She left message after message but got no reply until she called her sister Ella who had checked up on them. She said that her mum and dad had been sleeping during the day and been awake throughout the night. Veronica begged her dad to get her mum to a hospital. Paula was totally incoherent and didn't know who she was, let alone recognise her husband. He had been getting frustrated with her as she wasn't responding to him and refusing to eat.

Ella went around to see for herself, she said her mum would just sleep, then when she woke up, she would be very confused and not know where she was or who anyone was.

Ella convinced her dad to get Paula to the hospital. Finally he did, four days after Ella's wedding he turned up at Kings College Hospital at 11 o clock at night; he said it was difficult to get his wife dressed and to the toilet, and that it was exhausting for him as he hadn't eaten properly for weeks and was tired having been up night after night trying to console his crying wife who was in pain and scared.

Veronica felt frustrated with her dad for leaving it so long; Paula had needed to get to the hospital sooner. She felt sorry for her dad too as it had obviously taken its toll on him, but he hadn't helped himself by leaving it so long to get his wife to the hospital; and this is where Veronica grew impatient with him. The doctors could get no sense from Paula at all, they got her into a bed and she seemed to slip away as if in a coma.

The next day, Philip called his daughters to tell them to get to the hospital as soon as possible.

The doctors had said that her liver was not working and that the build-up of toxins in her body due to this, was causing her to be nonresponsive. It didn't look good, her breathing was shallow and the doctors told Philip that the next 24 to 48 hours were crucial, as they didn't know if Paula would pull through or not. Veronica couldn't believe it, surely it wasn't her time yet, she had only just had her chemo a month before. The consultant had said she could have up to two years with treatment, how could this be right? Veronica was crying hysterically.

Rae tried to calm her, "Vron you've got to be strong now, whatever happens you need to be strong. Your family need you and the children will wonder what's going on."

Veronica cleaned her face and took a deep breath. They dropped the children off to their nanny Irene's and rushed to London as fast as they could. It took forever to get through the midday traffic but when they eventually arrived, Veronica was called on her mobile by her dad.

"It's not looking good Vronx," he said with an emotionally broken voice.

"Oh my God, Dad don't say that please," Veronica cried. Rae parked the car and put his arm around Veronica. "I'm here Dad, I'm outside the hospital and I'm coming to find you." Her dad was crying down the phone, Veronica told him she loved him and would be with him in a few minutes.

As they got out of the car, Veronica got a rush of blood to her head, she felt dizzy and her heart was racing a million beats per second! Or so it felt. She wanted to be sick. It felt so wrong, so scary and so, so sad.

"Come on babe," said Rae, "let's just get to the ward and you can be with them."

271

They rushed through the hospital entrance, hurriedly looking for signs to her mum's department and wards. They waited impatiently for the lift then made their way to a corridor where they found the nursing station. They asked for Mrs Baker's room and were led to her bed; Ella, Paulette and their dad were sitting around the bedside. Veronica hugged them all, tears welled up in all of their eyes and Paulette ran out of the room. Veronica held her mum's hand as she lay practically lifeless in the bed. She kissed her mum repeatedly on her cheeks, whispering that she loved her in her ears. "Mum I know you can hear me, it's Vronx, you need to wake up, you've got us all worried and we need you to wake up." There was no response from Paula; all you could hear was the sound of her breathing.

Ella, Philip and Veronica started to discuss what had happened to Paula. Philip was telling everyone that Paula was talking nonsense in the waiting room of A & E when they arrived in the night. She asked Philip why there was a dog in the waiting room but there was nothing of the sort. Paula was convinced she could see it, Philip thought she was hallucinating which scared him, but the doctors assured him it was caused by the toxins in her brain. The girls were crying uncontrollably so in the end they had to leave the room; one of the nurses showed them to a bereavement room and told them to wait there for a doctor to come and speak with them. Paulette started to gasp for air; she was struggling due to her asthma and was quite hysterical. Veronica grabbed her with both arms and cradled her in her lap, stroking her hair. "I can't live without my little mum Vron, I am not ready to live without her, she is only young and so am I, how am I going to live without her, how is Dad going to cope without her?" Their dad was in tears, Rae put his arms around Veronica's dad and he too got quite choked up, everyone just cried.

The doctor came in and introduced herself. She explained that Paula's liver was potentially shutting down; and that sometimes the process could take weeks or months, but in some cases it could also happen quite suddenly. Due to Paula's weakness it was hard to say if she was strong enough to pull through, so the next 24 to 48 hours were crucial. Paulette struggled to breathe, reaching into her pocket for her inhaler.

Veronica tried to calm her sister, "Come on everyone, we just can't give up on her yet," she said. "We don't know, she may wake up, so let's sit tight and cuddle up to her. We can't let her hear us getting distressed because it will upset her too. Let's try to stay positive, that's all we can do isn't it?"

They all agreed. They wiped their tears, straightened themselves out and went back to Paula's bedside. As they walked down the corridor, they were met by their mum's two sisters, Beverley and Pat, with Beverley's husband Eddie. Veronica hadn't seen her Aunt Bev and Uncle Ed for years, not since she was around ten years old; and she had never met her Aunty Pat before. They all greeted one another and hugged. This caused everyone to break down again, crying outside Paula's room.

"Shoosh!" Philip exclaimed, "I don't want Paula hearing us because if she does wake up, she will wonder why we are all crying; and it will frighten her." Everyone agreed and they all walked back down the corridor towards the family room where they could get some privacy. Rae offered to stay by Paula's bedside to keep her company while the rest of the family talked.

Everyone broke down again. Paulette was inconsolable; Veronica couldn't bear seeing her little sister so distraught. What had she done to get such a raw deal in life? Veronica wondered. She was the youngest, the one who's life was still not settled; she still lived with her mum and dad, had no job, was on the dole and was a complete puff head, heavily addicted to marijuana despite her asthma. She had dropped out from school at a young age, refusing to go and try to better herself. She had low self-esteem and a temper that she found difficult to control. How would she get on without her mum there to pick up after her as she had done all these years? Veronica felt terrible, she felt sick to her stomach and the feeling would not let up.

After a chat everyone agreed to go back to Paula's bedside. Veronica enjoyed cuddling her Aunty Bev. There was something about her presence that reminded her of her mum and her Nan Rose. As they got to the entrance of Paula's room they were surprised to see Paula awake sitting up smiling. Everyone sighed with relief. Rae told them that this beautiful lady in this bed just opened her eyes and smiled at me. Paula chuckled.

"She was so happy to see me," he joked. Paula found it funny and so did everyone else. She said she heard everyone crying and it startled her.

"What was all the crying for?" she asked.

"What crying?" Philip replied.

"You know what bloody crying, don't try and fool me, I heard you all getting upset and the girls," she said.

"Phew, Paula was back to her old self," Veronica thought with relief.

Just then the nurse brought in a list for lunch. Paula chose soup and a sandwich, with a cup of tea. Everyone cuddled her and kissed her, none more than Philip, who was relieved that his wife had pulled through after all, so soon after they had been given their devastating news. "You frightened us woman," Philip told his wife, "we thought you were leaving us."

"I ain't going nowhere yet mate!" Paula responded, "Don't give up on me that easily."

"We didn't Mum, we knew you'd come through didn't we Ella?"

"Yes," Ella replied trying to show a positive upbeat posture, but their mum wasn't stupid and you could tell that she had taken it all in. She knew they were just trying to protect her.

Were they though, or was Paula herself starting to feel a bit isolated? After all, who could she relate to, who did she know who was going through what she was enduring? No one! It must have been painfully difficult for Paula, who also tried to put on a brave face for her entire family whilst suffering the pain and anguish of facing her terminal illness.

Veronica was due to fly to Mexico within 36 hours; she did not want to go, she had told Rae on the way to the hospital that she would not board that plane with her mum so close to death, but somehow she'd miraculously pulled through. Veronica didn't feel entirely sure that her mum was out of the woods just yet though. Rae begged her to go, and the next day Veronica's mum called her on her mobile and told her to go.

"You may not get a chance for a break for a while Vron, what with losing Masterstores," she said, "take my grandchildren away and give them a good time, they deserve it too. Don't worry about me I'm okay now, you just go, I love you babe and Rae and the kids."

There was something different about the way she spoke of Rae, she seemed to have got closer to him, almost like she had opened her eyes wide and could actually see the decent man that he was for the first time. Although she had always spoken of her respect for him as a doting dad for Jade and Charlie, and then Ashley and Sienna, and had always respected the fact he worked extremely hard to give his children and wife a better life, she had not really clicked with him. She had hidden a large part of her personality from him all those years, due to the drugs, but now it didn't matter anymore. She knew it didn't matter and the veil was lifted, she had almost given herself permission to just be natural and she was definitely more relaxed in that sense, when in Rae's company. This too helped Rae to see Vron's mum in her true light and he respected her honesty and her bravery. They had a mutual respect for each other that was calming, and Veronica was very much aware of this.

Veronica took her mum's advice, as she was torn between wanting to stay for her mum and to go for her husband and kids. She still felt uneasy about it, but Rae promised that if anything went wrong whilst they were away, he would get Vron back home on the first flight.

CHAPTER 74

Mexico, 2012

Veronica, Rae and the kids had booked an overnight hotel near Gatwick airport as they had an early morning flight. They decided it would be less stressful with the kids if they spent a night there prior to their flight. Veronica was still feeling very apprehensive about her mum's health.

She called her dad constantly to find out how she was doing. Miraculously, her mum had perked up a lot, she was eating and awake; and more chatty than she had been in a few weeks.

Veronica spoke with her on the phone whilst in bed in the hotel. "Are you sure you are okay Mum?" Veronica asked.

"Of course I am babe, now you go and enjoy yourself and have a good holiday with Rae and the kids. You've both been under a lot of stress what with your business and selling the house, and me frightening the life out of everyone, so go; and I don't want you to feel bad in any way about it," she said.

Veronica was relieved that her mum was a lot better, but she knew only too well that things could change overnight; she went along with her mum anyway.

"Rae has worked hard for this holiday, you both have; and there is no point in losing your money as you may not get a chance to go away for a while, so you must make the most of it Veronica," Paula said.

Veronica agreed, "But I love you so much Mum and I'm going to be worried about you, I just want to spend every moment I can with you that's all."

"I know you do babe, and you will when you get back, now look after them gorgeous kids and your man; and enjoy yourself do you hear me?" Paula said in jest. Veronica agreed and told her mum she loved her and wished her a comfortable night.

The holiday was a pleasant surprise for Rae and Veronica, the hotel where they were staying was really lovely and the food was fantastic. Rae had upgraded the couple's suite to a ground floor which had a personal plunge pool. It was perfect and it meant that the couple could enjoy some privacy with the children when they didn't fancy sitting around the main pool with all of the other hotel guests. Veronica felt very relaxed and didn't realise how much she needed to unwind from all of the stress the family had been through, but she felt a sense of guilt for being in the situation she was in whilst her sisters and parents were back in north London facing the reality of Paula's cancer.

Every day, Veronica wanted to hear from her parents, but it was expensive to call so she would text instead and wait for their response. As the days went by, Veronica found herself wishing the holiday away so that she could be with her mum. It didn't feel right that she was thousands of miles away from her mum when she was dying.

Rae understood his wife's feelings, he had seen for himself how close it had come to losing Paula, he too had come to understand her more and they seemed to have a sudden mutual love and respect. Veronica was happy about this, if only things could have been better between them years ago, maybe Paula's relationship with Veronica and the grandchildren would have been closer. Perhaps Paula felt ashamed around Rae, that was the feeling that Veronica got, but it was never discussed. Rae tried to distract Veronica's thoughts.

"Let's take the kids to the water park in Cancun," he suggested.

"Yes, that's a great idea," Veronica agreed, so they set off to Cancun in a taxi.

The day was as hot as ever in Mexico and the water park was lots of fun for both Ashley and Sienna. Rae and Veronica took it in turns to go on various slides with the kids. Ashley loved going on the Kamikaze with his dad and his mum, it was a really scary slide.

Ashley went on and on with his dad, whilst Veronica took Sienna into the baby pool.

As she stepped down holding Sienna, she slipped. The step was very slimy, as if there was mould or algae on the step. Veronica bent her toes back as she landed and she heard a click.

The pain in her foot was immediate, and all she could do was to sit in the pool trying not to cry, with all her might. Sienna let go of Veronica's hand and went off in the pool. Veronica panicked calling Sienna back to her, "Please don't go off honey, Mummy has hurt herself and I need Daddy."

Luckily Sienna must have sensed the urgency in Veronica's voice and came back to her mum. Veronica wriggled about in the water as the pain in her toe had become intense. She was too scared to look at her foot as she sensed she had broken something and was a big baby when it came to anything like that. She could be as cool as a cucumber if it was someone else hurt, but not when it was herself! She waited in the pool hoping that Rae and Ashley would come soon and find her. She was too scared to get out of the water for fear of seeing the damage.

A few minutes later Rae came along with Ashley. "What's the matter Vron?" he asked. "I think I've broken my toe, I slipped down the step and heard a crack in my toes," she replied.

Rae called for assistance, he managed to get the attention of a pool attendant and they tried to get Veronica to walk out of the water. Rae asked her to lift her foot out of the water and her toe was clearly broken and sitting at a right angle. Veronica couldn't bear the sight of it and started to feel very weak and faint! The pool attendant got a wheelchair and Rae lifted her out of the water. Veronica was sat slumped in the wheelchair struggling for air as she was gradually passing out. Rae was telling her to take deep breaths and asked for a brown paper bag for her to breathe into; Veronica was having a panic attack.

She had endured many over the years but they had been much fewer and further between since being with Rae, he had a way of making Veronica listen to him and he was very good at nursing her. Veronica knew that no one else would be able to handle this aspect of her behaviour, not like Rae, he was special, he was her knight in shining armour and she was never going to give him up for anything!

The pool attendant took the family to a treatment room where there was a doctor on hand, to have a look at Veronica. Feeling even more panicked and full of worry, Veronica was feeling sick and weak. The doctor offered her some gas and air which she accepted. Ashley and Sienna were both worried about their mum; it frightened them seeing her looking so ill in a wheelchair with an air mask across her face. Within around ten minutes Veronica was feeling a lot better, she had got herself worked up because she thought the doctor was going to bend her toe back into its rightful position. She had heard of this being done before but couldn't bear the thought of it. This is what made her have a panic attack.

He told her she needed to go to the hospital for an X-ray as it was difficult to know if the toe had just come out of its socket or if it was broken, so the family took another taxi to a hospital where Veronica had an X-ray costing £300, to confirm that the toe was in fact broken.

It was strapped alongside the neighbouring toe and Veronica was sent away with anti-inflammatory medication and pain relief. Then they laughed the whole night through about her broken toe. She had flown down dangerous water slides with Ashley half the day, but broke her toe in the baby pool and they found this hilarious! Not to mention nearly passing out at the sight of it. This certainly took her mind off of her mum's situation for a while though.

Veronica spent the next few days limping around the hotel complex, preferring to stick close to their room and make use of the plunge pool. The children loved being able to fall out of their room and into the pool, but Veronica had to be constantly on watch as Sienna had no fear whatsoever of anything. Veronica on the other hand, would panic at the slightest move Sienna made towards the pool.

The holiday was nice for the family as a whole, as they had quality time together without the usual interruptions of their business which had always been a huge responsibility and intrusion into the family home. But Veronica grew eager by the day to get home so that she could see her mum.

Whilst they were away, Rae and Veronica had bought presents for Paula and Philip. This was Rae's idea as he could see how much Veronica was missing them, so to cheer her up he took her into a Pandora shop in Cancun where they chose a man's leather bracelet for her dad and a special diamond charm for Paula, to fit a bracelet she already had.

Upon their return to the UK Veronica made plans to visit her parents the following day. Her dad seemed to be choked up by the Pandora gift. Veronica told him it was from Rae as he had chosen it, there were two silver charms with the letters P and B for his initials. Philip was overwhelmed and thanked them. Paula was mesmerised by her diamond charm, it was the design of a rope, made out of gold and silver, with tiny little diamonds. Paula smiled, kissed the couple and asked Paulette to fetch her bracelet.

Veronica told her mum about her escapade at the water slide and how she had broken her toe in the baby pool and was carted out of the park in a wheelchair. Paula found this very amusing. Veronica had always panicked

279

at the slightest thing, even as a child when the doctors put sweat patches across her back to try and find out why she kept getting pneumonia, she would scream the hospital down and it would take half a dozen doctors and nurses to hold her.

Veronica was just relieved to be by her Mother's side again. She was at home in bed, she couldn't do much as the swelling in her tummy had come back and it was now in her legs too.

Veronica wanted to cry, but she had to remain strong for her mum, she liked to distract her Mother's attention from her illness with stories of times gone by; and things that she knew would make her mum laugh! Veronica loved to be a bit of a joker, and her mum always seemed to get Veronica's sense of humour more than anyone else in the family.

Paula would often tell her daughter, "Veronica you do make me laugh, you cheer me up and help me forget." This was priceless to Veronica. She may not have had a magic wand to take away her mother's pain and the cancer, but at least she could take her attention away from it, even if for only a short moment at a time.

CHAPTER 75

Paula's Health Deteriorates

Veronica and Rae had a lot to contend with now. Their contract with Masterstores had ended and they were just relying on work they had coming from their advertising and from a small contract they had with DHL and with Bouygues UK; at least this gave them something regular. It wasn't a lot and they would have to do more to find other work, but at least it brought in something. They had two people working for them and were eager to continue using them on a self-employed basis. They were still waiting for the sale of their house to go through too, but the people at the bottom of the chain were holding everything up.

Meanwhile, Paula's health continued to deteriorate. The swelling in her tummy and legs had got so bad she could barely walk and she struggled to breathe and get comfortable. Paula was completely and utterly fed up and depressed; and before anyone knew it, she was back in Kings Hospital. Philip had been in A&E all night with her as she had become confused due to the toxic build up in her body and brain again.

Paula had woken up in hospital not remembering how she had got there. She found her phone by her bedside and tried calling her husband but got no reply. She called Veronica who answered immediately. Paula was crying down the phone to her daughter, she said she was frightened and that she had woken up not knowing where she was or how she had got there.

Veronica explained to her mum that she had become confused again because of the toxic build up in her brain. Paula cried, "Why does it keep happening to me, I just wish it would stop Veronica. I went to sleep knowing what was going on one minute, and then I wake up here and I don't know where I am or how I got here, let alone what day of the week it is."

Veronica welled up inside herself; it was awful to hear her mum so upset. "Where's Dad?" Paula asked, "He's not answering his phone to me."

"He's asleep Mum, he's been up night after night with you as you've been so unsettled."

Paula's confusion made her act like a child, she was very dazed and uneasy on her feet. Philip had literally caught her in the nick of time attempting to go downstairs. She couldn't get comfy on her back or on her side, the only thing she could do was walk around sometimes, but then when the confusion kicked in, this made matters worse and Philip found it very difficult controlling his wife and protecting her from harm.

"I just hate being here Veronica," Paula said. "I'm frightened that I won't leave, that I will die here in hospital, I just want to be at home with your dad and be with all of you."

Veronica couldn't hold back the tears any longer; she burst, but tried frantically to control herself for the sake of her mum.

"I hate being here all alone; it frightened me waking up in hospital without any of you by my side."

Veronica couldn't bear to hear her mum like this. "Mum, just sit tight, I am getting ready and I will be with you as fast as I can," Veronica assured her. "There are trains leaving Newington every half hour and it takes roughly fifty minutes to get to Kings Hospital once on the train. It's 9am now so I should be with you by 11am."

Paula sobbed, "I'm so sorry Veronica, I don't mean to bring you down, you've got enough going on."

"Don't you dare apologise Mum," Veronica said, "What you are going through is far more important than anything I've got going on, trust me, so don't you dare apologise Mum. You are the world to me and all I want to do is be there for you, so you've done the right thing to call me. Is there anything you need, are you hungry Mum? I could bring some fresh sandwiches for you."

"Ooh yeah if you like, that would be nice as the food in here isn't great," Paula replied. "Mum please don't get upset. I know it's hard and it's easy for me to say, but I just don't want you getting worked up so just try to relax and wait for me. I will be with you before you know it."

"Okay babe," Paula said, "I love you Vronx."

"I love you too Mum, more than you will ever know, we all do. I will be there soon, love you, Bye." Paula said goodbye and hung up.

Veronica fell into Rae's arms and cried. "She's so upset babe, I've got to get to her, I need to make sandwiches." Rae helped Veronica to get ready and out the door, and as she got to the station just twenty minutes after speaking with her mum, the train was just pulling in.

Veronica's journey took fifty minutes on the nose and Veronica was by her mum's bedside by 10.45 am. Her mum wasn't in bed when she got there as she had gone to the toilet, so Veronica waited for her return. Paula was surprised to see her daughter by her bed. "Hello babe," Paula said, "you got here quick." Veronica hugged her mum tight and helped her back to bed.

Veronica got out the sandwiches she had brought her, but Paula wasn't feeling hungry just yet.

"I will have them in a bit babe," she said. "I've not long had breakfast. I'm so glad you are here, I just wish I could go home Veronica, I'm scared I'm gonna go to sleep and not wake up. Sometimes I just lay awake for hours trying my hardest not to drop off because I don't want to wake up back in hospital again, or worse, not wake up at all. I'm so scared Vronx."

Veronica didn't know what to say, what could she say? There was nothing anyone could do to take away Paula's fears. She was the one now facing her death, it was awful, it was painful to watch, but what was even worse was that no one could change it. Veronica lent across to her mum and cuddled her. "I'm so sorry for all of this mum," Veronica said.

"Why are you sorry babe?" her mum asked.

"I just am Mum, for everything you have gone through these past few years, what with being so unwell with the hep C and now this. It just isn't fair and you don't deserve any of it."

"I know," said Paula, "but life is unfair and there are little innocent kids out there facing what I'm facing, so when you put it into perspective, what's fair?"

Veronica agreed, kissed her mum and then changed the subject. She spoke about Sienna and Ashley to try and take her mind off things. Within an hour Paula was feeling tired and went to sleep. Veronica sat by her bed stroking her arm.

A little while later, Paula's sister Pearl turned up with her daughter Amy. It was a pleasant surprise for Paula who hadn't seen her sister in a few years, they cuddled and chatted. Then Ella turned up with her husband Petros, and then a little later, Paula's other sisters Bev and Pat turned up with Bev's husband Eddie. Before Paula knew it, she had a lot of family around her which cheered her up no end. "I can't believe how popular I am she chuckled!"

"You've got a lot of people around that love you Pauline," said Bev.

"My friends at church have been praying for you."

"Oh that's nice of them," Paula said. "I need to get out of this place. I want a cigarette."

Veronica helped her mum put her dressing gown on and got her into a wheelchair. They wrapped a blanket around her legs and Veronica wheeled her out of the room along the ward and towards the lift. Veronica stopped to tell one of the nurses they were taking Paula outside for some fresh air and left her mobile number with the nurse in case they needed to bring her back to the ward. The doctor was on her rounds and Paula was in line to be seen, so Veronica didn't want it to mess up her visit. The family all followed into the lift and they went towards the hospital exit where there was a designated smoking area outside. Paula had a pack of cigarettes stashed in her dressing gown, she felt like a naughty school girl puffing away on her fag, but was also relieved to be outside in the sun.

The family all chatted and joked happily with each other, Veronica took the opportunity to take some pictures on her phone of her mum with her sisters. It was so sad to see Paula look so frail and old, but at least she was smiling and she enjoyed a rare moment of affection with her sisters as they held hands and cuddled. It brought a tear to Veronica's eye.

When Paula was finished, they wheeled her back to the ward. It was nearly 4pm and Philip still hadn't arrived at the hospital. He was on his way, driving through the manic London traffic, but it could take a few hours to get from Edmonton to Kings Hospital.

Everyone kept Paula's spirits high and she was able to forget about her illness during these moments. The family happily chatted about each other's lives, jobs and relationships, their kids, etcetera. It was a great distraction for Paula who seemed so much brighter.

It was nearly 7pm when Veronica had to say goodbye and get a train back to Kent.

Her dad, Philip, had just turned up with Paulette. Paula was very happy to see them.

Beverley, Pat and Eddie had gone a couple of hours before, heading back to Surrey.

Pearl and Amy left with Veronica to get a bus back to Edgware Road. Paula had experienced an eventful day, considering how it had started with her waking up all alone, frightened and confused. All she needed was reassurance and her family around her as much as possible. Veronica could see the positive impact this had on Paula's outlook. It was obviously horrendous what Paula was facing, but it was made so much more bearable with the love and support of her family around her.

CHAPTER 76

The Results of Chemoembolization

Paula was discharged from King's hospital a couple of days later. She had been on an antibiotic drip to help get rid of the toxins in her body. The doctors had also given her various drugs to help with going to the toilet, the downside to her anti sickness drugs was constipation, which contributed to the toxic build up.

Feeling a lot better, Paula was sent home and she was relieved to be back there; so too was Philip who hated being alone in the flat and away from his wife. He couldn't function without Paula, they had done everything together and had spent thirty eight years of being with each other every day, apart from the times when Philip was in prison.

Although he had been working full time in recent years as a plumber, Philip had spent twenty four years on the dole, dealing drugs with Paula by his side. He was completely and utterly lost without her. He wouldn't cook for himself let alone eat.

Ella had made a point of checking up on him and sending round cooked food for him, but she was heavily pregnant and about to give birth any moment, so it was hard for her too. Everyone was relieved that Paula was home safe and sound.

A few days later, Paula had an appointment at Kings College Hospital to find out the result of her treatment. Veronica had decided to be there to support her parents. It was difficult for her dad as he was also painfully thin and gaunt; he needed looking after as well. Veronica had pleaded with them to stay with her and Rae. "Please come and stay," she begged them, "let me and Rae do some running around for you both. Dad you need a break too, you need to be able to rest up and relax. You can't do that when Mum is awake every night, so you must come and stay with us." Philip agreed, and so did Paula, they promised that they would stay once they had seen the consultant for Paula's chemo result.

Veronica arranged to meet them at Kings Hospital half an hour before Paula's appointment.

It was pointless for Veronica to keep driving to North London, then through London to Kings, and back to North London to drop her parents' home, before returning to Kent. It was much easier and cheaper for her to get the train. Veronica arrived ten minutes early so she went for a coffee. Her mum and dad turned up shortly afterwards and they made their way to the consultant's waiting area in the liver department of the hospital. Paula was shown to a set of scales, where she was weighed by a nurse who recorded the weight on Paula's notes. Then she was sent to a phlebotomy room where her blood was taken, after that the family were led to the waiting area to wait for the consultant.

Paula started to shake uncontrollably. Her arms were so thin they were like a child's. Veronica just wanted to cry but she knew she had to be strong for her mum and dad. She put her arms around her mum and pulled her into her neck for a cuddle. "It's okay Mum," she whispered in her ear.

"It isn't babe," Paula replied, "I just know it's not gonna be good news. I've had no let up since my chemo, look how ill I've been, look how thin I am, they ain't gonna give me any more treatment, I just know it."

Veronica kissed her mum on the side of her face, "Let's just see what they say Mum." She gripped her mum's hand tightly and cuddled her close, but her mum's body continued to shake. Veronica's heart sank into the pit of her chest, she too felt that fear. It was awful.

Opposite Paula and Veronica were other patients with jaundice and swollen stomachs, they had been here before only weeks ago, but the reality of Paula's illness was becoming ever more real. The specialist consultant nurse called Paula's name. She got up on her feet, her body still shaking frantically. Phil, Paula and Veronica followed the nurse into her room, "Hello Pauline," said the nurse.

"Hello," Paula replied.

"Please take a seat everyone," Lillian requested. She took a look at Paula's notes and logged into her computer, putting Paula's hospital number into her system.

"Okay," she said, "I have the results back from the Chemoembolization treatment that you received. I can confirm that the tumour that was treated by the drug has significantly shrunk." The family sighed with relief.

"However," Veronica, Philip and Paula froze, "because the beads inserted to shut off this particular part of the liver so that the drug could be delivered directly to that tumour, stopped the drug leaking elsewhere in the liver, unfortunately other tumours have now grown in those other areas which the drug could not work on. These tumours are smaller, but they are aggressive none the less; and because of how weak you are Pauline and how painfully frail, your body would definitely not sustain any further treatment." Phil, Paula and Veronica burst into tears.

"I knew it," Paula cried, "I just knew this was going to happen."

"What about taking a slither of a compatible liver and growing it in the lab?" Veronica asked, frantically scrambling for any tiny piece of hope that may still be available. "Why can't Mum have a liver transplant? If my liver is compatible you can take a piece of mine," she said to Lillian as she cried.

"I am so sorry for you all and to Pauline for what she is facing, but we are still at least another ten years away from using that kind of procedure; and giving Pauline a liver transplant would not be the answer. There is a phenomenal waiting list for transplants and the prognosis for survival for Hep C patients with the type of cancer Pauline has is zero, that's why we don't offer this.

"The cancer has spread through major blood vessels in her liver and there is a high probability that the cancer will have spread elsewhere in her body. We are so short of liver donors that we have very strict criteria about who is eligible; and I know it's awful for you all to be in this position, but Pauline would only suffer huge complications and even more pain only to end up with the same result. Pauline needs to be of a certain minimum weight to receive chemotherapy, and she was already under the weight we would normally consider for chemotherapy originally. We had hoped that she may be able to withstand the treatment, but that hasn't been the case and the cancer is spreading."

The family were left dumbfounded. "Why were we told up to two years with treatment then?" Veronica asked angrily.

"Babe it's not their fault," Philip told his daughter, "they've tried all they can honey."

"I just can't accept this," Veronica replied, "There must be something we can do."

"I'm very sorry that things have gone this way," Lillian said, "Of course, as doctors and nurses, we want to save everyone we meet, we don't like to be in this position but sometimes we just can't change it."

Paula had stopped shaking; she had a look in her eyes almost of acceptance, as if she had just come to terms with her fate right then in that moment. Veronica couldn't bear it, Veronica couldn't believe it, she didn't want to believe it or accept it. This wasn't meant to happen to her beautiful little mum. This was the kind of tragedy that happened to other people.

"I'm so sorry Mum," Veronica cried, "I wish there was something I could do."

"I know babe, but there isn't anything that anyone can do now, I'm in the hands of fate," her mum replied.

Philip sat dumbfounded, usually he was full of answers but he could say nothing, it was as if he was paralysed, he looked numb.

Veronica couldn't hold it back any longer, she sobbed, "This isn't fair, I hate this world."

"I'm so very sorry for you all, I truly am," said Lillian, "May I suggest that you liaise with Palliative care from this point."

Philip got up and cuddled his wife and daughter, then he thanked Lillian for her efforts to help Paula. The family left the room and walked out of the liver department, dazed. Veronica scanned the waiting room and looked at the other patients. They too were experiencing similar situations. It was quite obvious spotting the ones that were coming to the end of their lives, as they too were painfully thin with bloated stomachs. It was Veronica's mission now to make every minute count.

"We've got another weekend booked for a caravan in Whitstable Mum. Let's get everyone down there for a few days," Veronica said as they left the hospital.

"Ooh yes that would be lovely. I want to get to the coast and be by the sea," Paula replied.

"Well that's what we shall do then Mum. What do you reckon Dad?"

"Yeah, we need to get away from that depressing dingy flat, so let's do it," he said. "Do you want to come and sit in the car with us for a bit until it's time to get your train?"

"Yes okay," Veronica replied.

They walked back to the car and Phil and Paula lit a cigarette along the way. Veronica hadn't smoked for three years but right then, she wanted to. She could have smoked a whole packet, the way she was feeling. How was Philip going to cope without his number one woman by his side? How would he survive life after Paula? He had been a bully to her in their years of marriage but he also had a soft side that could be very loving and attentive when the drugs were not having a negative impact on his personality. He had put the whole family through hell with his habit, including introducing Paula to heroin so that they both became totally dependent on their habit together. The children's needs were often pushed aside for their next fix. This had become an everyday life for the couple and for the children, who learned to accept this and adapt to their unusual situation.

Veronica had become more aware of her parents' shortcomings since leaving the family home though, and having children of her own had highlighted the issues even more for her. She questioned her parents' love for her and her sisters, and why they had put them through so many difficult situations. The truth was that the drugs always came first, before anything else. The truth was that her parents' addiction was like an illness, they were beyond fault as they were victims of heroin too. Veronica had understood this for her entire life, but it was now the reason why her mum's life would soon come to an abrupt end; and she would be taken prematurely from Philip, Veronica, Ella, Paulette and also her grandchildren. All they could do now was to stick together as a family, support each other as much as possible; and make the most of whatever time they had left with Paula.

CHAPTER 77

Staying with Veronica

Though Veronica and Rae had booked a long weekend for the family in a caravan in Whitstable, they'd had to change the booking a few times as Paula had been quite ill. There were still a few weeks to go before the weekend away, but Philip was struggling with caring for his wife, so Veronica suggested they stay at her home for a few days. This would give her dad a break and allow Veronica to take over Paula's care.

Paula loved the idea of getting out of London; she hated living in the tower block in Edmonton for the last 12 years. "Yes please," she said eagerly when Veronica offered; and Philip agreed to pack a bag and get down to Veronica the following day.

The next day though, Paula was disorientated, she was confused and didn't know who she was. It was strange how she would be okay one moment; go to sleep and then wake up confused. It seemed to be an ongoing pattern that was becoming more frequent, but no one could tell when this would occur. Philip would for example wake up to find her rummaging through the washing basket, and when he asked what she was looking for, she would say she was looking for some tissue. He would try to get her dressed but she would refuse, he would try and get her to take her medication but she wouldn't, this was very frustrating for him.

He found it very difficult to manage her on his own, especially when he'd been up night after night with her in pain. He was tired and weary himself and in need of care.

Paula didn't want to go into a Hospice, just the idea of it frightened her. She begged Philip not to let her die in hospital or in a hospice; she just wanted to be in her own environment with her family around her. He promised her that he wouldn't let that happen and so he tried hard to cope alone.

He called Veronica that morning practically in tears, "I can't cope anymore," Philip cried down the phone, "I just find it so hard."

"Do you want me to come and help you get Mum ready and pack some things?" Veronica asked.

"No it's okay, I've got some things I need to sort out before I come, but I need to have a couple of hours of shut eye before I can even think about coming," Philip said.

"Okay," Veronica replied, "If you need anything Dad just call, you know I am just an hour away. I can get to you if you need help."

"I know babe, thanks, I will be okay, I'm just tired that's all. I know this may sound awful but sometimes I wish this would end, I wish some nights that she would slip away peacefully. I love her so much but I can't bear the agony of it all. I will call you later when I'm on my way."

Veronica was a little shocked at what her dad had just said, but in a way she could understand his torment, having to watch his wife go through so much agony must be torture for him too.

Philip turned up to Veronica's quite late that evening. Rae had cooked them a lovely meal, but Paula was unresponsive and just sat at the table slipping away into a dazed sleep. Philip was getting a little frustrated with Paula as he was trying to spoon feed her and she was spilling it down herself. It was obvious that Philip was at his wits' end and was clearly tired himself.

Rae offered to help out, "Let me help her," Rae suggested to Philip, "You just enjoy your meal and I will feed Paula."

Philip agreed and moved over, Rae spoke softly to Paula. "Look at this tasty food we've got here for you Paula." She opened her eyes and smiled at him. "Would you like to try this delicious meal I've cooked for you?" he asked her.

Paula nodded her head in agreement and opened her mouth wide. Rae spooned some of the chicken and potatoes into her mouth. As she chewed she said, "Mmm."

"Is that nice Paula?" Rae asked, she looked at him and smiled, "Yes that is lovely."

"Great," Rae responded, "Would you like some more then?"

"Oooh yes please," Paula replied. Rae continued to feed and coax Paula and before they knew it, Rae had managed to get a whole plate of food into Paula.

Veronica was mesmerised by her husband's patience and his attentiveness to her mum, and Philip could not believe how easy Rae had made feeding Paula look.

"She's not like that for me," Philip said, "She just refuses to eat and is very argumentative."

"Don't worry Dad," Veronica said, "Just relax and let us help you out for a while, it's what we are here for, to give you a break and let you recuperate. You look so tired Dad, why don't you just relax."

"Thanks babe," Philip replied, "You don't know what this means to me."

Meanwhile, Ella had gone into labour. Her husband called Philip on the phone and told him that Ella was in a lot of pain and crying for her mum. He asked if there was any way that Paula could get to the hospital to be by her daughter's side. Phil couldn't believe the request.

"Are you joking man?" he asked, "We have come away for a few days because Paula is so ill, Ella knows how sick she is, there is no way she could support Ella. Paula needs looking after herself and to be honest mate, so do I."

Petros agreed to keep in touch and let them know how her labour progressed. Phil gave the family their love and put the phone down.

Veronica had sat listening intently to what was happening. "Can you believe it?" Phil remarked, "He says Ella is crying for Mum and wants her by her side. What planet are they on? She knows how sick your mum is, how could she expect her to be there? How bloody selfish of them to even call me and ask. They know how difficult it's been for me these past weeks and when I finally get here, they are calling me to go running with Mum now she's in labour."

Veronica couldn't understand either; it was pretty obvious that Paula was in no fit state to be of any assistance to Ella. Veronica on the other hand had given birth to both her children without her mum's support, but Ella was different, she'd had her mum by her side when she gave birth to Helen. Paula had wiped her head and fussed over her then and she obviously felt the need to ask for her mum again, but things were different now, Ella had a husband this time, so everything was different now.

A few hours later when everyone had gone to bed, Phil received a text and a photo of Ella and Petros's baby boy Sammy. Phil called Veronica into Ashley's room where they were sleeping, he showed her the photo and they all cooed over the cute photo of the new family addition. It was a proud moment for Phil and Paula as grandparents, but Paula wasn't herself, she was in and out of consciousness and not completely aware of what Ella had just gone through. It was a very bittersweet moment in reality, as although it was lovely to have a new life born into the family, the reality of Paula's fate tainted this. Sammy would be a grandchild who Paula would not see growing up, so it was a happy, but also very sad time.

The next couple of days gave Veronica some insight into Paula's condition and how Phil was coping. Luckily he had been left to sleep throughout most of the day. Veronica waited on her parents, bringing them tea and breakfast in bed, helping her mum to the toilet and assisting her to wash herself. Paula was so confused that she didn't know where the toilet was and would often walk into the wrong room, so Veronica had to keep a constant eye on her mum.

When Phil woke up he seemed a lot brighter and more upbeat. He had Ashley around him eager for some attention from his granddad, which Phil loved, as he got to be a big kid and amuse himself playing with his grandson. This was a rare moment as they had never had any quality time together without Helen. Whenever Ashley saw his Grandad, it was always when Veronica brought him and Sienna up to London to stay at Ella's.

Ashley was used to fighting for his attention because Helen was always quite clingy and jealous whenever Phil showed his grandson any attention. Veronica thought it was sad that it had taken nine years for this to happen, and that it was only because of the awful circumstances that the family was now in.

Later that morning Veronica got a call from her aunts, Bev and Pat, they asked if they could visit Pauline at Veronica's. Her parents hadn't wanted them to go to their flat in North London because of the state it was in, so Philip had asked Veronica if it was okay to have Bev and Pat round to see their sister whilst they were there. Veronica was happy to go along with whatever suited them and agreed. "Yes of course you can come over," Veronica replied. Her Aunts said they would like to see them all later that day. Paula was still very much out of it, she had spent all day sleeping, only waking for the toilet or a drink; and on the rare occasions that she thought about it, a cigarette.

Veronica and Ashley sat close to Paula cuddling up to her at every opportunity. Phil was also lapping up the attention he was getting from Ashley and Sienna, who had also started to warm towards her Grandad. He would play with her and tease her, she liked the attention and he liked the distraction from Paula's ordeal. Rae had been fantastic, making sure everyone was well fed and serving up some scrumptious dishes when he was not at work.

Then before they knew it, Bev, Pat and Ed were at their door. Veronica was pleased to see them all and invited them in. They were eager to get close to their sister and cuddle her. Pat sat beside Paula and cupped her sister's hand tightly in hers, she spoke softly to Paula to try and get her to open her eyes. When Paula eventually did, she looked surprised. "What are you doing here?" Paula asked. "I've come to visit my beautiful baby sister, is that okay?" Pat replied.

Paula smiled and chuckled, "Of course it is." Pat kissed Paula on the side of her face and they cuddled. Paula quickly fell back to sleep where she remained for most of the time her sisters were there. Veronica could see that it troubled them greatly to see their sister so fragile.

Phil went out into the garden to roll a spliff, Pat and Bev followed him thinking he was having a cigarette but they were astonished to see him blatantly roll a joint in front of them.

"Phil, haven't you grown out of all that yet?" Bev asked him.

"Nope, and nor will I," he exclaimed jokingly. Pat and Bev shot a look that said it all, they were disgusted, but there was no point causing friction so they changed the subject. Veronica's aunts were amazed at the size of Veronica and Rae's home; they couldn't believe how well they had done for themselves.

Bev kept repeating herself by saying, "You've done so well Veronica, you and Rae. You should be very proud of what you've achieved."

Veronica was flattered, but they were actually about to sell up and move. They would quite possibly end up losing much of what they had worked for, due to losing their biggest contract with Masterstores. She explained this to her aunt but it didn't change Bev's opinion.

"You have still worked very hard to be where you are right now and you should be proud of yourself."

Veronica had been full of pride but none of it mattered now, all that mattered was her mum.

It was soon time for her aunts and uncle to make their way home, they kissed everyone goodbye and cuddled their sister. Veronica could see how upset her aunts were by their youngest sister's poor health. After they left, everyone had dinner and went to bed. Paula was still very sleepy and confused.

"I might take her home tomorrow," Phil told Veronica, "If she's still like this, I think I need to get her to the hospital."

Veronica didn't want her mum and dad to leave, she had enjoyed looking after them and waiting on them, but she knew that her dad had to do the right thing and get her mum seen to.

The next day, Philip busied himself helping Ashley with a school project. Ashley had to make a model space craft using bits and bobs around the home, the project was about NASA so Ashley and Grandad spent all day cutting, painting and gluing.

It turned out to be a really good distraction for Philip from the worry of his wife. Veronica had spent all day looking after her and making both her parents breakfast and lunch. It was also an eye opener for Veronica seeing just how ill her mum was, but Veronica felt more at ease having her mother with her than she did when she was all the way in London. At least here, she could see her and be close. The family had another successful evening meal together and although very drowsy and confused, Rae and Veronica managed to get Paula to eat another plateful of food. This made Veronica feel relieved, as at least she could see she was eating, if nothing else.

Later that evening, Philip decided to have a bath with his wife. Veronica ran it for them and put some bubble bath in the water. A little while later, Philip took his wife to the bathroom and asked Veronica to help him get her undressed. She was quite dazed and unresponsive at this point and Phil had decided to leave the next morning to take her back to Kings College Hospital.

Veronica realised how difficult it was to manage Paula. Philip was so thin and frail himself, he could hardly hold his wife up, let alone get her undressed. Veronica helped him. They struggled to get Paula's top and bottoms off, but when they did, Veronica was shocked at the sight of her mum's bony body. Her clavicle was very prominent and her rib cage was showing, even though her stomach was really swollen from the ascites. Veronica helped guide her mum into the bath, then once she was in, Veronica left her parents alone in peace to continue their bath together.

They had bathed together for years, spending sometimes a couple of hours in the bathroom together. Half an hour later, Veronica heard an almighty bang coming from the bathroom. She was downstairs with the children and Rae.

"Oh my God," Veronica said. "What was that?"

She went running up the stairs to see what had happened. Veronica banged on the door, "Are you okay Dad?"

"Can you come in and help me?" Philip cried out to his daughter.

Veronica could hear from his voice that something was wrong. Veronica opened the door and was shocked to see her mum lying naked on the floor and her dad was gripping his rib cage and looked like he was in agony.

"What happened?" Veronica asked. "I told her to stay in the bath but as I turned to get some shower gel she got up and tried to get out of the bath," her dad said.

Veronica picked her mum up from the floor.

"Put your arm around me Mum," Veronica said, but Paula was not responding. Veronica gripped her mother around both armpits and lifted her off the ground. It took all of Veronica's strength to do it but she managed to get her mum to her feet.

Paula was wet and shivering; Veronica pulled a towel around her mum's body and patted her dry. Paula had a huge bruise across her head and her arm, which had come up immediately, quite dark and purple.

"Oh my God Dad," Veronica exclaimed, "look at these bruises."

"I told her to fucking stay in the bath," Phil said, "but she ignored me and as I tried to reach out to stop her falling I caught my rib cage on your taps." Veronica could see he was in a lot of pain.

Paula was still confused and upset by her fall and was crying. Veronica cuddled her close and told her not to worry. "Are you okay Mum? You've fallen out of the bath and bumped your head quite bad." Paula couldn't get any words out and just cried. Veronica was worried about her head.

Her dad was really angry, calling Paula a fucking idiot and shouting at her.

"Stop shouting at her dad, it's not her fault, she's confused," Veronica told him.

"I know," he replied, "but why can't she just fucking listen? If I say sit still it means sit still, not get up and get out of the fucking bath, it's not difficult. This is what it's like for me, she doesn't fucking listen, it's like having a child."

Veronica could see he was at his wits' end but where had his patience gone? Why had he become so worked up?

"I think I've broken a rib or two as I slipped to try and save her and cracked my ribs on your taps, I can barely breathe."

Veronica asked her dad if he wanted her to take them both to the local hospital to get checked.

"No it's okay babe, I'm taking her back to Kings in the morning."

Veronica felt bad for both her parents, but she felt awful for her mum. Philip had clearly lost his patience with his wife, and caring for her had become an issue. Veronica didn't want her mum to leave; she wanted to care for her 'til the end. At least she would be by her side and give her the understanding and patience she needed. Veronica took her mum into Ashley's bedroom where they were staying, dried her and got her dressed.

"Thank you," her mum mumbled in her confused state. "I'm sorry for this," she added.

"You've got nothing to apologise for Mum," Veronica replied. "None of this is your fault, you are not well Mum and it's our job to look after you. I'm sorry you slipped; it's my fault for putting bubble bath in the water. Maybe you wouldn't have slipped if I hadn't put it in the water," Veronica said.

Philip came in to the bedroom at this point and overheard Veronica talking to her mum. "It's not your fault either Vron," her dad said, "I don't think it was the bubble bath, it was just one of them things, she got up and tried to get out but didn't know where she was, so she should have just stayed sitting in the bath."

"It's not Mum's fault either dad, she's ill and dying of cancer, she asked for none of this, you know that."

Phil sat on the bed and huffed, he was fed up and tired and run ragged with all he had endured over the weeks since learning his wife was dying of cancer. It was plain to see that it was wearing him out and he was at his wits' end with it all.

Phil got dressed and Veronica helped guide her mum downstairs so that Phil could have a spliff in the garden. Veronica made them both a drink and stayed by her mum's side, cuddling up to her. Veronica got a cold pack from the freezer, wrapped it in a tea towel and applied it to her mum's head. She didn't want to let her mum out of her sight, but it was getting late and was soon time for bed. Veronica helped her dad take her mum back up to bed, and helped her to get ready and settled. Veronica kissed her parents and went to bed too.

In the morning she woke to find her mum being sick in the bathroom. Her dad was fast asleep and so were Rae and the kids. Veronica knocked on the bathroom door and asked her mum if she was alright. Paula told Veronica to let herself in. Paula was trying to steady herself as she was being sick in the toilet. Veronica put her arm around her mum and tried to hold her steady. Paula was bringing up a thick yellow substance. It looked very strange, not like normal vomit. It was thick and it was difficult for Paula to bring it up due to its consistency, which made Paula cry.

Veronica couldn't help but cry too. Her mum's head was purple from her fall the night before, she was thin and frail with barely any hair, and now she was crying due to the agony she was in and her sickness. Veronica wanted to take it all for her mum right in that moment. She wished she could go through the pain and sickness for her mum; it was just unbearable to see her suffer so much. There had been no let up since her diagnosis; she had endured one issue after the other and being carted back and forth to hospital. What could anyone do for her? They couldn't bear seeing her so unwell, but there was nothing anyone could do to make it better.

Veronica helped wipe her mum's mouth and got her some water. She helped her mum back to bed and tucked her in, then woke her dad and told him what had happened.

She made them some breakfast and got Paula's tablets ready to take with some water and a cup of tea and toast. Paula still felt sick and didn't want anything. Veronica could understand, it was so difficult for Paula, she was dazed, confused, bruised, swollen, frail and in constant pain with her liver. Veronica wished she could take it all away for her mum but she couldn't.

Paula shut her eyes to try and sleep it off. Veronica went to see to Sienna who was now wide awake and wanting breakfast.

Later that day, Philip asked Veronica if she would take them to Bluewater Shopping Centre to get Paula some new trainers. Veronica was happy to go and got the kids ready. Ashley enjoyed pushing his Nan around there in her wheelchair. Philip was quite happy for everyone to take turns.

Although she was confused, Paula was still smiling. She seemed to be enjoying being out and about with her family. Phil told Paula that she was going to get a new pair of trainers, she smiled in appreciation. They tried a few different sports shops, but it was difficult for Paula to focus and make a choice. Then she stood up from her wheel chair and walked towards a bright green pair of trainers and selected them.

When Veronica asked her why she had picked them up, Paula told her she wanted them. Veronica called her dad over, he'd been looking at some sports caps with Ashley.

"Dad, Mum wants these," she said. Phil looked confused, Paula generally hated anything bright coloured and would never in a million years pick up a bright green pair of trainers.

"You don't like those kind of shoes Paula," he said, "let's look somewhere else and find you something more suitable."

Paula agreed, and they helped her back into her wheelchair. Eventually they found a nice pair of grey Vans that had tiny little white embroidered anchors all over them. They were very stylish, and Veronica picked out a pair for herself. Phil liked them because they were very nautical.

"Paula will like these too," he said. Veronica agreed that they would suit her, so they bought two pairs. Veronica also spotted a navy t-shirt with tiny anchors all over it, which she picked out for her dad. He liked it, so she bought it for him as a treat.

Once they had finished shopping, Philip asked Veronica if she fancied driving them back to Edmonton to see Ella and her newborn son, Sammy. Veronica thought it was a good idea, so they returned to the car, then onwards to North London.

When they arrived, Ella had her in-laws over. Petros's mum was there holding the baby and there were gifts everywhere. Veronica had never seen so many gift bags, cards and balloons; there wasn't even any room to sit down with it all. Ella cleared a space and took baby Sammy from Petros's mum and gave him to her dad to hold. Phil smiled and cooed over the little bundle of joy. Everyone took turns holding him and Veronica eagerly waited for her turn. Many photos were taken of little Sammy that evening, but Paula was still very confused and not really aware of her new grandson.

Veronica sat beside her and tried to help Paula hold Sammy, but she was very drowsy and not with it. Veronica couldn't let go of them both and helped steady Sammy in Paula's arms for photos. It was a very bitter sweet moment, it was very sad to see Paula in this position; Ella had tears in her eyes.

A couple of hours later, Veronica, her parents and kids said goodbye to Helen, Ella, Petros and his mum; and headed back in the car to Kent. It had been a long day, but Rae had prepared another wholesome meal for everyone when they got back. Paula ate well again with help, but she was still unresponsive and drowsy. They all had an early night as it had been a long day, and Veronica was exhausted too.

Phil and Paula stayed another couple of days. Paula's condition remained the same, but Phil was feeling refreshed after being able to sleep lots at Veronica's. He had been able to unwind a little, knowing he wasn't alone in caring for Paula. Veronica was more than willing to continue, but Philip had things he had to do; and one of them was to get Paula to hospital.

Next day, Veronica's parents were dressed, packed and ready to head back to London. Paula was still semiconscious and confused, but Philip looked a little more refreshed from the break. Being able to sleep whilst Veronica and Rae helped care for Paula, had made a huge difference to Philip, he needed longer, but had to leave to take Paula back to Kings.

Veronica helped her dad to the car with the bags and Paula's wheelchair. It was crazy how her mum had gone from being a normal healthy looking woman to a shadow of herself, now dependant on a wheelchair.

Veronica kissed her dad as they got into the car and welled up with tears. It was awful for her to say goodbye, she wanted them to stay so badly, but Philip wanted to get Paula seen to at the hospital.

Veronica kissed her mum tenderly and whispered in her ear that she loved her and to be careful and listen to her dad. Veronica then kissed her dad again and told him to call her as soon as he got home, and to let her know how he got on at the hospital.

CHAPTER 78

Philip Takes Paula Home

Veronica didn't hear from her dad all day. Every time she called his mobile it went to answerphone, and her mum's landline just kept ringing. Veronica left messages but her calls were not returned. Veronica assumed that her dad had taken her mum straight to Kings' and that there was no reception on the mobile there.

Later in the evening, when her dad called back, Veronica asked him where he had been. He said he had been getting some prescriptions sorted for Paula and did some shopping. Veronica asked if he had taken her mum to Kings'. He hadn't, and told Veronica he was going to leave it for another day to see how she was, as Paula just wanted to go home.

Veronica was disappointed, there was no good reason for him to have left Veronica's house when he did, other than to take Paula to the hospital. Veronica could have picked up the prescriptions for them and had plenty of food to feed them both. Veronica didn't believe her dad and thought he was making excuses. She had a feeling that he had gone home to score drugs and had carted Paula around with him all day whilst he got them. Veronica's heart sank at the thought; her mum would have been better off staying in Kent if that was the case. If he had wanted to get his drugs why didn't he just leave his wife with Veronica where she was well cared for?

Philip always denied taking heroin, claiming he had stopped years ago, but his body language told a very different story. He had also been growing a skunk farm in Paula's lounge, and had all sorts of lighting set up in there. He had told Rae and Veronica that the equipment to run it belonged to an ex-boyfriend of Ella's, who had made a deal with her dad to set up the farm and look after the plants for a 50% share of the profits. Veronica and Rae couldn't believe what he was doing, he had only told them when Rae visited the flat one night with Charlie, to give Philip £1000.00 to help pay bills whilst he wasn't working. He had told his daughter and son-in-law that he had no income whatsoever, and he hadn't got around to claiming benefit because he was busy looking after Paula. They felt terrible about his circumstances, so they tried to help in every way they could. Rae and Veronica had managed to save well over the years their company had been successful. This was one of those times where they thought their savings would go to a good cause. At least if they could contribute to the bills, it would make life a little bit easier on Philip, who said he was only interested in his wife's welfare. This way, he could concentrate more of his attention on Paula's needs instead of worrying about paying the bills-or this is what they were led to believe. Philip had told them that his plants would net him an income of around £10,000 once they were fully grown. The process would take approximately 12 weeks. Veronica was beside herself with worry over the situation her dad was in; and Paula too, who was in the middle of a drugs' den whilst dying from cancer. The Palliative Care Team had offered home support, but Philip had turned it down, insisting he could cope alone. Philip had fitted a push button lock on the living room door for added security, but it looked suspiciously out of place. You could also hear the sound of the extractor fans whirring from outside the room and smell the distinct scent of marijuana as soon as you entered the flat.

Veronica couldn't believe how brazen her dad was; he made a point of saying that he needed a way to earn money whilst being able to care for Paula but this was ridiculous. If someone suspected and shopped him to the police, what good would he be to his dying wife then? What if the police arrested Paula too and put her in jail, dying from cancer.

Veronica begged her dad not to continue growing the plants but he shrugged it off, saying he would use the excuse of holistic medicinal purposes for his wife's disease to get him out of trouble if the worst came to the worst. Veronica could not believe her dad's attitude and behaviour. He didn't have to do this, she and Rae were happy to support him financially, they had given him money and paid some of their bills but it didn't make a difference. Veronica even wondered if her dad was doing it to get some money together for his wife's funeral. She spoke to Rae alone regarding this.

"When the time comes I want to help with my mum's funeral." Rae agreed. "I know you will want to send your mum off properly Vron; and when that time comes, I am behind you all the way. Your mum deserves a

303

good send-off and I wouldn't stand in your way to make sure she gets it. You know your dad isn't going to do it don't you?" he asked.

"Do you think?" Veronica replied. "Why is he growing a skunk farm then? Why else would he need that money?" Veronica asked her husband.

"He isn't doing that for your mum Vron, he's got no intention of sorting your mum out, he knows when the time comes, that we wouldn't sit back and do nothing. He knows you will want to sort your mum out and do right by her like you always have."

"Well I do want to send her off properly, like a princess," Veronica told Rae.

"And your dad knows that Vron, he knows how to play on your feelings and mine. He's got us right where he wants us at the moment but I am only going along with it, because it's what your mum deserves and she wouldn't get it otherwise."

Veronica knew in her heart that her husband was right, but she hoped her dad would prove them wrong and do the right thing when the time came. Either way, all that mattered at this time was that Paula got the care that she needed and deserved.

Veronica spent all night feeling upset and worrying about her mum. "There is nothing we can do babe," Rae told his wife. "We can't control the situation, it's down to your dad to sort this out; and if he chooses not to take her to the hospital, what can you do? It's out of our hands babe."

Veronica knew her husband was right but she wished she had more say over her mum's care. Her dad was Paula's legal next of kin; he was the one responsible for Paula. Rae was right, there was nothing anyone could do other than to offer support and hope that Philip would accept it.

It was another few days before Philip took his wife to the hospital. All they could do was give Paula antibiotics via a drip to clear any infection. She was soon sent home and seemed more alert after receiving the antibiotics, but it was a continuous vicious circle that Paula endured. The drugs she was given would build up in her system and as her liver could not break down all of the toxins caused from this in her body, she would eventually become confused again as the toxins affected her brain. Paula was understandably depressed and fed up; she knew there was no end to her problems. She knew that the result of all of this was death; and it was clear for everyone to see, that she was beginning to give in to the disease.

Philip was exhausted, Paula was exhausted; and the family as a whole were completely exhausted by the whole experience. The hospital had already told them that there was not much they could do for Paula now. The truth was brutal but it was still hard to accept.

CHAPTER 79

Paula Nearly Loses Her Battle

Two days later Phil called Veronica early in the morning, he told her that Paula had gone to sleep the afternoon before and she had been unresponsive since then. As Paula had been in so much pain, the Palliative Care Team had finally been allowed to visit and they had attached a line to administer pain relief. Phil told Veronica he thought they had given her too much of the morphine like drug and that her liver wasn't coping. He said she looked like she was slipping away, her heart rate was slow and her breathing didn't seem so strong. He had got so scared that he removed the line because he panicked. He had called the doctor to assess Paula, who told him that the next 24 hrs were crucial as it looked as though Paula's body was shutting down. He said that her liver wasn't functioning and that her other organs were possibly shutting down too. The doctor told Philip he would bring a form for him to sign, to agree that if she did not wake up, then her body would not be subject to a post-mortem as she was dying of natural causes.

His voice was broken with emotion as he tried hard to stop himself from crying. "I think this is it now Vronx, I don't think she is going to pull through this time." Veronica panicked; she told her dad she would be with him within the hour.

Rae didn't waste any time in arranging for Sienna to be looked after by his mother, and got Veronica on the road. Her heart was racing; she was scared that her mum would pass away without her being there to tell her she loved her. She thought of the little break away in Whitstable that the whole family were due to go on, and how much Paula had wanted to be by the sea. Veronica had a lump in her throat, everything had been so overwhelming and negative for Paula, the little break was supposed to be an escape from the reality of her dying in the dingy flat in Tottenham, which had become her existence for the past twelve years. Veronica cried in the car, all the way to North London.

Veronica and Rae soon arrived at the flat, the doctor was there too. He got Philip to sign a form to agree to no resuscitation if Paula slipped away, which was the harsh reality they were facing now. Veronica got all choked up and had to sit down.

Paula was lying in bed and her breathing was very shallow. Veronica waited for her dad to see the doctor out and then climbed into bed and cuddled up to her mum, holding her hand. She told her mum how much she loved her and didn't want her to suffer, but that she thought there were things that she still wanted to do. Veronica talked to her mum about the little holiday they had coming up in Whitstable, and that she knew how much she was really looking forward to being by the sea, describing how pretty the beach was. But Paula continued to lie unresponsive for hours. Although she was very worried, Veronica felt relaxed by her mum's side. There was something calming about it; and Veronica held her mum's hand all the time whilst she lay talking to her, not wanting to move, not even to go to the toilet.

Philip seemed more at ease too, having his daughter there for support.

Rae offered to go and get some lunch for everyone and brought back sandwiches and drinks from the local shop. Then he had to go back to Kent, to pick Ashley up from school, and said he would cook a dinner at home and bring it back to London for Phil, Paula and Veronica.

Veronica was amazed at Rae's suggestion and thought it was a lovely idea. Veronica stayed by her mum's side cuddling up to her and kissing her all day.

Later that evening, Rae turned up with a plastic container, inside of which were three plates of dinner covered over with top plates and wrapped tightly in cling film. He unwrapped the dishes and warmed the food in the microwave. Rae had cooked a full roast dinner with chicken, roast potatoes, broccoli, cauliflower, cabbage, roast mushrooms and Yorkshire puddings with delicious gravy.

Philip was surprised at how Rae had managed to bring it all the way back to London in the car intact, and Veronica and Philip ate theirs in no time. Then Paula started to stir, moving her body.

Rae had brought the food up to the bedroom as there was nowhere to eat downstairs. The kitchen was so tiny there was no room for chairs or a table, and the living room was occupied by a skunk farm. Before anyone

307

could say anything else, Paula sat bolt upright and looked at everyone, surprised that Rae and Veronica were there. She smiled at Rae and said, "Hello."

"Hello Paula, would you like some of my famous roast dinner I've cooked especially for you?" Rae asked.

Paula smiled and nodded in agreement, "Mm yes please, it smells gorgeous," she replied.

Rae told her he was going downstairs to warm her plate of food through and would be back in a moment. Veronica and her dad were surprised at Paula's sudden recovery. She had been lying virtually lifeless all that day and much of the day before and then suddenly sat up talking, as if she had just been asleep.

"Would you like a drink Mum?" Veronica asked.

"Yes please," Paula replied. Veronica went down to the kitchen to join Rae; she put the kettle on and prepared a cup of tea.

Rae cuddled his wife, "She's pulled through again Vron, your mum is not ready to give up yet, she is a strong woman, I'll give her that!" Veronica had tears in her eyes but she smiled and agreed.

They took Paula's dinner and tea up to the bedroom, propped Paula up with some pillows, then gave her the dinner on a tray. Paula started eating, she couldn't get enough of the roast potatoes and chicken, so soon it was all gone.

"Wow that was really tasty Rae thank you," Paula said.

"You are welcome Paula, any time at all."

"You gave us all a shock today Paula," Philip told his wife. "We thought we were losing you again."

Paula couldn't believe it, she was shocked herself that she had been in such a lifeless state. "Veronica has spent all day lying in bed with you, by your side holding your hand." Phil told her.

Paula smiled at Veronica. "I am a lucky girl," she said. "I wasn't letting you go that easy Mum. I was willing you to wake up because you need to get to the seaside and have a nice break away with us all."

Paula agreed and smiled, but her smile hid her pain, her torture and her truth.

CHAPTER 80

Whitstable, September 2012

Finally the family break away in Whitstable was happening at last. Veronica and Rae had cancelled and rebooked the caravan a few times due to Paula's ill health, but there didn't seem to be any real let up in Paula's condition and so they agreed to just go ahead with the booking.

Paula had been eager to be by the sea since her chemotherapy at the end of May, but she had been too unwell to go. Philip phoned Veronica that morning. "Hi babe," he said. "I'm just getting some breakfast together for your mum and then I will start packing. I will call you later when we are ready to leave."

"Okay Dad," Veronica replied. "We will wait for you to get here and in the mean time I will go and get some food for us all to have at the caravan." Phil agreed and said goodbye.

Veronica busied herself all morning packing the bags, then went shopping in the afternoon.

Phil didn't call until late afternoon to say he was leaving. Paula had been in pain all day and her swollen stomach was causing her a lot of problems. She had been sick on and off, and she just couldn't get comfortable. Paula suffered terrible constipation due to her medications and she had spent the morning on and off the toilet.

Phil had found it hard to get her out of the flat but he finally managed to leave around 5pm.

Veronica had booked a large caravan to sleep the whole family including her sisters and the children, but Ella had decided not to come until the following day with Paulette.

Phil and Paula turned up around 6.30pm at Veronica's and they all left together. They arrived at the caravan park around twenty-five minutes later. Veronica wasted no time in unpacking and making the main bed up for Paula so she could relax.

The sea front was a short walk away, but with it getting late, Veronica prepared a meal for everyone. It was a nice evening and Paula looked a little more relaxed being away from North London, but it wasn't long before her pains kicked in and overwhelmed her. It was soul destroying to watch this little lady fade away and suffer so much, and it was just as soul destroying for everyone who loved her. Veronica felt useless because she couldn't do anything to help her mum. For most of her life she had been someone who could ease Paula's problems. When Philip was in prison, she was there to help with her sisters when Paula had no one else to rely on. She could make her mum laugh and forget her troubles, cheering her up and singing to her as a kid, but this time, she couldn't take away the pain and she couldn't give Paula hope for the future.

After the family meal, they all retired for an early night to give them a head start the next day.

Veronica woke up early to the sound of her mum shuffling around in the caravan. Veronica got up to see if she needed anything. "Are you okay mum?" Veronica asked.

"Oh morning babe," she replied. "I've been in pain all night and I just can't get comfortable. It doesn't matter if I sit down, lie down or walk about; I just wish I could have a day without pain." You could hear by Paula's voice that she was suffering and close to tears.

Veronica remembered her own ordeal after having Sienna; she thought about the pains she endured all day every day for months due to infections and her operation to put her bowel and bladder back in place. Having that kind of enduring pain was something that Veronica had never suffered before and she found it relentless. Veronica had thought about suicide on a few desperate occasions, not because she was someone to just give up but because she just couldn't bear the pain any more.

Then she thought about her mum's situation, Paula's pain would eventually lead to her death, even though this wasn't what Paula wanted. Veronica felt bad that she had even contemplated suicide, actually Veronica wasn't brave enough to end her own life and she knew it wouldn't be fair on Rae and the children, but she felt bad nonetheless because here her mum was experiencing severe pain and she had no choice.

Veronica offered her mum a cup of tea and made her some porridge. Paula didn't feel like eating anything, which was completely

310

understandable, but Veronica asked her mum to try and eat as the tablets would make her feel worse without food to line her stomach.

Phil was still asleep, so too were Rae and Ashley, but Sienna was stirring and soon got up and wanted breakfast. Paula wanted a shower, she said it sometimes helped with the pain to have water running down her back, but she had to wait for Phil to wake up and help her as she couldn't wash properly because of her swollen stomach.

Veronica offered to shower her. "Let me help wash you Mum, you don't have to wait for Dad. I've brought some fresh clean towels and I've got some toiletries too," she said.

"I feel bad you helping me in the shower," Paula replied.

"Why Mum, you've got nothing at all to feel bad about, I'm your daughter and if your daughter can't help you in the shower who else can?" Veronica asked.

"You've got enough on your hands with Sienna, you don't need me taking up your time, it's not your responsibility I just wish I could manage on my own."

"I am more than happy to wash you and help you get dried and dressed, it will take no time at all and Sienna can go and cuddle Rae whilst I help you." Veronica persuaded her and Paula agreed, she smiled at Veronica and stroked her face.

"I always said you were an angel," she said.

"Why is that?" Veronica asked.

"Because you've always been a good girl and you've always been helpful," Paula told her.

Veronica smiled and cuddled her mum. "That's what daughters are for," she said. "Let me get the towels and I will help you into the shower."

Veronica got everything ready and helped her mum into the bathroom; she put the water on and got the temperature to the right setting, then helped her mum undress.

Veronica held back the tears and cleared her throat as she undressed her mum. Her frail body and hard swollen stomach was almost unbearable to see, but Veronica couldn't show her shock to her mum and had to pretend that everything was normal. Paula couldn't look at her daughter. Veronica knew her mum was embarrassed by her appearance.

She helped her mum into the shower and cuddled her gently. "You do know I love you so much Mum, don't you?" Veronica asked.

"I know you do babe and I love you too, more than you'll ever know."

As Paula stood under the shower, Veronica realised just how helpless this little woman was.

All her life she had been tough, even through the years Philip was in prison. Now here she was frail and helpless. Veronica was breaking down inside but she had to smile and keep calm and make her mum feel as comfortable about the situation as possible.

Paula couldn't bend to wash herself because of her tummy and she began to cry. "It's not fair Vronx; I can't even wash myself properly anymore, why did this all have to happen to me? I just want to be normal," she said.

"I know Mum, it isn't fair at all, you don't deserve any of this, you are a beautiful woman and I would give everything to make it all go away," Veronica replied. "Here let me wash you Mum, let me help you." Veronica grabbed the shower gel and washed her mum's back, bottom, legs and feet.

Paula sobbed as her daughter washed her. "You shouldn't be doing this Vronx; it's my job to look after you not the other way round," Paula said.

"Don't be silly Mum, how many times did you look after your dad when he was ill? Nanny had a heart attack and passed suddenly so no one had a chance to look after her, but you did with your dad, and what about Dad's mum? We all helped to look after her when she was poorly.

"It's what family is for Mum so stop beating yourself up. I love the bones of you woman and if I can't look after you then what's the point. Anyway, you've washed your top half, you are all done now Mum." Paula was starting to go blue in the lips and was shivering as Veronica got her out of the cubicle. She wrapped two large towels around her mum and began to dry her. Veronica sat her on the toilet seat with the lid down and helped to get her dressed. It was a long process as Paula's legs were also very large and swollen from the ascites but Veronica remained patient and soon had her mum dressed.

Paula went in to the bedroom to lie down for half an hour as she felt tired. Philip was still asleep so Veronica busied herself with washing up the breakfast dishes and getting Sienna showered and dressed. Morning had almost passed and lunch time was fast approaching, but there was still no sign of Ella and Paulette. Ella's baby Sammy was just a few weeks old; Veronica knew it would be difficult for Ella getting down early with a new baby in tow, but this weekend was undoubtedly the last time Paula would get away and the last time that she would see the sea. Veronica kept her fingers crossed that her sisters would arrive soon.

Philip had got up and had a wash. Veronica made him coffee and his usual Weetabix.

Rae had helped to get the caravan cleared and organised so that the family could head out down the beach. It was a sunny day with clear blue skies, but there was a definite chill as autumn was fast approaching. Paula felt the cold easily, so Philip got her coat from his car and they wrapped her up.

Veronica had bought her mum a thick soft fleece blanket which she went everywhere with.

It was useful to cover her up when she was out and about in the wheel chair. Paula was eager to get to the beach even though Ella and Paulette hadn't arrived. "Come on its getting late, "Paula said, "let's get going, I want to see the sea."

Rae helped Paula outside and into her wheel chair. Veronica covered her up with her fleece blanket and they all set off towards the beach. When they arrived, Paula's face lit up, she smiled from ear to ear and gazed at the sea. "Ah how I've missed the sound of the sea," she said.

"I know, isn't it lovely and calming," Veronica replied. She loved being by the sea too, the sound of the waves and the bubbling water was very therapeutic and Veronica was so happy to see her mum smile.

Philip busied himself chatting to Ashley and Sienna, whilst Rae pushed Paula along the sea front with Veronica. They walked for what seemed like miles along the coast.

Veronica reminisced about the days on the boat and the good times they had. Paula was still smiling and seemed to be taking it all in. She was also in deep thought, but she looked content and happier than Veronica had seen her mum in months. "I love the smell of the seaside," Paula told Veronica and Rae. "It reminds me of when I was a kid and I used to go to the seaside with my mum and sisters." Just then an elderly man on an electric mobility scooter came past, overtaking Paula in her wheel chair.

Rae laughed and said, "Look at speedy Gonzales there overtaking us, shall we speed up and show him?" Paula giggled and Rae began to jog pushing Paula along to overtake the man. Veronica was laughing too, it became a race and Paula found it hilarious.

Veronica and Rae jogged along the sea front for a few minutes and Paula sat contentedly taking in the surroundings, then, they saw an ice cream van up ahead. Rae asked if everyone wanted an ice cream. Paula fancied a cherry brandy ice lolly. "Ooh I haven't had one of those for years," she told Rae excitedly. The smile on her face showed how happy she was at that point; just for a moment she had forgotten her pain, forgotten her illness and all that she was facing. Paula was remembering good times gone by, for Veronica this was priceless.

Phil and Ashley were still a way back along the sea front, so Rae ordered Paula's ice lolly and some ice creams for Veronica and Sienna while he waited for Phil and Ashley to catch up.

Rae unwrapped Paula's ice lolly and handed it to her. "Ooh thank you Rae," she said as she sucked it. Phil and Ashley had caught up, so Rae asked them what they wanted and ordered more, then the family continued along their way.

They arrived at Whitstable harbour where there were many stalls selling anything from mulled wine to bric-a-brac. One stall in particular sold handmade jewellery and silver. Phil went to have a browse with Ashley whilst Paula continued to enjoy her cherry brandy lolly.

There were fish restaurants lined along the quayside; one in particular sold battered prawns with sweet chilli dip. Veronica, Rae and the kids had eaten here a few times before and loved the battered prawns. "Would you like to try them?" Veronica asked her mum and dad.

"Yes please," Paula replied.

Phil's phone rang, it was Ella, she and Paulette had arrived at the caravan, it meant that someone would have to rush back to meet them as they had Helen and baby Sammy with them.

"I will go back to the caravan and meet them," Philip said.

"Can't we direct them here?" Veronica asked. Paula was eager to sit outside the fish restaurant and try the battered prawns.

"I think they want to just relax in the caravan as they've had a long journey with the baby in the car," Philip replied. "I don't mind going back to let them in. You all stay here and enjoy the food and I will catch you up later."

Rae found a number on the internet for a local taxi firm to pick Philip up and take him back to the camp site. They had walked for miles along the sea front, so a cab would be far quicker.

Veronica asked her mum if she wanted to go back to the caravan or stay at the harbour.

Paula was enjoying herself and was eager to stay, so Rae ordered a taxi for Phil.

A few minutes later the taxi arrived and Phil set off. Veronica felt disappointed; she had wanted the weekend to be a complete family affair. She had envisioned everyone together, making an effort for Paula as this was going to be the last time she went away, but everyone else seemed to have their own agenda. Paulette was wrapped up in herself and her relationship with her Afro-Caribbean boyfriend, Ella had just had Sammy who was only a few weeks old and her husband Petros had his own agenda too, ducking and diving and wheeling and dealing.

Veronica thought he likened himself to a Greek version of Arthur Daley and came across as still quite immature for a thirty year old. Paula looked disappointed too; all that were left were Veronica, Rae, Paula and the two kids.

Rae went and queued up at the fish bar to order the battered prawns; Veronica found a table with chairs outside and pulled Paula's wheelchair up to the table. As the afternoon was wearing on it was starting to get chilly, so Veronica pulled Paula's blanket up around her body, cuddled her arms and stroked her hands as they sat at the table.

Paula looked like she was deep in thought. "Are you okay Mum?" Veronica asked.

Paula smiled at Veronica and replied, "As okay as I will ever be." Veronica was gutted that her dad had gone back to the caravan; surely they could have directed her sisters a few minutes on to where they were. They could have joined their mum for some fish and chips by the water's edge, it was lovely just sitting there, taking in the surroundings, watching the fishing boats lined up along the quay; and the hustle and bustle of all the people walking along happily enjoying the atmosphere.

There was a live band playing along the way, and there were many different smells of food coming from all of the restaurants and fish bars. Paula looked quite relaxed, and she thanked Veronica and Rae for getting her away from Tottenham.

"It's lovely here," she told them. "Just what I needed." Veronica was relieved too that Paula was enjoying it as best as she could but she was disappointed in her dad and sisters for not making more of an effort for Paula.

It should have been a whole family affair. Everyone should have been around her but it wasn't to be. Rae brought out the king prawns in batter, with fresh chips and a sweet chilli dip. Paula tucked right in and enjoyed it, Veronica was pleased to see her mum eating.

Nutrition had been an ongoing issue with Paula's illness as she couldn't stomach a lot with her sickness, so it was really nice to see her relaxed and enjoying her food.

The temperature started to drop as the afternoon wore on and Paula soon began to get cold and tired. It had been a lovely day for her, but her pains were also starting to kick in again and she wanted to lie down. Rae called a taxi and arranged a meeting point a short walk away.

"Thanks babe for a lovely day, thank you Rae, it's been really nice," Paula said. "I'm sorry for spoiling it by cutting it short."

"Don't be silly Mum, you haven't spoilt a thing, this break is all about you. We are happy and here to do what suits you, so no need to apologise."

"Thanks babe, I would stay here longer if it wasn't for the pains I'm getting."

"Well hopefully the cab will be here soon and we can get you snuggled up in the caravan," Veronica told her mum.

For some reason, the taxi seemed to be taking ages, the wind had picked up and there was a definite chill in the air. Veronica worried about her mum getting too cold, as she looked uncomfortable and her face was pale. Veronica asked Rae to call the taxi firm to see where the driver was and to make sure they hadn't forgotten them. The taxi was on his way but had got stuck in traffic. Five minutes later, he arrived and they all boarded the taxi bus. Rae and Veronica helped Paula out of her wheelchair and got her onto the bus and seated. Veronica got the children seated and buckled up and then sat beside her mum and cuddled her.

"I hope this wasn't all too much for you Mum?" Veronica asked.

"Of course not babe, I've had fun with you all today and I just wanted to be by the sea. I feel content now thank you." Veronica kissed her mum on the side of her face and rubbed her arms to warm her up. The journey back seemed to take forever, they had walked from the campsite to the harbour in no time, but getting back seemed a lot longer. Maybe it was because they were eager to get Paula comfortable and in the warm. When they eventually arrived, they thanked the driver and got inside.

Ella was busy changing baby Sammy's nappy and Paulette was rolling a spliff on the coffee table. Phil was also rolling a spliff.

Veronica helped her mum to the toilet and took her coat off. "Hello you two," Veronica said to her sisters. "You found the campsite alright then did you?"

"Yeah it was alright as I was navigating," Paulette replied.

"Yeah it would have been a nightmare on my own, trying to find it with the baby, but Helen was good and helped by looking after Sammy," Ella chuckled.

"Do you like being a big sister now Helen?" Veronica asked her. Helen nodded in agreement.

Veronica gave them all a kiss and put the kettle on to make everyone a drink.

Paula was in the toilet for quite some time, Sienna was still in nappies and needed to be changed, so Veronica went into the room they were using and changed her.

It was nice that Paula had all of her daughters and grandchildren around her, but it was such a shame that she was now in a lot of pain. Phil got her painkillers ready with a glass of water for her to take them. She still felt unwell and in lots of pain when she came out of the toilet. "I'm really sorry everyone, but I need to lie down." Everyone told her not to be silly and helped her to her room. Phil passed her medication and a glass of water.

"You better take these Paula," he said. "You are overdue these now."

Veronica felt bad that her mum had missed her tablets and was now in pain.

Paula got undressed and got into bed, she was tired and just wanted to rest, so she shut her eyes and before long, was fast asleep.

Rae felt it was time for him to leave the family alone to have quality time and said his goodbyes. Veronica didn't want him to leave, Paula had enjoyed Rae's company and was so at ease around him, but Rae didn't feel the same around Phil. He had caused a lot of upset between Veronica and Rae over the years. Veronica respected Rae's wishes and kissed him good bye, then she spent some time with her sisters, catching up with conversation and holding her baby nephew.

They ordered a takeaway and sat together for dinner, Paula wasn't hungry and just wanted to sleep as she was in pain. Before long Ella announced that she was heading back home with Paulette. She hadn't brought enough supplies for baby and so needed to get back.

Veronica kissed and cuddled them and said goodnight.

With her sisters gone and her mum in bed asleep, her dad went to bed too. Sienna had also gone off to bed, and so Veronica got herself tucked up. It had been a long day, with some very emotional moments and some laughter too, but it was all still tainted, Paula's cancer was never far from everyone's minds. Veronica went to sleep sobbing quietly into her pillow, she could see how sick her mum was, she had deteriorated so quickly and there was no denying it.

As Veronica lay trying to clear her mind to fall off to sleep, she could hear her dad shuffling around in the bedroom next door, then she heard him go to the toilet.

A few minutes later she could hear him sparking his lighter, then she could smell the distinct smell of heroin. This was something she hadn't smelt in years, she hadn't been around her parents' drug taking for a while. They seemed to have stopped doing it in her presence from the moment she moved in with Rae. She had asked them on numerous occasions over the years if they were still using but they just denied it, claiming they only used methadone. Veronica was shocked; here she was lying in a tiny narrow bedroom with Sienna, while Ashley and Helen were sleeping in another room next door. The smell of the heroin was potent and the caravan quickly filled up with smoke, the children were all sleeping and passively smoking. This made Veronica angry, she wanted to get up and bang on the bathroom door. She wanted to tell her dad to go outside if he wanted to smoke, but it would only cause a huge row which would undoubtedly erupt to the point where her dad would wake everyone up and upset everyone.

Veronica could not allow this to happen. He would no doubt make Paula leave the caravan in the middle of the night; and in her state of health there was no way Veronica could do this, so she had to just pretend she wasn't aware, close her eyes and go to sleep.

The next morning, Paula was up early. She was hungry, so Veronica got up and made her a small bowl of porridge and a cup of tea. This was enough to enable Paula to take her anti sickness tablets, her water tablets for the ascites and her pain relief.

They spent an hour or so just talking in the lounge and Veronica decided to prepare a cooked breakfast. Paula had missed dinner the night before, so Veronica wanted to get something a bit more substantial down her.

"Would you like some egg and bacon Mum?"

"Yes please," she replied. "Not too much though Vronx, because I've had porridge and I can't eat too much without it making me feel sick." Veronica agreed and got cooking. Phil was still asleep in the bedroom and the kids were all playing and watching a film on his iPad.

Veronica cooked for the kids and then her mum. She fried up some egg and bacon with a slice of toast. Paula got tucked in, surprisingly she ate the lot. "That was really tasty Vronx thank you," she said.

"You're welcome Mum," Veronica replied, as she took away Paula's empty plate and began to wash up.

Paula sat at the table and watched her daughter. She was smiling. "Look at you," she said. "You are a good mum."

"Really?" Veronica asked. "Of course you are, fussing over everyone and making sure we are all fed. You are a good girl."

"Thanks Mum." Veronica felt happy for that moment, her mum had complimented her and it meant a lot.

As the morning turned to midday, Phil was still asleep. Veronica was still angry for what had happened in the night. Her dad had no regard for the children breathing in his smoke, but then he never did in all the years he and Paula had chased heroin on foil day in and day out when Veronica and her sisters were growing up. She had even wondered if she had had a passive habit breathing it in for all those years. It certainly wasn't good and it wasn't fair. With the knowledge around about passive smoking now, there was no excuse for it; and it said a lot about her dad's priorities.

Just then, Rae knocked on the door, he had come back to spend the day with Veronica and the family. "I didn't sleep well at all last night," he said.

"Why was that babe?" Veronica asked, as she cuddled him, pleased he had turned up.

"I tossed and turned all night, it felt wrong not having you in bed with me," he said.

Veronica smiled, "Well you are here now."

Paula said good morning to Rae and went into the toilet as she had a pain. Just then it started to pour down with rain, the sound of it tapping the roof of the caravan was quite therapeutic. The kids were happy watching films on the iPad and cuddling up in their quilts. Phil was still fast asleep.

Paula eventually came out of the toilet and went back into the bedroom to lie down. "I'm sorry Vronx," she said, "I am in agony at the moment, I just want to lie down."

"That's okay Mum, no need to apologise or explain Mum, you do what you need to do and just get comfortable."

Rae helped Veronica occupy Sienna and the kids. He helped her tidy everything away and clear the beds. They swept and washed the floors and put all the dishes away and wiped the sides.

It was quite late and the kids were getting hungry. Phil got up and said "Hello" to Rae.

Veronica made her dad some breakfast and coffee. "Paula's in a lot of pain," Phil said. "I think we are gonna head back to London today, we've got some appointments next week and I've got some things to sort out. They had the caravan booked until the following day but Veronica needed to get back that evening anyway, as the kids were back to school the next day.

"Okay Dad," Veronica said. "Would you like to have a Sunday dinner somewhere in a restaurant before you head home?"

"Let me ask Paula if she feels up to it, and I will let you know babe."

Veronica agreed. The rain had stopped, so Veronica and Rae began to pack the car up with their bags.

Paula had got up and got dressed. "I will come out for dinner before we leave," she said.

"Oh that's great Mum." Veronica was pleased. Rae had driven past a local pub on his way in to the campsite, so they packed up their things, locked the caravan and set off to the pub. They all enjoyed a Sunday roast dinner together before setting off home.

When they got outside, Veronica cuddled her mum tight. "I don't want to let you go," Veronica told her mum. "I wish you could come back with me, I could happily look after you," Veronica added. Paula chuckled.

"I know you could babe and I wish I could come back with you. I've enjoyed being with you and having you and Rae look after us. It's been a nice break from the flat. I hate it there and I wish I didn't have to go, but we've got things to sort out." Veronica could see the look of disappointment in Paula's eyes.

"Why don't you sort out your appointments next week and then come back to me Mum?"

"I'd love to babe, but you've got enough things to worry about. You've got your house move coming up any time now, you've got packing to do and Sienna is a handful. You don't need me in the way," Paula told her daughter.

"Don't be silly Mum; you are the best distraction I could possibly ask for. Having my beautiful mummy by my side is all I want. I want to look after you and spend quality time with you. We never get much time on our own together. In the years I've been with Rae I've had no time with you really, apart from our holiday in Lanzarote, Xmas 2007. Please come and stay Mum, I know you would like to get away from the flat and it's nice here in Kent." Paula nodded in agreement.

"Okay babe, you are right. I hate it in the flat, it depresses me, so I will come back once we've sorted everything out and I will let you know." Veronica kissed her mum and told her she loved her. She kissed her dad and told him she loved him and to look after Mum. He got Paula into their car and everyone drove off down the road.

Veronica welled up with emotion, she couldn't believe her little mum was gone again; it ripped her heart out being apart. The only time Veronica could remain strong, was when her mum was near, the moment she was gone, Veronica fell apart. She was scared that every time she said goodbye, it would be the last time she would see her mum.

CHAPTER 81

Staying in Kent Again

Veronica had a lot on her plate. She and Rae were waiting to receive a phone call confirming exchange of contracts for the sale of their house. They were clinging on to hope that they would find more work soon, having lost their main source of income two months ago; and Veronica had practically packed up the home single-handed whilst Rae continued to go out and carry out works for a small contract they still had with another company. Rae had one person left working for him and he was determined to keep them both out working.

Veronica missed her mum, she had enjoyed their time together at the caravan but it was only for two days which passed too quickly. Paula was increasingly tired and in pain, she slept most days and was struggling with her pain and sickness. Veronica knew in her heart that they were running out of time, which made her apprehensive and she yearned to have more quality time with her mum. Paula had also enjoyed the time spent with Veronica and wanted to come back to Kent. She felt more at ease with Rae than she had ever been, perhaps it just didn't matter anymore. She had nothing left to worry about so her guard was down. Rae had shown nothing but compassion, understanding and patience with Paula and she realised the depth of Rae's personality. They had reached a mutual understanding of one another and found a sudden bond. It was quite lovely for Veronica to see this evolve and her only regret was that it didn't happen years ago. Paula had told Veronica that she and her dad would go home to sort some prescriptions and medication out, then they would return in a few days. Paula kept to her word and a few days later, Phil and Paula headed back to Kent to stay with Veronica and Rae.

Veronica had expected her parents to come late in the evening but as midnight passed and there was still no sign, Veronica was getting worried. She called, but their phones went to answerphone. She left messages but there was no reply. Rae had cooked them a roast dinner hours before and the gravy had congealed where it had stood for so long.

By 1 am Veronica went to bed, but she couldn't sleep for worrying about her parents' whereabouts. At long last, Veronica received a text from her mum. It read: "Hi babe, sorry it's got so late, we've been stuck in traffic and are on our way. Will be with you in an hour."

Veronica couldn't understand why they had not answered their phones earlier. Why were they stuck in traffic at 1.30am? It didn't make sense and it didn't add up, but Veronica just wanted her parents to hurry up and arrive safely. Her mum was in no fit state to be carted around at this ridiculous time of the night and Veronica was feeling angry about it. What the hell was her dad doing, she wondered. In her heart she knew. She had visions of him high on heroin and gouching out somewhere. Had he gone out to score before heading to Kent? This was the kind of thing that would normally slow her parents down in the old days and Veronica knew her dad was still taking it as he'd smoked out the caravan only a few days before.

Veronica had to grit her teeth and say nothing; she couldn't afford to argue about it when all she wanted was to give her mum a break from the depressing flat in north London, and to look after her. Veronica had almost dropped off to sleep, when her phone buzzed.

It was a text from her mum telling her they had arrived and were outside. Veronica went to the window and could see her dad's car parked across the road. Veronica got her jacket and trainers on and went over to help get Paula inside with the bags. She crossed the road as her dad got Paula into her wheelchair. Her mum looked tired and drained. Veronica kissed her parents and wheeled her mum across the road and into the house.

"You look exhausted Mum, where have you been all night? I've been really worried about you."

Paula had a fed up look on her face, "I wanted to be here hours ago Vronx, but you know what your dad is like, he's got no idea of time and I've been frustrated waiting for him."

Veronica knew exactly what she was talking about! "Have you eaten, Mum?" she asked.

"No, I haven't eaten all day, I'm starving."

Veronica's heart sank. It was 3am and Paula hadn't eaten any dinner and probably not even had a decent lunch either. She wondered what her dad had been up to all day and why he hadn't even bothered to feed his sick wife. She needed as much good nutrition as possible; she needed regular healthy meals to give her the best fighting chance at maintaining her strength. How could she cope without even being fed? Veronica was furious with her dad. Just then, he came walking through the door with some bags.

"Sorry we are so late babe, I've had a really hard day, your mum has had me up night after night and it's taken its toll on me. We got stuck in some horrendous traffic."

Veronica went into her own world. She shut her dad's voice out and couldn't even listen to his excuses and lies, in her heart she knew, he'd either been getting high or driving around scoring to get high with Paula being carted around. Veronica could tell by her mum's body language and the fed up look on her face that her dad was lying and making up excuses.

Veronica warmed their food through in the microwave and sat Paula down at the table to eat.

She made her parents a coffee and sat next to her mum to help her. Paula looked pale and washed out. "You look really tired Mum."

"I am babe," she replied. "I just want to go to bed."

Veronica helped her mum to eat as much as possible and then helped her to bed.

She helped her undress and put her nightclothes on, then tucked her up in Ashley's bed.

Paula sighed with relief as she lay down; Veronica stroked her mum's face and kissed her.

"I love you Mum, thank God you are here now, I will look after you." Paula smiled and shut her eyes. Phil was downstairs rolling a spliff in the dining room; he asked if he could go outside to smoke it. Veronica kissed him goodnight and went up to bed.

Veronica knew that Sienna would have her up in a couple of hours and she would be tired all day, but she was relieved to have her mum by her side again. As difficult as it was to see her mum in such pain and suffering, it gave Veronica some peace to know at least she was safe and in good hands with her and Rae.

Veronica was happy to wait on both her parents hand and foot, it gave Phil a chance to recuperate and unwind a bit. The pressure wasn't completely on him when he had help and support. There must have been some comfort for him knowing that he could rely on others too, at least that's what Veronica and Rae hoped.

The next morning, Sienna woke up early as usual. Paula was also awake, she was being sick in the bathroom. Veronica got Sienna out of her cot and gave her to Rae. "I need to check on Mum as she is being sick," she told him. Rae took Sienna down to the kitchen to get some breakfast whilst Veronica checked on her mum; Phil was still fast asleep in the bedroom.

Veronica knocked on the bathroom door. "Are you okay Mum?" she asked.

"No not really," Paula answered.

"Can I come in?" Veronica asked her mum.

"No babe, I can manage. I will be out in a minute."

"Okay, just call if you need me Mum." Veronica wanted to cry, it was obvious that Paula was struggling, but she tried so hard to remain strong.

When she came out of the bathroom she went back to bed to lie down.

Veronica made her mum a small bowl of porridge and a drink. Paula wasn't really feeling up to eating, she tried a few small spoonfuls, but that was all she could manage. Veronica didn't know what to do for her mum, she looked so uncomfortable and in so much pain.

Paula just wanted to sleep, so Veronica kissed her mum and let her be.

For most of the day, Paula stayed in bed and so did Philip. In fact they both stayed in bed for a couple of days, only getting up for food or to go outside in the back garden to smoke.

Paula was continuously sick. There was no let up at all for her, and they all knew that the cancer was taking hold. "I've really had enough now Vronx," Paula told her daughter. "I am just fed up with being ill all the time. I am never going to get better," she said.

Veronica didn't have any words of comfort; there was nothing she could say. The consultant had told the family that there was nothing more they could do for Paula, it was a waiting game and even Veronica had had enough of seeing her mum so down and depressed; being sick all the time.

The house phone rang, it was Ella, she was calling to see how her mum was. Veronica told her how sick she had been, Ella was depressed about it all. "I can't bear being away from her Vron," Ella told her. "I need to be near her and I need a cuddle," she continued.

"I just can't cope with her being so far away from me. I know she wanted to stay with you and get away, but I just wish she was here Vron, I

325

really miss her." Veronica knew how her sister felt, this was exactly how Veronica felt when her mum was in London and she was stuck in Kent.

Veronica had an overwhelming sense of relief wash over her when she drove to London to be by her mum's side. She could cope with the harsh reality of her mum's illness better when she was with her, than she could when they were separated and miles apart.

"I know how you feel Ella," Veronica told her sister. "That's exactly how I feel when you are all together in London and I'm stuck here in Kent. You just need to be with her, don't you?"

"Would it be okay if me and Petros drove down to you for a few hours so I could give her a cuddle?" Ella asked.

"Of course Ella," Veronica replied. "We've got Petros's three children as well, so is it okay if we bring them?"

Veronica paused. Petros's children had come round to visit before; they were particularly noisy children and were quite hard to manage. They had lots of energy and didn't stop running around the house, thudding loudly up and down the stairs all day. Veronica remembered this and thought of her mum. She was in so much pain and tired and had spent all day being sick. The last thing she needed was three crazy kids stomping around the house in her condition.

"Well Mum is really sick Ella and I don't know if she could handle all the noise of the kids running around. As long as they are quiet and well behaved, then that should be fine," Veronica told her sister. Ella took offence from this.

She snapped at Veronica, "You go on like they are naughty kids Ron, but they are just kids, I will keep them in the garden or something so they don't even come into your house okay?" she said harshly. Veronica didn't mean anything by it; she was just concerned for her mum.

"There's no need to be like that Ella, as if I want them outside. Don't be silly, I just want to keep the peace for Mum because she is so sick," Veronica told Ella.

"No I know you don't like Petros and his kids Vron because you said about it before. You complained about his kids after they came up for the day with us."

Petros's kids didn't listen to Veronica and Rae when they asked them to stop running up and down the stairs and slamming doors. They were asked to eat only in the dining room as this was their house rule, which Ashley and Sienna had learned to abide by. But Petros's kids ignored them and Veronica had to take a banana away from Petros's daughter when she found her upstairs in the bedroom with one; and there was banana up the stairs and hall squashed into the floor where they had stepped in it. Petros hadn't even told his children to behave and instead let them run riot all over the place. Veronica had tried to broach the subject gently with Ella after they had gone home, but she didn't like it and now she was creating a nasty atmosphere because of it.

"Don't worry Vron, we won't stay long, I just want to cuddle my mum and then we will get out of your way," Ella snapped. With that she put the phone down.

Veronica's heart sank, where had this all come from? She only wanted to keep her mum comfortable. She was more than happy for Ella to drive down and see her mum, but Ella had been nasty. Rae was in the room and had listened intently to the conversation between the two sisters.

"What did I do wrong?" Veronica asked.

"Nothing at all, you were thinking of your mum that's all. Your sister is being selfish, she doesn't like the fact you have some quality time with your mum and she wants to upset it. Why does she have to come down? Your mum is only staying for a few days; your sister sees her every day of the week and has had your mum by her side like this since I've known you Vron. Why can't she just let you and your mum have some time together? It's always been about Ella."

Veronica could totally understand how Ella felt being apart from her mum, especially now she was so poorly and dying, but when she thought about what Rae said, she did wonder.

Veronica went into Ashley's bedroom where her parents were. She told her mum that Ella and Petros were on their way to visit. Paula seemed pleasantly surprised, then Veronica told her that Petros had his three other children with them as well as baby Sammy and Helen. Paula looked disappointed.

"Why have they all got to come in tow?" she asked.

"Well I did think that; and I asked her if they could be quiet around you as I know you've been so unwell, but she has taken offence where there was none intended," Veronica explained.

"That's typical of Ella," Paula said.

"I'm sorry Mum, I didn't want to cause any upset by it, I was only thinking of you."

"I know you were babe, don't worry about it," Paula said.

She continued to get up frequently to go to the toilet to be sick, while Philip was downstairs smoking a spliff in the garden summer house. Veronica asked her mum if she needed anything, but she just wanted to lie back down and try to sleep off the sickness.

Veronica went back into her bedroom where she had been packing up boxes of clothes all day, in preparation for the house move. They were expecting a moving date at any moment and they had to be prepared to go. Veronica had found some clothes in the cupboard that she no longer wore as they were quite big and fitted her when she was pregnant with Sienna.

She asked her mum if she wanted any of them. Veronica had a long tweed coat from Guess, which was lined and particularly nice. It was huge on Veronica but she thought it might come in handy for her mum as the weather was getting increasingly cold.

Paula loved the coat and even got out of bed to try it on; she was amazed that she could do it up regardless of her swollen stomach. She smiled and said, "I feel like a queen in this Vronx! Are you sure you don't want to sell it? You could get some good money for this."

Veronica didn't care about getting any money, she only cared for trying to help her mum in any little way she could. "No Mum, it's made for you and really suits you." Philip had come back in from the garden and came into the bedroom.

"What do you reckon Dad?" she asked him, pointing to her mum in the coat.

"Wow!" he said, "you look gorgeous in it Paula."

"See Mum, I told you, so you must keep it," Veronica continued.

Paula thanked her daughter and gave her a kiss and a cuddle. Paula's face had lit up and she had forgotten the sickness for those few moments. For Veronica this was priceless.

"I've got some more clothes you might like Mum," she said, "and there are some jackets of Rae's that are way too small for him since he's filled out over the years. Would you like to have a look Dad?"

"Yeah okay," Phil replied.

Veronica spent the next couple of hours sorting, folding, packing and sealing boxes with clothes and shoes. Every time she found an item that she thought may be of interest to her parents, she took them into Ashley's bedroom for them to try. Veronica had found the suit jacket that Rae had married her in. It had a 'granddad' collar which Phil particularly liked. Veronica took it into her dad for him to try. The jacket suited him although it was quite big on the shoulders. He had lost loads of weight himself and looked very frail. Veronica didn't want to tell him this as she didn't want to upset him; instead she insisted that it suited him even though the jacket was a bit big. Phil looked at himself in the mirror, he loved it.

"Are you sure you don't want this Rae?" he asked him.

"No mate, it was made for you!" Rae said. Phil was chuffed to bits with his new jacket and posed in the mirror with it a little longer. Veronica felt good about gifting their designer clothes to her parents; they were after all as good as new.

Veronica continued to pack for another hour or so, whilst Rae decided to go shopping at the local supermarket as they were running out of food. He asked Veronica if there was anything specific she wanted and went on his way. He took Sienna with him to allow Veronica the time to carry on packing and look after her parents.

A few minutes after Rae left the house, Phil walked into the couple's bedroom where Veronica was in her wardrobe sorting through clothes. "Can I have a word with you a minute Vronx?" Phil asked.

"Yeah of course," Veronica replied. She had a dozen hangers with clothes on around her arm as she walked out of the cupboard. Phil's face had completely changed.

Instead of the friendly smile he had been wearing only moments ago when Veronica was passing him clothes, it had turned disdainful.

"What's the matter?" Veronica asked her dad.

"I need to talk to you about the way you make people feel like shit and how you have made your sister feel unwelcome in your home," he said. Veronica could not believe it, was she imagining this conversation? Was this like a bad dream? Her heart sank and she felt confused and upset.

"What are you talking about Dad?" she asked.

"You told Ella you didn't want the kids round and made her feel completely uncomfortable about driving down to see her mum for a cuddle, why are you so insensitive Vronx? Why is it that you don't give a fuck about anyone's feelings but your own?"

Veronica felt her stomach churn, she went from feeling gutted to angry in a second, and she was fuming. "You've got it all wrong Dad, I never said she wasn't welcome at all, I told her to come because I knew how it felt to not be near Mum. I understood her anxiety completely and told her to come. When she said she was bringing Petros's kids I just asked her to keep them quiet for Mum because she's so sick today and doesn't need loads of kids running around screaming and shouting as they are very loud."

Philip's face had curled with anger; he even had hate in his eyes. "You can't fucking admit nothing can you Vronx, it's always everyone else. You treat people like shit and act like a cunt and you are not even big enough to apologise for that are you?" Phil scorned.

Veronica wanted to burst into tears but she held it together, she wasn't going to let her dad intimidate her like this. Where had his anger come from all of a sudden? Why would Ella cause an argument like this? She didn't have time to work any of it out before her dad started again.

"When are you gonna stop treating your sister like shit and say sorry Vronx?" he said.

"I have got nothing to apologise for," Veronica shouted. Phil was almost spitting with anger.

"She is going to turn up here any minute with Petros and the kids. You better apologise and don't make her feel unwelcome."

Veronica didn't even want her, Petros and the kids in the house now. She wished she could throw her dad out as well. His spiteful behaviour said it all; he looked at Veronica like she was a bit of shit on the floor. Veronica couldn't believe it, or how quickly he had turned on her the second Rae left the house. Why didn't he start on her like this in front of Rae? Well it was obvious, Rae would have thrown him out and he knew it.

"You and Ella are bullies. I've done nothing to her apart from ask the kids to be quiet for my sick mum, you should understand that Dad. Why are you calling me a cunt? You've got no right to treat me like this," she said.

"Why, because I'm in your house?" Philip shouted sarcastically.

"Well actually, it is my house yeah!" Veronica told him. Philip didn't like it one bit.

Just then Paula came shuffling into the room as she struggled with her swollen legs, stomach and pains. "Philip can you calm down and stop shouting please?" Paula said.

"So because it's your house you can do what the fuck you like can you?" Phil asked Veronica.

"Well yeah I can, and I don't have to take any shit from you either!" Veronica snapped.

"Paula, pack the bags we are leaving," Phil said. "I hope you are happy with yourself now Vronx, you've upset your sister and made her and her husband feel unwelcome in your home, you refuse to apologise and now you've upset your mum too and ruined this break. You are the most selfish person I've ever known," he said.

Veronica was full of adrenaline, she was so angry and emotional all at the same time, she didn't know what to do for the best. She didn't want her mum to leave, she had been so relieved to have her by her side, but her dad was making things impossible. Veronica had had enough of him. She always felt like she was walking on eggshells where he was concerned, but he had overstepped the mark now.

"Go on then go, I'm not gonna put up with you treating me like shit in my own home. I've done nothing but show my love, I've helped as much as I can and you've thrown it in my face, belittling me and calling me a cunt. If anyone is a cunt it's you. Look at you, how dare you treat me like this and then blame me for it all. I never meant a thing regarding Ella. Rae was in the room when I was talking to her, he heard me, you ask him if I made her feel unwelcome. If you want to leave, that's down to you not me. I'm sorry for this mum, I never meant for any of this," Veronica said as she burst into tears.

Paula was in shock at the whole affair. "I ain't fucking staying here a minute longer, you disrespectful bitch," Phil said. "Come on Paula we are leaving."

"Oh grow up will you." Paula shouted at Philip. He couldn't believe it and stood with his mouth open in disbelief that Paula wasn't supporting him.

"I am not going anywhere," Paula told him. "Veronica was only thinking about me and didn't mean anything by it, Ella has blown this out of proportion and you know what she's like when she's on her period, she can be a nasty bitch." Philip was stunned, so was Veronica. She was so relieved that her mum had stuck up for her and supported her.

Philip walked out of the bedroom disgusted that his wife wasn't on his side.

Veronica was crying and shaking, it was at this moment that Veronica realised how little her dad really thought of her. She had seen the bitterness in his eyes, he meant every word he had said to Veronica and she knew it. There was nothing sweet or genuine about his behaviour towards his daughter, for Veronica it was like a curtain had been lifted.

There was no more front, no more Mr Nice Guy, just the real Phil Baker. All she could do was keep apologising to her mum.

Just then, the doorbell rang, Veronica knew it was Ella. Philip made his way towards the stairs to go down and let them in. "You better not carry this on," he yelled to Veronica. "You better not make her feel like shit," he continued.

Veronica stayed in her bedroom, shocked and upset. She grabbed her mobile phone and rang Rae. She whispered down the phone in tears as she tried hard not to be overheard.

"Babe, I've had a fall out with my dad. He started to have a go at me the second you left the house." Rae was also shocked.

"Why?" he asked. "You were getting along so well when I left."

"He called me names and said I made Ella feel unwelcome in my house because I 'told' her to keep the kids quiet. She told him that, I've just seen a 'what's app' text she sent through our group thing, so she wanted me to see it! I was busy packing when he came into our bedroom and started. He said I'm selfish and I need to apologise to her. I refused because I never did anything wrong, you heard me talking to her didn't you, was I nasty?" she asked Rae.

"No Vron, you were reasonable about it, you couldn't have asked her in any nicer way. I just knew she would twist it, they are so predictable your family. She's a bitch, couldn't just leave you to have time with your mum, she had to spoil it. How dare they treat you like this after everything you've done for them?" Rae said.

"My dad demanded I apologise to her and called me a cunt, they've just turned up downstairs. I'm in the bedroom and I actually feel completely uncomfortable in my own home. I don't want to go downstairs," she said.

"Vron if your mum wasn't so sick, I would throw your dad out. How dare he, who does he think he is? I hope you stood up to him," Rae told Veronica.

"I did, it made me angry then he threatened to leave, telling poor Mum to pack their bags, and said 'look what I've done'. Mum told him to grow up and said she wasn't leaving."

"Good for her," Rae said, "she backed you up for once, about time too. How pathetic of your dad!"

"I feel awful now," Veronica said. "Just when I felt okay having Mum here and now I just want him to leave, but that means both of them leaving. What a horrible situation. Please hurry home babe, I don't feel right on my own with them. They are all downstairs; I bet he's slagging me off to Ella and Petros."

"I am coming now babe, I will get the rest of the food tomorrow. I am not having them treat you like shit in our home. Your dad is a spineless prick Vron, look how he waited for me to leave before he started on you. Why didn't he do that in front of me? Because he isn't brave enough babe, I wouldn't be able to contain myself if he spoke to you like this in front of me and he knows it. I will be back as quick as I can. I love you; don't let him or Ella get away with it."

Veronica said goodbye and hung up. She felt too paranoid to leave the bedroom; she couldn't believe that her dad had made her feel so awkward. Veronica carried on packing her clothes, she thought she would stay out of their way and wait for Rae to return.

Five minutes later, her dad called up to her. "Your sister and her husband are here Veronica, are you going to come down and say hello or what?" he shouted sarcastically.

Veronica wanted to tell him to fuck off but she couldn't cause another scene and make things any worse for her mum. "I am packing up a box at the minute, I will be down soon," she replied as she bit her tongue. Veronica continued to pack, although she had lost all concentration and was listening intently to hear what they were talking about downstairs, but Veronica couldn't make out their conversation. She couldn't bring herself to go down to them; she was so angry with her dad and sister. She wanted to ask Ella why she had created an argument but it would only end up with a screaming match and Veronica could not be responsible for this, it was bad enough as it was. Rae seemed to be taking ages, Veronica knew she would have to go down and face the music. She decided to try and put on a front, as if nothing had happened.

As uncomfortable as it was, it was the only way, she didn't want to upset her mum in any way, shape or form and that was her priority. In fact, Veronica realised from this point on that her mum was the only person she would worry about. She was exhausted by her sister and dad's antics and downright disrespectful treatment of her. It almost seemed too surreal that an argument like this had erupted from nothing. Veronica began to wonder if it was premeditated. Was her dad looking for an excuse to leave Veronica's early? Perhaps he wanted to rush back to north London to get some drugs? Veronica wanted nothing more than to spend the last precious moments she could with her mum and she would do anything and put up with anything, to be able to see that wish through.

Veronica said hello to her sister and her husband Petros, they couldn't give Veronica eye contact and barely acknowledged her, talking to Paula and Phil instead. Veronica sat down next to her mum on the two seater sofa in the dining room. Veronica's dad and Petros sat opposite on the three seater. Petros's kids were in the garden playing and baby Sammy was asleep in his car seat.

Ella decided she wanted to cuddle her mum and sat on top of Veronica pushing her out of the way so that she could get beside her mum. Veronica wanted to tell her she was rude and childish but instead kept her mouth shut and got up and walked out of the room.

Paula looked pale and sick, but she also looked uncomfortable with the situation.

Veronica went back upstairs to her room; it was as if she had been summoned to be humiliated by her dad and sister. He had called her down to say hello, only to be ignored and pushed aside.

Veronica was full of mixed emotions, she wanted to cry and scream all at the same time.

Just then the front door opened and Rae had returned with Sienna and Ashley. Veronica immediately felt relief, her dad and sister couldn't continue their antics with Rae around. There was no way that Rae would stand for any of it. Rae was particularly quiet with Veronica's dad and Ella. When anything upset Rae, you knew about it, his body language spoke volumes and he was going to let them know that he wasn't being taken for a fool.

Rae unpacked the shopping and asked Paula what she fancied for dinner. He continued to be attentive towards her, but he made no effort with the others. Paula didn't feel up to eating because she still felt sick, so Rae agreed to make her something small and bland.

Once he'd finished putting the shopping away he went upstairs to see Veronica.

Veronica was sitting on the bed, upset and still shocked at what had happened, Rae put his arm around her. "Do you know it's taken all of my might to hold my tongue, down there? The only reason I won't say anything Vron, is because of your mum. She doesn't need this and your dad is a selfish bastard. Do you know that up to now, he hadn't just sucked you in; he'd also sucked me in. I felt his pain and anguish and I really felt for the man, but this has opened my eyes Vron. The whole thing has been a front, he only wants to use us for every last thing he can get out of us, you know that don't you?" he asked his wife.

Veronica knew deep down he was right but she didn't want to admit it to herself. Instead she wanted to make excuses for her dad's behaviour. "It's his way of coping," she said.

Rae laughed. "What, by treating his daughter like utter shit, when she has been trying to do as much as she can for him and her mum? Is that right then Vron, would you treat Sienna like this if it were her?"

Veronica shook her head. "No I know you wouldn't," Rae said. "You would treat her with love and understanding and most of all respect. You wouldn't abuse her like he does you. No, no, no, this has opened my eyes; never again will I fall for his bullshit. All he cares about is himself Vron, he don't even look after your mum. What has he been playing at, turning up here at 3am with her, making her wait days on end before getting her to a hospital? You don't do that to someone you love Vron?"

Veronica began to cry. Rae put his arm around her and pulled her close. "I'm sorry babe but you need to hear the truth. You know I will put up with a lot, I have put up with more than most men ever would where your parents are concerned over the years, but your dad is an utter piss taker; and he is using you and me both. I will keep it together for your mum; you need to be strong for her. I feel sorry for her Vron, she's been controlled by your dad her whole married life. He took her down the path that has led her to this point in time, you know that, he knows it, but he will never face up to it. He will always blame everyone else and anything else. That's not a real man; he could never look himself in the mirror Vron, and own up to what he's done. He should be begging for forgiveness not treating you like shit."

Veronica nodded in agreement as she wiped her tears. "All I want is to do right by my mum, I have to keep my mouth shut otherwise I won't be able to spend time with her. Also, he says he's skint. I'll have to make sure she has the send-off she deserves when she dies," Veronica told Rae, and he agreed.

"I am right behind you babe, we will make sure she gets what she rightfully deserves. All your dad keeps saying is that he's skint. He says he hasn't signed on to get help from the benefits department but why has he left it so long? All these months he hasn't worked, knowing his wife is going to die anytime soon. Why has he not tried to do something to prepare for that?" Veronica didn't have an answer. "It's obvious babe, because he knows we will do the right thing. If it was me in that situation and you were in your mum's shoes, I couldn't sit back and just expect everyone else to pick up the pieces. I couldn't sit back and watch our kids foot the bill. What kind of a man would that make me? No, it would be my responsibility to do right by my wife." Veronica agreed with Rae again,

"Take my parents Vron; if they died tomorrow, they have money set aside for their funerals. They wouldn't expect me and my brothers and sisters to pay for it."

Veronica became defensive of her mum. "My mum didn't know she was going to be facing a premature death though did she? My dad didn't know six months ago that she was going to be told she was dying of cancer," she said.

"Of course not Veronica, they weren't to know. However they've had nearly six months to sort this out. Your dad turned the flat into a skunk farm inhibiting your mum from receiving the proper care she needs. They've been turning away the Palliative care team because of his ridiculous skunk farm. You haven't stepped foot in that flat for years, how long have they been growing it for? They could have been doing this a long time. All those weeks that we have known he's been cultivating those plants and then suddenly they disappeared. What did he tell us? That they had spider mites and he never got much money from them. What an absolute pile of rubbish Vron. Do you seriously believe that story?

"He's full of it. I don't believe for a second he never got anything from that grow. If that was the case why has he set up another lot? When the time comes, you know he isn't going to do a thing for your mum to send her off, you do know that don't you?" Rae asked. Veronica shook her head in agreement and disappointment. She still clung on to the hope that her dad would surprise them and have something prepared, but only time would tell. Either way, Veronica was happy to pay for her mum's send off. She would do it right and with pride.

Rae cuddled Veronica close. "I feel so sorry for your mum Vron, for everything she is going through, it isn't right and it isn't fair, but your dad could make things a lot easier and could have done more for your mum and you girls. Instead, he takes it out on you, the eldest, and the one who could always be relied on. The one who took risks with her own life to protect her parents. Your dad's attitude stinks Vron. He should be proud

336

of you and all you've achieved in life, he should be singing your praises but instead he abuses you. I'm sorry, but you know if he were my dad, I would have fucked him off years ago but he isn't; he's your dad and you've got to do what you think is right for you," he said.

Veronica knew Rae was right, but at this point in time, she couldn't do anything, all she could do was bite her tongue and pretend it never happened. She had to keep the peace the best way she could for her mum. It was clear that her dad wanted to leave, but her mum didn't, so Veronica would keep things simple and comfortable for as long as her mum wanted to stay.

Rae went back down to the kitchen with Veronica. Ashley and Sienna were busy playing with Helen and Petros's kids in the garden. Paula looked tired and pale as she sat on the sofa.

Veronica's dad and Petros were happily chatting as if nothing had gone on; Ella was cuddling her mum with baby Sammy on her lap. Veronica wanted to be the doting auntie but it couldn't come natural with her feeling so upset with Ella. Even Paula had a vacant stare about her, as if she shouldn't have been there.

Veronica just got along as best as she could and eventually Ella and Petros got ready to leave and said goodbye. Ella kissed the kids and Paula, but bypassed Veronica, choosing to leave her out. Veronica didn't care, she was too angry for a fake kiss anyway.

When they left, Veronica was relieved, but she still felt overwhelmed with emotion. She couldn't even bear to look at her dad and decided to ignore him and pretend he wasn't there.

Veronica helped her mum back up to bed and got her settled, then she went into her bedroom with Sienna while Rae prepared dinner. Rae was very quiet and barely spoke to Phil, but Phil seemed to be either thick-skinned or too ignorant to even notice.

CHAPTER 82

Dinner was a Quiet Affair

Paula didn't eat much, still feeling very sick, she struggled with only a small portion and went back to bed. Phil sat for ages eating his, he had always been very slow to eat a meal and Rae always gave large portions which were too much for him to eat. Phil made conversation with Rae at the dinner table as if nothing had happened that evening. It was as if the monster that had erupted earlier had completely disappeared and the nice guy was back again, but Veronica was seething inside and she could tell that Rae was too. Rae just went along with the act, keeping everything peaceful for the sake of Paula.

As soon as Rae had finished his food, he got up to clean the dishes away and Veronica got up to help him. Philip continued to struggle with his food whilst playing with his iPhone. Veronica and Rae finished the dishes and said good night to Philip. Normally Veronica would have kissed her dad goodnight, but she couldn't bring herself to do it, just the thought of it made her stomach churn. She didn't want to kiss him after the way he had behaved; she was disgusted with his attitude and deeply hurt. She went upstairs, kissed her mum, who was in bed asleep, and checked on Sienna and Ashley; kissing them both goodnight.

Veronica didn't sleep too well that night; she knew her mum's cancer was taking hold. Paula was so frail and tired that she could barely take herself to the toilet to be sick. Veronica cried silently on and off all night. She was faced with her mum's imminent death and the aftermath of her dad's outburst and Ella's stirring. Veronica's stomach churned and she felt so sick with anxiety, somehow she had to be strong for her mum, but she was completely falling apart inside.

Paula had been up and down throughout the night being sick again. Veronica felt exhausted by the sight of what her helpless, little, frail mum was going through; and wondered what her mum must be feeling. She found it was just unbearable. She heard her mum shuffling along the hallway and got up to see if she needed anything, Paula had her dressing gown on with her hood up and a pack of cigarettes in her hand.

"Good morning Mum," Veronica whispered, trying not to wake Sienna or anyone else.

"Oh, good morning babe," Paula replied. "I didn't wake you up did I?"

"No Mum, I was awake anyway. Would you like a cup of tea? I'm coming down to make myself a coffee," Veronica asked.

"Ooh yes please babe, I want a fag and was gonna go in the garden," Paula replied.

"Well let me come with you and I'll put the kettle on," Veronica responded. She helped her mum tackle the stairs; they were a bit tricky for Paula who wasn't so steady on her feet with the swelling in her stomach and legs.

As they reached the kitchen, Veronica grabbed her mum's slippers and helped her put them on. She took her mum outside into the garden where there was a canopy to keep under cover. Paula lit her cigarette and puffed away. Veronica grabbed a garden chair for her mum to sit on and went back in to the kitchen to make the tea and coffee.

A few minutes later, Paula came back inside, she sat in the dining room on the sofa and Veronica brought her tea to her. She sat opposite her mum and drank her coffee. Veronica told her mum she was sorry for the argument that had erupted the night before. She told her that she never meant for any of it and never meant any harm to Ella or her husband, and only wanted for her mum to be comfortable. Paula told her, "I know that babe; you haven't got to explain that to me. I know you were only thinking of me. I've had time to really think about things and I just can't get my head around your dad sometimes. I don't know what it is with him. I love him so much but it's like there's something wrong with him, like he's got something missing in his brain. His brothers are the same; they are all full of bullshit." Veronica was stunned, had she heard right, was she imagining this conversation?

Paula carried on, saying, "I want to tell you something but do you promise me that you won't say anything to him or to anyone?"

"Of course I won't Mum, if that's your wish, I will not say a word," Veronica assured her. "The other week, your dad went out, he said he was getting some bits from the shop and wouldn't be long. He was gone for ages and ages Vron, he was gone for hours. I had been lying in bed in agony, I couldn't get up I was in so much pain and I couldn't figure out where my tablets were. Your dad had taken control of my medication because of how confused I had been. I was so upset and frustrated because I wasn't able to look after myself." Veronica was stunned, this was exactly what she had feared was going on.

"When he finally came back, I told him I was thirsty and hungry," Paula continued. "He said he was going to make me something and went downstairs, but he was taking forever. I was so fed up with waiting that I got up and went down to the kitchen. He was in the living room and hadn't even started to make me any food, so I put the kettle on and noticed that there weren't any clean cups and dishes, so I started to wash up. A few minutes later your dad comes into the kitchen and he comes right up into my face and screams at me, 'What the fuck do you think you are doing, I told you I was making you something, what are you doing down here?' I couldn't believe he was shouting at me like that and he was right in my face and he was so angry Vron, he really frightened me, it was like he was someone else. He'd changed, I think he'd been out getting gear and I think he's been taking cocaine again. Ella's bloke has offered it to him and George, who he gets his gear from, has it and offers it to your dad. I hate it when he's on that stuff. I told him I was hungry and had been on my own for hours waiting for him and I just wanted to help him by washing up, but he continued to shout at me. He said, 'Go back up to bed and stay there and wait 'til I am ready, don't fucking come down here sticking your oar in. I fucking started washing up, why are you doing it?' I burst into tears Vron, because it was like a monster standing there; he was so nasty to me. When I cried, he shouted again saying, 'Oh that's it, go on, start crying like a fucking baby, go on put on the water works you fucking idiot. What are you crying for?' he yelled. I thought he was going to hit me Vron, he intimidated me so much I didn't know what he was going to do. He was coming out with all this stuff, putting me down and making me feel so awful. I wished I had the energy to pack a bag and leave right then but I didn't, I was so ill and I didn't have the energy to do anything."

Paula had tears streaming down her face as she told Veronica this, and Veronica had tears streaming down her face as she was hearing it. Veronica wanted to run upstairs, drag her dad out of bed and beat him; it was completely sickening, how could she look at him now? At that moment, Veronica hated him. His wife was frail and dying of cancer and all he could do was leave her to suffer and get high and then abuse his dying wife.

It was obvious; this must have been going on all along. This was why Paula wasn't getting seen to at hospital promptly. Philip was getting off his face, and all the while Paula was left facing and fearing her death alone. Veronica cuddled her mum and they both wept together.

"I can't believe he's treated you like this mum. He's supposed to be looking after you, that's what he's led us to believe."

Paula became defensive of him. "He has babe, as best as he can. He hasn't done this since and he did apologise after, it's just that it scared me and I wanted you to know that it's not just you he starts on. I just don't think he can cope with what's happening to me and he's getting on the drugs to escape it because he can't cope. He's always been like it, I used to believe everything that came out of his mouth but I've realised he's full of shit. His brothers too, they are all the same, they are born liars. It's like they've all got something wrong with their brains, they can't tell the truth to save their lives, but I love him regardless. I am so worried about him Vronx. How will he cope when I'm no longer here? How will he look after himself? I've always done everything for him, from the household bills to his washing and cleaning. I even used to put his socks on for him in the mornings when he struggled to wake up for work! How will he survive?"

Veronica didn't have an answer. What could she say to that! Veronica was seething at the thought of him screaming in Paula's face when she tried to help wash up, how could he be so mean? Why should Veronica feel sorry for him now? He never treated Paula the way she deserved to be treated. Sure, he loved her in his warped, messed up, drug fuelled way but it wasn't a normal kind of love, not like the love Veronica had from Rae.

All Veronica could do was to tell her mum she was sorry and put her arms around her.

Paula had tears streaming down her frail, thin face. Veronica wiped them and kissed her mum's cheeks. "I am so sorry that I wasn't there the day he left you alone Mum. I wished you had called me; I would have come straight down. You know that don't you?" Veronica told her mum.

"Of course I do babe, but you've got enough on your plate. You've got your hands full with Sienna and moving house and losing your livelihood. Same with Ella, she's just had baby Sammy and settling down with him. You've all got your lives to live. I can't keep calling on you all," Paula replied.

"You absolutely can Mum, I will drop everything at a second's notice to be by your side and help you. It doesn't matter what I've got going on, what matters to me at this point in time the most is you, Mum. I've got Rae to lean on and he is totally behind me, he feels the same and wants me to support you, so don't ever feel like you can't call on me. You could have."

"I know babe, I just kept thinking your dad would come home at any moment and the time just dragged. Promise me you won't say anything to him, please?" Paula asked again.

"Of course I won't Mum, I wouldn't put you in that position," Veronica replied. She wished though, that she could hold her mum to ransom and not let her go back to the dingy flat in Tottenham. Veronica wanted to keep her mum with her for as long as she could, even though it meant putting up with her dad, it was better than the thought of Paula being left to suffer whilst Phil went out to score drugs. Veronica was livid with him, what a bully he was to pick on her little mum like that. It was disgusting and Veronica knew she could never forgive such an act. Paula wanted to go back up to bed, so Veronica helped her upstairs and got her into bed. Her dad was lying there fast asleep with his mouth wide open as he snored; Veronica wished she could slap him and wake him up, screaming in his face just like he did to her mum, but she had to bite her lip. Veronica kissed her mum and went back to bed.

Though Phil spent some quality time with Ashley whilst he was there, playing and discussing interests he had as a young boy, the atmosphere remained tense. Rae stayed by Veronica's side the whole time her parents remained at the house, as he didn't want to give Phil any chance to bully his wife, so when Rae went out, Veronica went with him. Ashley had never spent so much time with his granddad before though, and Phil seemed to be enjoying time with his grandson.

Paula continued to be sick for the following couple of days, and Veronica and Rae were always on hand to help her as much as they could. Rae continued to prepare wholesome meals for all the family.

Phil soon decided it was time to head back to north London though, as he had things to take care of. Veronica was dreading her mum leaving, she felt panicked inside. What if Phil was only going back to get his drugs? What if he left Paula to suffer alone in silence again?

Veronica took her mum to one side, "Promise me you will call me if he goes out and leaves you again Mum. Call me or even Ella, Mum, don't feel any way about it. We can't have you suffering and alone, that's not the deal, Dad is meant to take care of you and if he doesn't, I need to know."

Paula promised she would call and told her daughter not to worry. Veronica helped her parents pack their belongings and put them in their car. Phil was taking ages with getting himself together. Paula was fed up waiting for him and sat on the bottom step in the hall.

Veronica sat beside her and cuddled her close. "I really don't want you to go Mum," Veronica told her. "I could take care of you forever."

Paula smiled and stroked Veronica's arm. "I know you could babe and I could stay forever," she said. "I feel so much better having stayed here, and I've got to know Rae better too."

Veronica was happy that her mum had seen the real Rae and had time to get to know him in his true light for the person he really was, not the arsehole that her dad had always made him out to be. "You've got a good one there babe, hold onto him," Paula said, "I will Mum, I love him so much," Veronica replied.

"I'm so sorry that I didn't spend more time with you all, I'm sorry that I never did this sooner, and I'm sorry that I haven't been there for you. I love you Veronica more than you know. I'm so sorry for everything," Paula told her daughter. Veronica gripped her mum and sobbed, she couldn't hold it back.

"You've got nothing to be sorry for Mum," Veronica assured her. They both cuddled each other tight and Veronica wanted this moment to last forever.

Suddenly, Philip made his way down the stairs interrupting the mother and daughter's special moment. Veronica and Paula kissed and let each other go, getting up and moving out of the way for Philip to come past. Veronica wiped her tears and led her parents to their car; it was a very difficult moment saying goodbye. Veronica knew her mum was nearing the end of her life, the signs were obvious. Paula knew it too, and that's why she said the things she had said to her daughter. It was a very emotional time and Veronica had very mixed feelings. She was very upset at the thought of her mum passing away, having not fulfilled her dreams and her promise to her daughters, of a drug free existence and a normal life. Veronica was devastated at this reality that was looming ever closer.

The agony was too much to bear; the mere thought of her mum suffering in silence took Veronica over the edge. She couldn't cope with her feelings, she couldn't cope with the anger and with everything else going on in her life, she felt like she was dying inside herself. As the car pulled off and drove down the road, Veronica waved her mum goodbye and blew her kisses. She welled up with tears and as she walked back to the house she fell apart, her heart was breaking, it was so sad.

CHAPTER 83

The Last Days

Within a few days of Phil and Paula returning to London, Paula had ended up back in hospital.

Her swollen stomach had become too much to bear and the sickness wasn't easing, so Phil took Paula back to Kings College hospital, where she was given a private room on the ward. They had more specialist expertise in dealing with Paula's liver problems there, than their local hospital in north London. She was there for nearly two days before they could give Phil any answers. Then the doctors told him there was nothing more they could do for Paula. They could only try to ease the pressure of the ascites by taking fluid off of her stomach using a syringe, but the swelling would return just as quickly as it was taken down. There had been no let up for Paula since the day she had chemoembolization, she had suffered constantly with one issue after the other and it was clear for all to see that it was wearing her down. The doctors wasted no time in telling Phil that Paula was now in the late stages of her disease and that she would not survive another fortnight. He didn't want Paula to know the extent to which her cancer had spread, but unfortunately the doctor had told Paula this when she was alone in her room.

Phil had gone home to get some sleep and the doctor had visited Paula on his morning rounds and told her her imminent fate. When Veronica and her sisters arrived to see her with Phil, she told them that the doctors had written her off. She looked tired and fed up but there was almost a look of acceptance in her eyes. As much as she didn't want to be where she was, she had accepted that there was no way back and that she couldn't change it. The girls welled up with tears. Ella changed the subject and tried to make Paula laugh, then Phil joined in, distracting Paula with his morning events. Veronica looked on, dazed by what she had just learned.

Paula was being so brave, and Veronica could not take her eyes off her mum, she was mesmerised by her mum's bravery. This tiny woman had been through so much in her life and now here she was facing her final journey, the thing we all fear the most, and she still managed a smile. Paula welled up with emotion, her voice cracked as the tears rolled down her face.

"I'm so lucky to have such a lovely family, to see you all sticking together and supporting me like this, I'm so lucky to be so loved," she said as her voice broke. Veronica was crying already, there was no way the tears could be stopped; it was just too much to handle.

"We love you so much because you are a beautiful person," Phil told his wife.

"I'm sorry for putting you all through this," Paula said. "I know I haven't got long left now, I just want you all to know that I love you all so much."

Ella and Paulette were crying too, Phil's voice had broken and he was fighting hard to hold back his tears. At that moment, everyone knew that every second counted. Paula wanted to get out of the hospital and get home.

"I don't want to die here," she said. "I want to come home, I want to be with your dad, and I want to be in my own home. I don't want to die alone in here with no one around me; I just want to be at home with everyone with me."

Veronica felt like someone had driven a knife straight through her heart and twisted it slowly; it was agonising and never ending.

At that moment everyone knew they had to do what was right by Paula, as much as she wanted to be home, she hated the flat. Philip had never got around to painting it for her and making it look homely inside. Veronica thought it would be a lovely idea to paint Paulette's old room, as that was where the Palliative Care Team had arranged to deliver a hospital bed for Paula.

Rae and Veronica had also offered her parents some solid pine bedroom furniture which consisted of a chest of drawers, a wardrobe and a book case, all that was needed was a van to drop the furniture to the flat; and some paint for the room. Veronica asked her mum and dad if they liked the idea, and Phil agreed it would be nice to create a calming space for Paula. Rae organised the hire of a transit van and materials.

Over the next few days, Paula returned to the flat but she was getting increasingly weak and in constant pain. Ella's 30th birthday was also fast approaching. She called Veronica to tell her she was thinking about having a BBQ at her house for friends and family to celebrate her birthday. She told Veronica that it might be a good distraction for their mum, but Veronica wasn't so sure. Paula was in terrible pain and was constantly being sick; she could barely walk, needing assistance to go to the toilet.

"Don't you think it might be a bit too much for Mum, Ella?" she asked her sister. Ella paused, obviously disappointed by Veronica's reaction. Veronica couldn't imagine her mum being able to go to a party; and even if she found enough energy to go, would she feel comfortable around Ella's friends, being so unwell? Veronica told her sister that if their mum was well enough, then she would come along, but if she was too ill, then she would spend the time with her at the flat. She asked Ella if she could come to the flat and have a little family celebration there if their mum wasn't well enough to go out. Ella agreed, and the sisters said goodbye.

A couple of days later, it was Ella's birthday; and coincidentally Veronica and Rae were about to exchange contracts on the sale of their house, so they had to be ready to leave at a moment's notice as they were expecting to move within a few days. They had been anxiously waiting for the call, but were also worried as Paula was deteriorating rapidly.

Rae had spent weeks renovating his mum's bungalow, which she had bought in August. Rae had worked tirelessly for six weeks, labouring and organising various other trades to carry out the works to his mum and Dad's new home. This had taken a toll on the couple, along with dealing with their own imminent move and Paula's illness, how they had juggled everything so well was beyond them. They were mentally and emotionally exhausted from all of the responsibilities they carried, but Veronica and Rae were determined to do all they could to support Paula and Phil.

The morning of Ella's birthday, Rae had planned to take the furniture to Phil and Paula's flat, with Charlie to help him lift it all up the seven-floor block of flats; and then paint Paulette's room and move the furniture in. He had already loaded the hired van the night before so they could get an early start.

Veronica called her dad at 6am to let him know that Rae and Charlie were on their way.

Phil told his daughter that Paula had been in agony and was still being sick, he told her that it would be too much for Rae and Charlie to paint the room and asked if Rae could leave the furniture down stairs in the living room. Veronica felt disappointed. "She's really not up to having anyone around her, she's too ill Vron," Phil continued, "I know Rae and Charlie have made an effort and all that, but what can I say, she just doesn't want any disruptions right now."

Veronica accepted what her dad had told her and said she would tell Rae to just drop the furniture off.

Veronica was meant to be heading down later to spend time with her mum and get together with Ella at some point as it was her birthday. Veronica called her husband to tell him the painting of the room was off; Rae was just as disappointed as Veronica, but accepted what he was told.

A few hours later Veronica called Ella to wish her a happy birthday and to arrange times to meet up later. Ella told Veronica, "I've cancelled my BBQ because Mum isn't well and what you said about me having a party made me feel bad so I've called it all off."

Veronica couldn't believe it, she hadn't expected Ella to cancel anything, she just wanted to spend as much time as possible with her mum; and if Paula wasn't well enough for Ella's party then she would stay at the flat with her mum and celebrate with Ella another time.

Veronica had started to feel sick herself, she had been extremely anxious with her life up in the air and her mum's about to come to an end. Veronica felt uneasy about the unfolding situation, Phil had turned Rae and Charlie away from the flat due to Paula's sickness and now Ella had cancelled her 30th birthday BBQ which she had been so excited about only a couple of days before. Veronica needed time to digest everything that was happening.

"Okay Ella, I will call you later as I don't feel too well myself, I will call you in a few hours and see how I feel." Ella said "okay" and the sisters said goodbye.

Veronica called her dad and asked how her mum was. He told her there was no change and Paula had been sleeping for the last few hours. He told his daughter that all she did was sleep and when she wasn't, she was in pain and being sick. Veronica wondered if she were better off leaving her mum and dad for the time being and got on with finalising the packing up of their home. Veronica told her dad that if he needed her for anything to just call.

Rae had already returned home with the empty van, he told Veronica that he couldn't understand why it would have been an issue to paint the spare room. He said he would not have been in Paula's way as they could have shut the door whist painting and left her and Phil in peace. Veronica agreed, she so wanted her mum to see a lovely painted room with beautiful furniture in it for her. In the 14 years she had lived in the flat, she hadn't had so much as a wardrobe.

The couple had lived out of boxes surrounding their bed in their room, but it wasn't to be.

Veronica was upset because they had paid out over £200 to hire the van and get it down to Edmonton. Rae had also turned down a job he had been offered on that day to carry out the work on the flat. At a time where every penny counted, it turned out to be a complete waste of time, as Paula would not benefit from any of the effort. Veronica called her dad one last time; he said there was no change with Paula. Ella was also at the flat with her parents, so Veronica asked to speak with Ella. Veronica asked Ella what the plans were for her birthday, she told Veronica that she was just going to have a quiet night in with her husband Petros and the kids; and have an early night because she was feeling tired as she had been up the night before with her baby Sammy.

Veronica told Ella she wasn't feeling too good herself and would leave driving down to London until the next day. Veronica told her sister she loved her and her parents and said goodbye.

Veronica felt very uneasy, Ella had sounded quite off with Veronica but she knew she was very sensitive, so she didn't want to dwell too much on it. Feeling disappointed but anxious, Veronica got on with packing. Later that evening, Veronica noticed Ella's best friend had posted a birthday cake with a message for Ella, Veronica wondered what was going on; maybe Ella was having a party after all. At around 11pm a group message came through on 'what's app'. Veronica had created the group between herself, her sisters and parents to help keep Paula's morale high when she had been lonely in hospital. The girls could all send group messages to their mum to cheer her up. The message was from Philip, it read: 'To my sugar coated, honey dipped daughter Ella. Thank you so much for the lovely BBQ. Mum thoroughly enjoyed it. Happy birthday we love you so much.' Veronica's heart sank, at that moment she realised that everything that had happened that day had been planned. From stopping Rae and Charlie from painting the room for Paula; to telling Veronica that the party was cancelled. How hurtful of them all, why would they treat Veronica like this after everything she and Rae had done to help the family?

Veronica and Rae had paid the mooring fees on yacht Nova for the next six months so that her dad didn't have to worry about it. They had given him lumps of cash so he could pay for necessities and food for himself and Paula. Paula was claiming end of life benefits so they did have some money coming in, but Phil had told his daughter and son–in-law that he had not claimed anything for himself and didn't know what he would do when the time came and Paula would need a funeral. The couple couldn't imagine being in such awful circumstances, regardless of his drug problems, he needed help and they had been there to support him, yet he had abused their generosity and sincerity; and had broken his daughter's heart. Veronica went to bed in tears, she cried all night, waking frequently and suffering anxiety attacks. She felt her dad and sister hated her.

The next morning Veronica woke up feeling terrible, even worse than she did the day before.

She couldn't get over the fact that her dad had told her that her mum was too ill to have Charlie and Rae around to paint in the flat, yet a few hours later they had gone to Ella's house for a birthday BBQ after telling Veronica it was cancelled. It was so blatantly obvious, and Veronica wanted to scream at her sister and dad for it, but she couldn't cause a scene for the sake of her mum. Veronica had to bite her tongue and pretend she hadn't noticed, but it was too much for her to handle, just the thought of being in their presence made Veronica feel sick to her stomach. She desperately wanted to be with her mum, but she couldn't handle being around the others. Veronica got ready to go to London, but as it got closer to leaving the house, Veronica had a massive panic attack. She couldn't cope, she felt like she was in a dark hole and she couldn't get out. She thought about Ella and her dad and she thought about what they had plotted against her.

It was too much, Veronica couldn't face them; she was feeling too insecure and vulnerable. She was shaking from head to toe with nerves as she called her dad to find out how her mum was and to tell him she felt too ill to visit. His reaction was, "Oh don't worry Vron, you relax and get better; and we will see you whenever you are better." Veronica thought her dad was being sarcastic and false with her, but she didn't care, she wanted to be a million miles away from him and was relieved she didn't have to face him or Ella. At the same time she was guilt ridden, because she wanted to be near her mum and felt she was missing out on her last moments.

Paula had been sleeping constantly and was practically non-responsive; Veronica got off the phone and cried. The panic attack returned, with Veronica feeling short of breath and anxious. She got in her car and drove to Irene's. She showed her the messages on WhatsApp and told her what had happened with Ella's birthday. Irene was livid. "Your family are nasty, your dad is twisted, for all what you've done for your family and him; and he treats you like a bit of shit. You deserve so much more my darling," she told Veronica, as she cuddled her close.

Veronica was crying, she felt so unloved by her dad and sister. Why did they have it in for her, why did they treat her like this? Veronica couldn't get her head around it; she thought she was imagining it all and needed Irene and Rae to reassure her. She felt like she was losing her mind. Irene told Veronica to call her counsellor to see if he could help her. He was willing to drop everything and meet Veronica at home within half an hour.

Veronica couldn't believe how helpful he was, it was a Sunday morning after all, but he was happy to assist Veronica. Veronica kissed Irene goodbye and drove back home to meet Steve, her counsellor. He had helped Veronica to get a grip of her thoughts and control her emotions when she went to see him after having Sienna; he had already got to know about Veronica's life with her parents and their addiction. She trusted him more than she had trusted anyone, apart from her husband. He had helped her come to terms with a lot of her past and to put experiences that had been traumatic, such as her operation, into perspective. Veronica got home and waited for him. A few minutes later, Steve knocked on the door. Veronica invited him into her lounge and offered him a coffee. Steve asked Veronica what had happened, and then spent some time getting Veronica to relax and telling her to imagine herself in a place that was calm. He practiced some mental exercises which helped Veronica immensely. She told Steve she was full of guilt because she should be by her mother's bed-side, he told Veronica that she could still send love and compassion at a distance. Veronica felt much more at ease and thanked Steve for his kindness and help.

For the next couple of days, Veronica continued to pack boxes for their imminent house move.

Paula had been nonresponsive since coming home from Ella's BBQ. She had only got out of bed to use the toilet, but the Palliative care nurses had told Philip by Wednesday morning, that Paula's organs were shutting down. He called Veronica to tell her. She couldn't believe it, there was no turning back. Paula hadn't spoken for a couple of days; Veronica knew she would never hear her mum's voice again.

Rae called his mum to arrange her assistance with the children. They decided to take Sienna to London with them but asked Irene to be on standby to pick up Ashley from school.

Veronica cried all the way to north London, the agony Paula had endured for years had finally come to this, the moment that Veronica had feared her whole life, losing her mum because of heroin. She always knew it would be the death of her, but she had lived in hope that somehow she would get away with it, that she would miraculously escape its consequences and live a relatively long life. Now it was certain, there was no masking the truth, nowhere to hide; and Veronica found herself to be inconsolable.

CHAPTER 84

Paula's Last Hours

When Veronica and Rae arrived at the flat, Paulette opened the door to them. Veronica put her arms around her sister and kissed her, then they went upstairs to Paulette's old bedroom where Paula was lying in the hospital bed supplied by the Palliative Care Team. Her breathing was very deep and loud.

Veronica's dad was in his bedroom, he came to say hello to Veronica and Rae. Veronica couldn't take her eyes off of her mum, although she looked so painfully thin, she still looked beautiful, Veronica kissed her on the side of her cheek. Her dad told her that Paula's loud breathing was nothing to worry about, he said her organs were shutting down and that they didn't know how long she had. Veronica asked if Paula could still hear; and Phil said that although she couldn't speak, she could hear everything. Veronica cried, she knew that her mum's voice was now a distant memory. She just wanted to curl up beside her mum; she wanted to cuddle her close one last time.

"Can I get into the bed with her?" she asked her dad.

"Of course you can babe," he replied. Veronica didn't waste a moment, she took her coat and shoes off, gently climbed in and lay there cuddling her mum. She watched her breathe, it sounded so loud and painful, but her dad assured her it was normal and part of the body's shutting down process.

Veronica repeatedly kissed her mum's cheek. Rae offered to go and get some sandwiches and drinks from the local shop for everyone. Sienna was confused. "What's Nanny doing?" she asked.

Veronica told her that Nanny wasn't well and that Mummy was giving Nanny lots of cuddles.

"Is she going to get better?" Sienna asked. Veronica didn't know what to say and tried to change the subject, asking her to get her toys to play with.

"Why is Nanny making them noises?" she continued. Veronica was stuck for words, maybe she shouldn't have brought her, perhaps it was too much for her to take in at her little age, but then Veronica knew how resilient she was as a child. She also thought Sienna would not remember much of this when she was older; most of it would go over her head.

"Nanny isn't in pain darling, she just has loud breathing, and it's nothing to worry about." Veronica told her.

"I don't like it," she said.

Phil came into the room and offered to sit Sienna in the other room and put the Children's Chanel on the TV for her. Off she went happily with Grandad while Veronica continued to cuddle her mum in bed.

Veronica whispered into her mum's ear. "I love you Mum, more than you'll ever know, can you hear me?" Paula's breathing continued to be loud. Veronica wanted a sign that her mum could hear her but she wasn't sure. "Don't be afraid of anything now Mum, you haven't got to suffer in pain anymore. Nanny Rose is waiting for you, all of your family are there waiting for you. You will probably have a big celebration party when you meet them." Paula's breathing changed, and Veronica thought she heard her mum chuckle, then the breathing pattern resumed. "They will all be so happy to see you, tell Nanny Rose I miss her and I love her."

Veronica's tears rolled down her face, she couldn't stop them, there was no way back now, these were her mum's final hours of life and Veronica felt angry inside. It wasn't fair; her mum didn't deserve any of the pain she had endured, or all of the suffering. Paula had always done the best she could as a mum, she had made mistakes but she had owned up to them and apologised. She had never meant to hurt anyone, least of all her children. Unfortunately her actions had broken Veronica's heart, but Veronica knew it was never intentional. It was the sad truth of how her mum's addiction had ultimately consumed her, it had owned her all these years and now it was taking her forever. Veronica hated heroin, heroin was her biggest enemy, it had taken so many before but now it was claiming Paula.

Veronica stroked her mum's hair; she repeated, "I love you so much. I hope you can hear me Mum, I hope you know I'm here. I'm staying by your side, I'm not going anywhere. I just want you to know that I'm here and I love you." Paula seemed to mumble in response, she couldn't speak but her depth of breathing changed for a moment, maybe she was letting Veronica know that she was aware of her.

Rae came back with the sandwiches, but Veronica could not bring herself to move, she wanted to stay cuddled up to her mum. It was comforting for Veronica, her way of dealing with the situation, she hoped it wasn't too much for her mum; she just didn't want Paula to feel alone. She wanted her to know that her daughter was close and with her. "I'm right by your side Mum," she whispered in her ear. Veronica cuddled her mum for hours.

Rae decided to head back to Kent to get Ashley, it was going to be a long day and Sienna would be much better off with her Nanny Irene. Rae said goodbye and kissed Paula on her cheek.

Philip seemed to spend more time downstairs and in the other bedroom, Veronica didn't know what he was up to but she was happy to be alone with her mum.

Paulette was watching TV in the other bedroom and came in to see her mum from time to time before heading out briefly to meet her boyfriend. There was no one in the flat apart from Veronica and her parents. Veronica got out of her mum's bed to use the toilet. When she came back, her dad was sitting beside Paula stroking her face.

"She's so beautiful isn't she?" he said. Veronica nodded in agreement. "She doesn't deserve any of this; it's me who should be in her position now."

Veronica looked out of the bedroom window at all of the buildings beyond the flats, she could see right across London. Her dad was waiting for a response from Veronica but she didn't have anything to say. What did he want from her?

"This is all my fault isn't it?" he continued. "You blame me for all of this don't you? I know you are angry with me," he said.

It was Philip who'd got Paula involved with the drugs, but there wasn't any point in blaming him. He may not have been the best husband or the best dad but he never meant for any of this to happen to Paula. Veronica was angry with him for a lot of things but not for Paula's fate, she was responsible for her own actions in life, the same as Phil was responsible for his. If you looked back over the years and how he had got Paula into drugs, you could say he was to blame, but Paula had her own mind, they were both responsible for their mistakes.

Veronica thought her dad's timing for this conversation was all wrong, and all she was concerned about was her mum. Paula could hear everything, her breathing became more rapid and she sounded like she was getting a bit distressed. Veronica told her dad that she didn't blame anyone, and this was not the time to have this kind of discussion. All she wanted was for her mum to be at peace.

"She knows I love her, she knows how I feel; and I don't want her to be upset so please don't talk about this now," Veronica said; and Philip changed the subject.

Veronica waited for him to leave the room before getting back into the bed beside her mum. "I'm here again Mum," she said. "Don't you worry about a thing; you've got nothing to worry about now. I love you and everyone loves you." Veronica stroked her mum's face gently. Paula's breathing slowed down and Veronica spoke of the good times she had with her mum as a child. If her mum could hear everything around her, then she wanted her to hear nice things.

The Palliative care nurses turned up to top Paula up with pain relief, they told Veronica and her dad that Paula probably wouldn't last the night. They asked if Paula would like a Priest to visit and say a prayer for her. Veronica liked the idea, what harm could it do, she thought, but Philip quickly told the nurses that Paula was not religious in any way; and would not appreciate it.

Veronica and Rae had spoken to Ashley about his Nan dying, he wanted the opportunity to say goodbye when the time came, so Rae was bringing him back to north London to see his Nan for the last time. Phil decided to call Ella and ask her if she wanted Helen to do the same. Ella wasn't sure if Helen could handle it, but she agreed to let her come round. Ella soon turned up with Helen; as they came up the stairs and into the room, Philip told his wife, "Paula, look who's come to visit you, it's your number one grandchild Helen." Veronica was disappointed in his comment. Even if it were true, he didn't have to say it, not in front of Veronica anyway, it wasn't nice, it was hurtful. What had Ashley done to deserve only second best?

It was a good job he wasn't there to hear that himself, but Veronica felt bad about it. Philip turned around realising Veronica was in the room and had heard him. "I was only joking; she loves them all the same," he said. Veronica gave her dad a dirty look. It wasn't nice to even think it let alone say it. She knew he was fully aware of her presence, he just didn't consider her feelings at all.

Helen stood next to her Nan; she looked frightened by the sound of Paula's loud breathing. "Why is Nanny making that noise?" she asked. "Is she in pain?"

Philip explained that Nanny wasn't in pain because she had been given lots of medicine by the nurses.

"It's a horrible noise," she said. Helen became quite emotional, realising that her Nan was dying all got a bit too much for her; and she became quite distressed.

"I knew it would be too much for her," Ella said.

Ella put her arm around Helen and took her out of the room and into the other bedroom to calm her down. Half an hour later Rae returned with Ashley. He too, was shocked by his Nan and her breathing, but he seemed to deal with it with maturity beyond his years. Veronica was surprised, but she knew her son would handle the situation, he had a few tears in his eyes, but he was happy to sit next to his Nan and stroke her hand and arm.

Helen came back into the room and said hello to Ashley and cuddled him. She got very distressed again and cried uncontrollably. Ashley welled up with tears too but he fought hard to compose himself.

Rae told Helen, "Nanny can hear you darling, and she doesn't want you to be upset. Why don't you give her a cuddle?" Helen didn't want to; she found the sound of Paula's loud breathing quite scary. She nuzzled into Ella's arm, but Ella was the same, she wouldn't touch her mum. Veronica couldn't understand it, she had always been so close to her mum, yet now she was scared to be close.

Rae told Ella not to be afraid. "She's still the same woman, your mum. Why don't you hold her hand?"

Ella was hesitant but she did hold her mum's hand, Ella got quite emotional too. Veronica felt sad for her sister; she had given birth to baby Sammy only eight weeks before. Having a baby is a demanding time for anyone but having to deal with the imminent death of a parent at the same time was just unthinkable.

Veronica felt sad for Paulette too, she was the baby sister who relied on Paula the most. How would she cope without her mum around? Then there was her dad. He and Paula had been inseparable for years; the pair could barely function without each other. How would he cope without her?

After holding her mum's hand for some time, Ella left the room. She was crying and inconsolable but didn't want Paula to sense her anxiety. She went into the other bedroom to compose herself. Philip talked to Ashley about Nanny and times gone by; he told him about when they were younger and the things that they did together. Then he mentioned Paula's personal sentimental belongings and what he would give to Ashley. He went into the other room and got a gold chain of Paula's and gave it to Ashley.

"Your mum and dad bought this for Nanny for her birthday years ago," Philip said. "You can have it now, but you must look after it."

Ashley was surprised; he didn't know what to say. "I will give something special to Helen as well," Philip continued. He looked at Veronica, "You don't mind if I give him that do you?" Veronica felt very uneasy about it; she couldn't understand why he was giving Paula's things away whilst she was lying in the bed, still alive and able to hear everything around her. Veronica found it all a bit morbid but it was about to get worse.

Philip continued to talk about what would happen to Paula's body once she passed. He said he would have her cremated and that he was considering having her ashes made into some kind of figurine that he wanted to mount near the helm of his yacht Nova. Veronica could not believe what he was saying. Paula's breathing changed, it became louder, faster and more erratic, she sounded like she was agitated. This upset Veronica immensely.

"Dad how can you even discuss this with Mum still here? You can't do this now, you are upsetting Mum, please stop."

Veronica was furious with her dad, he had no tact at all and she wondered if he even had any feelings. Rae looked horrified at what had been said too, he shook his head in disbelief.

Philip changed the subject again. "Do you mind sitting with your mum whilst I run a bath?" he asked. Veronica agreed it was okay, so Philip went into the bathroom.

Veronica and Rae both made an effort to talk about nice things around Paula, but her breathing remained loud and erratic. It didn't matter what they said, it seemed to make no difference. Paula had gurgled, almost like a choking sound a few times throughout the day, bringing up some blood. Veronica had sat her mum up with the aid of the electric bed, to try to keep her airways clear, clean her up and make her comfortable. It was quite distressing to see, but Veronica remained calm at all times to avoid upsetting her mum. Paula's breathing was very loud and the children were getting very upset by it. Veronica wondered if Paula was in pain, so she knocked on the bathroom door and called to her dad.

"Dad I think Mum is in pain, how long are you going to be?"

"Not long, I will be out soon," he replied.

Veronica went back into the bedroom to be with her mum. Rae was holding Paula's hand and stroking her arm. Paula's breathing was still very loud and faster than it had been all day; Veronica couldn't relax for worrying about her mum.

"She sounds like she's in pain babe," she told Rae. "Mum if you are in pain please give us a sign."

Paula's feet moved, her toes seemed to curl. Veronica remembered when she was in labour with Sienna, that she curled her toes when she was in a lot of pain.

"Look at her toes babe they are curling up like mine did when I was in pain having Sienna, it's been hours since the nurses came and topped Mum up," she told Rae.

He nodded in agreement. "Ask your dad to call them," Rae said.

Veronica went back to the bathroom and knocked on the door. "Dad I'm sorry to bug you, but Mum is in a lot of pain, we need to get the nurses back to top her up with pain relief."

"Okay Vron, give me a few minutes, I will call them when I'm out. I'm sure she's okay, they know how much to give her and they are not due back yet."

Veronica wasn't so sure; Paula looked like she was suffering. Veronica went back to the bedroom; Rae was still holding Paula's hand. Paula was still breathing fast and making lots of noise. Rae asked Paula to squeeze his hand if she was in pain. Veronica and Rae both watched intently as Paula gripped his hand as hard as she could. Veronica welled up with tears, it was obvious then that Paula was uncomfortable and she couldn't say anything. This made Veronica cry. Rae whispered to Veronica to hold herself together. Veronica agreed and fought hard to hold back the tears, she had to be brave for her mum and not make things worse. Philip had been in the bathroom for ages, Veronica and Rae thought he'd been there too long. Philip had always taken an age to do anything, but this was due to being under the influence of drugs. There was no doubt in Veronica's mind that her dad was getting high in the bathroom whilst Paula was suffering. This was obviously Philip's way of dealing with things, but it wasn't fair on Paula and this made Veronica impatient with him. Veronica went back to the bathroom and knocked on the door again.

"Dad you really need to hurry up, Mum is in pain, she's told us, we need to get her some more pain relief fast. Give me the number for the Palliative care team and I will call them."

Philip told Veronica he was coming out and would call them. A few minutes later he emerged looking high, wearing a pink dressing gown and talking erratically. Veronica could hear by the sound of his voice that he had taken heroin, there was a very distinctive tone to a person's voice when they had taken it and Veronica knew this better than most, as she had lived around heroin her entire childhood and early adult life. His voice was croaky and at times slow, as if he needed to clear his throat. That was a typical tell-tale sign for Veronica; as was talking a lot of rubbish. Maybe that's why he discussed Paula's imminent cremation and dividing her personal items up, while she was still very much alive and breathing. He was somewhat oblivious to everyone else's feelings due to his intoxication. Veronica was feeling even more angry, but overwhelmingly emotional at the same time.

She made sure her dad called the nurses and waited for them to return. Rae went out to buy some pizza for everyone in the meantime, as nobody had eaten any dinner.

Eventually there was a knock at the door. "That's either Rae or the nurses," Philip told everyone. "I will answer it," Veronica said as she went downstairs to open the door. It was the Palliative care nurses, returning to give Paula a top up of her pain relief. As Veronica opened the door and let them in, she was suddenly very aware of the fact that they were standing directly in front of the living room door which was locked with a digital lock. You could hear the sound of the extractor fans and smell the distinct smell of skunk. Veronica had an overwhelming feeling of guilt wash over her at that very moment, she was of course completely innocent, but being aware of what her dad was up to, was enough to make her feel like a guilty culprit. She felt nervous and hoped the nurses didn't suspect anything. She closed the front door and led them upstairs to the room where Paula was.

The nurses got to work on her immediately, Veronica felt relieved that her mum would soon be pain free. She told the nurses that they suspected

Paula was in pain. The nurses tried to assure Veronica and Rae that the noises were very normal and all part of the natural process of the body shutting down, but Veronica wasn't convinced. She knew her mum; Paula had squeezed Rae's hand when asked if she was in pain. The curling of Paula's toes alone was enough to confirm to Veronica that her mum was not in a comfortable place. "Please can you give her a stronger dose of pain relief?" Veronica asked.

Paula had told her daughter over the years that doctors and nurses were often not aware of Paula's strong threshold for pain relief. Many did not know of Paula's drug tolerance, as she had played her habit down and even denied it time and again over the years. It was obvious to Veronica that whatever the Palliative care team were administering, it was not enough to keep her mum comfortable.

It was heartbreaking to be aware of this and not be able to do anything to ease her mum's discomfort. All she could do was to hope that Paula's pain would soon come to an end. As much as she didn't want her mum to die, she couldn't bear to see her suffer anymore.

Once the nurses left, Veronica kissed her mum and told her dad that they needed to get back home for Sienna. She told her dad to call if there was any change in Paula's circumstances. It was the most difficult moment in Veronica's life that day. It was something she had seen coming her whole life but she had hoped it would not come so soon. These were Paula's final hours.

Veronica had feared this moment her whole life and now there was no way of denying it.

She told her family she loved them all, kissed them and left with Rae and Ashley to drive back home to Kent. It had been a very long day and Veronica was emotionally exhausted.

CHAPTER 85

The Last Breath

Veronica and Rae left the flats and walked towards their car. Rae noticed a huge scratch along the entire length of a door panel on one side. That was the price you paid for leaving a nice car parked in Edmonton all day. It could have been worse, the windows could have been smashed and the car burnt out, which wasn't an uncommon occurrence in this area. Rae was fuming, but Veronica had more important things on her mind. The journey home was a sombre one, Veronica cuddled Ashley as he laid his head on her lap to sleep, but she did not speak a word. Veronica was emotionally wrought, her life flashed through her mind all the way home.

Rae called his mum on the mobile, she said she had put Sienna in her bed and told Rae not to worry about picking her up, so they went straight home to bed. It was 12.30am by the time they reached home, so everyone was exhausted. Veronica helped Ashley to bed and then went to bed herself.

It seemed as though only ten minutes had passed when Veronica's phone rang, she must have gone to sleep as soon as her head hit the pillow. She picked up her phone, it was 4.15am and it was her dad calling.

"Hello," Veronica said. "Hi babe, it's me, Dad. Mum has gone; she took her last breath at around 4am. Paulette was out when Mum's breathing became very shallow, I knew she was leaving us so I called Paulette on her mobile to tell her to get back to the flat quick. I told Mum Paulette was on her way. She could hear Vron, she knew, she wanted her baby with her, she waited for Paulette. As soon as she got back to her side, she mumbled something, it sounded like 'I love you' and she took her last breath. It was so sad Vronx, she was so beautiful. What am I going to do without her now?" Philip was crying.

Veronica burst into tears, she yelled "Noooooooooo," as she cried. "I'm so sorry Dad I don't know what we will do without her. I want to come and see her; we will get ready and be back with you within the hour."

Veronica told her dad she loved him and put the phone down. Veronica cried and cried like a baby, she was beside herself. Life would never be the same without her mum; it was strange, almost surreal, this stuff happened to other people. Ashley woke up hearing Veronica cry; he came into the bedroom and hugged his mum.

"Nanny has died hasn't she?" Ashley asked. Veronica nodded yes, even though she didn't want to believe it herself.

"I hate this house Rae; everything went wrong in my life the day we moved here. The problems I had giving birth to Sienna, all of the problems with our business and now my beautiful little mum has died. I can't wait to see the back of this house," she said and with that she shouted, "Get me out of here."

Rae consoled Ashley and his wife. "Come on babe," he said. "You've got to be strong now for your kids, for your dad and your sisters. We've got to do the right thing now and give your mum a good send off."

Veronica agreed and cuddled Rae. "Thank you for being by my side; I don't know what I would do without you." Veronica kissed Rae and Ashley and got up to get dressed.

She did not bother with her usual routine of putting on her makeup and spending ages on her hair before she left the house, she wanted to get on the road as quickly as possible.

"What should we do about Ashley?" she wondered, so Rae asked Ashley if he wanted to go to school. He didn't, he was very upset and wanted to be with his mum.

Rae called his mum to tell her the news. Irene gave her love and condolences and told her son not to worry about Sienna. She told Rae that Sienna had been content playing at her house and had eaten well the day before, she was still fast asleep. Irene told Rae just to concentrate on helping Veronica.

Before long, they were in the car and heading back to north London. Veronica felt completely empty, she couldn't stop thinking about her mum and all that she had endured. How sad that she had not had any let up from the pain, not even for long enough to enjoy the little break away in the caravan.

Veronica and Rae decided to drop Ashley off at Ella's as they didn't want him to see Nanny now that she had passed. There was no point, and they thought it might affect him too much. Ashley would at least be with his cousin Helen. Veronica and Rae were soon at the flat. As they went in, Veronica buckled and her tears flooded. She cuddled her dad close, he was numb, there were no tears, just shock on his face. He led Veronica and Rae upstairs to the bedroom where Paula was lying so still.

"Look at her beautiful face." Philip said. "All of the worry and pain has gone; all of the lines in her face have vanished, even her swollen stomach has gone down."

Veronica touched her mum's face. It was so cold to touch, no warmth left in her. Veronica kissed her cheek, but her tears were streaming fast and landed on Paula.

"Sorry Mum," Veronica cried as she wiped her own tears from her mum's cheek. "I'm so sorry for everything you've been through. I'm sorry that I went home and didn't stay, I love you so much and I always will. Life will never be the same without you I will always miss your smile, your laughter and your soft voice. Rest in peace now Mum, no more pain."

With that, Veronica nuzzled her head into her mum's bosom and cried. Rae stroked Paula's hair and face as he cuddled his wife. Veronica looked up at him. "My mum is gone."

"I know," Rae replied, "But she is at peace now, look at her face, she isn't suffering anymore."

Philip had left the room and was sitting on his bed in shock. It was 8.45 in the morning; Paula had passed almost five hours ago. Veronica went into the bedroom and sat on the bed next to her dad, he had his head held in his hands. "I can't believe she's gone, but I am relieved Vron. I'm relieved because it had become so unbearable. She couldn't sleep; night after night she was getting up and wandering around in pain. She could never get comfortable. The confusion was very difficult to deal with. You couldn't explain anything to her when she was in that state. It was hard to control what she was doing," he said.

Veronica didn't feel comfortable about his comments, especially when her mum had made her aware only days before that Philip had left her alone for hours after disappearing to get high on drugs. Then upon his return, he shouted in her face making her cry. This wasn't the understanding, loyal, patient husband that he should have been the whole way through. There was no denying that looking after Paula had been a difficult and enduring job, but this was the one time that Philip needed to be strong for his wife; and from what she confided in Veronica, he had let her down. Veronica wondered what to do now. Phil hadn't called a funeral director to arrange for Paula's body to be taken away. Rae came into the room and sat next to Veronica.

"What do we do now?" Veronica asked him. Phil still had his face hidden in his hands. Rae looked at Veronica.

"There's a Funeral Director on The High Road, it's a Cooperative Funeral Director," Rae said. "Me and Veronica will head over there and arrange for them to take Paula," he continued.

Phil could barely look at Rae and his daughter; he continued to bury his head in his hands.

"I don't know what to say," Phil said.

"Don't say anything," Rae told him. "You look tired Phil, shut your eyes and we will go and get things organised."

With that, he stood up and said, "Come on Vron, let's go." Veronica put her coat on, kissed her dad and told him they wouldn't be long. As they headed out of the flats on to The High Road, Veronica felt faint. The air must have got to her. "I feel sick and dizzy," she told Rae. "I can't do this," she said.

Rae put his arm around Veronica and kissed her cheek. "Yes you can," he said. "Take a deep breath, we've got to get your mum sorted and you want her to have the right send-off don't you?" Veronica nodded in agreement.

They crossed the road and looked through the window of the Cooperative Funeral Director's. It looked like it was closed as there was no one in sight. Rae checked on the door and saw an open sign, next to it was a message that read; please ring bell. Rae pressed the bell and a moment later, a lady appeared and opened the door. "Hello how can I help you?" she asked.

"Hello," Rae said, "my wife's mother has just passed away and we need to arrange for her body to be collected and for her funeral."

"Okay, come and have a seat and I will take some details," the lady said, as she got an A4 sized book out of a drawer in her desk. She asked for the deceased's gender, name, age, D.O.B, address, and details of time of death etc. then she told them that she would arrange for an undertaker to collect the body within a couple of hours. She asked what Mrs Pauline

Baker's wishes were for her funeral; and Rae explained that she had not discussed any of this with them and that his wife's dad didn't have any income as he had given up work to care for his wife. He told the lady that he and his wife would be paying for the funeral and that they needed to discuss arrangements with his father-in-law and let her know.

The woman was very helpful and gave them some ideas of prices for the ceremony and a price list for coffins and hearses. Veronica wondered if they could arrange a horse and carriage instead of a hearse.

"I don't like the idea of Mum going in a hearse," she said. "Well we can arrange for a horse and carriage if you prefer, but it will cost you a lot more," the lady said.

"How much more?" Veronica asked. The lady explained that the price of a hearse was included with the funeral package, but if she wanted a carriage it was an extra £1000.00. Veronica then had the option of paying £600.00 for a funeral car to carry the immediate family. The lady gave the price lists and quote to Veronica and told her to have a think about it. Veronica had to pay an initial deposit to have Paula's body picked up and taken to their mortuary. She took her credit card from her bag and handed it to the lady, who went off to get a card machine. When the payment had gone through, the lady told Veronica to come back within a couple of days, once she and her family had decided what they wanted for Paula, to make the necessary arrangements for her funeral. Veronica thanked her for her help and the couple left the shop.

Veronica felt very weak and numb, she could not believe that this was happening; it felt like a bad dream. She wished she could wake up and everything be normal again but this was reality.

Veronica and Rae returned to the flat, Veronica went upstairs and checked on her mum.

It was so strange to see her lying there so lifeless. She went into the room and kissed her again, then she went into the bedroom to check on her dad, who was watching telly. He still looked totally shocked and pale, and very frail and tired.

"We've arranged for Mum to be picked up within the next couple of hours," Veronica told her dad.

"Okay babe," he said.

"The funeral directors will call you just before the undertakers come to make sure you are here," Rae told Philip.

"Okay thanks Rae," Phil said. "I can't thank you enough for all you have done lately both of you," he said.

"That's what family are for," Rae told him. Just then the phone rang.

Veronica jumped, it couldn't be the funeral directors already she thought, but it was Mum's sister Beverley. "Okay Bev, yeah get off at Silver Street, I will send Vron over to meet you and bring you back to the flat. See you shortly, bye." Phil hung up. "Your Aunties, Bev and Pat, are on the train. I told them they could come, they wanted to say goodbye to your mum."

Veronica was shocked, why would he let them come over to the flat? What about the skunk farm she thought? Beverley was an inquisitive woman, she hated mess and dirt, she was the sort of person who opened your cupboards and disdainfully pointed out any dust. How would he explain away the locked lounge with the sound of fans and smell of skunk? Oh well, this was his mess not Veronica's, he would have to deal with it.

Veronica did what she was asked and walked over to the train station with Rae, to meet her aunts. When they arrived at the station, she saw her relatives walking towards them; there was Bev, Uncle Ed, Cousin Penny and Aunty Pat. They all hugged Veronica and Rae, and everyone cried.

Beverley wiped Veronica's tears. "Come on my darling, it's okay, you have a good cry," she said as she cuddled Veronica, who wept like a baby. It was like a release, her Aunt's words and reassurance allowed Veronica to let it all out. They cuddled as they walked towards the flat.

"You may get a bit of a shock when you go inside the flat," Veronica told her family. "It's not the nicest of places I'm afraid."

"Don't worry," Pat told her. "We are not here to see the flat; we just want to see our sister and our family."

Veronica wasn't so sure though, she was panicked about the skunk farm and worried that they might suspect something. She knew when they stepped inside they would be horrified that their sister had been living in such a run-down flat. She was right; the shock on their faces when they got inside, said it all. They tried to hide it but Veronica knew. Beverley scanned her surroundings, the horror in her eyes was evident. Phil led everyone upstairs to the bedroom where Paula was lying.

As Pat and Bev entered the room, they burst into tears; they sat beside Paula and stroked her face. "Oh my God," Pat said, "look at our baby sister. This should be me in her position not her," Pat cried; everyone cried.

Paulette came into the room and Penny cuddled her, they both cried.

"It's okay baby, you cry," Penny told Paulette. "She's not in any pain now, she has wings now," Penny continued. Paulette let her guard down and cried out loud.

"What am I gonna do without my little mum?" she said.

"I know baby, I know," Penny told her. "You've got to be strong for her now; you've got to look after your dad."

Veronica wondered how they would all move on from this, life would never be the same; a chapter had come to an end. The family talked about Paula and her illness, the struggles she had endured and the pain she had suffered. Phil told them how difficult the last months had been caring for his wife. Veronica and Rae decided it was time to go and get Ashley; Veronica hadn't seen Sienna since the previous day and needed to get back. She gave everyone a kiss and said goodbye.

Veronica didn't want to see her mum's body being taken away in a body bag; the idea was bad enough without seeing it. Pat and Beverly had offered to stay and help Phil and Paulette deal with the undertakers. Veronica felt bad leaving, but she couldn't bear anymore. They returned to Ella's, where Veronica gave Ella and baby Sammy a hug. They cried together for what seemed ages, then Veronica said goodbye and made her way back to Kent with Rae and Ashley.

CHAPTER 86

Coming to Terms

Veronica felt completely numb as she looked out of the car window on their way home. She looked up at the grey sky, how could the sun ever shine without her mum in this world she wondered. Where was she now?

Veronica was certain that her mum had joined her mum Rose and her relatives that had passed before her. She envisioned her Nan welcoming her mum into heaven, it was a sweet thought and one that Veronica needed to hold on to. She was emotionally exhausted and drained; the stress of the past five and half months had led to this day. The doctors had given Paula 6-9 months without treatment and up to two years with treatment, but Paula had just one dose of chemo that ultimately finished her off. Her body hadn't been fit enough to withstand the treatment and Paula never recovered.

It had been a roller coaster from start to finish. The entire family had found it difficult to accept and cope with Paula's circumstances and inevitable fate. There had been tears, some laughter, but mainly anguish in watching this person they loved so much suffer such debilitating pain. Veronica wanted to put her issues with her dad behind her as Paula had become the main focus and priority at the time, but every now and then the issues would rear their ugly head.

Veronica could not pin point what it was that agitated her dad so much, or why he would pick a fight with her for no apparent reason, like he did when he and Paula stayed with Veronica and Rae only days before Paula's death.

Veronica knew only too well what her issues with him were; she disliked him for being a bully. He had always been abusive both verbally and physically; he was heavy-handed with Veronica and her sisters as kids, particularly with Veronica in the early years. He would fly off the handle for something quite trivial and smack Veronica hard, often across her head. She had learned to flinch whenever he was angry, and he would shout at her. She had also witnessed him attack her mum, he would put Paula down and call her nasty names. He often said it was him who had the desire to do something constructive with his life, like sailing around the world; and that Paula made no effort to educate herself or to take any interest in anything other than the everyday mundane chores of being a housewife.

He had made Veronica feel downtrodden too. He was always quick to point out where she was failing, but slow to pat her on the back when she got something right. The feeling of walking on egg shells when around her father was something that Veronica had come to accept. Upsetting the apple cart would only upset everyone and cause a huge argument. Veronica would keep quiet most of the time for an easier life, but as the years had gone by, biting her tongue had become very difficult. She didn't live by his rules anymore, she didn't feel the need to impress him or look for his acceptance or approval. Philip knew this by Veronica's evolving change in attitude, and this had obviously become a threat to him. He was able to pull the wool over Paula's eyes and his other daughters, but Veronica could see right through him. Perhaps this was why Phil was always quick to pick on Veronica. What he didn't realise was that he was digging himself into a proverbial grave which eventually he would not be able to get out of.

Veronica spent the next couple of days in her pyjamas. She couldn't bear to face the outside world and walked around the house in a constant daze. Veronica could not get her head around the fact that her mum had gone, every time she thought about her, she burst into tears. Veronica had lost her appetite and couldn't stomach anything. She found it hard to concentrate on anything without her mum creeping back into her mind. All she could think about was how suddenly everything had changed.

The family had not even managed to get their head around the fact that Paula was terminally ill let alone deal with her dying. Now she had gone like a flash of light, there one second and gone the next. How delicate life was she thought. The very thing we take for granted, breathing and living, yet it could be taken away in a moment; and it had been. Veronica was beside herself with grief. Somehow, she had to pull herself out of this mode and continue to live her own life. She was expected to get on with the day-to-day things, as if everything was still the same, but it wasn't. Veronica felt as though her life had ended. The life she had known from birth was now changed forever, the very person responsible for bringing her into the world was gone forever, yet Veronica still had to get on with her own life and pack up the rest of her house. There were over forty boxes packed with household items, which she'd done at any spare moment she had between looking after the kids, finalising company paperwork and bills, keeping the house in order and travelling back and forth to London to help with her mum.

Veronica and Rae had waited months for the sale of their house to go through; and life for the couple was particularly stressful as they had both lost their incomes and were just living off their savings, with only minor work coming in. It seemed as though the world was against them as they strived to stay positive and battle against the odds. The costs of the company were still mounting, so were their personal costs of living, but the work had dried up. To top it all, they had supported Veronica's dad financially, helping him to pay his bills so he could focus on Paula; and now Veronica was faced with the cost of her mum's funeral.

Phil had said all along that everyone would contribute when the time came. He had told Veronica and Rae that Ella had savings and that she and her husband Petros would chip in. He had also mentioned that Paula's sisters were happy to help and that he would ask his brothers. Veronica just went along with what he told her, after all, it was his wife and he was her next of kin. It was his right to deal with the impending funeral whatever way he saw fit, but Veronica was there to provide financial support at any moment necessary.

As Veronica continued to pack boxes, the phone rang, it was her sister Ella calling to discuss the funeral arrangements. "I know you said you and Rae would pay for Mum's funeral," Ella said. "I don't really have any money Vron, me and Petros are skint since paying out for the wedding" she said.

"I know Ella; we are all in the same boat. Rae and I have lost our contract, we barely have any money coming in but we've got a lot to pay out for. We are all going through it right now," Veronica replied.

Ella snapped, "Why are you going on about money Vron, why are you making me feel bad? I will sell my fucking wedding ring if I have to."

Veronica was shocked at her sister's response, she was only saying that they were all in dire financial situations, Ella didn't seem to comprehend Veronica's problems. She had never had the huge expenses that Veronica had hanging over her; the mortgage alone was £1700 per month. With no regular income, it would soon mean that Veronica and Rae would lose everything, but Ella couldn't comprehend it, she was only concerned with her own situation. Veronica couldn't believe how nasty Ella was being, as if Veronica would ever want her sister to sell her wedding ring! It was a ridiculous statement. All Veronica had ever wanted for her sister was to see her getting on in life; she wanted the best for her, which is why she had bought her a car and helped her furnish her home, she wanted to share her good fortune with all of her family. Now things had changed dramatically for Veronica and Rae financially, but they both still wanted to help the best they could.

"Why are you being so nasty Ella?" Veronica asked her sister. "I would never expect you to do such a thing as to sell your wedding ring, I was just saying that we are all struggling right now. We had said all along we would help Dad with the funeral. He was the one who said you would contribute, I never asked for anything Ella. Why are you shouting at me?"

Ella tried to play it down but Veronica had seen right through her sister, she expected Veronica and Rae to do everything because they had achieved more than Ella. It did not make a blind bit of difference that they were quite possibly on the verge of losing everything; Ella did not have an ounce of sympathy for Veronica's situation. In fact Ella's jealousy of Veronica's success was very clear to see. Veronica was disappointed yet again for being so blinkered. "Rae and I will sort out Mum's funeral; you can sort out some flowers if you like?" Veronica said.

Ella agreed to arrange for some flowers as the mother of her good friend she had known since school, was a florist. She had offered to supply flowers at cost price. Ella asked Veronica if she was going to order her own flowers for Rae, the kids and herself, but Veronica thought that Ella could arrange the flowers from everyone. Paula wanted to be cremated so there was no point in getting too many flowers either. Ella then went on to say that they could arrange for a collection from all the family for cancer research or the Macmillan team. Veronica thought this was a good idea and agreed. Veronica was still upset by Ella's angry outburst and wanted to get off the phone to her.

"Sienna needs changing Ella so I'd better go," she said, "I will speak to you later in the week at some point. Love you all, goodbye."

Veronica put the phone down, she was confused. Ella's overreaction had taken her by surprise, much the same as when she'd reacted to Veronica asking that Petros's children behaved quietly around her mum when Ella came to Kent with them all. Veronica began to feel paranoid, she wondered what her sister would be saying to her dad, whether she would misconstrue the conversation regarding the funeral. She didn't have time to worry about it all anyway, as there were too many stressful things happening. Veronica and Rae had a solicitor chasing them for £8000.00 for outstanding fees through the company, they had £7500.00 VAT bill they couldn't pay; and they had finance agreements and bills for the company, which they were struggling to pay due to the money running out.

It upset Veronica so much because her sister was completely oblivious to the reality of Veronica and Rae's circumstances, and she was quite nasty about it as well. Veronica went downstairs to confide in Rae what had just happened. Rae wasn't one bit surprised by Ella's outburst.

"Nothing surprises me about your family anymore Veronica," Rae told his wife. "Don't worry about it, bite your tongue and just get on with it. You know what we need to do."

Veronica nodded in agreement. Rae kissed Veronica and put his arms around her. "Your family have never stood back and looked at what you've done and what you do. They can't bring themselves to even treat you with an ounce of respect Veronica. That's the most annoying thing about them; they show you no true love and respect. They think the world owes them something, they think you owe them something because you've had a better life than them. They can't see that you've actually worked hard for everything you've achieved. They expect it from you and when you can't give it, you see their true colours."

Veronica agreed with him, finally after all these years, she was realising just how far her family would go to use and abuse her.

CHAPTER 87

Registering the Death

Veronica went to work on planning her mother's funeral with pride. Regardless of everything, she wanted to make sure that her mum had the send-off that she deserved.

A few days after Paula died, Veronica returned to north London to pick up her dad and sister Paulette to take them to get Paula's death registered. Phil was not with it at all, he had asked Veronica to be by his side to register Paula's death. He was worried about tripping himself up when asked questions by the registrar. He needed Veronica to keep him calm and collected.

Phil hadn't told the authorities that he had been living with Paula. She had claimed benefits as a single mum for 14 years, since Phil had 'left her' to go and live on his boat. Now that Paula had passed away, there was a good chance that the flat would be repossessed by Enfield council and Phil would find himself with nowhere to live. Paulette was still technically living at home and Paula had arranged for her name to be put on the rent book. Maybe she thought this would protect Paulette in some way in the future, but Phil had made no effort to tell the authorities about himself. Paula had begged him to for years; she hated living with the worry of someone telling the council that her husband was in fact living with her. She had to deal with her hepatitis C and worry about her husband's lack of responsibility. As he had no fixed address for all those years, he could not even register at a doctor's; and his bad timekeeping had made sure that he was kicked off the rehab clinic where Paula was registered. She had kept them both in supply of methadone for years, by making out to the clinic that her addiction was twice as bad as it was. Philip had five months from Paula's terminal diagnosis to finally put the record straight, to do the right thing even if it was so late in the day, but he continued living his same old habits.

He told the Palliative Care Team that he had been living apart from Paula for fourteen years, but when he realised she was terminal, he moved back in with her to care for his estranged wife.

Paula had no energy to care, she was too ill to even notice what was happening around her for those last months. Phil's addiction would still win over everything else. During Paula's final months, his addiction was what kept him going; it was what he escaped to, his way out.

No one wished this on Phil. To lose your wife to the most debilitating disease and to watch her deteriorating so rapidly before your eyes is something no husband should ever have to witness or endure, but Phil could have been stronger. He could have done the right things, when they counted the most. Instead, he continued getting out of his head.

Veronica drove her dad and Paulette to Paula's doctor's practice to collect the medical certificate needed to register Paula's death. It was a very emotional experience for all three of them. It almost seemed surreal, like a bad dream. They almost had to pinch each other as they couldn't grasp the reality of what they were doing. Phil was so thin and pale; he looked like he hadn't eaten in months himself, his bones were jutting out from everywhere. Although he had always been quite skinny, he now looked incredibly gaunt and pale, he actually looked like an addict, but he also looked like a cancer victim.

Veronica worried about him, he had never had to cope alone with anything in the years he had his wife by his side. Now she had died; what would he do without her?

They made their way to the registry office and waited for Philip's name to be called.

The last time they had walked into this registry office was back in June, when Ella married Greek Petros. That was a sad event too, as Paula had lost a lot of hair and weight due to her recent chemotherapy.

As they sat waiting they discussed that day. Phil told of how proud Paula was, seeing Ella in her wedding dress. They remembered how sick Paula was that day; and how she had managed to withstand the whole day and most of the evening, despite having had such powerful drugs injected into her body. She had been determined to stick it out for her daughter.

The girls cried and huddled together with their dad. "She was such a brave little fighter," Philip said, the girls both agreed.

Just then, a lady emerged from behind a door and called out Philip's name. They were lead into an office and asked to take a seat.

Philip told the registrar that he had brought his daughters for moral support as he was struggling with his grief. The registrar understood, she asked Philip to confirm his name, his occupation, his wife's name and occupation, her D.O.B, marital status; and address.

She asked for the cause of death, the date and time of death, then she asked for the doctor's certificate for confirmation. She typed the information into her computer system.

She must have logged onto a database, as she knew that Paula lived in council accommodation and asked if Philip lived at the same address. He told the registrar that he hadn't lived with his wife for years until he discovered she was terminally ill. He continued to explain that he had given up work as a self-employed plumber to care for his wife. The registrar told Philip that she could see on her computer system that Paula had a 'blue badge' for disabled parking. She went on to say that it was Philip's responsibility as next of kin to contact various bodies and departments to confirm Paula's death; and to return the blue badge.

She gave Philip a reference number relevant to Paula's death registration, and a phone number. She explained that if he called the phone number, and gave Paula's reference number then it would notify every single department of Paula's death, which would save him from ringing the benefits department, housing department and so on, separately.

Once all the information was entered into the system, Philip was handed a green form. This was needed to arrange Paula's funeral; a fee was payable for Paula's death certificate. It was a very sombre moment indeed. Veronica had felt completely panicked throughout the interview.

Perhaps she was paranoid because of all the lies her dad had told once again. Did he not realise the stress that these actions had caused his wife for so many years? Did he not think to care about the impact his lies had caused his children, not just now but their entire lives? No, he didn't.

For the first time ever, Veronica was seeing her dad in his true light, without the veil of lies and exaggerations. It was as if her mother's death had lifted the veil completely; there was nothing left to disguise the truth. No mixed emotions to confuse the situation, everything was so clear and Veronica was dumbfounded. The interview with the registrar had seemed like it had lasted for hours, everything seemed to be in slow motion as Veronica looked at her dad as he lied to the woman behind her computer. When they walked out, he breathed a sigh of relief and said, "I'm not gonna make that call just yet to all the departments, I'm not ready, I need some time to come to terms. They will understand that won't they?" He asked his daughters, looking for their agreement. Veronica could see what he was doing, the longer he left the call the longer he didn't have to face losing the flat or losing Paula's benefits.

It was so sad for Philip to be in this position; he was like a complete victim, yet he was a victim of his own making. His wife had tried to steer him in the right direction many times over the years, but now it had come to this. Veronica led her dad and sister back to her car and drove them back to the flat. Philip had a prescription for methadone in his jacket; it was in Paula's name. Phil asked Paulette if she would go into the chemist and pick it up. The chemist knew that Paula was terminally ill; he had come to know the family over the years and often gave Phil cash work. Phil had done the chemist's plumbing at his house and other shop; he had also done work for other relatives of the chemist over the years. He knew that Paula was a recovering addict because of her methadone, but somehow Phil had disguised his habit from the chemist.

Veronica wasn't sure of all the ins and outs but this was what she was told by her parents.

The chemist was an Indian guy and he and his wife had apparently grown quite fond of Philip and Paula, inviting them to their home for food and cooking them Indian cuisine. Philip had joked how they couldn't handle the hot curry and would accept it kindly to take home, only to throw it away because it burnt the skin from their mouths it was so hot.

It was clear that Philip and Paula had also become quite fond of the chemist and his family too.

They felt they were never judged by them and were accepted for the people they were. The chemist quite often told Philip he was like family.

Here Phil was now, asking his youngest daughter to pick up a prescription from the chemist in her mother's name, straight after registering her death. Paula had died 4 days before; it was possible that Paula's GP would have telephoned the pharmacy to confirm Paula's death, but this was a risk that Philip was willing to take.

He told his daughter to keep her head down in the chemist's and pretend to be talking on her phone as a distraction from being questioned by the chemist. He told her to hand over the prescription and tell them she would come back in five minutes to collect it. Paulette looked panicked. "What if he asks how Mum is though, Dad, what am I gonna say?" she asked.

"Just say you've been away with your boyfriend for a few days and you haven't seen her, but you've had the prescription on you to pick up on your way home. I wouldn't ask you to do this if it wasn't necessary, you know that don't you babe?" he asked Paulette.

Veronica sat behind the wheel of her car dumbfounded by what was being discussed, she felt like she was an accomplice in a despicable act. Veronica was so angry inside; looking at Paulette was like looking back at herself when her dad told her to weigh up the heroin for his punters and she begged him not to make her do it. Now he was asking Paulette to lie and cash in on her mother's death, for the sake of her dad's addiction. Veronica started to shake with fear. "What if the chemist already knew?" Veronica asked her dad.

"Then he will not give Paulette the prescription and he will tell her to go home, there will be no harm done."

But Veronica wondered how long it would be until the chemist was informed and said this to her father. "Then would the chemist suspect anything and call you to say that there had been methadone given out in Paula's name after the time of her death?" Veronica asked her dad.

Philip seemed to have an answer for everything. "If that happens, I will tell him that I destroyed the methadone and threw it away. I don't have a choice right now, how else am I going to get through the next week without any money and without methadone?"

Again, Phil was playing the victim very well but Veronica wasn't buying any of it at this point.

He had had years to claim benefits if need be, years to tell the authorities he was living with his wife; but now everyone was expected to feel sorry for him, even though he didn't even care for doing right by his wife or his children; and even in death, he couldn't do her right.

There was no way he could disguise himself, Veronica was drained by him and his abusive destructive personality. He had taken every last ounce of pity, respect, compassion and love that she had for her dad. All she felt now was completely numb, like an empty shell. Philip had thought nothing of putting his youngest daughter through the trauma of walking into that chemist and collecting her mum's methadone. The fear in her eyes was evident to see, she was nervous and told her dad she didn't know if she could do it. Veronica sat at the driving wheel in shock.

"Of course you can do it, you know I wouldn't ask you if I wasn't desperate don't you?" Phil asked Paulette, who nodded in agreement, took a deep breath; and headed off towards the chemist. Veronica was parked only feet away, along the road from the shop entrance. She felt anxious for her sister, inside she was trembling; she wanted to tell her dad he was selfish to put Paulette in that position, but all that would have happened was he would have erupted in anger, as he always did in defence of his actions. He would have twisted everything and turned it around to make Veronica look like she was the one in the wrong. She couldn't afford to have a family row at this point in time, so she had to bite her tongue. Veronica needed to arrange her mum's funeral and so she kept quiet and said nothing.

Paulette seemed to take forever, but eventually she appeared with a prescription bag in her hand. She had a huge look of relief on her face. As she got into the back of the car, she said, "I done it, it's cool."

The chemist was on the phone when Paulette went into the shop, so she gave the prescription to a shop assistant, who handed it to the chemist, who prepared it out the back whilst still on the phone. Veronica was relieved for her sister but angry with her dad.

Veronica drove them back to the flat and they had a cup of tea. "We need to pop into the funeral directors again Dad and organise Mum's send off," Veronica reminded her dad.

"Okay babe, let me just roll a joint and finish my tea and we will get going," he said.

Half an hour later they made their way across the road to the funeral directors. Philip had told Veronica that he was going to ask his brothers to contribute to the funeral, but Veronica found this all a bit strange. Philip had barely spoken to, let alone spent time with his brothers in years. He had distanced himself from them when his mum, Emily, had died from cancer in 1997. He felt that his brother Michael had taken control of Emily's possessions and divided them up to his and his children's advantage, having no thought for the rest of the family, or anyone's feelings. Phil had been beside himself with his brother's selfish actions. Now he was apparently going to ask him to contribute to his own wife's funeral. They reached the funeral directors and as they walked in to the reception area, the lady came out from an adjoining room. "Hello can I help you?" she asked.

"We've come to finalise the funeral arrangements for my mum, Mrs Pauline Baker," Veronica replied.

"Okay, I'll get the details, please take a seat," she said. Philip looked uncomfortable, his face was still very pale and he looked like he hadn't slept in weeks.

The lady looked up Pauline's details to familiarise herself with them, and then asked Veronica what they had in mind. She showed Veronica some booklets with different caskets to choose from, and gave her an outline of the costs involved for a funeral car and the service. Veronica had been feeling disappointed by the argument she had had with Ella the previous day on the phone. Ella had made Veronica feel terrible about her not having any money to contribute to the funeral, and almost made it seem as though Veronica had an issue with paying for it all herself. For this reason, Veronica didn't want to pay for the cost of a family car; and thought instead, that it would be a beautiful idea to pay twice as much for Paula to be carried in a horse and carriage whilst everyone else travelled in their own cars. Veronica and Rae had two nice vehicles anyway and would happily use them to take her dad and sisters.

Veronica asked her dad what he thought about her idea. He agreed that it was a lovely idea but it was up to Veronica as it was a lot of money. Veronica wanted her dad's input; she wanted him to be happy with the choices and encouraged him to give his opinion on the type of coffin etc. Veronica asked her dad if he objected to the idea of everything being in white. Veronica didn't want the traditional black theme for her mum's funeral; she wanted her mum to be in a white coffin, in a white carriage, with white horses. Only the horses' headdress feathers would be in black as a mark of respect.

Phil sat quietly throughout; Veronica found the whole experience quite difficult.

Maybe her dad felt uncomfortable because he wasn't taking control of his wife's funeral. Veronica didn't have the time to figure it all out, they had to make a decision, Paula's body was resting in a mortuary and she needed to be put to rest. Veronica asked her dad one last time if he was happy with what she had chosen. He nodded in agreement, although still appearing to be dazed. Veronica felt extremely awkward, the woman in the funeral directors also seemed a bit uncomfortable, as she didn't know what to say or do for the best.

"So you would like the white carriage, with two white horses; and the white wooden coffin with silver furniture. With the order of service, the doctor's fees, the cremation fees and minister fees. Is that everything Mrs Cook?" Veronica agreed.

Flowers needed to be arranged and ordered, but that was down to Ella to organise. The lady led Veronica out to the shop front where her card reader was. She was offered the option of paying a deposit and balance within seven days or full payment. Veronica didn't want the cost of her mother's final day left outstanding, so decided to pay in full. She looked over towards her dad, who was sitting in the office adjacent to the reception desk. He was holding his head in his hands still, and Veronica felt sorry for him. Even though he had let Paula and everyone around him down, she still felt sorry for him. The lady gave Veronica the details of the times and date of the funeral, and the receipt for the payment. Veronica thanked her for her assistance and called her dad to leave.

Once outside, Phil soon got distracted by a phone accessory store. He had just upgraded his iPhone and needed a car charger for it. Veronica thought that he seemed to have perked up quite a lot in a short space of time, perhaps he couldn't handle being in the funeral directors, it was like he had become a different person sat there so solemnly, but outside on the high road he had other distractions.

Veronica went into the shop to try and find what he needed but they didn't have the charger. Then they went into a bakery and Veronica bought some sandwiches to take back to the flat with them. Phil thanked Veronica for what she and Rae had done for him and his wife. Veronica gave him a cuddle and told him that she wanted her mum to have a good send off.

They ate their sandwiches and talked about Paula's last days, then Phil's phone rang, it was his brother Michael. Phil told his brother how devastated he was at losing his wife. Then he told him how he and Veronica had just come from the funeral directors and asked his brother if everyone could club together to help out.

Veronica was stunned by his audacity, and embarrassed when her dad said, "Whatever anyone can give would be really appreciated Michael. I just don't have any money as I've not worked since caring for Paula and I'm really just relying on Veronica and her husband to help out. They've just lost their contract and are about to move house. They are not in a great position themselves, so anything anyone can give would be really helpful Michael."

Veronica wanted the ground to swallow her up there and then. Did Phil not have an ounce of self-respect or pride? Veronica kept her thoughts to herself as she couldn't say anything. She knew that Michael was the tightest man ever when it came to money, as if he was going to contribute to his brother's wife's funeral, what planet was her dad on in thinking that he would?

After a few minutes of conversation with his brother, Phil said goodbye. He told Veronica that he was sure his brother would help contribute; and that he would also ask Paula's sisters Beverley and Pat. "I don't want you and Rae paying for all of this, they are family and they can help out too," he said, but Veronica found the whole idea very strange; maybe this was his way of making himself feel better for not paying himself. He had grown skunk plants for months and boasted that one grow could net him around £20,000 yet he didn't seem to have a penny now.

Veronica was disappointed with him but there was nothing she could do, all she could do was go along with it and avoid a confrontation with him. All that mattered now was her mum's day, and by hook or by crook Veronica was going to make sure that it all went ahead and ran smoothly.

It was late and time for Veronica to head back to Kent to get on with the tasks of looking after her children and getting ready to move house. Veronica and Rae were on tenterhooks waiting for a date to move. She kissed her dad and sister Paulette goodbye, then made her way back home on the long journey to Kent.

CHAPTER 88

A Stressful Time

Veronica was relieved to be back home in Kent with Rae and the kids, but her mind was in a whirl. The past five months had been unrelenting, and she had so many thoughts in her head as she tried to make sense of it all. She had started to come to terms with many things about her life. Veronica's childhood and upbringing had been very unusual, and she had found it very difficult to reconcile her emotions about it all. Losing her mum to hepatitis C caused by sharing a dirty needle, was right now the biggest thing that she struggled with though. From the time she had heard the diagnosis six years before, to the moment her mum passed away, Veronica could still not accept it. She had hoped that her mum would be one of the lucky few who managed to overcome the virus with treatment, but it wasn't to be.

The constant question in Veronica's mind was how had her mum become infected? She wondered who had shared that dirty needle with her. Was it her dad, did he infect her? As Phil refused to get himself tested, even when Paula was dying, this added to Veronica's stress because she was forever worrying about his health. He said he was only interested in his wife's welfare and not at all concerned for himself, but Philip's lack of responsibility; and nobody knowing either way whether he had the virus or not, only put more pressure on the family as a whole.

Paula had desperately wanted him to be tested; and his other daughters were worried sick about him too. As Veronica tried to make sense of it all she felt angry and let down. She didn't have the power to change anything, but she had exhausted herself with the worry. She had given so much of herself to her parents throughout her life to support them, only to realise now that all she had done was enable them to continue on their destructive paths, which was just as painful as watching her parents deteriorate.

With Paula gone, how would Phil continue, what would become of him? He had never cooked or cleaned, Paula had done everything around the home. This man, husband and father who had been so controlling and dominant, seemed so fragile now without Paula, and that worried Veronica and her sisters. Despite Veronica feeling angry about everything that had brought Paula to her premature death, she still loved her dad and was concerned about his future. Having a normal relationship with him was becoming increasingly difficult though, his behaviour towards Veronica was intolerable at times. He took his anger out on her, and it felt like she was being treated like a scapegoat. But she'd endured this kind of abuse on and off for years, there had never been any let up from it; and it seemed that he only ever treated her reasonably when she was giving him something. At no time before, had this become more apparent than now. She felt as though he was using her and manipulating her emotions to get what he wanted. He knew that Veronica could never turn her back on her mum; he knew that she would do right by her mother.

Veronica felt uneasy around him, she felt like he wasn't being at all sincere with her; and she felt exactly the same when she was around her sisters too. In fact she had even felt the same with her mum sometimes, before she became so ill. Every time she went to north London to see them, she felt as though she was pulling knives out of her back when she left their house and shut the door. If she was handing money over to her dad to pay the bills though, he would be full of compliments and praise for his daughter. But the moment she said something he thought out of turn, or that he didn't like for some reason, he would switch and come down on her like a ton of bricks. He had a split personality, one minute he was Mr Nice Guy, the next a complete monster. His tongue could shred Veronica to pieces within seconds, and she felt extremely unloved by him.

The moment she moved out to begin her life with Rae, he became very disdainful towards her.

He had even blamed her for everything going wrong with the dealing, as they lost their punters shortly after Veronica moved out. She never knew exactly why, because her parents had never told her. All her mum had said was that they stopped dealing because people were fed up with waiting around for Phil to get his act together to go and score, so they found someone else to supply them. Veronica thought her absence may have contributed to that, because she wasn't there to support her parents with the running of the house and looking after her sisters, but that wasn't her fault. Her dad had given her an ultimatum when she returned from Mexico in 1998. He had told her to be part of a team and help them with their plans to sail around the world, or move out and find her own way in life.

Veronica was 24 years old when she finally made that break and was entitled to live her own life with her own ideas and her own ideals. Phil had clearly never accepted this, which showed through in his behaviour towards Veronica. He was a control freak, he had controlled his wife and his daughters, but he had lost his grip on Veronica when she met Rae, and he couldn't accept it. Phil had always put the blame for his attitude on Rae. He had said it was Rae who didn't like him and Paula, that Rae had never accepted them. He blamed this on Veronica as he suspected that she had told Rae too much about the drugs, but Rae was no stranger to the drugs scene. He had witnessed one of his uncles deteriorating due to heroin and eventually dying of an overdose, so Rae did not judge Veronica's parents on their addiction or lifestyle, but on the mistreatment of their daughter over the years he had been with her. Phil had always made Veronica and Rae feel uncomfortable whenever there was a family get-together; and the constant feeling of unease was very tangible, even Rae's mum had felt it whenever she was around them. She had noticed that Veronica was uneasy around her family, and that she was more relaxed without them. This was because Veronica felt like she was walking on eggshells with her family all the time, the slightest thing could set off their paranoia; and her dad could start on her at any given moment. In the end, Veronica preferred to avoid any get-together with Rae's family and her family, because she couldn't stomach it. Irene had once commented on Veronica's family's behaviour when they came to a BBQ when Ashley was a baby. She said that they huddled together in their own corner of the garden only talking to each other, as if they were the only people there. Irene thought it was quite rude that they had made no conscious effort to mingle with Rae's parents and family.

In the years that followed Veronica leaving home and making her life with Rae, Ella had become Phil's golden daughter. Maybe because in his eyes, Veronica had turned her back on her family. Ella had stayed with Veronica and Rae on many occasions over the years they lived in Kent though, and there was nothing that Veronica loved more than having her sister and niece Helen stay with them. She loved taking them to the nearby beaches and spoiling them on shopping sprees. Ella always came across as quite sweet and innocent around Rae, but he had always said to Veronica that he found it a bit false, as she could start a full-blown argument between Phil and Veronica with the snap of her fingers.

Veronica remembered how her dad and Ella had broken her heart when they deliberately caused an argument while she had her parents stay for a few days, when Paula was extremely sick. Ella had also deliberately told Veronica that her birthday party was cancelled as she was tired and Paula was too ill anyway, only to go ahead and have the BBQ a few hours later and invite her friends and her mum and dad. It was all planned and premeditated to hurt Veronica, because she had made Ella feel selfish for wanting a party when Paula had a matter of days left to live. Veronica had paid the highest price as she had missed out on being with her mum the last time she went out, as Paula died just over 3 days later.

Veronica could not understand why her dad and sister wanted to hurt her so much. All she had ever done was to love them so much and try her best to help them, in any way she could. She thought of all those years she had spent as a child in that awful drug fuelled environment. The years she had kept her mouth shut to protect her parents from going to prison, even smuggling drugs for them. Why had it all come to this? Veronica was totally beside herself with grief.

As Veronica reflected on all of this, she felt heartbroken, not just because she had lost her mum, but because her mum's illness and death had highlighted her dad's true personality and the family dynamics with her sisters.

With all of this going through her mind, Veronica still had to concentrate somehow on her children, their needs, her husband's needs and the upcoming house move.

Rae told Veronica that they had been given a date for exchange and that they would be moving house on 6th November. Veronica was relieved to be finalising the sale of the house and to be moving to a new home where she could make new memories. Losing their contract with Masterstores supermarkets had been a major blow to Veronica and Rae, they needed to sell the house fast, as they were running out of funds to pay the mortgage, so this at least, was some good news. However, Paula's funeral was set for the 2nd of November, meaning that Veronica and Rae would be moving only four days later, so Veronica had no time to wallow in self-pity. She wanted to, she wanted to fall apart and just cry, but there wasn't time. Veronica had eight years' worth of office paperwork to pack up still. There were dozens of binders full to the brim with invoices and company details. There was office furniture to dismantle and box up and shelves to take down. Veronica found it to be a good distraction from wallowing in her grief, and her daughter Sienna also took up much of her time. She was at the typical two year old stage where she was into everything. Veronica had to keep her eyes on her constantly, whilst trying to pack up. There were so many things to tie up before they were ready to move, that Veronica and Rae really had their hands full in the days leading up to the funeral.

CHAPTER 89

The Funeral, 2nd November 2012

A few days later, Veronica's dad phoned to say that the vicar had called to discuss the service arrangements. Phil had arranged to meet him at Ella's house, as he didn't want him to come to the flat. He asked Veronica if she could come to the appointment too, which was scheduled for the next day. Although very busy, Veronica wanted to meet the vicar and be involved with Paula's arrangements as much as possible, so the next day she drove to Edmonton and met her dad and sisters at Ella's. Veronica was surprised by the potent smell of skunk when her sister opened the door to her; it literally hit her in the face. As she sat on the sofa in the lounge, she wondered if the vicar would be aware of the smell too.

When he turned up half an hour later, he was greeted by Phil who shook his hand and introduced himself as Paula's husband. He ushered the vicar into the lounge and introduced him to his daughters. He sat down and began to go through the details of the service and asked the family if they had any preferences for the hymns. They agreed on a few choices and some music that Phil wanted to play in memory of his wife. Veronica didn't say much during the meeting as she was stunned by the strong smell around them and felt uneasy with a vicar in this situation.

Phil gave some background information about Paula's personality, and told the vicar that she was not religious in any way. The vicar came across like he was quite down to earth and on everyone's level, but Veronica wondered if that was just part of his job. Veronica suspected that he could smell the skunk. It was so strong you'd have to have had sinus trouble not to! It made Veronica feel completely at odds with the situation, but Phil didn't seem to care. He chatted away so much it was as if he was on speed. Veronica looked at her dad's behaviour and body language. It did seem like he had taken something. She wondered if the vicar suspected anything, but there was nothing she could do about it if he did.

Shortly after the vicar left, Veronica made her way back to Kent. Paula's funeral was less than a week away and Veronica would be moving house four days later. Veronica was rushed off her feet and overwhelmed with grief, but the days passed quickly with the last of the packing to do.

Phil had asked Veronica if she wanted to view her mum the day before the funeral to say goodbye. Veronica did not like the idea of seeing her mum in a coffin all made up cosmetically. Seeing her mum lifeless the day she passed had been enough for her to take, Veronica had said goodbye to her then and she wanted to leave it at that. Her dad was a bit disappointed but it was Veronica's decision. "I want to remember Mum how she was before she got ill, already I can't get the image of her thin pale face out of my mind. I know it will take time to get over it, but seeing her again two weeks after passing away, just isn't a comfortable thought for me," she explained to her dad.

Also, what Veronica was already dealing with was stressful enough; she didn't need another journey to London and back the day before her mum's funeral. She felt bad for not being by her dad's side, but she assured him that she would be by his side the following day to finally say goodbye to her mum. Later on, her dad called again to tell Veronica that Ella's husband Petros had split up with her. He had told her that he needed some time to sort his head out because he couldn't cope with the stress that was caused by Ella's family circumstances. Veronica was stunned. Of all the times to walk out on someone, he chose to walk out on her the day before her mum's funeral. Veronica was furious, so too was Phil as he was telling Veronica about what had happened. Ella was in the process of going to view her mum's body when her husband dumped her. They'd only been married 3 months, Veronica was so angry with him.

"Poor Ella," she said to her dad. "What must be going through her mind right now? She's not long had a baby with him and he's left her at a time like this. What a selfish bastard," Veronica added.

Her dad agreed. "I know," he replied. "He doesn't want to come anywhere near me, I will fucking knock him out," he told Veronica. "I just wanted to keep you in the loop as to what's happened, because she's going to need us to be strong for her tomorrow and support her. You've got Rae to lean on but she's got no one now thanks to that." Veronica agreed.

"Don't say anything to her about this; I don't want her to get any more upset than she already is. It's going to be bad enough with what we are all dealing with without his antics. So please keep quiet about it." Veronica agreed, she didn't want to make anything worse.

She got off the phone and told Rae what had happened. Rae wasn't in the least bit surprised.

"Nothing less than what I expected to be honest babe," Rae said, but even Veronica wasn't expecting this. Anyhow, all she could do was be as strong as she could for her family and do right by her mum like she had intended.

The next morning, Veronica and Rae got up fairly early to shower and get the kids ready for what was to be the most emotional day in Veronica's and her family's life ever. Sienna was dropped off to Irene. She was far too young to be going and Veronica needed to support her dad and sisters without worrying about Sienna. Ashley however was older and able to understand, he wanted to be able to say goodbye to his Nan and wanted to support his mum. He looked so smart and handsome in his suit.

All the men wore pink ties and the girls had pink tops with the traditional black attire. Helen had decided on this pink element of the dress code in memory of her Nan, and Veronica thought it was a lovely idea.

Rae went out early to put petrol in the cars and get them washed, so they were all shiny clean for the funeral. Unfortunately Veronica's Audi was playing up, there seemed to be something wrong with the electrics. When she put her foot on the gas pedal it didn't seem to want to speed up at all. Veronica was worried that the car may not make it to north London and the funeral; of all days to play up she thought, this was just typical.

Due to this, Veronica and Rae gave themselves plenty of time and left early. Veronica couldn't drive too fast so Rae followed slowly behind her, so that if the Audi did break down they would leave it and continue on in the Range Rover.

The sun began to shine as they headed up the motorway. Veronica thought how lovely it was that the sun was shining and the sky was quite clear and blue. She looked up to the sky and said to herself, "Come on, don't let me down, don't break down on me now." Luckily the Audi made it and Veronica felt relieved.

The horse and carriage was due to pick Paula up from the funeral director's in Edmonton then get to Ella's house for around 1pm. The service was booked for 2pm. This would give enough time for the horses and carriage to make their way from Ella's, through Hertford Road and up to the crematorium.

Veronica, Rae, Charlie and Ashley got out of their cars. As they walked towards Ella's front door, they saw some flower wreaths lying on the front drive, one said Mum, another said Nan and there was a heart with roses. Rae stopped to look at the messages on them, but Veronica found it all a bit emotional and knocked on Ella's door. Ella looked tearful when she answered but Veronica thought she looked beautiful. Paulette looked just as beautiful too, so did Helen who wore a black dress with black tights and had a pink flower broach pinned to her dress. Veronica cuddled them all. Phil came downstairs, he was wearing a smart black Armani shirt that Veronica had bought for him, she thought he looked smart too and gave him a kiss and a cuddle.

He was wearing lots of aftershave; Phil always spent an age cleaning and pruning himself and making himself smell good. A few minutes later, Michael and Kathy knocked on the door with their sons, Gary and Paul. Kathy had her granddaughter with her, who was the same age as Helen.

Paul and Gary had their girlfriends too, and the family were all introduced to each other and cuddled. Veronica had not seen any of them since Xmas 1998 after returning from Mexico; she didn't really know what to say. What should have been a nice occasion to be reunited with her aunt, uncle and cousins after all those years was tarnished with grief and sadness for the loss of their mum, Paula. Veronica did not much care for the banter; she was only interested in sending her mum off with dignity and pride. She went outside to see if she could see the horses and carriage coming down the road but instead she saw Ella's husband Petros. Rae was outside talking to him; Rae's body language told Veronica that he was having a serious conversation with him. There was no doubt in Veronica's mind that Rae was giving Petros a telling off. After all, how could he dump Ella so soon after getting married and having his baby, let alone the day she was viewing her mum's body and the day before the funeral?

Veronica wanted to walk out and punch him in the face, but it was the wrong time.

Veronica's dad had called Veronica on the mobile minutes before she pulled up outside Ella's house to say that Ella and Petros had made amends over the phone, and that he was on his way over to support Ella at the funeral. Veronica's dad asked that she kept her mouth shut and didn't get involved in her sister's marital affairs.

Veronica had more than enough to worry about without Ella's feud with her husband. If Ella was crazy enough to forgive him so easily, it was down to her, Veronica did as she was asked and said nothing. She went back inside Ella's house and waited. 1pm came and passed, there was no sign of the carriage. 1.30pm came and passed, there was still no sign of the horses and carriage, Veronica felt agitated. She was worried about her mum.

"Does anyone know if Mum is on her way here?" Veronica asked. "Have you called the funeral directors to see if she's on her way?"

"It's probably taking a while because of traffic," Phil said. "She's coming by horse and carriage, so it's bound to take longer. She will be here soon," he said.

Veronica joked; "Mum spent her whole married life waiting for you Dad, now she's making you wait for her!"

It was 1.45pm before the horses and carriage came down the road. Everyone gathered outside Ella's to watch, it was a breathtaking, beautiful yet sad moment. Veronica felt full of pride to see her mum being carried in such style. Paula loved animals and nature; she was a true hippy at heart, believing in looking after the environment and being kind to nature. She would have loved the idea of being carried by beautiful horses. These two white horses looked perfectly groomed, their headdress made them and the carriage look fit for a princess. The family stood with their mouths open in wonder at these beautiful horses heading towards them, with Paula in a white coffin in a pretty white carriage.

Veronica and her sisters cried as the coachman stopped the horses outside the house. People from neighbouring houses who had seen the carriage looked on intently. The horses stood perfectly still, they nuzzled each other as if cuddling. Everyone witnessed this moment of affection and sighed; it was as if these two beautiful creatures were in love and their tenderness was reciprocated in a synchronised fashion, they looked so elegant.

Phil's voice broke as his emotions overwhelmed him. Veronica and her sisters huddled around their dad to support him, but found themselves joining him with tears.

They walked to the back of the carriage to open it and put the flowers inside with Paula's coffin; it looked so small, which only added to the sisters' and Phil's upset. They all held the coffin and cried; they all kissed each other and agreed to be strong for Paula.

They wiped their tears and told family and friends to follow the procession.

Rae put his arm around Phil and led him to the car. Rae was following behind the carriage, with Veronica following behind him with Ella and her husband Petros. Paulette followed behind Veronica in her boyfriend Gavin's car. Although very emotional, Veronica was filled with pride as the beautiful carriage went on ahead, with Rae behind in his Range Rover and Veronica behind Rae in her Audi; the procession looked fit for royalty. Even Paulette's boyfriend was following behind Veronica in his Audi TT. All the other relatives and friends followed behind them. They had to drive very slowly and keep a fair distance between cars. Veronica was relieved about this as her car was still playing up.

The horses, carriage and procession of cars reached the junction to turn right into Nightingale road. The horses and carriage made their way out with Rae following behind.

As Veronica edged out, a double-decker bus cut her up and got between Rae and Veronica, with the remainder of the procession behind her.

Veronica's car had a large funeral car sticker attached, but the bus driver either hadn't realised or didn't care. Veronica beeped the bus driver, yelling at him to pull over and allow the procession through. He ignored her, continuing all the way up Nightingale road. Paulette and her boyfriend were beeping and yelling as well, and so too were other members of the funeral precession. Veronica was fuming. How disrespectful of the driver and how typical that Paula had endured being mugged and attacked in the years she lived in Edmonton, and now, on her final journey, a bus driver cuts into her procession just to disrespect her one last time.

As they reached the traffic lights to turn right onto Hertford road, the bus moved into the next lane to go straight on. Fuming but relieved to be back behind Rae and her mum's carriage, Veronica turned right into a very busy high street. The street was filled with pedestrians, people of all ages and of all cultures, who stopped to take note of the passing carriage. People everywhere took their hats off as a mark of respect and made the sign of the cross. This was a far cry from the rude bus driver that had just cut them up.

The funeral precession continued through Hertford road and turned left onto Turkey Street.

From there it made its way along to the A10 and turned left for the crematorium which was just up on the left. The carriage pulled up alongside the chapel, there were cousins and aunts and uncles from Paula's side of her family already waiting for them. As Veronica, her sisters and dad walked towards the carriage, Paulette decided that she wanted to carry her mum's coffin, with the help of Veronica and Ella, into the chapel. Phil's brother Tom offered support too; it was an extremely emotional affair. The entire family watched intently as the girls got into position, lifted the coffin and placed it firmly onto their shoulders. Phil walked behind the coffin, the three sisters wept simultaneously as they carried their mum into the chapel. Veronica could barely see for tears falling heavily from her eyes.

As the girls reached the catafalque they placed the coffin gently down, it had no weight to it at all. The vicar handed roses to Phil and each of the girls to lay across the coffin, then they were asked to take a seat. The girls were breaking down at this point and Veronica struggled to let go of the coffin, she kissed her hand and rubbed it on top of the coffin. "I don't want to let you go Mum," Veronica mumbled under her breath, as she was encouraged to sit down.

Veronica looked at her dad who was wearing blacked out sunglasses; he took her by the arm and led her to a seat. He, Veronica and the girls sat in the front row, Phil gripped Veronica tightly and didn't let go.

The vicar spoke briefly of Paula and her family life, before leading everyone in singing some hymns. It all seemed very surreal for Veronica, like a bad dream from which she wanted to wake up, only it wasn't a dream, this was reality.

After the hymns, Phil went up front to speak about his wife. He was still wearing his blacked-out sunglasses. Were they to hide the dark rings around his eyes, or maybe mask his dilated pupils from the drug fuelled night before? He looked uncomfortable up there in front of everyone, he looked almost guilty. His head almost hung in shame and his body language was very sheepish. He talked about his boat and the wonderful experience of sailing through the Med. He told everyone that Paula was timid and afraid to push herself to do new things in life, but that he had encouraged her to get involved with learning to sail and being a skipper's mate. He joked about her fear of heights and how he had pushed her to sit in a bosun's chair and hoisted her up to fix a sail. Yet when she got to the top she froze, unable to do anything.

He spoke only of some good times they had shared during the years they spent on yacht Nova.

Veronica was disappointed by his speech; it was more about his boat than his wife.

He spoke of his dreams and aspirations, not of hers. He didn't say a lot about Paula as a person and how sweet and soft natured she was. Veronica wished she had got up and spoken about her mum. The trouble was, what could you say about this woman's life? There were some good times, mainly the ones they spent on the boat, but for her span of 56 years they were few and far between. Veronica wanted to recognise her mum's strength when she was left alone to cope with two young children and being pregnant, when Phil went to prison. Veronica wanted to speak of the things she had learned from her mum growing up as a young teenager. Paula had taught her daughter to cook, clean and look after herself. Paula had encouraged her to be self-sufficient when Phil was in prison. Veronica wanted to tell people about her gentle personality and of how affectionate she was.

Paula made many mistakes in life due to her addiction, but she also left behind her three beautiful daughters and grandchildren. Veronica wanted to recognise her mum's strength when faced with life's difficulties and challenges. How brave she had been throughout her illness and how she'd managed to smile and laugh through all her pain. Paula didn't feel sorry for herself and accepted her fate, always reminding everyone how many others were worse off than her, like the millions of children around the world who suffered disease and cancers, or the young parents who would not live to see their children grow up. Veronica so desperately wanted these aspects of her mum's personality to be recognised, but Phil really only spoke of the time they had spent on their boat. Veronica was angry with her dad for this.

For 38 years she had been a loyal wife to him and stayed by his side, regardless of how many other women he cheated with, but how could this be brought up, how would that make Phil look?

After his speech, Phil sat back down. The vicar continued to speak, then there were more hymns and before they knew it, the service was over and they all went outside.

The vicar gave a rose to Phil and shook his hand; Veronica thanked the vicar as they left the chapel. They all stood outside and cuddled each other: aunts, uncles, cousins and friends were all there for Paula. Phil thanked everyone for coming and gave people the address of the pub for the wake that Ella had organised, with her husband.

Phil asked if he could drive Veronica's Audi to the pub. Veronica wasn't entirely happy about it as her dad never had insurance, but it was only down the road and he couldn't speed around in it as it had an electrical fault. Veronica would follow him in the Range Rover with Rae, so she agreed. Phil offered his niece Jenny and partner Ian a lift as they had made their way to the crematorium on public transport. Veronica thought it was strange that her dad wanted to drive her car and thought he just wanted to show off in it. When they arrived at the pub, Phil was obviously disappointed by the car's lack of power!

"What's the matter with the Audi?" he asked his daughter, "I put my foot flat to the floor on the gas, but it wouldn't move."

Veronica chuckled to herself, "I did tell you it's playing up Dad, it started this morning. I have to get it looked at when we get home."

Everyone made their way inside the pub, it wasn't a big pub, very small and old fashioned, it looked like it could have done with updating. Ella had ordered some finger food; there were some sausage rolls and pick bits. Veronica's cousins from Paula's sisters side were very quick to tuck in, taking huge platefuls and leaving little for anyone else, Veronica and Rae only managed to get a couple of sausage rolls.

The food was sparse and disappointing; and Veronica and Rae could not drink due to driving home, but they stayed for as long as they could. Veronica chatted to all of her cousins, and Ashley got a lot of attention from all of the family. Veronica felt so out of place, all of these people that surrounded her were as good as strangers. Her mum's family had not featured in their lives for years. There had only been a few occasions that Paula had met with her sister Pearl over the last 15 years but she had nothing to do with the rest of her sisters, and Veronica had only met Pat at the hospital back in July. She had not known her Aunty Pat her whole life, Paula was terrible for keeping in touch with everyone but it was due to her lifestyle; and Phil was as bad. Although in the early years, Veronica spent more time around her dad's side of the family who lived in Hampshire and Wiltshire, she hadn't seen any of them since 1998. Veronica was emotional and tired. Rae also looked out of place; he told Veronica that her uncle Michael had not even acknowledged him all day, treating him like an outsider. Rae never liked Michael for this and found him rude. Phil kept disappearing into the toilets. Rae walked into the men's to have a pee and found that Phil was blatantly snorting cocaine in there; Rae was disgusted by his behaviour. When he came out, he told Veronica it was time to leave. Rae had had enough.

When Phil came up to his daughter to say goodbye, his nose was dripping and he looked like he was on drugs. He'd removed the sunglasses and dropped the pretence; here he was, now on display for all to see, the true Phil.

He cuddled Veronica and Rae and told them how his wife would have had a pauper's funeral had it not been for them. Rae looked at Phil with utter disappointment. Rae patted him on the back and told him, "You'd better get saving for yours or you'll have a cardboard box and a wheelbarrow!"

But Rae wasn't joking; he was annoyed that Phil had no decency, no pride; after all that he had put his wife through over the years, he could not contribute to her funeral. Rae had, like Veronica, felt sorry for Phil throughout the months Paula was dying, which was why he had been so generous and wanted to support her dad in any way possible. But when his vindictive personality shone through and he abused Veronica, it was a wake-up call for Rae, realising that he had no respect for Paula or his daughters or for anyone else. He felt used by Veronica's dad, he knew that Phil had got money from his skunk plants but he just didn't want to part with it, not even for his own wife. There was no way Rae would pay for Veronica's dad's funeral after this and he made sure Phil knew it.

Veronica didn't know where to put her face or what to say, she still felt sorry for her dad; he looked so desperately helpless without his wife by his side. Yes, Veronica was angry with him for all the right reasons but she still cared about him, she loved him and worried about his future.

Veronica and Rae said goodbye to everyone and set off back to Kent. Rae told his wife how disgusted he was to find Phil in the men's toilets snorting coke and showing off to his nephews like he was Mr Cool.

He told Veronica that her dad was a sad human being, that he was not a real man in his eyes.

He had done nothing for his wife her entire life apart from abuse her, cheat on her and get her completely hooked on heroin. He had trapped her into this lifestyle, she could not go anywhere or leave him as long as she needed the drugs; and that's how he kept her until it became the death of her. Veronica broke down in tears, she knew he was right, there was no denying it, this was the reality of it all. Phil could still hide from it though and live in denial, as long as he had a fix or a line of coke, he could escape the reality. It was staring Veronica bluntly in the face.

CHAPTER 90

Marylebone, Where It All Began.

It had been a couple of weeks since the funeral, and Veronica had not seen her dad and sisters for over a week. She had been in her new home, concentrating on settling in and helping Rae with invoicing and paperwork for a couple of companies he still had some work from.

Their company didn't have much in the way of funds, yet the bills were mounting, so it was essential for Rae and Veronica to focus on getting in what work they could; and maintaining it.

As the weekend approached Veronica spoke to her dad on the phone. He was depressed and unable to concentrate on anything; he was completely lost without Paula. He spoke of the early days when he and Paula first started out when they were teenagers living in Marylebone.

He told Veronica there was a bush outside Paula's old house, and he'd taken a branch off it and given it to her. That's when they had their first kiss. It brought tears to Veronica's eyes.

With all he had done and all he had become, he still loved his wife and had always loved her.

"I really want to go back there and get a few branches from that bush if it's still there," Phil said.

"Ella's got a lot on her plate with baby Sammy and Paulette doesn't want to come with me. She's in her own world; you know what Paulette is like. I was wondering if you would come with me Vronx?" he asked.

Veronica was feeling emotionally affected by the story of her young parents having their first kiss; and she had not been to this part of London for years, so to see where her mum grew up would be a comforting experience for her, therefore Veronica agreed to go with her dad. She told him she would drive down in the next couple of hours and meet him at Ella's.

Phil suddenly cheered up somewhat. He was pleased to have his daughter's company and to be going back to his old haunt. It gave him something to look forward to, and Veronica was happy to oblige. Within a couple of hours, she arrived at Ella's; her dad was already there waiting for Veronica, which was unusual compared to Phil's normal behaviour. When Paula was still alive, Veronica would wait all day and evening sometimes, for her parents to turn up, but today her dad was obviously eager to get going. Paulette was meeting her boyfriend and Ella was busy with the baby, but had offered to cook her dad and Veronica dinner upon their return. So Veronica and her dad set off along the A10 and A406 towards West London. It took forever to reach Marylebone because of the traffic. When they reached the flats where Paula and Phil both lived as kids, they looked around for somewhere to park and stopped directly opposite the flat where Paula had grown up. Phil had lived in the exact same flat with his parents before they moved to another around the corner; Paula's mum and dad had moved in as Phil and his family moved out. The couple discovered this later, when they got together.

Phil told Veronica about this as they got out of her car and walked towards the flat, he pointed out a small window, which was Paula's bedroom. He said that he and Paula had spent days inside that bedroom making love, 'not leaving for nothing.' This was a bit too much information for Veronica, but it was something that Phil needed to talk about. He said that he had fallen in love with her the moment he set eyes on her, and that he had given her a branch from the bush outside as a token of his love. He said it should have been a bunch of roses but they were both just in awe of each other and it did not make a difference, it was the gesture that mattered.

Veronica thought it was very sweet and innocent; this is where their relationship began.

Phil was quite emotional as he stood by the front door of the flat and reached across to the bush and took a few branches of leaves. He passed them to Veronica to hold. He looked across the road to his right and pointed out to a large building. He told Veronica that that was where his primary school used to be. It had been knocked down and rebuilt some years later around the corner. Veronica was interested to know a bit more about her parents' early years. It was almost like going back in time with her dad as they walked along the road and he pointed out different houses and explained who lived where. His mum had lived in the same area during the blitz. She used to go to Edgware Road underground station where many local residents had taken shelter from the bombs. Phil talked about people that his mum knew well, who hadn't made it to the shelter and lost their lives. Then he pointed towards the railways behind the flats where he and his mates had played as kids. They had come across an unexploded bomb that had been partially buried since the war. Veronica found these stories of her dad's youth fascinating.

As they walked through the flats and around its grounds, Phil told her about a local police officer who always had it in for him. He would look for any excuse to stop Phil and search him, often giving Phil a slap just for the hell of it. Phil had got a bit of a chip on his shoulder because of the way he was treated, so he would deliberately cause mischief just to wind the officer up.

He would shout from a distance calling the copper a bastard and then run and hide behind a bike shed. He would watch, spying with glee as the copper got all frustrated trying to catch Phil.

Veronica realised that this little journey back to Marylebone was like therapy for her dad.

"Do you fancy getting a drink somewhere Dad?" she asked him. He agreed and took her to an old local on Church Street where Paula's dad used to spend all of his time drinking.

They walked in and Veronica went to the bar to order a beer for her dad. Suddenly she heard an Irish accent saying hello from the other side of the bar. Veronica and her dad looked across to see Paula's sister's husband Chris. He had lived in the Lisson Green estate for most of his life, and spent all his free time in the pub drinking. He had never known anything else and it was as if time had stopped still for him. He offered to buy Veronica and her dad a drink, and they sat chatting with him briefly. Chris was difficult to understand with his slurred drunken Irish accent, so having a conversation with him was hard work. Phil didn't want to stay too long in the pub; he had never been a fan of Chris, although he was harmless enough. They drank their drinks, gave their love and good wishes, then left the pub.

When they got outside, Phil wanted to find a newsagent to buy a pack of flints for his lighter, but nowhere seemed to sell them. He could only buy disposable lighters, which frustrated Phil.

"Why do they all sell clipper lighters, yet you ask them for flints and they don't know what you are talking about?" Phil mentioned that he didn't have any money and had to get himself down to the unemployment office to sign on. Veronica felt sorry that he was in this position but he had had plenty of time to get that in order. Why hadn't he done it before now? Veronica wondered.

She couldn't say anything to him about it though, as it would only end with him making a million excuses and he would make Veronica feel guilty for questioning his actions, or lack of.

Veronica saw a cash machine down the road, she took out £70 which was the last of her wages that remained in her account and handed it to her dad. Rae never had access to this account and so would not notice the money missing. Veronica felt like she was betraying her husband by doing this, but she felt so bad for her dad having nothing, that she did it anyway.

The moment she handed the money to her dad, she knew in her heart it would probably be spent on a fix. Now she felt even worse than she did before giving him the money. It was useless, when would this ever end? But she knew as long as he had a breath in his body, he would continue to take drugs.

It was dark and getting late, so they made their way back slowly towards the car. Phil told her some more stories along the way, while Veronica listened intently. On their way back to Ella's, Phil decided to play some music on Veronica's car stereo. He put on Snow Patrol and skipped through some of the songs to reach one that Paula loved. "Your mum loved this track Vronx," he said. Veronica welled up inside. She missed her mum immensely and still couldn't get her head around the fact that she was no longer with them. "You are a good girl Vronx, you've always put yourself out for others," he told her.

"I really appreciate you taking the time to bring me here today," he said. "You've got a lot going on what with losing Masterstores and moving home, and you've given up your time to be with me today. Thanks a lot honey," and with that he kissed Veronica on the cheek. Veronica smiled as the tears streamed down her face; at least he'd acknowledged what she'd done today. It was something and that was enough for Veronica.

When they reached Ella's, dinner was being dished out. Veronica sat cuddling baby Sammy as her sister plated the food. Ella's husband Petros came into the kitchen and started to show off about a skunk deal he'd just done, he was playing Mr Wide Guy, and showing Veronica that his feet were firmly under the family table.

"Here Dad, come have some of this, roll yourself a spliff!" He passed Veronica's dad a bag of skunk to help himself to. Her dad thanked him and made jovial conversation as he rolled his joint. They looked like a right pair, best of friends.

The man that had dumped his wife the day before her mum's funeral was now best of friends with her dad and all had seemed to be forgotten. Veronica couldn't stand him; she thought he was sly and false. She didn't trust him, or believe that he would be a good husband to Ella.

After all, he was growing skunk farms around north London and playing Mr Wide Guy.

It was obvious he didn't like Veronica, he knew she could see him for what he was; and that posed a threat. Veronica wasn't going to stand in his and her sister's way. She had married him, she had made her bed and she had to lie in it, but Veronica did worry about Helen and how she would cope with this man who had steamrollered his way into her life.

It was soon time to leave and Veronica was missing her own family, she hadn't seen Sienna, Rae and Ashley all day. Sienna would be fast asleep when she arrived home.

Veronica kissed her dad, Ella, Helen and Sammy goodbye. Ella's husband also approached Veronica for a kiss, she braced herself as she had to kiss him, but it made her stomach churn.

As she shut the door and headed for her car, she felt again as though she was pulling knives from her back. Ella had been off with Veronica since the fall out with her dad in Kent, before Paula had died. Their relationship was showing great signs of strain and Veronica found it difficult putting on a front for an easy life. But this was how things had come to be, it was hard to accept but it was staring Veronica in the face. She was desperate to get home to Rae, and felt immediately relieved when she got there.

CHAPTER 91

The Fall Out

It had been just over a week since Veronica had seen her dad and sisters. She woke up feeling very emotional, missing her mum like crazy, no matter what she did to try and distract herself she just kept crying. She decided to call her dad as she wanted to tell him that she was having a bad day and missing her mum.

"Hi Dad," she said as he answered the phone.

"Oh hi babe," he replied, he sounded like he was half asleep. It was around 10.30am which was late for Veronica as she had been up early getting Ashley to school, but then she remembered her dad's habits. He was always late to bed and late to rise.

"Oh sorry Dad, have I woken you up?" Veronica asked.

"It's okay, I've got to get up in a bit anyway. I've got things to do," he answered.

Veronica told her dad that she was having a bad day and couldn't stop crying, she told him she was missing her mum terribly.

"I know Vron, it's so hard. I can't believe she isn't here anymore. I wake up and look over expecting to see her lying next to me, but then realise she isn't. It's just awful."

Veronica had a pain in the pit of her stomach as her dad told her this. "Somehow I've got to learn to live on without her, but I can't Vron, she was everything to me, my soul mate. I don't even want to get up or go out. I have no purpose without her."

Veronica couldn't hold back. She cried down the phone. "I'm so sorry Dad; I wish I could bring her back. What are we going to do without her?" Veronica continued to cry.

"You'll never guess what your sister Ella has done." Phil's voice suddenly changed, now he sounded angry and agitated. Veronica didn't know what to think.

"No Dad, what has she done?" Veronica asked him. "She has accused me and Paulette of stealing money from her house," he said. Veronica was stunned. Why would Ella accuse them of stealing from her? After all, her parents had stolen from shops in the past but they had never stolen from their own family, even Veronica knew this was absurd, Phil had always made a big point about never stealing from your own.

"What do you mean she's accused you and Paulette of stealing money?" Veronica asked.

"She said she had some money in an envelope which she and Petros were given on their wedding day from all of their friends and relatives. She said there was about a thousand pounds there and when she checked it, there was a couple of hundred pounds missing. I can't believe she actually thinks that me or Paulette would steal her money. Can you believe it?" he asked.

Veronica was dumbfounded, after everything that has just happened. "I am lost for words Dad, I can't believe she would ring you up and actually ask if you took her money."

Veronica began to feel angry with her sister. *How dare she make such an accusation at such a time? Where were her priorities, is that all she cared about?* she thought; then the penny dropped and Veronica became even angrier.

"Hang on a minute Dad, Ella told me she never had any money a few weeks ago. When mum died and you said that we would all chip in for Mum's funeral and to speak to Ella about the arrangements, she was really nasty to me. She screamed down the phone at me Dad. She said she never had any money to contribute to Mum's send-off; and when I told her that me and Rae were also in a predicament financially, having lost our livelihood and having to sell up and move, she screamed that she would sell her fucking wedding ring if she had to. Now you are telling me she had money from her wedding back in July, really? She made me feel like an utter cunt, what a joke," Veronica said.

She was expecting her dad to be understanding towards her feelings, after all, Ella had lied and been nasty, but all of a sudden, Phil let rip.

"So you expected Ella to give you the little bit of money that she had got from her wedding day to pay for Mum's funeral did you Vron? The little bit of savings that she had got for herself and her kids, after just having baby Sammy, you wanted her to give you the little bit of money she had then, is that right, is that what you are saying?" he snapped down the phone.

Veronica was not prepared for his reaction; she did not expect him to be so defensive of Ella.

A minute ago he was complaining that she had accused him and Paulette of stealing from her!

Veronica could not win no matter what she did or what she said, and now she realised this more than at any other time. Ella could walk all over her dad but Veronica couldn't even speak her mind.

"No Dad, I didn't expect Ella to give her last penny, you said she was willing to chip in, but when I spoke to her she said she had nothing, then screamed about selling her wedding ring if she had to. Obviously she wasn't that bothered about contributing to it as she lied to me, she said she had nothing; she didn't have to do that. She could have said she had a little bit of money but didn't want to part with it not make me feel like a cunt for making her feel as though she should sell her wedding ring. You are missing the point."

Phil didn't listen and shouted over Veronica as she tried to defend her reaction. He wasn't listening to a word that Veronica was saying and instead hurled abuse down the phone at her. "I can't believe what a selfish bitch you are Vronx, everything is you, you, you. None of us have a pot to piss in yet all you go on about is how you've lost your business and how you've had to move. We've lost everything; if Ella said she never had the money to contribute then that's it. Whether she told you about her little bit of money or not is beside the bye; and none of your business. You and Rae said you'd pay for the funeral and now you are complaining that Ella never contributed. Now you've made me feel like a complete cunt. Thanks Vronx, this is typical of you." Veronica's head was in a spin, what was she to make of all of this?

Veronica felt the need to defend herself, how dare her dad treat her like this after everything.

It seemed that the more she did for her dad, the more he treated her like a door mat. She was after all, defending him; yet when she realised Ella's deceitful and hurtful actions, Phil got on Ella's defensive and attacked Veronica. It seemed to her now that she and Rae had been totally used and abused. Veronica had just sent her mum off like a princess, but this was the treatment she received from her dad! It didn't add up or make sense, but Veronica suspected that his behaviour was due to his own guilt because he hadn't contributed in any small way to his wife's funeral. That wasn't Veronica's fault but all of a sudden she was made to feel like it was.

"How dare you talk to me like this after everything I've done for you Dad, I've bent over backwards these past months to support you and the family in every way I possibly could. Even my husband has bent over backwards for you all, even though you've always treated him like shit. We've given you everything we could give, our time, our love and every penny we could. None of you have even cared about what was happening in our life and that's fine, because we were all losing Mum, but you've only considered your own circumstances. You said everyone was chipping in with the funeral, we said we were there to support you, we never said we would pay for everything. You said your skunk plants failed due to spider mites and Ella said she was skint after paying out for the wedding. If me and Rae didn't pay for it, then who was going to, what would Mum have had? I wanted to make sure she had a good send-off, she deserved that. What I don't deserve is you treating me like shit, I can't believe what a cheek you have, how dare you Dad."

Phil was livid. "Oh it all comes back to poor ole Vron again doesn't it? I've just lost my fucking wife and you are screaming down the phone about fucking money. Is this all you care about Vron?" he retorted.

Veronica was spitting feathers, he hadn't listened to a word she said, he was twisting everything.

"Why are you always twisting everything Dad? Why are you blaming me for all of this; I never accused you of nicking off of me. It was your precious daughter Ella!"

Phil continued to shout. "I can't believe you've called me up Vron complaining that you paid for Mum's day. If I had known you were going to do this, I would never have let you pay for it." Veronica had more luck talking to a brick wall than trying to get her dad to understand her. He didn't want to listen and he didn't care, he had made this quite clear and Veronica had had enough. Phil was still shouting, "Don't fucking ring me Vron until you can apologise. You've completely ruined everything. Just like you always do."

"What the fuck are you talking about now?" Veronica asked her dad.

"It was your fault we lost our dealing when you fucked off and moved out, it's your fault we ended up in this shitty tower block in Tottenham, even all what happened with stabbing Steve, that was all your doing," he said.

Veronica would have smacked her dad in the mouth had he been standing there in person saying this.

"You are blaming me for everything that went wrong in your life: so I put a knife in your hand and made you stab the bloke did I? I made you live in a tower block even though you said you were sailing around the world did I? I can't believe you are blaming me for all your mistakes. I've had enough Dad, I won't be calling with an apology because I have nothing to apologise for. I'm sorry that everything in your life went wrong. I'm sorry that we've lost Mum but I'm not sorry for things I haven't done."

With that, Veronica hung up. She burst into tears, adrenaline rushed through her body, she was stunned, shocked, angry, emotional and confused. How had it all come to this, how could this ever be fixed? It couldn't, all she had ever been to her dad was his beating post. Veronica couldn't take it anymore, this was the last straw. With Paula gone, the one person she couldn't live without, what was there to fight for? It was clear Phil had no feelings for Veronica, now for the first time ever she could see it clearly, he had used Veronica, abused her and discarded her.

CHAPTER 92

Moving On

Veronica was beside herself, she felt so unloved by her dad. What had she done to deserve the treatment she'd received from him? She cried and cried. Veronica was alone in the house, Rae had gone to London that day to do a job for another company, Veronica wished he was at home with her. She called him on his mobile and told him what had happened. Rae told Veronica that she hadn't done anything wrong in trying to defend herself. He told her, in the years he'd been with her he'd never known her dad to treat her right.

"Your dad doesn't care about anything other than himself," he said. "If he were a decent person and father, he would be pulling you in close as a family. He would be doing the right things for his daughters. Any normal dad would show you all love and consideration and try his hardest to be strong for his family, not abuse you and push you away. What daughter does what you've done for your parents? I'm not talking about just the last few months, but your whole life Vron. Throughout everything both your parents put you through you stayed loyal to them and loved them unconditionally. You've put up with their drug taking, their dealing, the raids, the prison sentences, the fights, the affairs and all of your own torment that their behaviour caused you. You've tried to help them, you were there for your sisters and you've been there to support their lifestyle, and all your dad has done since I've known you, is to bring you down and treat you like utter crap."

Veronica was sobbing; she knew her husband was making sense.

"They've never made an effort for you or your children over the years, everything has been about them. If you didn't get in your car to drive up to see them, you would never have seen them and Ashley would never have got to know his grandparents. To be honest with you Vron, and please tell me if you disagree, but in my eyes your dad isn't even a real man. A real man stands by his family and works hard to provide for them. A decent husband would have provided for his beloved wife's funeral. He sat there and did nothing Vron. Not a single thing. He never even made an attempt to provide for the funeral because he knew full well that he could manipulate you, so that you would sort it out; and instead of showing his appreciation for the amazing way you sent your mum off, he abuses you down the phone and expects you to apologise for it. That is a complete joke Vron, don't you dare waste your tears on him. If he dropped dead tomorrow, I wouldn't give a penny for his funeral. I went along with your wishes to help your mum Vron because I realised at the end that she was as much a victim in all of this as you. He lured her into a life of drugs and got her hooked so that she could not get away. Once she was in that same situation as him, she was dependent on him. She was caught up in it all Vron, he manipulated your mum all their married life and controlled her. He bullied her and he has bullied you for years. It's up to you what you do, at the end of the day he's your dad not mine, but if he were, you know my feelings about him, I would have fucked him off years ago. Your dad is protecting Ella over her lying about her having money because he's no doubt done the same. Those plants he had growing in his flat were healthy, there wasn't anything wrong with them, there is no way he never got any money out of that. But it was to his advantage that he led us to believe he had nothing, so that we would feel sorry for him and pay for the funeral," Rae told Veronica.

"Doesn't he have a conscience though babe?" Veronica asked Rae. "Doesn't he feel any remorse for not trying harder to provide for your mum's funeral? He didn't have to Vron; he had us to sort it out. If your dad had come up even with some of the funds, I would have thought more of him, but he never ever tried. How could you profess to love someone so much, in his words his "soul mate" and then not even bother to contribute to her send off? It's disgraceful Vron." Veronica had calmed down; she agreed with her husband, she knew he was right.

Veronica had disliked the fact her dad was almost begging his brother to put his hand in his pocket for the funeral. Where was his pride then, she thought? Her dad had no morals at all, he'd made that as clear as day when he got his daughter Paulette to get Paula's prescription of methadone five days after her death. He had also told Veronica on the phone that he had got Paulette to forge her mum's signature on a giro and cashed it because he was so desperate for money, excusing himself by making out it was backdated as they hadn't had time to cash it before when Mum was at death's door. All of these circumstances had built up in Veronica's mind, this was someone who had surely lost the plot, this person wasn't living in the real world and certainly never had any morals. Veronica found it quite sickening, not only was he stealing from the state, but he was cashing in on her mum's death, and here he was abusing her after she had done everything righteous; and more importantly she had been doing it out of the goodness of her heart. Veronica decided to stay away from her dad, she wouldn't call him, text him or go and see him, she needed to keep away.

She felt as though she couldn't take anymore, her mum's death was the one thing she had feared the most her whole life; and to see this come to pass was utterly painful, but now she had to deal with her dad's abuse, she felt like she had fallen into a deep dark hole. Veronica began to have a panic attack; apart from that time she broke her toe, she hadn't suffered these since meeting Rae. She started questioning her actions and reactions to her dad. Had she been hard on him? Should she have been more understanding towards his needs and addiction? Did she deserve the way he treated her? Then she started to spiral into a state of depression. Veronica did not want to leave the house, she couldn't deal with seeing anyone, and even dropping Sienna to nursery was a challenge. She felt on edge and paranoid that other mum's were staring at her because they somehow knew she was mentally struggling. She felt like everyone was judging her, even strangers, the only time she felt secure was when she was behind closed doors where she didn't have to put on a brave face and pretend. At home, she could cry all day and no one would know, and that's what she did.

Veronica received calls from her dad and her sister Ella but she ignored them, she couldn't face another conflict. When the phone rang and Veronica looked at the screen to see who it was, the second she saw her dad's name, she would panic. Her heart would race and she would spin out and feel sick. She just couldn't deal with another argument and she knew that he was phoning to demand an apology. In the end her dad sent her text messages, so too did Ella, her text was nasty. It said: "Veronica you wanted me to give you my last thousand pounds when you've got £20,000 worth of jewellery. Why didn't you sell that if you are so skint?" So Ella had taken Veronica's argument with her dad out of context. How dare she tell her to sell her jewellery, this was Veronica's engagement ring and eternity ring she was talking about. So that's what the comment about her selling her wedding ring was all about! There was no point in even having a discussion about it, Veronica knew where she was with her family, it was blatantly obvious, they were jealous of what she and Rae had achieved over the years. They thought it was their right to expect Veronica and Rae to pay for everything; they had no sense of responsibility for their mum and wife at all. Veronica felt so used. She was angry too, the more they sent nasty text messages, the more upset and angry she got. The last straw came when her dad tormented her with a barrage of text messages throughout the night. He was sending them at midnight, 2am and so on, it was obvious he was up getting high on drugs. What normal person would behave like this?

Veronica was in bed, she had to be up early to take the children to school but her dad had no consideration at all. One text read: "A cardboard box and a wheel barrow would have done and a tight-knit family. You are evil."

All Veronica wanted was to be left alone, she couldn't stand the bullying, all it did was make her angry and emotional. She texted her dad asking him to leave her alone and give her some space. She told him she was taking a step back to concentrate on her children and husband. Her dad didn't like it and kept calling. Veronica was left crying uncontrollably, she wished he would leave her alone but in her head, she was tormented by everything that had happened and everything that was said. It had got to the point where she locked herself in the bathroom with a knife, she envisioned the quickest way of ending her life. Veronica didn't like pain and if she was going to commit suicide then it would have to be done properly. Then Veronica thought about Rae and the children. What would become of them if Veronica gave up? How would Rae cope alone without his wife? The children would be devastated and it would have a massive impact on their lives. For these reasons Veronica couldn't do it, but the torment in her head would not let up, it would not pass. How could she start her life over? All she had ever known was loving her family and wanting to help them, it was unbearable to realise that they didn't even care. Veronica couldn't deal with them calling her phone, Rae told her to change her number.

"It's the only way you are going to have peace of mind," he told her. He called her mobile provider to get it changed. Veronica felt relieved that she couldn't receive any more nasty texts. But she also felt guilty for shutting her family out completely. After all, she still loved them and wanted to be a part of their life but she realised that she was never going to have the relationships with her sisters and dad that she wanted. They didn't treat her right and they were never going to.

Rae was worried about his wife; he hadn't seen her like this before. It was plain to see that Veronica was having a complete break down and there was nothing Rae could do to help her, the issues from her past had suddenly blown up in her face. What was once a strong willed, confidant and determined woman had now become an empty person that doubted herself and everything around her. Rae told her that she wasn't the same person anymore, she had completely changed. It was as if the light had gone from her eyes, she couldn't even manage a smile, Veronica was a broken person.

CHAPTER 93

Rebuilding Herself

It took months for Veronica's depression to ease. Luckily she had got quite close to a woman she'd known a few years but hadn't spent much time with until now, her name was Diane.

She was a very spiritual kind of person who was very much in touch with the spiritual world; she was also a very grounded and realistic person however. Veronica had met Diane through chance at a party in 2006 not long after moving to Kent. The two women met only a couple of times over the following six years, but Veronica got back in touch with Diane when her mum was dying. Veronica found Diane to be a great strength and they soon bonded. She had been through her own share of heartache with her family, and her advice and genuine friendship helped Veronica immensely. Diane was very intuitive and receptive to Veronica's circumstances, and she genuinely wanted her to free her mind of all the worries and guilt she had undoubtedly carried all her life. Diane encouraged Veronica to do right by her mum whilst she was alive, and to take a step back when her dad bullied her. She could clearly see that Veronica was being used by her dad; she could see him for what he was - an addict. Although this blatant fact hurt Veronica, she needed the support of friends like Diane to keep her strong. She had become so broken by her mother's illness and the abuse of her family that she had lost all of her self-esteem and confidence.

Veronica was also in close contact with her counsellor Steve Orwin, who had also been an amazing support for her during these difficult months. He advised Veronica to write everything down; he said it was a good way of dealing with hidden issues. He wanted Veronica to recover but realised that only by getting everything out onto paper, would she truly come to terms with all that she had experienced. It was also a very positive way of letting go.

Over the following year Veronica received emails from her sister, and Rae also received abusive calls from both Ella and Paulette, who had even shouted down the phone that she didn't even know why she was calling Rae as he wasn't even family! That said it all in Veronica's mind, they were never going to change, they were never going to face up to their own actions; and they would never see it from Veronica's angle.

Then a few months later, Veronica's uncle Michael called Rae on his mobile. He told him that he needed to speak to Veronica urgently. Veronica called her uncle back, who told her that her dad had apparently been ill with stomach cancer; he told her that Phil was riddled with it. This made Veronica agonise, she felt awful at the prospect of her dad having to deal with losing his wife and soul mate, then having to cope with all of the impending issues of losing Paula's council flat and having no income. This must have been awful with cancer as well. What was Veronica to do? Her instinct was to call him immediately, but if she did, she knew her call would be met with harsh words and guilt trips. She knew that her dad would play on his illness so much that Veronica would be manipulated to the point of another mental breakdown. She loved her dad desperately, but she doubted he had any feelings for her. If he truly did, cancer or no cancer, he would have made some effort himself to make contact and he would have done it months before. He had used his other daughters to try and manipulate Veronica's feelings and that had failed. If he really cared, he would have kept his daughter close and treated her with respect, Veronica no longer trusted her dad or her sisters. They had all lied and abused her so much that she just couldn't believe anything that came out of their mouths. Michael was a notorious liar himself, Veronica wondered who had put him up to calling her.

He told Veronica that she needed to let go of the anger and make amends with her father.

It was obvious to see that everyone had been led to believe that Veronica was in the wrong; no one knew the truth behind what actually happened. None of the distant relatives understood the real situation; Veronica was still very much upset and angry. She was still in no position to meet face to face with her dad; she was still hurt by his behaviour around Paula's death, she was angry that he had not even tried to do right by her. Paula's suffering was undoubtedly made worse by Phil's inability to cope due to his addiction, and his priorities being all wrong when he

415

insisted on growing skunk in the lounge and delaying the palliative care team getting to Paula.

All of these issues had made Veronica very angry towards her father; and the way he shut her out when it suited him, then reeled her in when he wanted something from her added to this feeling of mistrust.

Veronica doubted he had cancer, but she decided to wait and see if anything else should come to light. Veronica's Aunty Beverley had looked after a tea chest and some furniture of Phil and Paula's when they were living in temporary accommodation and Phil was meant to be preparing his yacht Nova to circumnavigate fourteen years before. They had told Beverley that they were between moving and just needed some storage space for a few months, Beverley ended up looking after these items for fourteen years. Veronica knew that her dad had wanted to collect the tea chest before her mum passed away. Inside the chest was a large amount of gold jewellery and expensive items of ornaments that had belonged to his mum, Emily, before she died. Amongst the gold were solid gold bangles that belonged to Paula. There were antique necklaces and rings with precious and semi-precious stones that the couple had acquired over the years they had been together. Some of the items had been acquired in exchange for heroin, so they had got them cheap. They had also dealt in antiques over the years and had a good eye for quality goods and knew what was worth holding onto. Phil had mentioned to Veronica and Rae before Paula died that he needed to arrange a suitable time to visit Beverley to collect the chest. He said that he would need to sell the items in order to raise funds for Paula's eventual send off. Obviously this had never happened.

A couple of days after Michael's call, Veronica got a call from her aunt Beverley; she told Veronica that her dad had called to arrange picking up the chest. It had been around eight months since Paula died and seven months since Veronica had fallen out with him.

A few days after this, Ella called Beverley to arrange a time, as she wanted to see Beverley as well. She told Beverley that her dad had been in hospital suffering a chest infection. Beverly told Ella that Phil had brought it upon himself with all of the drugs he consumed. Ella did not like Beverley's response one bit and snapped at her.

She told her aunt, "I have no idea what you are talking about. My dad has never taken drugs." With that Ella lost her temper and slammed the phone down on Beverley. A few minutes later, her phone rang again and it was Phil. He told her she had a cheek accusing him of being a drug user and told her he'd never done drugs! She couldn't help but laugh at the denial.

Beverley's husband Eddie could hear in the background, he said, "Please don't mock our intelligence."

Beverley had been told by Phil himself years back that he was a recovering addict and had been registered with a clinic. Somehow though, he had forgotten this. Phil was still not convinced and kept denying it. He told Beverley, "I don't want your sympathy anyway, for someone who is meant to be a devout Christian you've got a very cold and unforgiving heart." He said, "Don't worry, I won't keep you, I will be down to pick up my chest and I will be out of your way for good."

"That's fine," Beverley responded, and with that Phil put down the phone.

That weekend, Beverley waited in for Phil to turn up; she was a little concerned that he would be aggressive towards her so she and Eddie arranged for a friend, who had been a policeman, to be at the house just in case there was any trouble. Paulette was the first to arrive.

When Beverley answered the door to her she told her aunt, "If you were to come out here, I would disrespect you." Beverley ignored Paulette's troublemaking comments and let her in. A few minutes later, Phil arrived, he had also brought Ella's husband along with him to help carry the chest, but there was no sign of Ella and the baby.

Beverley had made some soup. Paulette told her aunt that she was hungry, so Beverley gave her a bowl of her homemade soup. Paulette took a spoonful and spat it out.

"That's disgusting," she said rudely. "Haven't you got any real soup like the tinned stuff? I don't eat that." Beverley was annoyed at Paulette's rudeness and told her she didn't have anything else.

Phil came into the house and behaved as though the conversation they'd had a couple of days before had not happened. He boasted about working on his boat to get the vessel ready to sail in the October. Beverley and Eddie never took much notice and just went along with his story. Then Phil asked for his chest, and he and Petros carried it down from the attic and left. Beverley called Veronica after to tell her of the events.

She told Veronica, "There is no way that man is riddled with cancer, someone who is riddled with stomach cancer would not be in that fit state. They are lying to get your attention. They know how to manipulate your feelings and they want to make you pay. Do not call him Veronica, he is a callous man and your sister, well she is utterly rude."

Veronica could not believe that her family would stoop so low to lie about having cancer, but then she remembered a time years before, when Rae had helped her dad get a job for a building company he worked for. Every week the men would drop their invoices into the office for wages. The staff had told Rae that they were sorry to hear that his mum-in-law had cancer. Phil had been late on numerous occasions going to work, no doubt due to his late drug fuelled nights. As an excuse, he had told his employer that his wife had had tests. The women in the office who worked there had somehow come to the conclusion it was cancer. It took weeks for Rae to broach this subject with his wife as he was scared that her parents were keeping it from her. He kept asking if her mum was okay. This was long before Paula discovered that she had Hepatitis C. This was the first time Veronica realised how far her dad was prepared to lie to save himself, but Phil dismissed it by saying the girls in the office had come to conclusions themselves and he hadn't told them Paula had cancer. Veronica had never been convinced by his excuse and now she wondered if this was all part of the real personality of Phil Baker that she had been in denial about her whole life.

Her mother had even told her he was a bullshitter just days before her death. Had she finally seen the light too, as her life was nearing its end? Veronica knew that her family were too poisonous, and she needed to stay away for her sense of normality and sanity. She couldn't believe anything anymore where her dad was concerned; so she remained silent and refrained from calling her family.

As the months rolled by Veronica gradually became more at ease. She didn't stress out over the least little thing and she didn't become agitated and angry so easily. She had started to write about her life just as Steve had advised. Veronica found this to be very therapeutic. Reading it back to herself after writing made her see everything from another perspective. Instead of having the troubled mixed emotions she'd carried all her life, she was beginning to see the situation for what it was. Everything was becoming clearer and making sense. More than anything, Veronica needed clarity, but the reality of the mental and emotional abuse she had suffered her whole life was also a shock. Veronica was now finally coming to terms with it. Some days she would sink back into her dark hole of despair and cry herself silly. The hardest thing for her was having severed her relationships with her dad, sisters, niece and nephew; she had always been a strong family-minded person. She had always put her family's needs first. Now she was making the choice of putting her own needs first and that of her own family, but it was difficult. She struggled every day with the mental torment. She would beat herself up for turning her back on her sisters and on her dad at the worst time in his life, then she would remind herself about their treatment of her. Paulette had not really done anything to Veronica, but she was dragged into the argument by her sister Ella and her dad. Veronica felt awful for the relationships that she had left behind, but there was no way she would ever free her mind and move on to a peaceful life if she continued to have her dad and sisters in it. It cut her to pieces, but she had to somehow learn to accept it and move on.

She busied herself with keeping fit. Veronica became a keen member of a local gym where she soon made new friendships. She entered The Race For Life, running 10K for cancer research. Veronica had never done anything like this before, but it gave her great satisfaction knowing she was doing something positive in memory of her mum.

She had struggled with grieving the loss of her mum; and having no other close relationships connected to her mum to share her feelings with, put a bigger strain on her. The grieving process therefore took a long time; Veronica knew that somehow she had to survive it and that's why she threw herself into anything and everything possible to keep her positive.

She entered Moon Shine for cancer research and walked 26.2 miles throughout the night in London. The route took her all around the areas she was born and started out, which was a therapeutic experience in itself. As time went on, Veronica became stronger, she could see the reality of her life more clearly as she became more detached and focused more on herself and her own children. She had become more confident and doubted herself less and less. She threw herself into some home study courses learning massage, anatomy and physiology to distract her from spiralling back into her negative thoughts. It was difficult some days but it worked, the more she concentrated on her own needs and positive endeavours, the more at one with herself she felt. Eventually, some three years after her mum's death, Veronica had reinvented herself. No longer was she manipulated and used, no longer was she angry and confused. Veronica had finally made peace within herself, she wasn't angry with her dad anymore, she realised that she could still care for him and love him, but from a healthy distance!

It was a real shame that his life had been wasted through the use of drugs. It was a shame that much of her own life was wasted due to the impact of her parent's drug abuse, but she was going to tell the world about it in her book.

She had a plan to shout it from the rooftops; she refused to be ashamed of her background any longer. She was proud to be the person she had become because of her struggles, and she wanted to encourage others in similar circumstances to make positive changes for themselves and their families.

Finally, Veronica's life had all made sense, this was her path, this was her unique story.

All she had ever wanted was to see her parents give up their destructive habits, but unfortunately both of their lives were destroyed and blighted by heroin.

Veronica realised that there aren't enough services to support people in this predicament, as much of heroin addiction is still very taboo, and addicts are unwilling to be open about their problems. She hopes that the issues illustrated by her story, particularly about the children of addicts, may contribute to a better understanding by agencies working in this field; and that her experiences will encourage addicts and family members to seek help early. Veronica has rebuilt her life and her self-esteem, though at one time she didn't believe it would be possible. She thinks that if one person reading this book is inspired to do the same, it will have been worth it.